The Rise of Nationalism
in Central Africa

Written under the auspices of
The Center for International Affairs
Harvard University

The Rise of Nationalism in Central Africa

THE MAKING OF MALAWI AND ZAMBIA

1873–1964

ROBERT I. ROTBERG

HARVARD UNIVERSITY PRESS

Cambridge, Massachusetts

1965

Distributed in Great Britain by Oxford University Press, London

Library of Congress Catalog Card Number 65–19829

Printed in the United States of America

Cikumbutsa ca Dunduzu Kaluli Chisiza

1930–1962

PREFACE

While the tinder of racial antagonism everywhere in Central Africa
was bursting into flame, white officials, businessmen, missionaries,
and settlers assured me that the animosities so apparent in 1959 reflected recent conditions and particular political mistakes only. They
blamed ambitious African agitators and a few irresponsible white
"communists" for fueling and setting alight the conflagration that
then appeared to have spread south from Ghana and Kenya to en-
flame Northern Rhodesia and Nyasaland. They said that "the natives" had always been happy under British rule. Never had the
Africans protested or complained. Indeed, in their eyes the ambitious agitators and white malefactors managed to exert an influence over events only after successive British governments had
demonstrated that they had lost their will to rule the subject peoples
of their far-flung empire, and had begun to submit to the pressure of
Indians, Palestinians, and Ghanaians.

True? I wondered. What had been the realities of colonial rule
and the nature of the African response thereto? Did the then current
expressions of African nationalism have deep or shallow roots? Did
they indicate the existence of widespread grievances or simply mani-
fest the aspirations of a few, clever, educated Africans? These were
among the questions to which answers seemed to be needed, and to
the partial explication of which this book is addressed. Clements
Kadalie, a Nyasa who at the end of World War I founded the radical Industrial and Commercial Workers' Union in South Africa,
once wrote, with particular reference to his own country: "I believe
that the white man will not preserve [the] genuine history of the
black man."[1] Nevertheless, this book also is intended to portray the
modern political history of the peoples of Malawi (formerly Nyasaland) and Zambia (formerly Northern Rhodesia) and to place the
achievement of independence within its immediate historical con-

[1] Clements Kadalie to Isa Macdonald Lawrence, 4 April 1925, Zomba archives.

text. (The pre-colonial history of Malawi and Zambia, although not entirely irrelevant, is consciously excluded from the discussion that follows. It receives a fuller exposition elsewhere.)

"A healthy nation," wrote George Bernard Shaw about Ireland, "is as unconscious of its nationality as a healthy man of his bones. But if you break a nation's nationality it will think of nothing else but getting it set again. It will listen to no reformer, to no philosopher, to no preacher, until the demand of the Nationalist is granted. It will attend to no business, however vital, except the business of unification and liberation. . . . Conquered nations lose their place in the world's march because they can do nothing but strive to get rid of their nationalist movements by recovering their national liberty."[2] Before the colonial partition of Africa, neither Malawi nor Zambia were nations in the sense of Shaw's Ireland. The accidents of white settlement, the presence of minerals, and, ultimately, the whims of diplomats in Europe, gave them the shapes that they now hold. These shapes arbitrarily contained peoples who spoke different languages and professed various ethnic loyalties. Yet, under colonial influence many of these peoples came to consider themselves Nyasas or Northern Rhodesians; they were "British Protected Persons" and, foremost, Africans. Providing that we remember that usage has broadened and popularized its meaning— in the process stripping the word of its narrowly Balkan and Irish connotations—Shaw's analysis of nationalism still serves to describe the emotions of the Africans who wanted to reclaim their heritage. In that sense, Shaw's statement also affirms the conceptually loose way in which the words "nation" and "nationalism" are used herein, and in almost every discussion of the phenomenon of nationalism in Africa.

My quest for explanations and documentation began in 1959/60, while I was primarily engaged in other research, and occasioned subsequent visits to Africa in 1961, 1962/63 and, briefly and for ceremonious reasons as well, 1964. From the very first, the leaders and followers of several political movements willingly shared their thoughts and their memories on an endless variety of occasions. On a Sunday in February 1959, Mr. Simon Katilungu, then the senior

[2] George Bernard Shaw, *John Bull's Other Island* (New York, 1908), xxxvi-xxxvii.

research assistant at the Rhodes-Livingstone Institute for Social Research and now the High Commissioner for the Republic of Zambia in Great Britain, guided me into the heart of Chilenje, an African suburb of Lusaka, to meet Mr. Kenneth Kaunda, then the president of the militant Zambia African National Congress and now the President of the Republic of Zambia. Our conversation took place in a tiny hut that served as the headquarters of the political organization that was soon to be banned by the governor. In later years, we talked together in Accra, Dar es Salaam, Salisbury, and Lusaka. Throughout, his courtesy and patience proved unfailing; he endured endless importunities, answered interminable questions, and permitted my wife and me to observe at close hand the transformation of Northern Rhodesia into Zambia. We remain much in his debt.

Similarly, from our first meeting in the United States until the celebration of his country's independence, Dr. H. Kamuzu Banda, now the prime minister of Malawi, welcomed my inquiries and investigations, granted a number of interviews, and encouraged wide-ranging research in the various districts of Malawi. He also read and commented upon my typescript. Mr. Aleke Banda, now *inter alia* the secretary-general of the Malawi Congress Party, proved remarkably responsive and sympathetic to our needs.

The present Zambian Minister of Local Government, Mr. Sikota Wina, with whom a dialogue began during his restriction at Luwingu, has continued to enrich my understanding of African life. The late Dunduzu Kaluli Chisiza, at his death Malawi's prospective Minister of Finance, was himself interested in writing a history of the Nyasaland African Congress. He shared his opinions and ideas, lent me the records that he had collected, and went out of his way to make my own task easier. Messrs. Augustine Bwanausi, Willie Chokani, and John Msonthi, all members of the Nyasaland cabinet in 1962, spoke freely on a number of formal and informal occasions. In addition, Messrs. Bwanausi and Msonthi materially facilitated one aspect of my research at a time of peculiar awkwardness for themselves. In Northern Rhodesia, Messrs. Simon Kapwepwe and Arthur Wina, both of whom subsequently became members of the Zambia cabinet, assisted my own efforts to reconstruct the past and appreciate the nuances of the present.

With characteristic generosity, Sir Stewart Gore-Browne, Zambia's foremost settler and long-time politician, permitted my wife and me to peruse and to quote from his vast collection of private papers. He submitted at irregular intervals to rounds of questions, read six of the following chapters in draft, and, despite a variety of impositions, continued cheerfully to welcome our visits to his manor house at Shiwa Ngandu. Mr. G. G. S. J. Hadlow, a sometime member of the Nyasaland Legislative Council, and Mr. Archibald H. Elwell, a sometime welfare officer in Northern Rhodesia, lent me their private papers and amplified the contents of those papers in conversation. The Rev. Mr. Charles C. Chinula allowed me to read the minutes of the meetings of the Mombera Native Association and spoke at length of separatism. Messrs. Harry Nkumbula and Job Michello, then the president-general and the secretary-general respectively of the African National Congress of Northern Rhodesia, permitted me to read the extant files of their organization and to discuss its history with them. Mr. Harry Langworthy brought a valuable unedited manuscript by Mr. Wittington K. Sikalumbi to my attention.

In 1962, the then governments of Northern Rhodesia and Nyasaland allowed me to examine a variety of closed files and materials in their respective archives and to read district records as well. In particular, I am grateful for the assistance of Mr. James Moore, the then acting archivist in Lusaka. Mr. B. Cheeseman, librarian of the Colonial Office, provided valuable help in London. I am also indebted to Mr. Patrick Mumba, who permitted me to read the political papers that he had collected in 1959; Mr. Rankin Sikasula, for long Dr. Kaunda's private secretary; Mr. Simon ber Zukas, who spoke at length of his own experiences in Northern Rhodesia and later constructively criticized a relevant chapter of this book; Chief Mwase Kasungu, who could not have been more hospitable; Mr. Donald Siwale, an early member of welfare associations and the Representative Council of Northern Rhodesia, who spoke and wrote feelingly of early political intrigues and the campaign against "closer association"; Mr. Iain Macleod, M. P., sometime British Secretary of State for the Colonies, with whom I discussed the final chapter of this book; Sir Glyn Jones, now the governor-general of Malawi; Sir Richard Luyt, then the Chief Secretary of Northern Rhodesia and now the governor of British Guiana; Dr. George Brooks, for research in Indiana; Miss Anthea Hall, who helped me to answer questions about Dr. Banda's sojourn in northern England; Mr. Arthur Westrop, who lent us a cottage atop Zomba Mountain; Mr. Edward Mulcahy, who contributed over the course of many years to my own attempts to understand diverse aspects of Africa, and others who would no doubt prefer to remain nameless.

The guidance of Professors Rupert Emerson and George Shepperson, who read the final draft of this book with great care and understanding, helped me to avoid a number of substantive and analytical pitfalls. I am grateful for perceptive readings and extremely useful comments, and for many other kindnesses as well, to Mr. J. David Rubadiri, now the Malawi ambassador to the United States; Mr. Ian Nance, for many years an administrative officer in Malawi; Mr. George Loft; Mr. Trevor Coombe; and Dr. Prosser Gifford.

Without the encouragement and support of Dr. Jo W. Saxe this book might never have been written. For a willingness to be content with the promise of deferred gratification, I remain deeply indebted to Professor Robert R. Bowie, the director of the Harvard Center for International Affairs. The Center specifically financed visits to Africa in 1961 and 1962/63 and to Britain in 1963. The Harvard Department of History granted me a leave of absence in order to complete the research in Central Africa on which this study is based.

In Africa, other friends provided a rich hospitality and that insight into local conditions that cannot be equaled by the activities of transients. In this connection, and for myriad kindnesses, I cannot refrain from mentioning Mr. Dennis Acheson, who first introduced me to Copperbelt politics; Mr. and Mrs. Richard Hall, whose home in Lusaka has always been the center of political and journalistic ferment; the Rev. Mr. and Mrs. Hamish Hepburn, then of Zomba; Mr. and Mrs. Sean Kelly, then of Lusaka; Mr. and Mrs. Ian Nance, then of Zomba; Mr. Ian Robertson, of the Malawi forests; Mr. Derek Rowe, of Kisumu and Nairobi; Mr. and Mrs. Clyde Sanger, of *The Guardian*, Salisbury, and Karen, who allowed us to benefit from their unrivaled knowledge of matters African, and Mr. and Mrs. Anthony Wilson, who introduced us to the politicians of Mzuzu and Nkata Bay.

Mrs. Mary Hodgdon and Mrs. Lillian Christmas speedily typed the final drafts of the present book and, together with Mrs. Jane

Tatlock, improved its preparation in innumerable other ways. Miss Yen-Tsai Feng and Miss Nancy Barber provided invaluable bibliographical assistance.

My wife Joanna deserves more than the usual end-of-preface citation. She drew the maps. She participated in almost every aspect of the research on which this book is based, read with me in the Zomba archives, joined me in a succession of interviews, and shared the joys and occasional discomforts of our visits to the remote districts of Malawi and Zambia. With great acumen, and while in the midst of maternal responsibilities, she also suggested important improvements to original and later drafts of the chapters that follow. This, more than any other, equally is her book.

R. I. R.

Harvard University
24 October 1964

In accord with accepted usage, I spell most Bantu proper names without pronominal concords, and use modern orthographical forms wherever possible.

Contents

CONTENTS

Illustrations

(*Unless otherwise credited, all photographs were taken by the author.*)

Following page 220

Maps

(*Maps drawn by Joanna H. Rotberg.*)

The Rise of Nationalism
in Central Africa

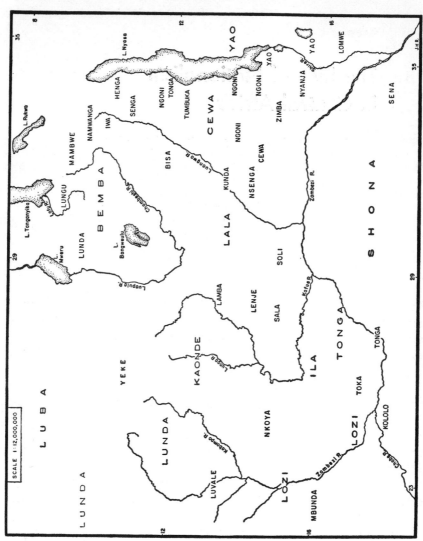

The peoples of Central Africa before the European conquest.

Chapter I

THE COMING OF THE EUROPEANS

Yet it must be borne in mind that the negro is a man, with a man's rights; above all, that he was the owner of the country before we came, and deserves, nay, is entitled to, a share in the land, commensurate with his needs and numbers; that in numbers he will always exceed the white man, while he may some day come to rival him in intelligence; and that finally if we do not use our power to govern him with absolute justice the time will come sooner or later when he will rise against us and expel us . . . .

—Sir Harry Johnston,
British Central Africa
(London, 1897), 183–184

Without the irruption of Europe, the course of tropical African history would have been very different. There would have been no scramble or partition. There would have been no struggle for self-expression in the form loosely called nationalism. But Europeans did come to Africa. They came to explore, to proselytize, to trade, and, in the final analysis, to carve out colonies. In the trans-Zambezi areas that were later known as Nyasaland and Northern Rhodesia, the intrusion of Europe was a phenomenon of the late nineteenth century. Britain gave the region the unity of colonial rule and the integrity of artificial borders. It offered a focus for the loyalties of disparate peoples. It channeled the aspirations of the subject population along new paths and provided a framework within which nationalism could eventually transform itself into African self-government.

The roots of nationalism in Central Africa are found in the rocky soil of British colonial rule. Although negatively expressed, the history of nationalism is as much European as African in its early stages. Thus, after the first wave of resistance to white control there came a period during which Africans attempted to adapt themselves to the West—to accept its demands, to internalize those demands, and, in time, to realize what they construed as the benefits of the acculturation process. Colonialism, however, did not accept the ultimate logic of this process. The concept of nationalism —of a redress of grievances—therefore did not spring full-blown into the minds of latter-day African agitators. The entire course of colonial history in a sense favored the development of nationalism.

THE EXPLORERS

Throughout the nineteenth century a collection of hardy romantics, visionaries, and adventurers crisscrossed Africa and disclosed the existence of peoples and geographical features of which the Western world had been previously unaware. Their "discoveries" stimulated a new European interest in the affairs of tropical Africa and led, ultimately, to partition. In central Africa, David Livingstone, about whom so much has been written, was the first European to travel extensively.[1] He personally encouraged the subsequent immigration of missionaries, traders, and administrators into central Africa, while providing a towering example of devotion to truth and scientific thoroughness that others strove vainly to equal. Livingstone's travels there were, however, anticipated by a number of Portuguese whose efforts had unfortunately failed to contribute measurably to the Western world's knowledge. In the early fifteenth century, António Fernandes visited what is now Southern Rhodesia; he did not venture significantly into the areas of modern Nyasaland or Northern Rhodesia, however, and left few records of importance.[2] In 1616, Gaspar Bocarro traversed Nyasaland, south of the lake, on his way from Tete to Kilwa as an emissary of the acting captain general of the Portuguese military expedition to the silver mines of Chicoa.[3] In the late eighteenth century, a Lusitanian physician, Francisco José de Lacerda e Almeida, reached the important town on the Luapula River of the Lunda chief Mwata Kazembe. There

[1] The best full-length biographies are William Garden Blaikie, *The Personal Life of David Livingstone* (New York, 1881); George Seaver, *David Livingstone: His Life and Letters* (London, 1957).

[2] Hugh Tracey (trans. Gaetano Montez), *António Fernandes, Descobridor do Monomotapa, 1514–15* (Lourenço Marques, 1940).

[3] R. A. Hamilton, "The Route of Gaspar Bocarro from Tete to Kilwa in 1616," W. H. J. Rangeley, "Bocarro's Journey," *The Nyasaland Journal*, vii, 2 (1954), 7–23; John Milner Gray, "A Journey by Land from Tete to Kilwa in 1616," *Tanganyika Notes and Records*, 25 (1948), 37–47.

he died of fever. Two half-caste slave traders, Amaro José and Pedro João Baptista, traversed the African continent from Angola to Moçambique between 1806 and 1814, and were detained for three years by the reigning Kazembe. In 1831/32, two majors in the Portuguese army, José Correia Monteiro and António Pedroso Gamitto, sought an easy route that would link Angola to Moçambique, but they were unable to proceed beyond Lake Mweru.[4]

For Livingstone, "the end of the geographical feat [was] the beginning of the missionary enterprise."[5] None was as indomitable— as restlessly driven by a passion for discovering the secrets of the heart of Africa. None unfolded its mysteries so dramatically or so well. Livingstone went to work in a Scottish cotton mill at the age of ten, and later studied medicine at Anderson's College, Glasgow. He joined the London Missionary Society, hoping to be sent to China, but the "Opium War" intervened and he was persuaded to go to Bechuanaland. In 1849, he guided the first successful European crossing of the Kalahari "thirstland" to Lake Ngami. Later, in order to provide a new outlet for evangelical enterprise, he trekked across the "thirstland" toward the Chobe and Zambezi rivers. Upon reaching the banks of the latter in 1851, he realized for the first time that the Zambezi might prove to be an accessible avenue into the unevangelized heart of Africa. No longer, he hoped, would missionaries and explorers be forced to travel overland across the waterless wastes of the Kalahari. At the same time, Livingstone obtained his initial glimpses of the trade in slaves that he spent the remainder of his life seeking to eradicate. "Providence," he wrote, "seems to call me to the regions beyond. You will see . . . what an immense region God in His Providence has opened up. If we can enter in and form a settlement we shall be able in the course of a very few years to put a stop to the slave trade in that quarter. . . ."[6]

Livingstone became obsessed with a desire to open up the heart of Africa to new forms of commerce and religion in order to end the slave trade, foster the Christian endeavor, and destroy the several obstacles of ignorance, poverty, and isolation that blocked, he be-

---

[4] Richard F. Burton (trans. and ed.), *The Lands of Cazembe* (London, 1873); Ian Cunnison, "Kazembe and the Portuguese, 1798–1832," *The Journal of African History*, ii (1961), 65–76.

[5] Seaver, *Livingstone*, 267.

[6] *Ibid.*, 144.

lieved, the growth of "civilization" in Africa. Between 1853 and 1856, he therefore investigated the "unknown" regions of central Africa. From Linyanti on the Chobe River, he traveled up the Zambezi River at the head of a small company of Lozi- and Kololo-speaking Africans. This, his first visit to Barotseland, prepared the way for the later settlement there of British and French Protestant missionaries. He entered Lunda country, in what became North-western Rhodesia, and thence crossed Portuguese territory to Luanda. After a much needed respite, he returned with his African companions to Barotseland, which he again reached in late 1855. A few months later, having embarked down the Zambezi toward Quelimane, Livingstone espied the waterfalls that he named after Queen Victoria. Then, avoiding the country of the warlike Ila, he trekked across the Tonga plateau and eventually followed the course of the Zambezi River through Moçambique to the Indian Ocean, where he arrived in 1856. In twenty months, he had nego-tiated the "dark continent" from west to east. Six months later, after the news of his travels had preceded him home, Livingstone arrived in London to receive the honors of Britain and to set in motion a series of events that in time resulted in the introduction of com-mercial and missionary enterprises into the regions that he had ex-plored and, ultimately, in the partition of Central Africa.

Livingstone completely captured the public sympathy. When he appealed for religious reinforcements and for a full-scale attack upon the slave trade, all Britain listened. A famous speech at Cambridge epitomized his sentiments: "I know that in a few years I shall be cut off in that country which is now open; do not let it be shut again. I go back to Africa to try to make an open path for Christianity. Do you carry out the work which I have begun. I leave it to you."[7]

The explorer returned to central Africa at the head of an expedi-tion sponsored by the British government. On this occasion, he specifically sought ways whereby Christianity and commerce could most expeditiously be introduced into the heart of Africa. An at-tempt to ascend the Zambezi River by ship proved impossible, and Livingstone therefore concentrated his efforts upon what became Nyasaland. In 1859, he became the first Briton to describe lakes

[7] William Monk (ed.), *Dr. Livingstone's Cambridge Lectures* (London, 1860), 168.

Chilwa and Nyasa. During the course of the next four years, he and his white companions came intimately to know much of what is now the Shire Highlands and the environs of Lake Nyasa. They assisted an abortive expedition to establish a station of the (Anglican) Universities' Mission to Central Africa in the Shire Highlands, and contributed to a growing British interest in this area before the expedition's recall in 1863/64.[8]

In 1866, Livingstone again reached Zanzibar on his way to trans-Zambezia. This time, he was even more determined than before to seek information about the slave trade and to obtain a thorough understanding of the configuration of the major watersheds of eastern and central Africa. Although John Hanning Speke and Samuel White Baker had viewed the "main" sources of the Nile River, Livingstone was not yet persuaded that its "true" origins had been found. He thought that Lake Nyasa might flow north into Lake Tanganyika, which again might be linked to Lake Albert, and the Nile. Livingstone furthermore sought the source of the Congo River and desired to trace its course to the sea. While growing steadily weaker in body and more obsessed in mind, he engaged in these pursuits from 1866 until 1873.[9] Livingstone's wanderings took him from Zanzibar to Lake Nyasa and on to Lake Tanganyika. Turning to the west, he "discovered" Lake Mweru—Lacerda had reached it in 1798—and Lake Bangweulu in 1867/68. Leaving the future Northern Rhodesia, Livingstone spent the next two years investigating the river system that flowed north from Mweru and, in 1871, he was "found" by Henry Morton Stanley in Ujiji. Together they learned that rivers flowed into the north end of Lake Tanganyika, not away from it toward Lake Albert. This information strengthened Livingstone's belief that Lake Mweru and branches of the Congo River system fed the Nile. Stanley urged the great explorer to return to Britain, but Livingstone, for the last time, plunged southwest toward Bangweulu and Katanga, where Africans said that he would

---

[8] David and Charles Livingstone, *Narrative of an Expedition to the Zambesi and Its Tributaries* (London, 1865); Owen Chadwick, *Mackenzie's Grave* (London, 1959); Reginald Coupland, *Kirk on the Zambesi* (Oxford, 1928). Lake Nyasa has since resumed its pre-Livingstone name and is now called Lake Malawi.

[9] See Horace Waller (ed.), *The Last Journals of David Livingstone in Central Africa* (London, 1874); Reginald Coupland, *Livingstone's Last Journey* (London, 1945).

find the "fountains" that would prove to be the source of the Congo and, as Herodotus had foretold, of the Nile itself.[10] After finding the fountains, he planned to go home for good. But Livingstone was again sick, and his last year in trans-Zambezia was painfully unrewarding. He died near Chief Chitambo's village in Lala country, southeast of Lake Bangweulu, during the first week of May 1873.

THE MISSIONARIES

Livingstone opened up the heart of Africa to white missionaries, settlers, and colonial governments. The circumstances of his death and the example of his life inspired those in Britain who had already demonstrated their concern with the evangelization of distant parts of the globe to turn their attentions to central Africa. In 1874, but a few short weeks after Livingstone's ceremonious burial in Westminster Abbey, the influential Dr. James Stewart, of Lovedale, proposed that the Free Church of Scotland should establish a mission in Africa that would carry the great explorer's name and be a living memorial to his ideals. Stewart suggested that a "Livingstonia" should be established "in a carefully selected and commanding spot in Central Africa," and that it should be "an institution at once industrial and educational, to teach the truths of the Gospel and the arts of civilised life to the natives of the country."[11] By the end of 1874, both the Free Church and the Established Church of Scotland had committed themselves to memorial missions; Stewart and Sir John Kirk, who had both traveled extensively in what was to become Nyasaland, recommended that the two Scottish churches should send their missionaries to "the slave-hunting region around Lake Nyasa."[12]

In late 1875, a mission party reached the southern end of the lake and built the first "Livingstonia" on an uncomfortably hot, isolated promontory near Cape Maclear.[13] A year later the Estab-

[10] Herodotus, ii, 28.

[11] James Wells, *Stewart of Lovedale: The Life of James Stewart* (London, 1908), 125.

[12] Quoted in Alexander John Hanna, *The Beginnings of Nyasaland and North-Eastern Rhodesia, 1859–95* (Oxford, 1956), 13.

[13] See Edward D. Young (ed. Horace Waller) *Nyassa: A Journal of Adventures* (London, 1877); Robert Laws, *Reminiscences of Livingstonia* (Edinburgh, 1934), 15–23; William P. Livingstone, *Laws of Livingstonia* (London, 1923), 72–104ff; Jailos Chingota, "An Autobiography," *The Nyasaland Journal*, xiv (1961), 14.

lished Church—whose emissary had disliked all of the possible lakeshore sites—dispatched a new group of men to establish a station at a place in the Shire Highlands to which they gave the name Blantyre, after the Scottish town of Livingstone's birth. At Cape Maclear the Free Church opened a school where the rudiments of reading and writing were taught and parts of the New Testament committed to memory. Dr. Robert Laws, the moving spirit of the mission, also began a medical practice that was to draw Africans to Livingstonia from distant centers of population.

At Blantyre, however, the missionaries of the Established Church were slow to teach or to minister to the medical needs of the predominantly Muslim Yao among whom they had settled. During 1879, they instead took the law into their own hands; they charged, tried, and imprisoned Africans accused of murder or theft, flogged many of the accused unmercifully and, in at least one instance, ordered the execution of an African without a thorough investigation into the circumstances of his guilt.[14] When these incidents were disclosed in 1880, the Foreign Mission Committee of the Established Church ordered its Blantyre staff to abandon the exercise of all civil jurisdiction and, later, to concentrate upon the education of Africans for useful trades—a function that the mission performed admirably.

Dr. Laws and the Free Church meanwhile had decided that the original site at Cape Maclear was too remote from the main concentrations of the country's population to serve as an evangelical center. In 1881, the mission moved to Bandawe, on the western shore of Lake Nyasa. Here, and at yet another "Livingstonia," farther north along the western shore, Dr. Laws and his devoted colleagues established educational and medical outposts and the beginnings of a truly indigenous church. Their activity, and that of the Established Church at Blantyre, provided the foundation upon which subsequent Westernization and nationalism was based. The existence of Livingstonia and Blantyre, and the joint agitation of the Free Church and the Established Church, also influenced Britain's formal extension of "protection" and colonial rule to the Nyasa region in the last years of the nineteenth century.

To the west, the vast woodland areas of what was to become Northern Rhodesia also attracted mission societies intent upon

14 Hanna, *Beginnings*, 29–32.

carrying forward the evangelical task that Livingstone had begun. In 1882, pioneers of the explorer's own London Missionary Society opened the first of several stations at the southern end of Lake Tanganyika; its outposts in time were established among Kazembe's distant Lunda, on the Luapula, and among the Bemba of Mporokoso. Roman Catholic White Fathers soon joined the London missionaries in a competition for the souls of the Mambwe and Bemba peoples and, before the end of the 1890's, the Free Church of Scotland's Livingstonia mission also opened branches nearby. Barotseland, along the upper reaches of the Zambezi River, had meanwhile been subjected to the evangelical efforts of Frederick Stanley Arnot, a Plymouth Brother who had followed Livingstone's footsteps to trans-Zambezia, and members of the Paris Missionary Society. Arnot, unsuccessful in Barotseland, left the Lozi capital in 1884 and later founded stations in Katanga. But the Paris Mission, which began its work among the Lozi a year later, stayed to provide Northwestern Rhodesia with a number of influential stations, schools, and dispensaries.[15]

A welter of denominations, each bent upon capturing souls for a Christ of its particular persuasion, followed these earliest missionary bodies into Northern Rhodesia. The Primitive Methodist Missionary Society, a group estranged from the orthodox branch of Wesleyanism, started work among the Ila near the Kafue River in the 1890's. The Dutch Reformed Church of South Africa, which in 1889 opened stations in central Nyasaland, began the first of many missions in Northeastern Rhodesia at the very end of the nineteenth century. The Plymouth Brethren moved from Angola into Northwestern Rhodesia, and from Katanga into Northeastern Rhodesia, early in the twentieth century. Along the central line of rail, the Society of Jesus, the Seventh-day Adventists (active near Cholo in Nyasaland from 1902), and the Zambezi Industrial Mission (active from 1892 in the Shire Highlands) all opened stations before 1910. The Universities' Mission to Central Africa, with its many scattered outposts, the Montfort Marist Mission in Nyasaland, and the South African General Mission, which spread the Gospel in the sparsely populated districts of Northwestern Rhodesia,

[15] For a fuller account, see Robert I. Rotberg, *Christian Missionaries and the Creation of Northern Rhodesia, 1880–1924* (Princeton, 1965), chs. 1–4.

completed the roster of missionary bodies that sought converts in trans-Zambezia before World War I.

The missionaries had demonstrated the main ways in which they had hoped to transform African life. They regarded many aspects of indigenous behavior as evil and naturally sought an eradication of what they termed "heathen" customs. Polygyny, beer-drinking, and drumming were clear indications of "paganism." For example, at Chitokoloki, a remote outpost of the Plymouth Brethren in Northwestern Rhodesia, the missionaries were asked if they objected to Africans dancing in order to propitiate the ancestors of a sick woman. They wrote of their reply: "We said we did not object to the dancing on our own account, but because we knew that in so doing they [the Africans] were not putting their trust in one who could help them, and spurning the real Lord and Giver of Life."[16] At Mporokoso, a London Missionary Society center, alcoholism appeared to be the main problem. "It is these public beer drinks that form one of the evil customs of these people. They drink and dance until beside themselves with excitement and intoxication, while all restraint is lost and unnameable wickedness is the result."[17]

The missionaries urged Africans to copy the white man's ways—to put on clothes, to purge themselves of sin and corruption, and to accept the truths of the Gospel as a complete code of conduct. Many methods of coercion were used by the missionaries to obtain compliance with their modernizing demands; they denied a place upon the ladders of material advancement to those who refused to comply with missionary dictates. They reserved the educational experience to nominal Christians. More significantly, they provided employment only for those who professed some seemingly sincere interest in the Christian message. In general, the missions and the over-all impact of European experience contributed profoundly to the outward and inward Westernization of the peoples of trans-Zambezia. And in this process of giving Africans the means to acquire a national rather than a parochial outlook, the missions unwittingly played a catalytic role in the struggle for home rule.

Their educational programs varied along a lengthy continuum according to the theological liberality of the denomination, the

16 George Suckling, *Echoes of Service* (September 1923), 205–206.
17 William Freshwater, diary entry, 26 December 1905, privately held.

character of the missionary in charge, the availability of teaching equipment, and the ability of the pupils. Some were no more than "a fence of grass, six feet high, surrounding some big tree," wrote one missionary. "A few poles laid across short forked sticks [served] for seats [upon which sat] a mass of wriggling, chocolate brown, youthful humanity."[18] Others, like the famous Overtoun Training Institution at Livingstonia, were a complex of brick buildings where gifted instructors produced the clerks, evangelists, and indigenous leaders of early trans-Zambezia. The village schools served up a limited fare: students memorized selected portions of Scripture and hymnal, learned to make their letters in the sand, and mouthed the phonetic sounds. But at Overtoun and in many of the senior primary schools (there were no real secondary schools until World War II) students were taught to read in the vernacular, to do arithmetic through simple division, to draw, to memorize the features of world geography, and to know the Bible thoroughly.

Schools were very important to the process of Westernization, but the missionary's contribution was also evident in innumerable other ways. His tours of the villages and an entrepreneurial role that has generally been underestimated played a large part in opening up the country to Western influence. The missionary was a trader; he stimulated African desires for Western products and supplied those wants by a complicated transport, sales, and service network. The missionary was compelled to protect his trade routes and to preserve order on the stations. He therefore became a lawgiver, a policeman, a prosecuting attorney, and a judge. As one missionary later wrote: "Many a little Protestant Pope in the lonely bush is forced by his self-imposed isolation to be prophet, priest, and king rolled into one—really a very big duck he, in his own private pond."[19] Excesses, like those attributed to the Blantyre missionaries in 1879, were not uncommon, and the London Missionary Society, in particular, was scandalized by the temporal powers that its missionaries exercised.[20] The missionary, whether trained or untrained, was also called upon

[18] William Lammond, letter dated 22 April 1920, *Echoes of Service* (August 1920), 185–186.
[19] Daniel Crawford, *Thinking Black: Twenty-two Years without a Break in the Long Grass of Central Africa* (London, 1913), 324–325.
[20] See Robert I. Rotberg, "Missionaries as Chiefs and Entrepreneurs: Northern Rhodesia, 1882–1924," *Boston University Papers in African History* (Boston, 1964), i, 204–209.

to heal the sick and comfort the dying. In general, missionary assistance gradually drew Africans into the Western orbit. They came to appreciate some of its advantages and, at the same time, to understand that the tenets of Christianity and Western civilization were ones that prescribed equality between men and of opportunity. By denying Africans such equality, by assisting in the conquest of Central Africa, and by generally condoning the discriminatory policies of government officials and settlers, the missionaries set in motion a rethinking of this ambivalence between precept and practice that, in time, contributed to the growth of indigenous discontent and the rise of nationalism.

THE CONQUEST

Livingstone's explorations and the presence of English-speaking missionaries provided an historical excuse and an important political pretext for the British diplomatic and military conquest of what became Nyasaland and Northern Rhodesia. The acquisition of these areas must, however, be viewed in the over-all context of the late nineteenth-century scramble for Africa and in the more specific rivalry between Britain, Portugal, and the Transvaal for the control of its riches.

Portugal had always asserted its sovereignty over Nyasaland and a wide swath of territory that theoretically tied Angola to Moçambique. But Portugal's interests, even in the late nineteenth century, were predominantly coastal; to the dismay of the British consuls stationed after 1857 at the port of Moçambique, it was primarily concerned with continuing the profitable slave trade. The consuls sought unsuccessfully to persuade the various Portuguese governors to accept British cooperation in the suppression of the trade in slaves and, after the Scottish missions were established near Lake Nyasa, attempted to work with them for the abolition of slave caravans at their source. In 1883, Captain C. E. Foot was appointed Her Majesty's Consul "in territories of the African Kings and Chiefs in the districts adjacent to Lake Nyasa."[21] He was enjoined to seek the suppression of the slave trade by persuasion and the encouragement of legitimate commerce. In reality, he had been sent partially at the behest of the missions—who had asked for a "kind of British

21 FO 84/1634: Foreign Office to Foot, 1 October 1883, Public Record Office.

Protectorate"—and partially as a maneuver whereby signs of Portuguese interest in the interior might be observed and, if necessary, forestalled. A note exchanged between London and Lisbon in 1877 had already denied Portuguese sovereignty in the interior wherever *bona fide* occupation and *de facto* jurisdiction "of a continuous and non-intermittent kind" did not exist. But Portugal continued to assert its claims to Nyasaland.[22]

Foot's appointment only increased Portugal's concern. After 1884, it tried persistently to impose its authority over Nyasaland and the Zambezi River, to the detriment of British commercial and evangelical freedom in the interior. In 1887, Portugal claimed all of the Zambezi basin, including Nyasaland and what is now Southern Rhodesia, and proceeded to obtain treaties with African chiefs with which to support its position. During the next two years, Portuguese officials in Moçambique interfered with the passage of vessels and equipment to Nyasaland, hindered the successful completion of a war against Arab slavers in which the African Lakes Company (later Corporation), a Scottish evangelical trading concern, was engaged, and sent expeditions inland to seize the contested lands.[23]

The Kirk and the Glasgow-based company grew alarmed. Lord Granville had already refused the Company's application for Imperial protection. Lord Rosebery and his successors at the Foreign Office had evinced a similar lack of concern for British territorial claims north of the Zambezi River. When he became prime minister, Lord Salisbury was willing to permit the local British consul to exercise influence only on behalf of the missions. In his view, the declaration of a "protectorate" was financially out of the question. Salisbury was then uninterested in the evangelical needs of the region. He wrote: "It is not our duty to do it. We should be risking tremendous sacrifices for a very doubtful gain. . . . We must leave the dispersal of this terrible army of wickedness to the gradual advancement of civilization and Christianity."[24] Nonetheless, in about 1887, the agitation of the missions and their influential British supporters coin-

---

[22] Quoted in Hanna, *Beginnings*, 111.

[23] For details on the war with the Arab slavers, see FO 84/1883; FO 84/1942; L. Monteith Fotheringham, *Adventures in Nyassaland* (London, 1891).

[24] Lord Salisbury, quoted in Ronald Robinson and John Gallagher, *Africa and the Victorians: The Climax of Imperialism in the Dark Continent* (New York, 1961), 224.

cided with an imperial attempt to prevent either Portugal or the Transvaal from occupying Matabeleland and Mashonaland. The alliance of Cecil John Rhodes and Henry Hamilton (later Sir Harry) Johnston finally persuaded Lord Salisbury to act decisively in Central Africa. In 1889, Rhodes, a 36-year-old imperialist who ruled a gold and diamond empire worth more than £20,000,000, came to London from South Africa. He requested the support and sanction of Her Majesty's Government for the annexation of Matabeleland. In return, he offered to pay for the colonization and administration of Matabeleland and the Bechuanaland Protectorate, to extend the existing rail and telegraph lines to the Zambezi River, and to obtain for the Crown all of trans-Zambezia. With that abundant resolution of which Livingstone would have approved, Rhodes proposed to paint the heart of Africa British red without cost to the Imperial exchequer. He promised to outdo Sir George Goldie of Nigeria and Sir William Mackinnon of East Africa and to gamble one fortune to protect others. In exchange for a few swift strokes of Salisbury's pen, Rhodes promised to forestall the Transvaal and Portugal in Central Africa, to obviate any disastrous entanglements with African warriors, to discharge all of the responsibilities of a government and, in short, to help himself by helping the Crown. How could the British government refuse? Humanitarian interests, concerned to prevent exploitation of Africans, sought to persuade the Government to do so, but, by the autumn, Rhodes's attractive proposal had been accepted. When a charter was granted in late 1889, it gave Rhodes's British South Africa Company full financial and administrative responsibility for much of Central Africa and authorized the Company to allocate lands and mining rights and to settle whites within its new domain.[25] The future Northern Rhodesia, in which Salisbury remained uninterested, and which he purposely excluded from the first draft of the charter, was in addition declared a part of the British sphere, probably because Rhodes correctly suspected the existence of copper there. In concert with Johnston, Rhodes also made possible the inclusion of Nyasaland, paying at once for treaty-making expeditions and promising to ab-

[25] For texts, see Edward S. Hertslet (ed.), *The Map of Africa by Treaty* (London, 1896), i, 174–182.

sorb other expensive activities in the future.[26] For more than three decades, practical sovereignty in most of Central Africa thus passed to a chartered undertaking, the activities of which remained effectively beyond the control of the British government.

Johnston had meanwhile accepted appointment as Her Majesty's Consul to Moçambique. During a dramatic May morning encounter, Rhodes and Johnston had reinforced each other's conception of what Britain's imperial role should be: "We settled as we thought the immediate line of action in South and Central Africa."[27] The financier gave the diplomatist a £2000 check to defray treaty-making costs; Johnston later in the day persuaded Salisbury to add official sanction to the arrangements. The diminutive consul's arrival on the lower Zambezi, at the end of July 1889, thus signified the beginning of a definite British forward policy in the Nyasa regions. Johnston quickly forestalled the forceful assertion of Portuguese sovereignty over much of trans-Zambezia by authorizing the unilateral declaration of a protectorate over the Shire Highlands (announced in September 1889) that was secured by an official British ultimatum. In January 1890, Salisbury rose from his sickbed to order the Portuguese to withdraw from the Shire Highlands Protectorate; if they refused, he promised to send gunboats to shell the capital of Moçambique. Portugal submitted, and to all intents and purposes Britain became the mistress of Central Africa.

Even before Britain's contest with Portugal had reached a successful conclusion, Johnston had met Alfred Sharpe, a London solicitor turned big-game hunter, had appointed him vice-consul, and, with his assistance, had negotiated the end of the hostilities with the Arabs. Together, Johnston and Sharpe thereafter concluded a series of agreements with indigenous chiefs throughout a vast unpartitioned region from the Ruo River west to Lake Mweru and north toward Lake Tanganyika. These treaties bound the chiefs in question not to cede territory or sovereignty to any other European power without Her Majesty's approval. They testified to the existence of "peace" between a tribe and the Queen of England, promised to admit British subjects freely, and to accord Her Majesty consular jurisdiction over all disputes that arose between the

[26] FO 2/55: H. H. Johnston to C. J. Rhodes, 8 October 1893. But see J. G. Lockhart and C. M. Woodhouse, *Rhodes* (London, 1963), 137, 142, 164.
[27] Harry H. Johnston, *The Story of My Life* (Indianapolis, 1923), 219.

indigenous inhabitants and Britons. These treaties did not confer or promise protection, however, and, when Johnston announced a further protectorate over the environs of Lake Nyasa, his action bore no juridical relation to the original understandings between the Queen's consuls and the chiefs. Nevertheless, in May 1891, after agreement had been reached with Rhodes over the extent of his financial support, and the geographical limits of Johnston's jurisdiction, the British Foreign Office formally declared that "under and by virtue of Agreements with the native Chiefs, and by other lawful means, the territories in Africa, hereinafter referred to as the Nyasaland Districts, are under the Protectorate of Her Majesty the Queen."[28]

As in the east, where Johnston had been successful in an area devoid of important chiefs, so it was in the west, where Rhodes sought rights to territory and minerals. There—along the Upper Zambezi—Mwanawina Lewanika, the paramount chief of the Lozi, ruled over most of what became Northwestern Rhodesia and a part of what is now eastern Angola, northern Bechuanaland, and the Caprivi Strip. Alone, of the missionaries who had been permitted to preach in his kingdom, François Coillard, the Paris Society leader, had achieved a measure of influence with the chief. Thus, when Rhodes wanted Barotseland, he found an ally in the pro-British Coillard, who feared Portuguese or German interference from the west and consequently desired British protection in order to further his missionary endeavor. Coillard in turn induced Lewanika, who feared the Ndebele, to request British protection and, in 1890, Frank Lochner arrived in Barotseland to treat with Lewanika on Rhodes's behalf.[29] The negotiations proved a tedious affair. The Lozi were in no hurry to sign away their prerogatives to the white man and Lochner, who sought to avoid the elaborate protocol of Lealui, the Lozi capital, was the least tactful of many possible emissaries. Yet, with Coillard's active assistance, he finally persuaded Lewanika to assent to what the chief and his councilors believed to

[28] Hertslet, *Map* (1909), i, 286.

[29] François Coillard to Sir Sidney Shippard, 8 January 1889, in *Africa South*, 372, no. 120 (encl.); Chief Kgama to Coillard and Lewanika, 17 July 1889, in Coillard Papers, Salisbury archives. See also François Coillard (trans. and ed. Catherine W. Mackintosh), *On the Threshold of Central Africa* (London, 1902), 141–373.

be a treaty with Queen Victoria.[30] When they later learned that a commercial company had in fact practically obtained control of their lands and subsoil rights, their alarm was understandable. Nonetheless, the Lochner treaty, however unscrupulously obtained, subsequently proved the basis for the British South Africa Company's assumption of direct rule in Northwestern Rhodesia and, wrongly, for its rights to the lucrative ores that later allowed Northern Rhodesia to become the world's second largest producer of copper. In 1891, it and the treaties obtained by Johnston and his representatives in Northeastern Rhodesia, permitted the Chartered Company formally to include these regions within its sphere.

For the next three years, Johnston governed Northeastern Rhodesia with Rhodes's money and, at the same time, attempted to make Nyasaland (from 1893 to 1907, officially called the British Central Africa Protectorate) a tidy part of the empire. He established a rudimentary government and attempted to advance his own ideal program for tropical Africa. It should, he thought, "be ruled by whites, developed by Indians, and worked by blacks."[31] To further his scheme, Johnston sought to cooperate with missionaries, to encourage the immigration of additional whites as officials and coffee planters, and to import Sikhs and other Asians to serve as policemen and traders. Unfortunately for him, Johnston's ideas were greeted inhospitably by Africans. Although many of the less powerful chiefs cooperated with his government, the stronger leaders resisted the European take-over. As a contemporary wrote approvingly, "the history of Sir Harry Johnston's Administration . . . while it records many notable civil achievements, is yet in its more salient features a history of successive military expeditions"[32]

In 1891, a small army, commanded by Captain Cecil Montgomery Maguire and containing Sikhs and Muslim Lancers from Hyderabad, readied itself for the military conquest of British Central Africa. The result was one little war of resistance after another. In July, Chikumbu, a Yao chief who had attempted to prevent the successful settlement of coffee planters near Mlanje, found that his own weapons were no match for those of Maguire's troops. In September, Johnston, Maguire, and the Indian army went north from Zomba,

[30] A copy is printed in *Africa South*, 414, no. 245 (encl.).
[31] FO 2/55: H. H. Johnston to Percy Anderson, 10 October 1893.
[32] Hector L. Duff, *Nyasaland under the Foreign Office* (London, 1906), 17.

the Protectorate's capital, to deal with several other powerful Yao chiefs. After the beginnings of Fort Johnston had been constructed near Lake Nyasa's outlet to the Shire River, the Commissioner resolved to crush Makandanji, a chief who had tied up and imprisoned Johnston's envoys. The chief's town was seven miles from the fort. Maguire, wrote Johnston, "resolved on the true Napoleonic policy of crushing our enemies singly. . . . He suddenly fell on Makandanji and drove him out of his village . . . scattering Makandanji's forces, which were never again able to take the field against us." Mponda, a stronger chief who resided closer to the fort, thereupon enslaved the Africans scattered by Maguire. Johnston explained: "Over seventy of the captives he had the insolence to drive through our camp at Fort Johnston, at a time when Captain Maguire was absent and I was left with only ten men. As soon as Captain Maguire was back and the little fort was completed, I summoned Mponda to set all these slaves at liberty. He declined to do so, and commenced warlike proceedings against us."[33]

The British contingent resolved to attack at night. "Accordingly at nine o'clock, on the evening of the 19th of October, 1891, one hour after the expiration of the term given for the restoration of the slaves, we fired a shell across the river into Mponda's town, perhaps a quarter of a mile distant. . . . A few more shells soon set much of Mponda's town on fire, and he called for a truce."[34] Fighting continued throughout the night until Mponda capitulated early the following morning. "Encouraged by this success," Johnston and Maguire borrowed a steamer from the African Lakes Corporation, sailed up the lake, and soon destroyed the villages of Makanjira, a "notorious" slave-raiding chief of the east coast. By November 1891, Johnston could congratulate himself upon the first of a number of successful battles that were to make "our protectorate a reality."

Winning Central Africa for the empire was not always accomplished so easily. In December 1891, Kawinga, a Yao chief who lived northeast of Zomba, took up arms against the administration. Maguire and the Indians therefore marched to Kawinga's stockade and opened hostilities. But they met heavy fire. Maguire was wounded and several of the troops lost their lives before Kawinga treated for peace. He was told that he must accept the sovereignty

[33] Harry H. Johnston, *British Central Africa* (New York, 1897), 100.
[34] *Ibid.,* 101.

of the Queen and advise his people to pay taxes and buy gun licenses. Shortly thereafter, Maguire and two other Britons lost their lives in an abortive attempt to capture Makanjira, whose men had regained their command of the southeastern section of the lake. At about the same time, Zarafi, a Yao chief who had initially agreed to cooperate with the new administration, successfully attacked Fort Johnston. He turned back a punitive expedition and even captured the seven-pound gun upon which the British forces so often relied. And, to make matters worse for the Johnstonian cause, the peoples of Chiradzulu and Ndirande raided the main road between Blantyre and Zomba with impunity while Makanjira emerged from victory to fame and extended his sway farther along the eastern shores of Lake Nyasa and to sections of the west coast as well. African resistance had seemingly stemmed the tide of the white advance. "This time," wrote Johnston, "may be taken as the nadir of our fortunes."[35]

The antagonistic Yao maintained their independence throughout 1892 and, except for chief Liwonde's capitulation in early 1893, until the last months of that year. By then, however, Johnston had obtained a pacification subsidy from Rhodes, a new detachment of one hundred Sikhs from India, and three small gunboats with which to patrol the lake.

Nyaserera and Mkanda, "troublesome" chiefs who lived near Mlanje mountain, were the first to taste the bitterness of Johnston's new strength. Chiwaura, a Yao ally of Makanjira who had constructed a fortified town about five miles inland from Kota Kota, next faced the gunboats and the Sikhs. The British forces bombarded and, after severe hut-to-hut combat, occupied the town. Across the lake, Makanjira meanwhile had continued to proclaim his resistance to the British occupation. But at this junction Makanjira's men proved no match for the Sikhs, who stormed and fired their town under the cover of another bombardment from the gunboats. Although the chief himself again escaped, the expeditionary force razed his various villages, and constructed a new fort, named after Maguire, as a center from which Johnston effected the occupation of Makanjira's country.

Many of the Yao leaders still refused to accept their defeat as final. In 1894, the chiefs Makanjira, Makandanji, and Zarafi raided

35 *Ibid.*, 107.

the settlement that surrounded Fort Maguire, fired a section of the stockade and murdered the chief whom Johnston had appointed to replace Makanjira. During the remainder of that year, Makanjira gained followers and fortified a new capital town and, in early 1895, Zarafi, Kawinga, and Matapwiri led the Yao in a series of inconclusive sorties against the British settlements in the Shire Highlands. Johnston believed that they had conspired to oust the British completely. His Sikh troops consequently proceeded to sweep the country from the southern slopes of Mount Mlanje to Fort Johnston. They defeated Kawinga, disarmed Matapwiri, and, after heavy fighting, forced Zarafi to flee permanently into Moçambique. Before the year was out, the Sikhs had even ended Makanjira's vaunted independence. Only then, as Johnston later wrote, did "a sense of security spread over the Southern portion of the Protectorate which was quite pleasantly unfamiliar."[36]

The north still remained largely outside of the official British sphere of influence. Mlozi, an Arab slave trader and the most powerful personage along the lake, ruled the Karonga district from a fortified town on the Rukuru River. After some years during which he had endured British attempts to end the transport of slaves to the Indian Ocean littoral and had generally seemed content to coexist with the few Britons who had resided in his district, Mlozi attempted to reassert his economic and political freedom from British constraint. In Johnston's calculations, his elimination thereby became essential. In late 1895, after the final victory over Makanjira, Johnston assembled a strong force of four hundred soldiers, transported them by water to Karonga, and laid siege to Mlozi's stockaded town. Cannon shelled it, but Mlozi's Nyamwezi mercenaries fought tenaciously for two days until the town lay in ruins. The opposing forces then engaged in fierce fighting at close quarters before the British-led detachment emerged victorious. Mlozi was captured and hanged, and British expeditions subsequently destroyed the remaining stockades in northern Nyasaland.

Meanwhile, to the southwest, the Cewa chief Mwase Kasungu had also demonstrated a determination to resist European rule. After a short battle, the British troops took his village, and Mwase Kasungu committed suicide to avoid arrest. In the following year,

36 *Ibid.*, 132.

after Nkosi Gomani, the chief of a section of the Ngoni, had led his people in raids on mission stations and had promised to prevent Britons from occupying or administering his part of Nyasaland, a troop of British-officered Sikhs routed the Ngoni on a high plateau in what became the Ncheu district. Gomani himself remained at large, however, until he succumbed to a ruse prepared by one of the British officers. Before his death, which virtually ended African efforts to resist the British occupation, he apparently voiced the question that must for many years have been implicit on the lips of fellow Africans—and to which no completely satisfactory answer was ever forthcoming: "I come to ask why the white man brings war to my country, kills my people, and burns my villages?"[37]

Britons conquered Northeastern Rhodesia (the financier's name was officially applied to this portion of trans-Zambezia only in 1897) with greater ease. As early as 1891, Johnston established a government station near Lake Mweru in order to forestall Belgian encroachments across the Luapula River. Abercorn, near the southern end of Lake Tanganyika, and Fife, on the road between Lake Nyasa and Abercorn, became British outposts in 1894 and were, for a time, the sole manifestations of Imperial control in that region. The Imperial presence was therefore exiguous, but missionaries and planters had started to settle in its outlying regions and, by 1896, they had come into conflict with the traditional prerogatives of some of the more important tribal rulers. The western Ngoni had begun to resent the demands for labor made upon them by white recruiting agents and farmers. They rightly sensed a clear and present danger to their position as the leading Africans of eastern Rhodesia. Sharpe wrote to the Foreign Office: "Matters in Mpeseni's [Ngoni] country are far from satisfactory: These expeditions organized by the British South Africa Company or their sub-concessionaires keep dropping into the [Ngoni] district, and Mpeseni and his . . . warriors are evidently beginning to get a little uneasy."[38]

In early 1898, a convenient pretext was arranged and a force of 100 Sikhs and 350 Tonga and Yao, led by Colonel William Manning, invaded Mpeseni's country and compelled the Ngoni to submit to

[37] Quoted in R. C. F. Maugham, *Africa as I Have Known It* (London, 1929), 176.
[38] FO 2/106: Alfred Sharpe to Clement Hill, 26 May 1896.

Company and British rule.[39] During the next year, an equally large force of troops, reinforced with machine guns, brought an end to the independence of the Lunda Chief Kazembe. According to Codrington, Kazembe had "received European traders in a hostile manner." Despite a telegraphed plea from the Foreign Office to avoid military action, Sharpe prepared to strike "the final blow for order in Northeast Rhodesia." He later explained: "I assembled [the army] . . . [and] informed Kazembe of the foolishness of his actions and that I did not want to use force. . . . He was told to destroy his stockade. . . . He replied that he was ready for war Further negotiations were useless."[40] Kazembe fled from his capital on the Luapula River and permitted the British army to enter his village unmolested. Finally, with the diplomatic help of the White Fathers, the Company easily occupied Bembaland, despite a minor skirmish with a relatively unimportant chief.[41]

In Northwestern Rhodesia, the British "Resident" appointed to Barotseland in 1897 was officially forbidden to exercise, or even to try to obtain, administrative powers for the British South Africa Company from Lewanika. Lord Salisbury envisaged a far simpler arrangement. He instructed the Resident:

The British South Africa Company has no rights of government in Barotseland. . . . The relations of the . . . Company to Lewanika are regulated [solely] by the agreement of 1890. . . . You should not try to obtain any administrative power. . . . You are sent to redeem a long-standing promise made for Her Majesty's Government by the British South Africa Company, and to assist him in maintaining order amongst persons who are subject to H.M.G. jurisdiction. You will do your utmost to remain on the most friendly footing with the King.[42]

In 1899, Joseph Chamberlain, the then British Colonial Secretary, proposed to Lord Milner, the British High Commissioner in South Africa, that Colin Harding should relieve Robert Coryndon as the

---

[39] Accounts of the war will be found in: LO 5/4/7, LO 5/4/8, Salisbury archives; FO 2/147, FO 2/148, FO 2/149, Public Record Office; T. William Baxter, "The Angoni Rebellion and Mpeseni," *The Northern Rhodesia Journal*, ii (1950), 14–24.
[40] FO 2/210: Sharpe to the Foreign Office, 29 December 1899.
[41] Details in FO 2/248; FO 2/388; LO 5/4/13; Rotberg, *Missionaries*, 33–36.
[42] FO 2/131: Salisbury to Coryndon, 8 April 1897.

Resident in Barotseland. "I presume," he wrote, that "Harding is not likely to go too fast or to force matters if Lewanika objects. We do not want any trouble in Central Africa on our hands." Milner assured him that he had issued the "most explicit" instructions. Harding was "to do nothing without [the] full approval of the King."[43] Nonetheless, the Company soon exercised an overweening influence in all of Northwestern Rhodesia and, specifically, in Barotseland, as a result of the Northwestern Rhodesia-Barotseland Order-in-Council of 1899 and a new treaty concluded with Lewanika in 1900. In that treaty Lewanika conceded administrative rights to the Company and "all such things as are incidental or conducive to the exercise, attainment or protection of all or any of the [mining and commercial] rights powers and [other] concessions hereby granted."[44]

By 1901 all of trans-Zambezia had become subject to the Crown. By the use of the expedients of treaty and warfare, Britons had induced a number of recalcitrant tribal monarchs to end their resistance to the imposition of foreign rule. During the same period, white men had begun to force people into the labor market, make and enforce new laws, alienate African-owned land to settlers, and introduce taxes.

GOVERNING THE PEOPLE

Northern Rhodesia and Nyasaland were protectorates. In practice, however, Her Majesty's Government and its local representatives tended to ignore the legal limitations presumably inherent in a "protectorate" and treated the Central African territories as conquered colonies. While his power was secured by force of arms, Johnston derived legal authority to rule Africans from the British African Order-in-Council, 1889, as amended. It empowered him to make so-called Queen's Regulations in order to promote "peace, order, and good government" and to establish courts wherein Africans could be tried and sentenced for transgressing the Queen's Regulations. Armed with a unilateral British declaration, a number

[43] FO 2/248: Chamberlain to Milner, 14 November 1899; Milner to Chamberlain, 16 December 1899.
[44] Copy printed in Lewis H. Gann, The Birth of a Plural Society (Manchester, 1958), 216.

of treaties of friendship, some cessions of sovereignty, a small troop of Indian and African soldiers, and the force of his own personality, Johnston thus began, in 1891, to govern Nyasaland and a part of Northeastern Rhodesia. At first he confined himself to the Shire Highlands, only gradually extending the influence of his government northward along Lake Nyasa to lakes Tanganyika and Mweru. By 1896, he had established a pattern of administration that by and large proved the basis for all later British rule north of the Zambezi River.

In order to establish and to maintain law and order throughout the protectorates, Johnston in 1892 divided his administrative area into districts and employed Britons as Collectors of Revenue and Resident Magistrates. As their titles imply, these individual imperial pro-consuls (twenty-seven were employed in 1896) were responsible for the raising of revenue and the over-all supervision of their districts. They became super-chiefs and, as agents of the Commissioner (later Governor), their word constituted local law. They settled disputes between chiefs, decided where roads should be built, conscripted labor for public and private employment, organized a postal service, and acted as a combination overseer of, and handyman for, the public weal.

Under such a system, the authority of the chiefs in Nyasaland became nominal. By 1904, they played "no real part in the affairs of their country." The Protectorate *Annual Report* recognized the problem but proposed no remedy: "A somewhat difficult question for consideration is the extent of power which should be allowed to native chiefs. Before British influence was established a chief had unlimited powers . . . [Now] . . . the tendency is for the old large communities to be broken up."[45] Eight years later, the government once again congratulated itself upon the success of its policy of direct rule: "The decay of the power of native chiefs and the tendency all over the Protectorate to the splitting up of villages into small family groups continues: this tendency is to some extent gratifying in that it originates in the native's sense of his complete security under the existing Government."[46]

[45] Quoted in S. S. Murray (ed.), *A Handbook of Nyasaland* (London, 1932), 126, 128.
[46] *Ibid.*, 128.

In Nyasaland, the growth of a central government was rapid. An accountant joined Johnston in 1892; by 1896 a small secretariat had been established in Zomba, the Protectorate's capital that Johnston had artificially created. An embryo judicial department was begun in the same year. A Principal Medical Officer was appointed; a Superintendent of Public Works, a Superintendent of Roadmaking, and a First Surveyor all had their own departments. Each had a part to play in the British development of Nyasaland—as slow and as superficial as that development was at first to be.

Johnston and his successors believed strongly in positive government. His policies were honestly imperial:

Firstly, to protect the rights of the natives, to see that their villages and plantations are not disturbed, and that sufficient space is left for their expansion; secondly, to discourage land speculation; and, thirdly, to secure the rights of the Crown in such a way that the Crown shall profit by the development of this country, and find in its landed property a source of revenue which may enable it to further develop the resources of British Central Africa.[47]

At the same time, he wanted to encourage white settlement, and he was never loath to approve the transfer of large grants of land if the European purchaser demonstrated *bona fide*, non-speculative, intentions. Furthermore, Johnston equated "the rights of the natives" with the interests of the Crown and, by a variety of means, reserved as much land as he could to the Protectorate.

He encouraged coffee planters to enter the Shire Highlands during this early period. They opened up a number of profitable estates and turned to the administration for assistance in obtaining a steady supply of labor. In 1895, Johnston made regulations for the employment of Africans. He also began to tax Africans in order to induce them to offer their labor to the settlers, and in order to defray the cost of administering the country. As European control gradually asserted itself in the highlands to the south of Lake Nyasa and, eventually, north and west of the lake, he compelled Africans throughout the Protectorate to pay three or more shillings a hut. Foreign Office officials feared that Africans would rebel if the tax was imposed too harshly; Johnston and Sharpe, who followed him

[47] Quoted in Hanna, *Beginnings*, 231.

as Commissioner, therefore enforced the tax regulations throughout the entire Protectorate only after 1904, when the northern Ngoni began to pay. By that date it seemed clear to Central Africans that the British government had come to rule them permanently.

Across the territorial boundary, the two separately governed protectorates of Northeastern and Northwestern Rhodesia were actually subjected to regular Company administration only after 1901. A few scattered officials attempted to govern isolated districts of Northeastern Rhodesia in the 1890's; Abercorn, Fife, and "Rhodesia" near Lake Mweru early were fortified outposts and, only after the humbling of Mpeseni and Kazembe and the acquisition of Bembaland, could the Company create administrative centers. Robert Codrington, the Deputy (later full) Administrator of Northeastern Rhodesia, transferred his residence from Blantyre to the new Fort Jameson, near Mpeseni's town, only in 1899.[48] In Northwestern Rhodesia, the Administrator did not establish a secretariat until 1901. But, by that date, Africans had reluctantly accepted the British presence throughout all of what was to become Northern Rhodesia. Thereafter, the agents of the ruling British South Africa Company governed the Protectorate largely on Nyasaland lines. They imposed taxes and regulated land holdings. Administrators, variously called Collectors, Residents, Native Commissioners, and District Commissioners, supervised African life, made laws and dispensed justice, and generally attempted to develop and to modernize the large districts for which they were individually responsible.

Northern Rhodesia was created officially only in 1911, when the separate administrations of Northwestern and Northeastern Rhodesia, first divided by the Kafue River and later by the railway, were amalgamated by the British South Africa Company in order to economize. The town of Livingstone, near Victoria Falls, became the country's trading center and administrative capital. Most of the few thousand settlers who had been attracted to the territory after the conclusion of the South African War lived on either side of what became the single railway, which reached Broken Hill in 1906 and Ndola, on the way to Katanga, in 1909. Along the rail line, Kalomo, Choma, and Mazabuka served the most important farming districts.

[48] For Codrington, see Lewis H. Gann, A History of Northern Rhodesia: Early Days to 1953 (London, 1964), 94–96.

Other significant economic activity was carried on at the Broken Hill lead and zinc mine, at the Bwana Mkubwa copper mine near Ndola and, far to the east and northeast, in small, scattered farming communities.

These settlers exerted an influence out of all proportion to their number (in 1921 only 4000 whites resided in Northern Rhodesia) and the Chartered Company, which ruled until 1917 without any formal concession to white representative government, listened carefully to their grievances. Although a Legislative Council, on which settlers were represented, was granted to Nyasaland in 1907, the white farmers and miners of Northern Rhodesia grew increasingly more powerful than their counterparts in the neighboring protectorate. As a result, the government of Northern Rhodesia never really attempted to safeguard African rights to the same extent as the government in Nyasaland. Northern Rhodesia, as its name implied, was ideologically no more than an extension of the commercially controlled colonial system of Southern Rhodesia. In such circumstances, settlers naturally received greater privileges in the one than in the other and, in the long run, Africans fared worse in Northern Rhodesia than in Nyasaland. Even so, the discriminatory ways in which whites ruled Africans were sufficiently similar to provoke an almost identical anti-colonial response. The seedbed of nationalism was fertilized in practically the same, rich way.

Chapter 11

THE CHARACTER OF WHITE RULE

We have governed the native and over-governed him. We have taken from him the power of self-determination and have hedged him in with a network of rules and permits, a monotonous, highly regulated and very drab existence. We save him from war and enslavement but we do very little else for him [and] in return for what we have taken away we have given him very little in exchange.

—Mr. Justice Philip Macdonnell, in a letter to the Administrator of Northern Rhodesia, 5 May 1919

Central Africans received their first European visitors warmly. The Portuguese were reasonably well treated; Mwata Kazembe protected and succored the expedition of Francisco José de Lacerda when it reached his village. David Livingstone was a man of peaceful and honorable intentions. Generally, therefore, Africans assisted his travels, and remembered his visits with pleasure.[1] Subsequently, when the initial mission parties came to Nyasaland and Northern Rhodesia, they too were welcomed. Africans saw them as potential allies in the inter-tribal conflicts of the time. They fancied the missionaries' new Western skills and Western products, many of which came to be desired even by the more isolated indigenous peoples. Missionaries thus were allotted plots of land and encouraged to open new stations. Indeed, during the later years of the nineteenth century, Africans accepted foreigners of all persuasions rather uncritically. At the same time, those who attempted to interfere with established practice—like the slave trade—were anathema, and were dealt with as such. Thus, the Yao attacked the first Universities' Mission at Magomero and battled with Harry Johnston. The Cewa, Ngoni, and Lunda similarly fought an unequal struggle against white men who threatened to upset established ways of life.

[1] David Livingstone, *Missionary Travels and Researches in South Africa* (London, 1857), 169.

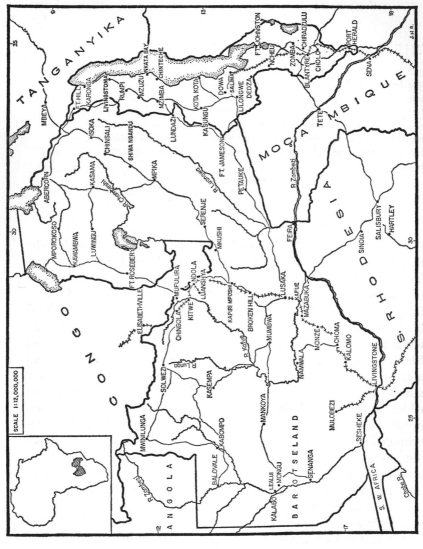

Northern Rhodesia and Nyasaland during the colonial period, showing important towns, administrative centers, rivers, railways, and roads.

That was really the point of African objection. Strangers were traditionally accepted into the African social system. Provided that they faithfully observed local customs, they usually went unmolested. But, when British laws and administrative regulations were introduced into Nyasaland and Northern Rhodesia in the 1890's, Africans began to think that the white explorers and missionaries had disguised their intentions. They became disillusioned and rued the day when they had allowed first a few, and later more, of these white strangers to settle in their country. As a Northern Rhodesian chief wrote long after it had become impossible to oust the whites without bloodshed: "When a white man came in this country he treated us as people but we have found out that he is leaving his first duty. . . ."[2] Why did white rule serve to disillusion Africans?

THE PROBLEM OF LAND RIGHTS

An agricultural and pastoral people regarded access to arable land as essential to their way of life. Before the coming of the Europeans, the inhabitants of Nyasaland and Northern Rhodesia grew millet, sorghum, maize, and a little tobacco and cotton, and grazed cattle in order to satisfy their own requirements. Throughout the middle years of the nineteenth century their land had changed hands; tribe fought tribe, African battled Arab, and newly arrived immigrant Africans squatted wherever they could find room. Then, in the years after Livingstone's visit, white missionaries, traders, planters, hunters, and concession-seekers began to arrive in trans-Zambezia. They either purchased land, often from "chiefs" who had no right to alienate tribal holdings, or persuaded African leaders to permit their unhindered settlement. Equally often, whites contentedly took land by force.

Johnston understood the importance of land to Africans. He also wanted to encourage the settlement of Europeans genuinely interested in the development of British Central Africa. After returning to Nyasaland in 1891 as its Commissioner, he attempted, with characteristic industry, to reconcile the needs of whites and Africans and to provide a rational basis for the future alienation of African-owned land. His task was initially hindered by the chaotic mélange of conflicting white land claims and counterclaims that purported to

2 Chief Musokotwani, Minutes of the Livingstone Native Welfare Association, 9 June 1930, Lusaka archives.

divide the more fertile parts of the Shire Highlands among a fairly small number of white owners. By taking advantage of African ingenuousness and inexperience, these individuals and companies had obtained ownership of land on which large numbers of Nyasas lived and tilled the soil. At Blantyre, Chief Kapeni, who sought protection from Ngoni raids, granted to the missionaries the right to settle and, in time, to purchase a site between the Likabula and Nasolo streams. Before long, most of what became the city of Blantyre-Limbe had been sold to eight persons for trifling amounts. The premier coffee planter John Buchanan, for example, purchased 3,065 acres of the future city for a gun, 32 yards of calico, two red caps, "and several other things." A British evangelist obtained 26,537 acres for "seven trusses of calico measuring 1,750 yards."[3] As Johnston reported to Lord Rosebery in 1892, after beginning his survey of land claims:

There are claimants whose demands it would be impossible for me to satisfy to the full unless I handed over to them thirty, forty or fifty square miles of territory, with all the native inhabitants as their serfs, with exclusive mining rights, road-making rights, and in some cases a "right to exclude all other Europeans from the land." Men who make claims like these have in most cases come up to Nyasaland rich only in their aspirations, have started with a few pounds' worth of inferior trade goods—flint-lock guns, gunpowder and cloth—and with these have induced some heedless young Chief or silly old savage to put his mark on a paper conferring vast territories and sovereign rights on the needy pioneer.[4]

Judge John Joseph Nunan, the British Central Africa Protectorate's chief legal officer, dilated upon these original claims in two judgments handed down by him in 1901 and 1903. He ruled that chiefs were not "landlords of the lands over which they rule," and that they could not, even with the consent of their people, dispose of freehold rights or easements. Furthermore, the chiefs, headmen, and other interested parties appeared to have surrendered the fee simple

[3] W. H. J. Rangeley, "Early Blantyre," *The Nyasaland Journal*, vii, 1 (1954), 37–42.

[4] FO 84/2197: H. H. Johnston to Lord Rosebery, 13 October 1892. Quoted in Roland Oliver, *Sir Harry Johnston and the Scramble for Africa* (London, 1957), 220–221.

of their lands with "a *gaîté de coeur* which must have endeared them to the traders in question."

The 60,000 acres which are the subject of this Judgment were sold for . . . a quantity of cloth, coloured stuff, guns, powder, brass wire, beads, and other things, being at the rate of one-fifth of a penny per acre. With equal cheerfulness and simplicity, the natives refrained from specifying any conditions on which they themselves might be allowed to remain on the transferred land.[5]

The 1903 Land Commission later estimated that the Shire Highlands had been alienated for about one-tenth of a penny per acre. Johnston set himself three tasks—to establish Crown ownership of land in order that he might be in a position to lease plots to settlers; to extinguish or to regulate private claims that conflicted with this aim; and to provide land sufficient for African villages and fields. If the Commissioner were satisfied that Africans had received a fair value for their lost lands, that there were no privileges or monopolies claimed that were inconsistent with the idea of British sovereignty, and "that the rights of the natives [were] sufficiently secured," he issued a Certificate of Claim to the European party concerned. Into these certificates he often introduced a section designed to protect Africans in the future. It read: ". . . no native village or plantation existing at the date of this certificate on the said estate shall be disturbed or removed without the consent in writing of Her Majesty's Commissioner and Consul-General." At the same time, the European proprietor was permitted to prevent the establishment of any new villages or plantations upon his property.[6]

By the end of 1893, Africans realized that Johnston had, despite his professedly good intentions, confirmed most of the important white-owned holdings and had acquired the remainder of the best land for the Crown. In his adjudication of the various claims, Johnston had in practice been unwilling to deny even the most unscrupulous private promoter some land to call his own. He dealt harshly

---

[5] Supervisor of Native Affairs v. Blantyre and East Africa Company, Blantyre, 28 April 1903, Zomba archives.

[6] Enclosure #2 in Acting Commissioner Pearce to the Marquess of Lansdowne, 7 July 1903; a slightly different version may be found in S1/411^{ii}/33: "Land Tenure and Tenancy," Zomba archives.

with absentee speculators but, by whatever standards Johnston used to divide up the densely populated Shire Highlands, more than half of the most suitable land was allowed to remain in white ownership. In North Nyasa, he was further constrained to approve the British South Africa Company's claim to 20,000 square miles of land near Karonga. This freehold was derived from treaties made on behalf of the Company and the Crown by Joseph Thomson, Alfred Sharpe, and other early emissaries. But, as the District Commissioner for Karonga later wrote, Africans who signed treaties with the early consuls and explorers could not—any more than Lewanika and Kapeni—have known what they were doing.

They were prepared to place themselves entirely under [European] protection and entered into an agreement to that effect, thinking these Europeans were the direct representatives of a greater power beyond the seas.

They could not possibly have understood the meaning or functions of a commercial firm and they could not have realized that the agreement they made was a sale, and that by this act they disinherited their tribe and deprived posterity of the right to their lands. I submit that this is tantamount to false pretense.[7]

Even so, in the final analysis Johnston permitted whites to control about 15 percent of the total land and water area of the Protectorate. This very control provided much of the basis for the subsequent growth of African unrest.

Johnston assumed, as he later did in Uganda, that he could arbitrarily design a permanent solution to the land problem. In Nyasaland, he thought that the inclusion of the non-disturbance clause in Certificates of Claim would prove sufficient protection for Africans. But the clause was enforced on neither side; little let or hindrance was placed in the way of African migration from place to place. Indeed, the European proprietors generally encouraged immigration onto their estates in order to obtain as large a supply of labor as possible. For the most part, they utilized only a small part of their holdings, and were content to allow Africans to cultivate and to reside anywhere on the undeveloped portion. By 1900, however, coffee prices had reached a comparatively high level and a number of the planters were only with extreme difficulty obtaining suffi-

[7] S1/1519a/28: J. J. O'Brien to the Northern Province Provincial Commissioner, 7 May 1930, Zomba archives.

cient labor during the planting period. They had, at that time, to compete with African devotion to the preparation of their own gardens. Planters thus began to charge Africans a rent for the privilege of residing upon and cultivating land owned by Europeans. The rental fee was not, however, expected to be paid in cash or kind. Instead, the planters hoped, indeed assumed, that Africans would choose to work upon the white-owned plantations for two months during the critical wet season. If so, their rent would be remitted and, in addition, they would receive the normal rate of pay with which they could defray their tax obligations to the administration.

By 1903, the *ad hoc* efforts of the planters had largely extinguished African land rights in the Shire Highlands. Whether he was an old or a new resident, and whether or not he was theoretically protected by a Certificate of Claim, the individual African had become a tenant at will. However, "he tends," said Judge Nunan, "to differ in one respect from the [unfree] mediaeval villein. If the latter were bound to the soil he had at least a fixity of tenure. The native, apparently, is to have eventually no tenure at all." The judge summarized eloquently:

The natives, in return for a past consideration—the fact that they have been allowed to change their gardens at some date not mentioned—surrender a freehold, or claim of freehold, and receive a tenancy at will, with the s[u]peradded condition that if they do not work for the landowner . . . for two months . . . during the rainy season (a period at which their labour is particularly valuable to themselves, as it includes two out of the three months of their own hoeing time), they are bound to pay 6s. annual rent . . . an annual payment equivalent to 120 per cent of the fee simple. The native has no security of tenure, must move without compensation when called upon . . . and can take up no fresh ground for his garden [without] permission. It is to this that British protection has brought the Central African native.[8]

Other abuses followed. Africans were paid only nominally for their induced labor. They received the equivalent of 3/- a month in calico, but the actual market value of the calico was apparently little more than 2/- a month. Africans were not allowed to sell the produce of their own gardens except to the proprietor of the estate. They could sell their labor only to the estate owner. And planters fre-

[8] Judgment of 28 April 1903.

quently paid the taxes owed by their tenants directly to the Collector without the personal appearance of the Africans concerned. This early, informal, "check-off" system assisted the administrative collection of the tax and, at the same time, permitted planters to exert an unfortunate influence over their tenants. It appears that proprietors were not above retaining the tax receipt as an "inducement" to encourage their tenants to comply with their demands for labor whenever called upon. Moreover, despite the claims advanced by the local Chamber of Agriculture and Commerce, Africans had no option. Cultivable acreage for gardens was available for the most part only on the vast, European-owned estates. Near Blantyre, the government earmarked all of the available Crown land for railway or official construction. Then too, Africans saw that the more important landholding companies refused to develop the bulk of their extensive holdings. By 1903, Europeans had utilized less than 1 percent of the total alienated acreage of the country during a peaceful period of relatively high world prices for tropical products. On the British Central Africa Company estate, for example, the owners had cultivated only 5,000 of its 367,000 acres. On the Bruce estates, against which John Chilembwe later directed his ire, all but 500 of its 160,000 acres lay fallow. In terms perhaps inappropriate for Central Africa, the Commission held that this inability or unwillingness to develop alienated lands virtually constituted mortmain, which deserved to be taxed.[9]

Despite the criticisms and recommendations of the 1903 Land Commission, the rights or lack of rights of Africans on alienated estates remained a source of indigenous grievance and national controversy for fifty years. Settlers successfully opposed administrative attempts to alleviate some of the main causes of African distress. According to Deputy Governor Francis Barrow Pearce, the European planter simply wanted cheap labor and disliked policies that tended to raise the natives above the level "at which they would be content to work for him at a pittance."[10] Pearce, when he acted as the governor, attempted to deny further white encroachments, but his successors were unwilling or unable to prevent renewed white

[9] British Central Africa Land Commission to Acting Commissioner Pearce, 6 May 1903, Zomba archives.
[10] CO 525/49: Pearce to the Secretary of State for the Colonies, 14 June 1913, Public Record Office. Pearce had earlier been styled Acting Commissioner.

alienation of African-occupied land and the perpetuation of the tenancy system.

In 1920, Claude Algernon Cardew, a district officer with many years experience in the Protectorate, sought to forestall white settlement in Central Angoniland. He explained at some length the reasons for Ngoni opposition to whites. "The Angoni are strongly opposed to Europeans residing in their midst, continually overlooking them and watching what they do, stopping their dancing and drumming on account of the noise, making trouble if their livestock wander on the estate, continually demanding labour, carriers, etc. from the neighbouring villages. . . . If the Europeans come the Angoni will be forced to move off."[11] But these protests, and those of Africans, were to no avail. By 1921, a large new influx of Europeans had leased large acreages throughout the Protectorate, thereby increasing the already aggravated problem of land ownership and tenant obligation.

In Judge Nunan's words, Africans who resided on white-owned estates remained little more than serfs throughout the period between the two world wars. By 1928, custom had even become enshrined in ordinance. Thereafter, the government officially excused African tenants on tea and coffee estates from the payment of rent so long as they worked for their respective proprietor whenever he requested them to do so. If Africans, whether original residents or not—and the distinction had become hopelessly blurred—refused to work, they either paid rent in cash or subjected themselves to eviction. Landlords told their tenants what and when they should plant, and purchased the resultant crops from them, in lieu of rental obligations, at contrived prices.[12] From the settler's point of view, the estates were private property, paid for by hard-earned money. Africans, on the other hand, claimed that they had been arbitrarily deprived of their lands and, in the process, unconscionably abused: Although their soils became exhausted, the estate owners refused them new lands for gardens. If they moved onto fallow land, the owner uprooted their crops. African tenants were not allowed to grow maize and other foodstuffs for personal profit.

[11] S1/378/20: Claude Algernon Cardew to the Chief Secretary, 6 May 1920, Zomba archives.

[12] See S1/411ii/33: Governor Harold Kittermaster to Secretary of State Philip Cunliffe-Lister, 15 December 1934, Zomba archives.

They could not cut down trees in order to build huts in the traditional manner. In an area where the customary pattern of settlement was matrilocal, Europeans forbade young men to settle on
the lands of the family of their prospective spouse. Men who lived
on an estate, but who worked and had their fields elsewhere, were
forced to pay rent for the land on which their hut was sited. Proprietors often compelled youths to leave the estates when they
came of age.[13] In short, if Africans distrusted white rule, they need
only to have resided upon a European-owned plantation for all
their worst fears to be confirmed.

The moderate white reaction to this problem was expressed in an
early missionary publication: "On the face of it, it is an anomaly that
the native should . . . have to buy back land which was once his
own. Where once he had fixity of tenure he now has to pay for it
at the rate of four shillings per annum. It is an anomaly but one
of those anomalies which must be allowed for."[14]

In Northern Rhodesia, meanwhile, there was far less pressure
upon the land. Although individual settlers immigrated there in
numbers greater than to Nyasaland, there was ample land for all.
The soil was, overall, less fertile than that of the Shire Highlands,
there were relatively fewer Africans, and the parts of Northern
Rhodesia most thickly populated by Africans were for the most part
distant from the main areas of white settlement. Thus, with the exception of one important area of white interpenetration, African
patterns of land use were little affected by the coming of the Europeans and by the subsequent alienation of much of the better and
more accessible tracts to whites. At no time did Northern Rhodesians agitate for the return of their land in the manner of Kenyans
or Nyasas.

The British South Africa Company acquired control of the land
of Northern Rhodesia by virtue of the Lozi concessions and the
treaties and Certificates of Claim approved by Johnston. The agreements with Lewanika permitted the Company to create townships
and to grant estates in Northwestern Rhodesia to prospective settlers. In the years after the South African War, whites began to oc-

---

[13] S1/411ii/33: the District Commissioner (Cholo) to the Chief Secretary,
13 June 1936, Zomba archives.
[14] Quoted in George Shepperson and Thomas Price, *Independent African*
(Edinburgh, 1958), 144.

cupy homesteads on either side of the single railway line from Livingstone to Ndola. They grew maize and grazed cattle and at first competed largely for local markets. Wherever African land holdings interfered with the tracts exercised by white farmers, Africans were moved. But, in the early years, settlers were happy to have a ready source of labor resident upon their farms. They made no distinction between resident and non-resident Africans; if Africans refused to participate when their labor was required, they could be evicted. If the treatment they received was too harsh, unalienated land was not far away, and Africans were usually content to migrate. Instances of individual hardship should not be minimized but, in broad social terms, the indigenous inhabitants of Northern Rhodesia felt the impact of white settlement less severely than did their fellow Africans in neighboring Southern Rhodesia or Nyasaland, or in Kenya.

Nevertheless, in order to attract new settlers, in 1913 the Company drew up elaborate plans for reserves that would confine Africans to lands well removed from the choice farm sites along the railway line. Although this scheme was modeled upon the South African and Southern Rhodesian precedents, and was motivated primarily by a desire to restrain Africans from permanently occupying lands suitable for whites, it also reflected the benevolent and romantic thoughts of those who saw in reserves a way of preserving African life uncontaminated by the demands and concerns of Western civilization.[15] But, only in 1928/29 were these reserves, and those in the northern and eastern provinces, actually created; the best half of the land in the administrative districts along the railway line was reserved to European settlements, the other half to about 300,000 Africans.[16] In 1938, the Pim Commission reported that almost 90 percent of the land from which Africans had been moved had not yet been taken up by Europeans and was consequently lying fallow. One-third of the Ndola district and two-fifths of the Mkushi district

[15] See correspondence for 1918/19 in the John White Papers, Methodist Missionary Society archives; A 3/2, on "Native Reserves," Lusaka archives; J. Merle Davis (ed.), *Modern Industry and the African* (London, 1933), 235–236.
[16] Philip Mason, "Land Policy," in Richard Gray, *The Two Nations* (London, 1960), 85; A. W. Pim and S. Milligan, *Report of the Commission Appointed to Enquire into the Financial and Economic Position of Northern Rhodesia*, col. no. 145 (1938), 57.

were, as a result, practically uninhabited. Meanwhile, in the newly demarcated reserves to which Africans had been sent, overcrowding and the resultant destruction of timber and soil resources—sheet erosion presented a further problem—testified to their inadequacy.[17] And the very distance of Africans from the railway line tended to arrest the development of their participation in the Protectorate's cash economy.

While these maneuvers were taking place on the line of rail, the Protectorate's only serious disagreement over land rights was being precipitated in Mpeseni's country. The defeat of the Ngoni, in 1899, had heralded a land rush; the North Charterland Exploration Company, the founders of which had wrung a concession from Mpeseni and had subsequently brought about the war that had resulted in his downfall, alienated large blocks of land to European stockmen. On these lands as many as 150 Ngoni frequently resided per square mile. This was the most densely populated part of Northern Rhodesia; thus, competition between white and black for available grazing land early threatened to become acute. In 1904, the first of many commissions investigated the situation and proposed that a Ngoni reserve be created. In 1907, the government gazetted a very small reserve, but no Africans were compelled to move into it.[18] Only after the arrival of white cotton and tobacco farmers, in the period from 1910 to 1913, did settlers agitate to expel Africans from white-owned land. Administrative officials moved a number of villages during this period, despite African protests, but this enforced transfer proved *ultra vires*, and no reserves were created.

At the conclusion of World War I, a new influx of settlers, and an attempt by the North Charterland Company to profit by its concession, combined to threaten African holdings once again. The Company and the settlers wanted to remove about 150,000 Ngoni, Nsenga, Kunda, and Cewa from their lands in order to make way for an undetermined number of whites who might be induced to purchase Company-owned lands in the Fort Jameson district at 1/- an acre.[19] The Anglican missionaries resident in the area protested

[17] *Ibid.*, 65–70.

[18] ZP 1/1/1, Lusaka archives. But cf. Lewis H. Gann, *The Birth of a Plural Society* (Manchester, 1958), 146.

[19] See the Campion Papers, Salisbury, for 1920; Msoro Papers, Northern Rhodesia, for 1921; John R. Fell, "Native Reserves," *Proceedings of the General Missionary Conference of Northern Rhodesia* (Kafue, 1922), 47–58.

on behalf of the indigenous population. They pointed out that Africans would be transferred from land that had been occupied for generations to a country quite incapable of sustaining them. Of one district, the Anglican Bishop complained: "it seems . . . a questionable proceeding to remove 2500 natives from a district which is admirably fitted for their requirements to another which is quite unfitted, in order that two or three Europeans may be settled."[20] A district officer confessed that the removal of Africans into reserves might cause discontent. "It is difficult to find a place for them to go where there is timber and water."[21] Even so, after two special land commissions had, at the behest of the Chartered Company, surveyed the land and reported, after the House of Commons had discussed the point, and after the Governor of Northern Rhodesia had listened patiently to missionary objections, reserves were delimited and Africans were moved away from the more desirable sections of the Charterland concession.[22] A government agricultural specialist later toured the reserves with a district officer and reported that the crowding of Africans into such agriculturally inadequate reserves had caused famine and periods of acute hunger. He also reported the existence of widespread African discontent.[23]

THE IMPOSITION OF HUT AND POLL TAXES

The principle of raising needed revenue from the inhabitants of overseas protectorates and colonies was common to all of the European empires. Although missionary opinion was hostile, Johnston held that "those natives of British Central Africa who were unable to protect themselves from the incursions of slave raiders, or who by their own misconduct compelled the intervention of the Administration for the maintenance of law and order, should contribute as far as their means allowed towards the revenue of the Protectorate, for

[20] Bishop May, in *Central Africa* (1922), 144.

[21] B 1/8/2: Report of an interview in Fort Jameson between the police and native commissioners, 30 May 1920, Lusaka archives.

[22] See *North Charterland Concession Inquiry: Report to the Governor of Northern Rhodesia, by the Commissioner, Mr. Justice Maugham, July 1932*, col. no. 73 (1932); *Report . . . May 1933*, col. no. 85 (1933).

[23] Sec/Nat/85: Report by R. H. Fraser and Kenneth Bradley, 21 July 1938, Lusaka archives; Pim, *Report*, 60–62; R. H. Fraser, "Land Settlement in the Eastern Province of Northern Rhodesia," *The Rhodes-Livingstone Journal*, iii (1945), 46–47. See also *Parliamentary Debates*, fifth series (1922), 155/1024, 156/269–270, 166/1642.

it was not to be supposed that the British taxpayer . . . could continue indefinitely finding subsidies for the support of the Protectorate."[24] In short, the Protectorate, like most colonial claims upon Her Majesty's reluctant Treasury, had to justify its existence by attempting to support itself. A yearly 6/- tax on an individual's huts, soon reduced to 3/-, was thus imposed in 1892 throughout the British-administered portions of the Shire Highlands. An African who owned three huts (each wife had a dwelling of her own) paid three times 3/-; one who had four wives paid four times. Gradually, as Johnston and Sharpe conquered and occupied Nyasaland, new British-protected peoples were compelled to pay part of the cost of their own pacification. Chiefs were at first employed to collect the tax. Later, administrative officials, the Collectors of Revenue, were employed primarily to secure the taxes, and only incidentally to govern their districts. By 1894, Johnston was collecting more than £1100 yearly. [25]

When the outlying districts of Nyasaland and Northern Rhodesia were in time subjected to European rule, they too were asked to contribute financially. In Northeastern Rhodesia, the administration began to collect hut taxes in 1901 without meeting serious resistance. "The natives," wrote Robert Codrington, "consider the tax inevitable."[26] In Nyasaland, the chiefs of the northern Ngoni met Alfred Sharpe, then the governor, at Ekwendeni in 1904 and agreed peacefully to join the Protectorate, provided that they were not compelled to pay taxes until 1906.[27] Meanwhile, in the years between 1904 and 1913, the principle of taxation by huts was extended slowly to Northwestern Rhodesia despite occasional African resistance.[28] In almost every instance the collectors initially accepted remittances in kind. "In those days a Government station must have presented very much the appearance of a farmyard; for besides grain, fruit, eggs, and other produce, quantities of live stock were brought in by the taxpayers, including many thousands of fowls. These latter were turned wholesale into runs built for their reception, from which naturally many escaped or were stolen, while others died from over-

[24] Harry H. Johnston, *British Central Africa* (New York, 1897), 111.
[25] FO 2/66: H. H. Johnston to Lord Rosebery, 22 January 1894.
[26] A 2/3/1/4: Codrington to the B.S.A. Co. (London Office), yearly report for 1902, Lusaka archives.
[27] 1a/1398: Sharpe to Colonial Office, 14 October 1904, Zomba archives.
[28] See A 3/14/1, Lusaka archives.

crowding and similar causes."[29] In some districts coin quickly replaced kind, thereby cushioning some of the more invidious effects of the early methods of tax collection. Yet a Portuguese traveler was shocked in 1909 to discover that Africans in parts of Northeastern Rhodesia were required—in a manner faintly reminiscent of the Congo scandals—to gather rubber in order to satisfy their obligations: "The natives are prohibited to sell rubber, and so are the traders to buy it. The natives can only gather it under the condition that they hand it over to the Government in payment of their hut tax, [although] for every additional pound the Government pays 6d a pound."[30] This form of compulsory contribution of produce was rare, however, for the taxation of Africans was intended to perform a very different function.

The pacification of trans-Zambezia attracted increasing numbers of immigrants and imposed new responsibilities upon a growing administrative staff. The immigrants—most of whom had obtained some experience in South Africa—wanted the services of African labor in order to assist the development of newly alienated lands. They early demanded that their governments should—by any one of a number of means—encourage Africans to forsake their tribal chores for employment opportunities on white-owned estates. The administrators themselves sought to obtain labor for the performance of a variety of routine tasks; they always needed head porters, for instance. But both the Foreign and Colonial Offices frowned upon methods of recruitment that approximated impressment. As a result, the governments of Nyasaland and Northern Rhodesia used the tax as an instrument with which to induce Africans to offer their labor to whites in return for artificial rates of pay that were geared entirely to the level of the prevailing tax assessment. They consciously set the rate of tax at a level that would successfully draw African males away from their homes to the usually distant centers of white agriculture and industry. Although a relatively few Africans had previously begun to migrate from their trans-Zambezian homes to South Africa before the coming of the Europeans to Central Africa, taxation became the compelling reason for a twentieth-

---

[29] Hector L. Duff, *Nyasaland under the Foreign Office* (London, 1906), 352.
[30] A 1/6/3: Teixeira de Mattos to Sharpe, 19 March 1909, Lusaka archives; Cf. A/2/5: The Administrator of Northeastern Rhodesia to Governor of Nyasaland, 17 May 1909, Lusaka archives.

century migration that transformed the countryside and destroyed a traditional way of life.

The taxation of Africans was the cornerstone upon which the subsequent structure of white rule and white prosperity was built. The governments of Northeastern and Northwestern Rhodesia were subjected to heavy pressure to tax from their own settlers, from their district officers, and from the British South Africa Company office in Salisbury. The Company, on behalf of farmers and gold miners south of the Zambezi River, sought to attract thither a steady supply of labor—generally unavailable in the Colony—from the northern protectorates. The difficulties of administering an undeveloped domain would, they believed, thereby be eased. Codrington put his case simply: "the natives are able . . . to pay the three shilling hut tax. It would prove, as . . . in the British Central Africa Protectorate, a means of getting a certain amount of work out of the natives, and would in this manner greatly assist transport difficulties."[31]

In 1902, the Administrator of Northeastern Rhodesia introduced a hut tax and reported that Africans who lived in districts bordering the Zambezi River were being encouraged to migrate to the Southern Rhodesian mines: "The tax has made labour generally plentiful."[32] Val Gielgud, an official stationed in the Hook of the Kafue River district, carefully informed Africans about the principles and purposes of European taxation and, throughout 1901/02, encouraged Ila tribesmen to go to Bulawayo in order to obtain the cash with which to pay their taxes.[33] In the Chambezi district, where Africans were once forced to work for the administration without pay, the general acknowledgment of tax obligations permitted British officials to renounce the *corvée* and various other techniques by which African workers had been introduced to the white man's employment. Unpaid labor for the government, in lieu of tax obligations, was also encouraged in Northeastern Rhodesia until the Foreign Office learned of this system and unequivocally ordered its cessation.[34] Initially, the monthly scales of pay were artificially

[31] FO 2/210: Codrington to the Administrator (Salisbury), 15 June 1899.

[32] A 2/3/1/4: The Administrator of Northeastern Rhodesia to the Colonial Office, yearly report, 1902, Lusaka archives.

[33] A 3/8/1: Gielgud to the Administrator of Northeastern Rhodesia, 1901/02, *passim*, Lusaka archives.

[34] FO 2/669: Minutes of 22 December 1902, by Cranborne, Lord Lansdowne, and Clement Hill, on Sharpe to the Foreign Office, 14 October 1902.

pegged to a level approximately one-half of the prevailing rate of taxation per hut. If a man had one wife, he usually found that he would need to work for two months in order to pay his taxes. Additional wives meant more months in employment. At times, too, wages alone failed to attract labor. For long, the African section of Central Africa's dual economy remained insulated from the price and wage mechanism of the cash sector.[35]

During Nyasaland's early years, the local supply of labor was more or less adequate for the needs of the small white colony. The tax obligations imposed by Johnston were sufficient to attract African workers to the new plantations, thereby fulfilling one of the critical items of the Commissioner's credo: "A gentle insistence that the native should contribute his fair share to the revenue of the country by paying his hut-tax, is all that is necessary on our part to secure his taking that share of life's labour which no human being should evade."[36] But with the introduction of a coffee industry and the consequent increase in the settler population, the demand intensified for carriers, for household servants, for roadworkers, and for agricultural labor of all kind.

The system then in practice seemed simple: if an African did not pay the required 3/- in any financial year, he was called upon to work for one month in private or government employment, at the ordinary rate for unskilled labor of 3/- per month. At the expiration of his month—usually the "ticket" month of thirty days, rather than a calendar month—the pay due him was made over to the administration in discharge of his tax. In time, this system encouraged Africans to pay their taxes punctually in order to evade requisition as defaulters. The number of those who could legitimately be compelled to work thus grew smaller, at a time when pressure from planters increased inexorably. The labor supply became dependent largely upon the good offices or, as a contemporary phrased it, "the moral influence" exercised by collectors over the inhabitants of their districts. But this influence was subject to abuse. The problem was best expressed by one of the administrators involved:

I am far from wishing to underrate the force of such [moral] influence, especially among a simple and amiable people like the Bantu negroes of

[35] See Robert E. Baldwin, "Wage Policy in a Dual Economy—The Case of Northern Rhodesia," *Race*, iv (1962), 74–79.

[36] Quoted in Oliver, *Johnston*, 270.

Nyasaland; but a certain inequality in the distribution of that noble faculty, which draws the good-will and commands the obedience of subjects, warns us not to rely upon it as a perfectly stable quantity in practical politics. When present in its fullest perfection, it can achieve wonders, no doubt; but hardly any two men seem to possess it in quite the same degree; and, at the worst, mischance may conceivably ordain that an Administration shall be largely composed of able and conscientious members in whom it is deficient.

Without wishing to agree with what others had implied—that Nyasaland had been guilty of abusing the privileges of tax labor— Duff concluded that "many thousands of natives, by a judicious admixture of authority and persuasion, [had been] induced to bestir themselves, [perhaps] against their immediate inclinations."[37] In 1902, as a result of these various demands and inconsistencies, Sharpe ingeniously doubled the rate of hut tax while simultaneously offering a 50 percent rebate to those Africans who hired themselves out to Europeans for at least one month in the year.[38] After 1911, those who sold 120 pounds of rice, 100 pounds of tobacco, or 36 to 56 pounds of cotton to white merchants were likewise exempted from paying the maximum amount. By this means Africans contributed heavily to the economic development of Nyasaland and Northern Rhodesia. Before World War I, for example an acting governor noted that Nyasaland depended directly upon the taxes of more than one million Africans for 70 percent of the Protectorate's annual revenue. They also worked to produce the crops grown by 107 planters, and made life more comfortable for the 200 missionaries and 100 administrators. He concluded that those who paid the most were being cheated.[39] After the war, an outspoken, experienced, district officer explained:

At present the natives of the Protectorate contribute the greater part of the revenue by direct taxation, irrespective of indirect taxation which they bear in common with all persons residing in the Protectorate. Europeans and Indians, who are in a better position to bear direct taxation, are not taxed directly. The natives get very little in return for providing the

[37] Duff, *Nyasaland,* 355–356.
[38] FO 2/605: Sharpe to Hill, 3 April 1902, fol. 322; FO 2/606, fols. 78–81.
[39] GOA 5/3/1: Pearce, "Confidential Notes on Nyasaland," August 1913, Zomba archives.

greater part of the revenue. They have peace and justice. . . . Apart from
that they are left practically unaided. Of education nothing except minute
Government contributions to Mission Funds. Of medical aid nothing
whatever. . .[40]

There is no reason to deny such observations or to doubt that these
views were shared by the leading missionaries and, indeed, by the
Africans concerned.

Throughout the colonial history of Nyasaland and Northern Rhodesia, the incidence and extent of African taxation remained an issue.
The principle remained the same: "If we owe a duty to the natives,
they also owe a duty to us. We are performing our part of the con-
tract loyally, and we have a right to expect that they shall assist us
with their labour in the performance of designs which tend to the
mutual benefit of all concerned."[41] As the available labor supply
shrunk, however, and the cost of colonial administration grew, so
were African taxes increased. In 1920, a flat rate of 6/- was imposed;
in 1927, the tax was raised to 9/- a year for those who failed to pay
the lower amount by the end of a fiscal year.

In Northern Rhodesia, the rate of taxation, although it differed
according to the wealth of the district in question, increased steadily
throughout the interwar period. The Protectorate's foremost settler
commented: "Poor villagers . . . their tax [has been] put up from 5/-
to 10/- a year as a reward for being loyal. It's the good old policy
of exploiting the black man, in this case it's intended to drive him
down to the mines in Southern Rhodesia, 1600 miles away, where
they're short of labour."[42] For those tribes which were troublesome,
the tax was likewise increased as a punitive measure: "Any [native]
tendency to trifle with the Government," said Governor Herbert
Stanley, "leads to unpleasant consequences."[43] Similarly, in Nyasaland measures traditionally used to collect taxes were improved. The
administration burned huts of tax defaulters, seized their wives
until the tax was paid, and continued the old practice of accepting
road labor in lieu of taxes. In 1921, the Government of Nyasaland

[40] S1/1365/19: Cardew to the Chief Secretary, 17 March 1920, Zomba
archives.
[41] Duff, *Nyasaland*, 363.
[42] Gore-Browne Papers: Stewart Gore-Browne to Dame Ethel Locke-King,
15 June 1921, privately held.
[43] B 1/1/1061: Stanley to the Secretary of State for the Colonies, 8 May
1926, Lusaka archives.

recognized the necessity of taking hostages in lieu of taxes.[44] In 1926, a Provincial Commissioner, later supported by the Chief Secretary, extended the practice. He wrote: "I approve of your demolishing the . . . huts of adult male defaulters . . . [and] . . . the huts of women whose husbands are [away] in Southern Rhodesia and who have not paid the hut tax. . . . I would add that the simplest way of destroying a hut is to have it demolished with poles. . . . If you burn and a wind gets up other huts are apt to catch fire."[45]

In 1930, when Lord Passfield (Sidney Webb) briefly became the Secretary of State for the Colonies, he declared that taxation should not be imposed to the extent that it would disrupt traditional life or, as he suspected were the intentions of the Government of Northern Rhodesia, to compel Africans to offer their labor to the newly opened copper mines. "Taxation," he wrote, "is not meant to change the life of a people."[46] Nonetheless, it soon appeared evident that taxation was responsible for decreasing the extent of polygyny, for driving men permanently from the rural areas, for thereby encouraging divorce, both urban and rural adultery and, in time, prostitution, and for giving rise to all the myriad ills that critics have lumped together in their attacks upon "migrant labor" and "detribalization."[47] The worker was furthermore compelled inequitably to pay taxes for the non-worker and to pay irrespective of his means or the extent to which he contributed indirectly or involuntarily to the government revenues. As the Chief Secretary of Northern Rhodesia privately expostulated in 1937: "I know of no justification for demanding that . . . a man shall leave his home and family in order to earn money."[48]

The governments of Britain, Nyasaland, and Northern Rhodesia were in African eyes identified intimately with the tax burden and its attendant consequences. Tax collecting was, after all, the major

[44] S1/312/21: Chief Secretary, circular letter, 24 October 1921, Zomba archives.

[45] S1/312/21: C. J. Brackenbury to the Resident (Chinteche), 11 February 1926; The Chief Secretary to Brackenbury, 16 March 1928.

[46] ZA 1/12: Lord Passfield to the Governor of Northern Rhodesia, 7 February 1930, Lusaka archives. This constituted a revolutionary departure from previous policy.

[47] See Davis, *Modern Industry*, 59–122; Gray, *Two Nations*, 120–127.

[48] P 2/3: Charles Dundas, minute of 26 April 1937, Lusaka archives.

preoccupation of the provincial administration. In Northern Rhodesia, district officers appeared at the mines and in sawmills on payday and collected a worker's tax from him at the moment that he received it. In Nyasaland, the planters continued to pay taxes directly to the government from the wages of their worker-tenants. Throughout the rural areas, the imprisonment of debtors was common (7589 persons in Northern Rhodesia in 1933) even after destruction of huts and the imprisonment of hostages had been ruled illegal. Whenever it needed more money, the colonial administration looked first to Africans. Obviously, a government that devoted most of its visible activities to collecting taxes was unlikely to be popular, especially if the methods employed were often somewhat unusual. Or, as this truism was expressed more directly in official circles: "There are causes for unrest: The native is getting nothing out of the white man; we give him no education, nothing, and screw 10/- out of him. The wages are usually 6/- per month. . . and calico you cannot buy."[49] Africans agreed, recognized their own large contribution to the local economies, spoke unsuccessfully against each increase in taxes, and slowly fanned the fires of protest.

COLONIAL GOVERNMENT, JUSTICE, AND DISCRIMINATION

Like colonial subjects elsewhere in tropical Africa, the peoples of Nyasaland and Northern Rhodesia suffered arbitrary rule by aliens. Officials, variously styled Collector, Resident, Magistrate, and Native Commissioner, prevented tribal warfare and local quarrels, eradicated the slave trade, collected taxes, and made themselves responsible for the introduction of Western concepts of law and order into their administrative districts. The Lozi excepted, these white officials deprived important chiefs of their traditional executive and judicial powers and typically guided tribal activities themselves. Recalcitrant indigenous leaders were deposed and "loyal" tribesmen appointed in their place. When his troops had occupied Bembaland in 1899, the Administrator of Northeast Rhodesia personally appointed a successor to Chief Mwamba: "I held an *indaba* with the headmen . . . and told them I had nominated Kalonganjofu to be their chief and called on them to recognize him as such. I also addressed Kalonganjofu [and told him] exactly what

49 B 1/8/2: Interview with Peter Cookson, Native Commissioner, 30 May 1920, Lusaka archives.

would be required of him in his position as chief, and directed him to enter on his inheritance without committing the barbarities customary to his tribe."[50]

White administrators were few, however, and at times "loyal" chiefs were paid to act as agents for the European government. Shorn of political powers and forbidden to exact tribute from their subjects or to exercise their most important religious functions, they were paid a small salary for doing police work.[51] The traditional role of the chief obviously declined and, in practice, British officials became "gods" whose responsibilities and rights appeared almost limitless. In the Abercorn district of Northern Rhodesia, for example, the Native Commissioner was officially "responsible for the welfare of the natives, for the collection of taxes, for compiling the census, for obtaining details of tribal customs, for [providing] speedy notice of any cases of disloyalty towards the administration, for the general well-being and order of his people, and for the hearing of all native civil and criminal cases." He supervised four chiefs and their subordinate headmen. When touring his district he made a prismatic compass survey, ascertained the precise location of all geographical features, made sectional maps, observed the condition of the African crops and stock, informed the people of the different regulations that affected them, and "generally note[d] the state and condition of the inhabitants."[52] On the whole, this was an *ad hoc* system of direct government that successfully subordinated the peoples of Central Africa to the Crown.

The destruction of the tribal authority was swiftly accomplished, particularly in Nyasaland. There, even the historic superstructure of chiefs and subchiefs was dismembered in 1912 and, by the terms of the District Administration (Native) Ordinance, an artificial hierarchy of Principal and Village Headmen substituted everywhere except in those districts where Africans squatted upon land owned by whites. The new scheme, "in no way intended to bolster up, foster, or perpetuate either governance by chiefs or tribal instincts," was an improvement upon the prevalent pattern of direct white rule.

[50] FO 2/248: Codrington to the Administrator (Salisbury), 15 June 1899.

[51] Leo Marquard, "The Problem of Government," in Davis, *Modern Industry*, 250.

[52] IN 1/12: "Memorandum on Native Administration in Northeastern Rhodesia," c. 1903/04, Lusaka archives.

Governor William Manning introduced it in order to give the administration a stricter control of "the rising generation" of rural Nyasaland.[53] The Principal Headmen, who were encouraged to regard the District Resident as the "only chief" to whom they were beholden, were appointed by the governor in recognition of their previous service to the colonial regime. According to the relevant legislation, the Principal Headmen were responsible for the maintenance of discipline, the encouragement of taxpaying, the reporting of crime, the apprehension of criminals, the provision of sanitation, control of cattle movement, and the general welfare of their administrative areas. Each supervised a number of Village Headmen and all met together, as a theoretically embryonic local government, in a council of headmen presided over by the various District Residents.

Neither in Nyasaland nor in Northern Rhodesia was direct rule a wholly satisfactory way of governing peoples who preferred to be left alone. Even Governor George Smith, in attempting to persuade the Colonial Secretary to strengthen Nyasaland's District Administration Ordinance, unwittingly appreciated the problem: "It is growing more and more apparent that something must be done to combat the increasing apathy of the indigenous races, attributable in no small degree, it may fairly be asserted, to the peace, good order and higher civilization resulting from the enlightened administration which European occupation has conferred."[54]

Direct rule was largely negative and disruptive; it took little or no account of indigenous political requirements and hastened the otherwise rapid pace of detribalization. Because Africans were governed, in practice, by whites, it also tended to "weaken tribal feeling," and, as a perceptive judge realized, "to foster and accelerate a race consciousness that may possibly have an anti-European tendency."[55] Moreover, the publication in 1922 of Lord Lugard's *The Dual Mandate in British Tropical Africa*, and the formal introduction into Tanganyika of a government modeled upon his conceptions,

[53] CO 525/43: Manning to Harcourt, 19 October 1912, Public Record Office; *Proceedings of the Nyasaland Legislative Council*, tenth session, 5–8 November 1912, 10; S. S. Murray (ed.), *A Handbook of Nyasaland* (London, 1932), 129.
[54] NC 1/19/1: Smith to the Secretary of State for the Colonies, 9 August 1922, Zomba archives.
[55] ZA 1/9/39: Macdonnell to Moffat Thomson, 13 February 1927, Lusaka archives.

made Central African and British officials think that methods of direct administration were conceivably a derogation of the principles of Imperial Trust by which they had originally justified the protection of trans-Zambezia.

Indirect rule, imposed in Northern Rhodesia from 1930, and in Nyasaland from 1933, was an attempt to transform chiefs and chief's councils into local governments by investing them with political, administrative, and judicial powers, without, however, granting them any financial responsibility or control. The ordinances concerning indirect rule were models of paternal benevolence. Chiefs and Principal Headmen were gazetted Native Authorities and were permitted to make rules and orders for the regulation of their own districts. This legislation was subject to the veto of a European district commissioner who could, if he so wished, compel a Native Authority to issue an order on any subject or to enforce any rules that were observed more in the breach than in practice. The governments of Nyasaland and Northern Rhodesia likewise gave the Native Authorities limited judicial responsibility under the supervision of European magistrates. Yet these new forms of colonial rule made little difference to the actual administration of rural areas. Again, with the possible exception of Barotseland, "indirect rule" was never real. District commissioners were reluctant to transfer any important governmental functions to the Native Authorities for fear that they would perform the required tasks inefficiently and incompetently. They did not want to "hurry" the development of the Native Authorities. They were unwilling to "jeopardize the success" of indirect rule by entrusting Native Authorities with responsibilities that they were "not fit to exercise." Despite Colonial Office insistence that the collection of tax revenues be transferred to the Native Authorities— "this not only enhances their importance in the eyes of the native population, but provides the most valuable part of their education in administrative responsibility"—the district commissioners and the governments of the protectorates regularly resisted such a devolution of power. Indirect rule therefore meant little to the peoples of Central Africa. As one official commented: "every service which has been 'taken over' by the chiefs is in actual fact largely carried out by the D[istrict] C[ommissioner]."[56]

[56] See NC 1/20/1–3, Zomba archives; Sec/Nat/274, Lusaka archives.

In the urban and white-owned farming areas of Nyasaland and Northern Rhodesia, such pretense proved unnecessary. Peripheral to the white trading centers and mining towns were locations, later townships, where Africans lived in overcrowded barracks or primitive brick huts. Accommodation, initially much inferior to that to which they were accustomed in the rural areas, was allotted to them by settler or company-run councils or committees. Their life within these locations was strictly regulated; a white superintendent supervised the locations, kept order, dealt with complaints, and combined within his own psyche the somewhat conflicting paternal qualities of policeman and counselor. Except in the mine compounds, Africans were not represented on administrative bodies. Furthermore, at the behest of white residents, the territorial government of Northern Rhodesia strictly regulated the movement of urban Africans. From 1927, permits were necessary for Africans who wished to reside, to look for work, or to visit towns along the railway line. Like his brothers in Kenya, Southern Rhodesia, and South Africa, each had to carry an identification certificate on his person and to produce it whenever required. No African who lived in municipally owned housing was permitted to receive visitors without the permission of the location superintendent. None could move freely at night without a special pass. As the Northern Rhodesian Secretary for Native Affairs said, "The Night pass had advantages; it keeps a lot of noisy natives from wandering around towns."[57] His Senior Provincial Commissioner offered a slightly different reason: "The main advantage [of the night pass] is that it reduces the number of natives in towns, and we ought to face the fact that these towns are European towns and the natives must be prepared to accept the fact."[58] In other words, if an African from Serenje—a rural district—chose to visit his brother in Lusaka—the national capital after 1935—he needed to obtain an identity certificate, a pass to enter the compound, and a third pass to be out at night. Such were a few of the restrictions with which Africans were beset. As sympathetic whites and the so-called Native Associations wondered: Why should the natives of Northern Rhodesia not walk about as they liked in

[57] S 1/103a/33: Moffat Thomson, in "Proceedings of a Conference of Native Commissioners at Victoria Falls," 13 September 1933, Zomba archives.
[58] E. G. H. Goodall, in *ibid.*

their own country? Is a man not supposed to have some sort of rights in his own country?

British government brought Africans many benefits and advantages. Yet an Afrikaans-speaking missionary, in commenting upon colonial rule in Central Africa in 1921, still could, with some justification, complain in a letter to the *Nyasaland Times:*

Government does bring peace to Africans but they say that there used to be long intervals of peace in the old days. Now their obligations are never ending: they labour for the government, they pay a yearly tax, they are bullied by *askaris*. They conclude that they are now practically all *akapolo,* or slaves, whereas the slave raiders, of whom the government has freed them, always left the great majority free.[59]

Compulsory labor for public purposes was condoned until the late 1930's; in Nyasaland "immemorial custom" permitted district commissioners to draft Africans for the carrying of mails or for the improvement of roads.[60]

To their credit, the governments of Nyasaland and Northern Rhodesia encouraged the education and medical treatment of Africans by Christian missionary societies and, in time, began to support these activities financially. Yet before World War II, most Africans were treated exclusively in mission hospitals. As the Nyasaland Medical Officer early concluded: "I am aware . . . that the work of the Government Medical Officer is principally confined to Europeans, but this I consider partly due to the fact that so little attention has . . . hitherto been paid to the maintenance of a decent Government Native hospital."[61] When Levi Mumba, a leading African—subsequently the President of the Nyasaland African Congress—in 1934 asked the Nyasaland Government to pay a part of his son's secondary school fees in South Africa (there was no local equivalent), the government reluctantly advanced £13-10-0 for the first academic year. The Chief Secretary's opinion accurately reflected the feelings of his administration: "Such cases will continue to be rare for some time to come, fortunately I think, since the slower the

[59] D. K. van Oesterzee, of the Dedza Dutch Reformed Church Mission, *The Nyasaland Times,* 17 March 1921.

[60] See S1/1550/25; S1/862/31, Zomba archives.

[61] S1/1268/24: The Medical Officer, Blantyre, to the Principal Medical Officer, 10 July 1924, Zomba archives.

progress—in the direction of higher education for the African—the better."[62]

Not until World War II was secondary education introduced into Northern Rhodesia and Nyasaland; prior to that time, in order to progress beyond the teacher-training institutions available locally, a few Africans went to South Africa and East Africa.[63] Privileged individuals spent short periods in Great Britain. For the most part, however, Central Africans were dependent upon the initiative of British administrators and missionaries who were as reluctant as the Chief Secretary of Nyasaland to extend the school system vertically. The colonial regimes succeeded in fostering an indigenous demand for further schooling and improved medical treatment. But when Africans were willing to accept fully the logic of Westernization by improving their educational and professional skills, many avenues remained closed to them.

In African eyes, the positive actions of the Colonial Government— the ending of tribal quarrels and the slave trade, the introduction of indirect rule, British justice, British medical care, and British education, and the expenditures on railways, roads, telegraph lines, and electric power—seemed negative expressions. On the one hand, Africans believed that they were better off before the white man came and imposed his restrictions; on the other, they believed that the white man had promised them that he would share his secrets and his medicines with Africans and, in time, that he would share his wealth and his government with those who were capable. Instead, he gave Africans few chances to participate fully in European life. He refuted therefore, what Africans had always been led to

---

[62] S1/478/34: Minute by Hall, 22 December 1934, Zomba archives.

[63] The government of Northern Rhodesia gave its first bursaries to enable Africans to attend secondary schools in 1938. It sent Alfred Hambayi to a junior secondary school run by the White Fathers in Tabora, Tanganyika; Cephas Kabeta to King's College, Budo, Uganda; Moffat Mpasela to an Anglican school in South Africa; Kenan Ngambi, a teacher, to the government secondary school in Tabora; and Hubert Siwale, the son of Donald Siwale, one of the earliest associationists, to the Alliance High School in Kenya. In 1939, the new Munali government junior secondary school near Lusaka admitted its first students, although at least three Northern Rhodesians, in addition to Mpasela and Siwale, were also studying in South Africa on government grants. (The Lubwa Presbyterian mission school in the previous year had enrolled eight primary school graduates in an advanced class.) Sec/E/40: the Director of Native Education to the Chief Secretary, 4 February 1938 and 19 March 1940. Mr. Trevor Coombe kindly supplied this reference.

believe about the nature of British rule. What is more, the white man also practiced discrimination widely.

No one can deny that Africans felt discriminated against both by white officials and settlers. And, in African minds of the day, there were no subjective differences between the various levels of discrimination. The treatment of Africans in Northern Rhodesia, because of its larger settler population and the type of district officer that it attracted, was probably inferior to that of Nyasaland. But Nyasas perceived and experienced discrimination to the same extent as their Northern Rhodesian contemporaries. They were subjected to a similar type of abuse from white foremen and policemen; even the best-dressed never attempted to enter a "white" hotel or restaurant. Africans in both protectorates addressed Europeans respectfully and were constrained to doff their caps to whites of every tation. In the mines they were called "black monkeys"; in the rural areas some whites lived with their wives or had children by their daughters. There was no redress. "Why, is it," they asked, "that only Africans need to carry passes in their own country?" "Why is it that the African trains do not provide places for us to eat?" "When a white man commits adultery with an African woman he is not punished. When a native is suspected of committing adultery with a European woman he is punished. Why?" The white railway station master at Kapiri Mposhi, Northern Rhodesia, was convicted of whipping and kicking African women. "Why was he not dismissed?"[64] In 1919, when Harry Kabango, a Nyasa working on the Glasgow docks, wanted to marry Isabella Paton, a white Glaswegian lass, why did the Governor of Nyasaland, the Church of Scotland, the British Home Office, and the Scottish police, fearful of the effect that such a marriage would have in Nyasaland, prevent him from taking her to the altar?[65] Answers to these questions were never forthcoming in a manner satisfactory to Africans. Long before, when the whites came to trans-Zambezia, they had been welcomed as friends. But soon the anguish of Africans expressed their resultant disillusionment. Their leaders prophesied the coming of a new political dawn.

[64] See Acc 63/1/57, Lusaka archives.
[65] See S 2/54/19, Zomba archives.

Chapter III

THE BEGINNINGS OF INDIGENOUS PROTEST

We are imposed upon more than any other nationality under the sun. [We] . . . have been loyal since the commencement of this government. . . . But in time of peace the Government failed to help the underdog. In time of peace everything [is] for Europeans only. . . . [We] hope in the mercy of Almighty God, that some day things will turn out well and that Government will recognize our indispensability, and that justice will prevail.

—John Chilembwe, *The Nyasaland Times*,
26 November 1914

Colonial rule, with its many coercive demands and regulations, encouraged a hostile response. In Nyasaland and Northern Rhodesia, Africans reacted very early to the cut and thrust of the perhaps well meant British intrusion: "Are we to set aside native . . . rights," a Scottish missionary asked of his kinsmen, "and conquer a country with no provocation, and take what is not our own and yet be just?"[1] This was the question that Africans also asked of the Imperial connection. The most articulate of the early mission converts contrasted Biblical teachings of equality with the performance of Europeans settled in their midst and, not unnaturally, queried their own initially rather mute acceptance of the superiority of the white man's approach to modern life. These seeds of thought, often influenced by the social or economic circumstances of particular Anglo-African confrontations or by external ideological stimuli, at first germinated slowly. In time, however, Africans grafted a wide range of political and religious expression onto the frail stock of such tentative protest, thus encouraging the first shoots of indigenous nationalism.

THE FIRST STIRRINGS OF DISCONTENT

Where the reaction to colonialism could not be expressed directly, or where healthy protest failed to bring about any appreciable ame-

[1] David Clement Scott, writing in 1892, quoted in George Shepperson and Thomas Price, *Independent African* (Edinburgh, 1958), 18.

lioration, the conquered people cloaked their rejection of colonialism in religious garb. Wherever there were no other outlets, Africans formed independent religious bodies to exploit or to remedy their grievances.[2] In both Northern Rhodesia and Nyasaland, a succession of indigenous quasi-Christian groups played upon this theme from the first years of the twentieth century. They expressed separatist or chiliastic ideas, subverted the tenets of established mission churches, defied the colonial governments, and acted as a major channel of nationalist sentiment.

The first of the Northern Rhodesian sects, the so-called Ethiopian Church of Barotseland, was planned in Lealui in 1900, at about the time that John Chilembwe had begun to lay the foundations of the Providence Industrial Mission near Chiradzulu in Nyasaland. Both Christian bodies traced their origins to the United States and asserted the primacy of independent African organizational control, but there any similarity ended. Willie J. Mokalapa, the organizer of the Barotseland Church, was a Suto evangelist in whom the Paris Missionary Society had placed great trust. He had studied at the Lovedale Institute in South Africa and had assisted François Coillard, the experienced Huguenot missionary, to advance the cause of orthodox Protestantism among the Lozi. Sometime in 1899, however, Mokalapa and several of his Suto colleagues publicly claimed that the missionaries treated them as inferiors. They agitated for and were refused an increase in pay, and therefore evidently sought a means whereby they could play a more significant role in the political and religious life of Barotseland. While on a visit to his home in Basutoland, Mokalapa apparently met or contacted representatives of the South African Ethiopian movement and, perhaps in Johannesburg, secretly joined the African Methodist Episcopal Church.[3]

Like so many religious ideologies that have appealed to Africans, the origin of the African Methodist Episcopal Church was American. The Negro preacher Richard Allen opposed the color bar of the

[2] See Robert I. Rotberg, "The Rise of African Nationalism: The Case of East and Central Africa," *World Politics*, xv (1962), 84.

[3] Coillard Papers: Coillard to Catherine W. Mackintosh, 26 May 1900, fols. 1750–1757, Salisbury archives; Josephus R. Coan, "The Expansion of Missions of the African Methodist Episcopal Church in South Africa, 1896–1908" (unpub. Ph.D. thesis, Hartford Seminary Foundation, 1961), 387–388. I owe this reference to Miss Pamela O'Neill.

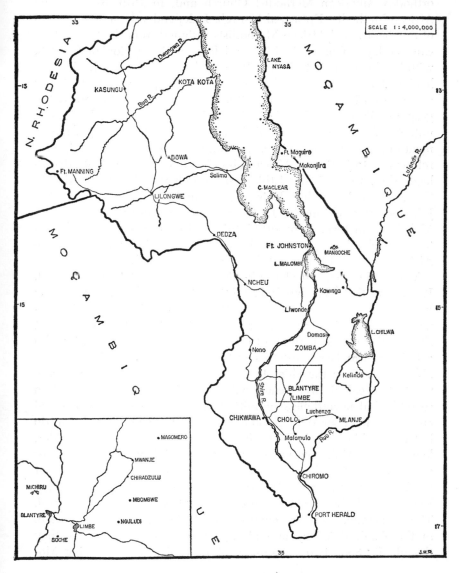

Southern Nyasaland with principal places, rivers, and roads (inset shows area of the Chilembwe rising).

orthodox American Methodist Church and, in 1816, founded the African Methodist Episcopal Church. Independently, a small group of mission-trained African Methodists resigned from the South African Wesleyan Church in 1892 and formed the Ethiopian Church, with headquarters in turbulent Johannesburg. Mangena M. Mokone, leader of the church, welcomed members from a variety of tribes and mission backgrounds and attempted consciously to spread the gospel of Psalm 68:31—"Ethiopia shall soon stretch out her hands unto God." Hence the name of the church, and the separatist movement in general; Mokone interpreted the Psalm, and other Scriptural references, to justify an African church, under independent African leadership. In 1897, the Ethiopian Church was incorporated into the African Methodist Episcopal Church, thereby linking the Johannesburg schismatics to their fellow separatists in America.[4] Mokalapa, in turn, transported this radical religious combination to Barotseland and, in time, became the Presiding Elder of the African Methodist Episcopal Church in Barotseland.

Very little is known of the Ethiopian movement in Barotseland. It appears that Mokalapa's first attempt to break away from the Paris Mission was abortive; his letters addressed to Lewanika demanded an "African church for Africans." But the Lozi Paramount showed them to Coillard and to Adolphe Jalla, the missionaries who acted as Lewanika's translators and advisors. Forewarned, they were able to persuade the chief to denounce Mokalapa and to expose what they called his "treachery." The mission reprimanded him severely, but nevertheless permitted him to resume his evangelical employment. "Poor Willie," Coillard wrote, "had nothing else to do but to humble himself."[5] The fires of revolt continued to smolder, however, for Mokalapa eventually persuaded Lewanika to sponsor an Ethiopian Church among the Lozi. He promised to provide what the Lozi had always wanted—a school where spoken and written English would be taught and a church that Africans would control. The Paramount therefore gave the Ethiopians a good mission site in the Zambezi Valley and abundant free labor to use as they thought fit. Soon two sons-in-law of Lewanika joined, giving Mo-

[4] Bengt G. M. Sundkler, *Bantu Prophets in South Africa* (London, 1961), 39–40.

[5] Coillard Papers: Coillard to Mackintosh, 26 May 1900. See also IN 1/7/1: Memorandum by the Secretary of Native Affairs, 6 April 1905, Lusaka archives.

kalapa his first "great victory." One of the converts explained that the Paris Mission had little except discrimination to show for its long residence in Barotseland. He told Coillard: "I have been at your schools and I am as ignorant as those who have never set foot in it. I cannot even salute in his own tongue the English man I meet. You have [furthermore] chased me away from school."[6]

By early 1904, Mokalapa and his Suto and Lozi supporters had gathered a fairly large following, many of the members of which had been rebaptized after being enticed away from the Paris Mission churches. The missionaries naturally condemned this invasion of their "preserve":

Our field of labor has been lately invaded by the Ethiopians whose leader is one of our former Basuto teachers. They have got the ear of the king; our schools are seriously threatened, our Christians partly won over and disturbed and our teachers give no small amount of trouble and anxiety. Thus the work of twenty years, in one of the hardest parts of the [mission] field, is threatened with destruction at the very time when we expected the harvest.[7]

The Ethiopians constructed a number of small schools where they taught rudimentary English and persuaded the Lozi that Africans could direct religious and secular ventures as successfully as Europeans. None of their sermons have survived, but Mokalapa and his lieutenants evidently preached in the "Africa for the African" vein. According to the government, "among the more pernicious doctrines being spread . . . [were] the equality of the white and the black races."[8] Robert Coryndon, the administrator of Northwestern Rhodesia, thereafter cautioned Lewanika to beware of the dangerous influence exerted by the Ethiopians. "I have told you plainly . . . that the Ethiopian Church is not a good church . . . I can see that the Ethiopians have been telling you what to say . . . and putting bad thoughts into your mind. . . . Once I find that they have been teach-

[6] Coillard Papers: Quoted in Coillard to Mackintosh, 24 March 1904, fols. 2482–2489. See also A 1/2/4: Gell to British South Africa Company, 10 January 1904, Lusaka archives.

[7] Coillard Papers: Coillard to J. Bruce, 26 April 1904, fols. 2504–2508. See also Catherine W. Mackintosh, *Coillard of the Zambesi* (London, 1907), 438–440.

[8] IN 1/2: Coryndon to Selborne, 24 October 1904, Lusaka archives.

ing you bad things I will send them out of the country."[9] "Warn
Mokalapa," the British High Commissioner said, "that he will have
to go if he exercises an injurious influence on the native mind."[10]
But the Lozi aristocracy, which had cherished its long-standing
connection to the Paris mission, welcomed the Ethiopian teachings,
and Lewanika personally resisted every attempt to hinder Mokalapa's
freedom of expression and movement.

Mokalapa established a strong church that demonstrated the
ability of Africans to guide their own destiny in defiance of established colonial authority. Unlike Chilembwe, the Suto evangelist
challenged colonial rule only indirectly and confined the appeal of
this mission to Barotseland. Within these limits he proved eminently
successful. Moreover, had Lewanika not sent him to Cape Town to
buy boats and other equipment for the mission and the Lozi *kuta*,
or court, there is no telling to what extent the Ethiopian movement
might eventually have served to focus the indigenous voices of
Rhodesian protest. But the trip resulted in disaster. About £750 of
Lewanika's capital, which had been entrusted to Mokalapa, was
swindled from him by auctioneers and other entrepreneurs in Cape
Town. Mokalapa therefore failed to return to Lealui and, without his
peculiar evangelical talents, the Ethiopian church slowly declined in
local importance.[11] By 1907–08, this early movement of protest no
longer provided a propitious channel for the expression of indigenous discontent.

Chilembwe had meanwhile made a great success of the Providence
Industrial Mission. His own history and that of the church have
received substantial treatment elsewhere.[12] Here it is necessary only
to add supplementary detail and to set the stage for a subsequent
discussion of some of the early manifestations of nationalism in
Nyasaland.

The story begins with Joseph Booth, a British fundamentalist of
apocalyptical religious vision. After a business and farming career in
England, New Zealand, and Australia, Booth heard the call of a

[9] IN 1/7/1: Coryndon to Lewanika, 3 January 1905, Lusaka archives.

[10] IN 1/7/1: Milner to Coryndon, 14 November 1904, Lusaka archives.

[11] IN 1/7/1: F. Z. S. Peregrino to the Transvaal Department of Native
Affairs, 23 January 1905; British South Africa Company to Coryndon, 10
December 1904, Lusaka archives.

[12] Shepperson and Price, *African*, 36–147.

missionary vocation. In 1892, aged 41, he arrived at the mouth of the Zambezi River determined to establish a self-supporting Baptist Church on lines pioneered by William Carey in India. The Zambezi Industrial Mission, with its main station near Blantyre, was the result. There Booth spread the egalitarian ideas that made him anathema to the established Scottish missionaries and to the colonial administration. Indeed, his criticism of the comfortable life led by European missionaries in the midst of African poverty indicates the extent of the ideological gulf that both separated him from other resident white men and foreshadowed the subsequent indigenous analyses of European Christian hypocrisy. Writing to London in 1892, Booth described the anomaly:

Candidly now, is it not a marvellous picture to see elegantly robed men, at some hundreds of pounds yearly cost, preaching a gospel of self-denial to men and women slaves, with only a very scrap of goat skin around their loins, compelled to work hard from daylight to dark six, but more often seven days in a week. . . . I have never felt so utterly ashamed of myself and my fellow countrymen as I have since coming here. Either we ought to stop spreading the Gospel or conform to its teaching amidst such a needy cloud of witnesses as Central Africa presents.[13]

By paying considerably higher wages than the missions or the government, Booth also earned obloquy from whites and lavish, excited praise from Africans.

Among the many Africans who came to know Booth, none was closer than John Chilembwe, possibly the son of a Yao father from the Chiradzulu district of Nyasaland.[14] In 1892, after studying at the Blantyre Mission, he became Booth's trusted servant. Booth's daughter later wrote: "The coming of John was to mean to us much more than merely having found, at last, a dependable cook-boy. . . . He had a great desire to learn and write, and to gain the Truths of Christianity. Being a cookboy was only a means to an end."[15] He acted as a nurse to the malarious Emily Booth, was a faithful companion to Booth's son, accompanied and interpreted for the mis-

[13] Joseph Booth, quoted in *ibid.*, 33.
[14] George Simeon Mwase, "A Dialogue of Nyasaland, Record of Past Events, Environments, and the Present Outlook within the Protectorate" (unpub. typescript, 1932), 5, says that Chilembwe was born at Sanganu, near Chiradzulu, of a Yao father and a Cewa mother.
[15] Emily Booth Langworthy, quoted in Shepperson and Price, *African*, 37.

sionary, and, in general, became the mainstay of the new church and of the Booth household. Thus, there is no doubt that Chilembwe was influenced fatefully by these early contacts with whites who regularly tended to speak and to act in a manner that can loosely be called pro-African. As such, Booth was outstanding in late nineteenth-century Central Africa. And consequently, Chilembwe could not help but appreciate that the typical British approach to African problems was not necessarily immutable.

Even before going to the United States with Booth in 1897, Chilembwe was associated with him in the formation of two Christian organizations. The objects of the proposed African Christian Union of Nyasaland were: "equal rights, political, social, and economic, for Africans as well as Europeans; the development of African education along the technical lines of the European world; independent African activity in all economic fields; a just land settlement; the encouragement of a pro-African press and literature; and the growth of independent African Christianity."[16] Such ideas were manifestations of Booth's radicalism and of the "Ethiopianism" with which he, and perhaps Chilembwe, had been infused as a result of independent African religious and political activity in South Africa, the rising of the Ndebele in Southern Rhodesia, and the defeat of the Italian army at Adowa by the true Abyssinian Ethiopians. Whatever the elements that were responsible for Chilembwe's later revolutionary spirit, a letter that he wrote, unaided, to a British mission director in 1895 or 1896, is indicative of a proud, African reaction to a poem about the servitude of Ham.

But am very pleased for the booklet which you sent to me . . . when I read it out . . . I hear some words . . . about Ham and his sons . . .

> "Cursed let HAM be, and HAM'S son,
> CANAAN to ages unending;
> Servants of servants they shall be;
> Servants to SHEM and to JAPETH!"

Yes, that is true to be so, if it was long times ago, but by this time, is not so to be, says one of HAM's sons. Now HAM'S son they shall be servants not to them now, dear white brothers and sisters.[17]

[16] *Ibid.*, 79.
[17] John Chilembwe, quoted in *ibid.*, 67.

In the United States, Chilembwe was set firmly on the path of radical protest. He could only with difficulty have avoided the intense social and political discrimination of the post-Reconstruction period in the South; his experiences at a small Negro Baptist seminary in Lynchburg, Virginia, and the ideological ferment common in Negro intellectual circles, would only have reinforced Chilembwe's approach to the white man in his African context. Whether or not his command of written and spoken English had been improved by two or three years in the United States, he returned via London to Nyasaland, probably in late 1900, "as a full-blown, round-collared, long-coated 'Reverend' of the regulation type."[18] Backed by the influential National [Negro] Baptist Convention in America, he acquired title to a small plot of land at Mbombwe, in the Chiradzulu district of Nyasaland, and began to give to "the children of Africa" the "quickening and enlightening influence of the Gospel of Christ" that would "lift them from [their] state of degradation, and make them suitable members of the human family."[19] He later explained to the government of Nyasaland that the station had been established in the following manner:

On my return [from America] I thought it was best as I knew too well that I was one of the subject of British flag, to consult the leading members of the kingdom and after [being] allowed to visit the House of Common where I obtained my right of getting a letter of introduction to Commissioner Sharpe. . . . After good conversation on the subject finally I was allowed to open my mission at Chiradzulu.[20]

With the help of Negroes sent by the National Baptist Convention, he gradually transformed the first collection of wattle-and-daub huts into a flourishing station. The Providence Industrial Mission gained adherents throughout the Chiradzulu and the neighboring Mlanje districts and, to some extent, even in Southern Rhodesia and Moçambique. He established a chain of independent African schools, constructed an impressive brick church, and planted crops

---

18 Joseph Booth, quoted in *ibid.*, 116.
19 Chilembwe, quoted in *ibid.*, 127.
20 S 2/22/34: John Chilembwe to the Resident (Chiradzulu), 12 January 1914, Zomba archives. It would be of interest to know from whom at the House of Commons he received an introduction to Commissioner Sharpe. George Shepperson suggests Keir Hardie, M.P.

of cotton, tea, and coffee. Chilembwe turned his station into an outwardly Western community; he insisted upon European affectations and the wearing of clean, neat Edwardian attire. As an African biographer of Chilembwe later reported:

He was always sober, he hated any kind of drink and abhorred the power of alcohol. He exhorted people from keeping themselves into strong drinks, and such like, he taught adults and children to keep on work, not to lounge about, even to advise headmen . . . to keep their villages nice and clean telling them that was the key to civilisation, also the key to a good health . . . he liked to see his country men work hard and prosper in their undertakings, also to see them smart, such as negro fellows he had seen in America and other countries. He preached against carnalist, murderer, robber . . . and thief. He warned his country men against the habit of begging, he explained that begging was very much disgraceful system on the face of the world.[21]

At this time, when Mokalapa was causing so much consternation in Lealui, Chilembwe and his followers were models of respectability. Even so, he complained that the settlers were cruel to their African tenants. Influenced by Booth, he objected to the employment of Nyasas in the wars of Europeans and publicly championed the rights of the landless and the oppressed of the Shire Highlands.

THE VISION OF A BLACK JERUSALEM

Although Chilembwe's mission grew in importance during the first dozen years of the twentieth century, the main threat to white rule in Nyasaland came from two other religious movements that owed their inspiration to Booth. The British evangelist had returned from the United States in 1899 and, characteristically, had busied himself with a number of projects that the government justifiably labeled seditious. By this time, after parting company with Chilembwe, Booth represented the small but well-established Seventh Day Baptist Church of Plainfield, New Jersey. Although the government prevented him from building near Lake Chilwa, he established a new mission station called Plainfield, thirty miles south of Blantyre, and then attempted, by means of an appeal published in the *Central African Times*, to seek a rapid redress of

21 Mwase, "Dialogue," 15–16.

what he believed were outstanding indigenous grievances.[22] His so-called 1899 petition was no less than a blueprint for the end of colonial rule. It demanded that the "whole Protectorate should revert to native ownership after twenty-one years," that hut-tax revenues should be devoted to educating Nyasas to British standards, and that free higher education should be provided for "not less than five per cent of the African population."[23] Alfred Sharpe, the Commissioner of Nyasaland, reacted swiftly to this challenge from an old adversary. He advised the chief judge:

I have a copy of Booth's document, to which he wants to get natives to put their marks, the whole thing being sent home to the Queen. I cannot allow Booth to tamper with the natives. To place these foolish proposals before them would be inexcusable and dangerous. They can never be carried out, and the whole thing is absurd and "cant" on the part of Booth. He must give it up at once or be deported.[24]

Booth evaded arrest. In a letter to the *Central African Times,* he termed the suggestion that he should be furnished with a "free passage to Chinde" as an interesting proposition. He did not, however, "see how it would accomplish much since there [were] abundant bases of operation . . . probably more desirable than British Central Africa. A far better plan would be to expel the Book which teaches [that] man should not covet, steal, or kill." From Blantyre, he was reported to have gone to Chikwawa, on the lower Shire River, where he evidently told enthusiastic African audiences that Queen Victoria had said that they were not to pay taxes.[25] "When we catch him and deport him," Sharpe wrote, "he can worry about his family, we won't."[26] But Booth slipped through the hastily drawn security net, and took up residence across the border in a relatively inaccessible part of Moçambique. Finally, at the beginning of 1900, Sharpe allowed him to resume his evangelical activities in

[22] Booth's appeal was published and condemned in the *Central African Times* of 5 August 1889; but Shepperson and Price, *African,* 120, give the date as 22 July 1899.

[23] The petition is summarized in J 2/9/2; Zomba archives, and in Shepperson and Price, *African,* 120.

[24] J 2/9/2: Sharpe to Wallis, 10 August 1899.

[25] The *Central African Times,* 12 August 1899; J 2/9/2: Telegram from the Collector (Chikwawa), 17 August 1899.

[26] J 2/9/2: Sharpe to Wallis, 14 August 1899.

Nyasaland after Booth undertook entirely "to abstain from any interference in any political matter whatsoever concerning the Natives of [Nyasaland] . . . [and to] abandon the . . . petition." Six months later he again promised Sharpe to "keep the peace . . . and to obey . . . regulations now . . . or . . . at any time hereafter published . . . under penalty of . . . an amount not exceeding £500 or . . . to suffer deportation."[27] These agreements to the contrary, there is no real evidence that Booth subsequently refrained from propagating his heretical "Africa for the African" doctrine; he preached the Seventh Day Baptist creed at Plainfield (later Malamulo), attracted Africans from all over Nyasaland to his station and, after a serious, protracted quarrel with the Negro Seventh-day Adventists who had been sent out from the United States in 1902, he left Nyasaland forever and settled in South Africa.[28]

It now appears that Elliot Kenan Kamwana Achirwa, whose prophetic mien later posed a serious threat to British rule, accompanied Booth as far as Durban in 1903.[29] Kamwana, a Tonga, had been a pupil at the Bandawe Mission of the Free Church of Scotland and later had been among the educated elite who had received further training at the church's Overtoun Institution. He broke with the Scottish church when it introduced educational fees, and then found his way to Booth's sabbatarian mission, into which faith he was subsequently baptized. Whether or not he and Booth actually traveled together, Kamwana followed the numerous Tonga who had already begun to migrate to the urban centers of southern Africa. There he almost certainly became acquainted with the various forms of Ethiopianism that had begun to serve collectively as a type of safety valve in an already tense racial situation. Booth meanwhile severed his connections to the Adventists, approached the British Churches of Christ, and in the United States became an ardent adherent of the group that is known today as the Jehovah's Witnesses. At that time, it was the Watch Tower Bible and Tract Society, the members of which believed in the Second Coming, in the Apocalypse (due by implication in late 1914), in a Final Judg-

[27] The undertakings are dated 27 January, and 23 July 1900.

[28] J 2/9/2: Pearce to Young, 14 February 1907; Hetherwick to the Governor, 26 June 1902. But see Shepperson and Price, *African*, 135, 148. In 1907, Booth made plans to return to Nyasaland but the government barred his way.

[29] Reports contained in GOA 2/4/14, Zomba archives.

ment, and in the everlasting kingdom of the elect, who would inherit the New Jerusalem.[30] Religious socialism and a peaceful uprising of the masses that would result in world-wide revolution and the overthrow of all law and order—essential parts of this millennial doctrine—clearly appealed to Booth and, in turn, to Kamwana. Sometime in 1907 or 1908, after Booth had returned to South Africa from the United States, Kamwana joined him in Cape Town and soon became a Witness and a subscriber to the colorfully written ("inflammatory" in the opinion of the colonial governments) pamphlets published by the Watch Tower Society.

In late 1908, Kamwana went home to proclaim the coming of the new dawn. His fellow Tonga, who lived near Nkata Bay, Chinteche, and Bandawe along the western shore of Lake Nyasa, were ready. Threatened by the warring Ngoni, they had followed missionaries of the Free Church. They had adopted Western ways, mastered the rudiments of reading and writing, and in time assumed white-collar positions throughout the urban areas of South and Central Africa (among others, Clements Kadalie, founder in 1919 of the militant Industrial and Commercial Workers Union of South Africa, was a Tonga). The Free Church had gathered many adherents, and from about 1895 it had encouraged a local spirit of revivalism into which Kamwana's message fitted admirably.[31] Like other Nyasas, the Tonga had wearied of paying taxes and of being forced to leave their farms in order to work elsewhere for white men. (A Kunda prophetess, about whom too little is known, had in 1907 gathered a large following by proclaiming the end of taxation and European occupation.)

Kamwana understood and capitalized upon his people's discontent; as such, he may be considered occupied Nyasaland's first prophet. To excited African audiences he described the new age that was expected in 1914. Then, at the time of the Second Advent, Christ would abolish colonial rule, whites would depart with their

---

[30] The fullest, if occasionally contradictory, statement of Watch Tower beliefs is contained in Charles Taze Russell, *Studies in the Scriptures* (Allegheny, Pa., and Brooklyn, N.Y., 1886–1904), six volumes. See also Royston Pike, *Jehovah's Witnesses* (London, 1954); George Shepperson, "The Comparative Study of Millenarian Movements," in Sylvia L. Thrupp (ed.), *Millennial Dreams in Action* (The Hague, 1962), 51.

[31] George Shepperson, "Nyasaland and the Millennium," in Thrupp, *Millennial Dreams*, 150.

hated taxation, and Africans would govern themselves. These officials, he said, "you soon will see no more. . . . We shall build our
own ships, make our own powder, and make or import our own
guns."[32] This was the substance of a religion that, like so many
subsequent separatist sects or chiliastic cults of Africa—and the
related cargo cults of Oceania and the ghost groups of Indian
America—corresponded to widely held indigenous aspirations.[33]

In open-air, revival-type meetings, Kamwana baptized all who
would come forward; he may easily have thus celebrated the cere-
monial rebirth of more than 10,000 Tonga, Ngoni, Henga, and
Tumbuka during the first few months of 1909. Scottish missionaries
noted that a reversion to "pre-European ways" accompanied his
evangelical successes—that "obscene dances," polygyny, and general
sexual license once again became common. In general, the new faith
provided a necessary outlet. But the Watch Tower successes frightened the government as well as the missions and, later in 1909, it
removed Kamwana from Tongaland and exiled him to South Africa.

Without Kamwana, the Watch Tower movement still continued to
flourish. Despite his prolonged absence from the country, Kamwana
was remembered and revered throughout Nyasaland, Northern
Rhodesia, and Southern Rhodesia. His teachings remained articles
of faith, even after the Second Advent failed to occur in 1914. But
Kamwana himself languished in detention. After returning from
South Africa in 1910, he was confined to the Mlanje district, where
the government could observe him and where the indigenous population spoke a language dissimilar from Citonga. Sometime toward
the end of 1910, he was taken to South Africa by William W.
Johnston, a Glaswegian sent by the Watch Tower leadership to investigate the movement in Nyasaland. Forbidden to land at Durban,
Kamwana returned to Chinde, at the mouth of the Zambezi River,
where he preached assiduously until 1914. Early in that year, he
was imprisoned for a month by the Portuguese government, thereafter returning to his place of detention at Mlanje. He was once
again closely watched, but the authorities nonetheless suspected that
Kamwana was responsible for the unwillingness of Tonga to assist
the military mobilization in August 1914. Very little is known of

[32] Kamwana, quoted in Shepperson and Price, *African*, 156.
[33] See Lucy Mair, "Independent Religious Movements in Three Continents,"
Comparative Studies in Society and History, i (1959), 135.

this period of his life, but a letter he wrote in October 1914 indicated that he at least believed that his prophecies were coming true. He prophesied, conceivably with some special knowledge of Chilembwe's own plans, that the government, which in typical Watch Tower language he called Babylon, would leave Nyasaland in April 1915, when all of the nations of Europe would simultaneously come to an end.[34] But even before this magic date, and before the rising fomented by Chilembwe, the Governor and his Executive Council decided to deport Kamwana to Mauritius after he and other Watch Tower pastors had been accused of preaching seditiously. The rising intervened, but Kamwana, Elliot Yohane Achirwa, and William Mulagha Mwenda, although absolved from any charges of complicity, were thereafter deported to Mauritius and, later, to the Seychelles. There Kamwana lived a quiet life; his first wife died and a second was recruited by followers in the Chinteche District and sent out to him. Eventually, Edward VIII of England abdicated, and Kamwana was allowed to celebrate the coronation of King George VI at home in Nyasaland, where his Watch Tower movement continued strong.[35]

At the time of Kamwana's deportation, the mantle of indigenous religious leadership passed to another of Booth's disciples. Charles Domingo, a Kunda born in Portuguese territory along the Lower Shire River about 1875, was taken in 1881 from Quilimane, where his drunken father cooked for the African Lakes Company, to Livingstonia.[36] There he served in the household of Dr. Robert Laws and, in time, became a protégé of the veteran missionary. He studied

[34] William Mwenda, who was deported with Kamwana, and who may have had a particular case to plead, later wrote that "The serious truth is that some months before Chilembwe's rising took place, Kamwana deserted the Watch Tower and became a trusted counsellor of Chilembwe, before whom Chilembwe and his colleagues had no secret. Chilembwe, knowing this, had no alternative but to send for his counsellor in that black night; but Kamwana's wife being a woman of strong determination spoke dogmatically against following Chilembwe and compelled her husband to reveal the matter to the Resident," S 2/8/26: Mwenda to the Governor of Nyasaland, 19 September 1926, Zomba archives.

[35] The new information regarding Kamwana that was unavailable to Professor Shepperson is contained in S 2/68ii/19; S 2/8/26; S 1/1179/19; S 1/46/19; GOA 2/4/14; Executive Council Minutes, 3 February 1915—all Zomba archives. But see Shepperson and Price, *African*, 156; Shepperson, "Nyasaland," in Thrupp, *Millennial Dreams*, 150.

[36] W. P. Livingstone, *Laws of Livingstonia* (London, 1923), 194–195; S 1/927/19 and GOA 2/4/13, Zomba archives.

in the local school and, for two years, at Lovedale, where he made contacts that were to influence his later separatist activities. At Livingstonia, he studied theology informally with Laws and, eventually, in company with two other prospective ordinands, Hezekiah Tweza and Yesaya Zerenji Mwasi (who eventually, like Domingo, led his own separatist church), he received instruction in Church history, Scriptural exegesis, and systematic theology and, additionally, a one-hour talk daily from Dr. Laws on the nature and function of government, the necessity of taxation in general and the beneficence of British colonial taxation in particular, the uses of money, the evil of debt, the necessity of encouraging industry and thrift, the importance of good housing and sanitation, "and other practical subjects." Domingo became an elder in the local congregation and the first African assistant in the mission school; as the biographer of Dr. Laws notes, he was "an ideal teacher [who] maintained order and discipline, and yet contrived to keep the pupils bright and happy."[37] In 1904, when Dr. and Mrs. Laws celebrated their silver wedding anniversary, Domingo appropriately conducted the thanksgiving service. Certainly by 1907, he was, in Western eyes, one of the leading Africans of the Protectorate.

Sometime late in that fateful year Domingo, like Kamwana, began to see the New Jerusalem in African terms. After a quarrel with the Scottish missionary Donald Fraser, Domingo began preaching on his own and then, through the good offices of a number of his former colleagues at Lovedale, he became acquainted with Booth's doctrinal approach.[38] During this same period he is said to have joined the American Negro Baptist Church and to have been intimately associated with Chilembwe's Providence Industrial Mission.[39] Contact with Booth may have caused Domingo to shift his allegiances somewhat. In any event, from about 1909 he was affiliated to both the Seventh Day Baptists (Booth in South Africa was again their agent) and, probably to a lesser extent, to the Watch Tower movement.

[37] Livingstone, *Laws*, 309.
[38] Domingo's own testimony, quoted in S 1/927/19: Duff to the Resident (Mzimba), 8 May 1916, Zomba archives.
[39] GOA 2/4/13: The Governor to the Secretary of State, 28 August 1916, Zomba archives.

From 1910 to 1916, Domingo directed the African Seventh Day Baptists (sometimes called, confusingly, the Church of Christ) in the old Mombera's District (now the Mzimba and Rumpi districts) —the home of the northern Ngoni. From his station at Chipata, near Mzimba, he organized a small network of separatist churches and a string of independent schools where colonial rule and white hypocrisy were subjected to criticism. Booth and the American Seventh Day Baptists supplied the funds and much of the literature for this movement (some came from the Watch Tower Society), but Domingo and his pastors attacked the government on its home ground and gave significant, albeit religious, expression to a fairly widespread animosity. In these congregations, as in Kamwana's and Chilembwe's, "the Bible became, as it has so often become in moments of social tension, a great source book for the criticism of established institutions, and a mine of authoritative texts which soon acquired the character of political slogans."[40]

Very little is known of Domingo's teachings. The best statement of his critical disaffection was contained in a telling leaflet circulated privately in 1911:

There is too much failure among all Europeans in Nyasaland. The three combined bodies, Missionaries, Government and Companies, or gainers of money—do form the same rule to look upon the native with mockery eyes. It sometimes startles us to see that the three combined bodies are from Europe, and along with them there is a title "CHRISTENDOM." And to compare or make a comparison between the MASTER of the title and his servants it pushes any African away from believing the Master of the title. If we had power enough to communicate ourselves to Europe we would advise them not to call themselves "Christendom" but "Europeandom." Therefore the life of the three combined bodies is altogether too cheaty, too thefty, too mockery. Instead of "Give" they say "Take away from." From 6 a.m. to 5 or 6 p.m. there is too much breakage of God's pure law as seen in James Epistle, v. 4 ["Behold the hire of the labourers who have reaped down your fields, which is of you kept back by fraud, crieth, and the cries of them which have reaped are entered into the ears of the Lord of Sabaoth."][41]

[40] Shepperson and Price, *African*, 162.
[41] Quoted in *ibid.*, 163–164, exclusive of the bracketed sentence from the Scriptures.

Domingo directed this last injunction to the condition of African tenancy and employment on white-owned lands; Chilembwe and his followers were to renew such criticisms in 1915.

Domingo himself seems to have played no part in the 1915 rising. "He [was] loyal to the Boma."[42] His preachings expressed the intellectual ferment of the age and, like Kamwana, he may have helped to provide a critical climate conducive to rebellion. Similarly, he was eventually deported in 1916 after the seriousness of his alienation was, possibly for the first time, revealed to the Administration. In a letter intercepted by the censor, Domingo endorsed Booth's so-called British African Congress petition of 1915 (not to be confused with Peter Nyambo's Rhodesia-Nyasaland Appeal of 1914, although couched in almost identical terms), which suggested that "educated Natives, as they become available in any part of British Africa, shall have equality of representation in the respective Legislative Assemblies or Councils, and be fully eligible for official posts of trust."[43] All "competent" adults signing the declaration attached to the petition became members, "without financial obligation," of the Congress and were to be "advised in due course as to meetings of the members thereof by the Executive." Domingo sealed his deportation order by joining the Congress and by openly declaring his sentiments, and the wishes of Africans everywhere in British Central Africa, in a long, prescient letter to Booth of 4 February 1916:

That the world should have equality of representation in the respective Legislative Assemblies or councils and be fully eligible to all sorts of loveliness is the commencement of the New Heaven [on] Earth. May his Majesty the King of Great Britain—Defender of the Weak ones and his Government attend to the pleadings of his African subjects—and angel's songs to its fulfillment.[44]

---

[42] S 1/927/19: The Resident (Mzimba) to the Attorney General, 26 June 1915, Zomba archives. A *boma* was and is the local name for any administrative headquarters.

[43] GOA 2/4/13: Enclosure in Buxton to the Governor, 19 October 1915, Zomba archives. For Nyambo, see Shepperson and Price, *African,* 203–209.

[44] S 1/927/19: Enclosure in Duff to the Resident (Mzimba), 8 May 1916, Zomba archives.

RESISTANCE AND REBELLION IN EARLY RHODESIAN SOCIETY

Antipathy toward taxes, the most directly felt manifestation of colonial rule, was a common feature of early Central African society. Although the first administrators imposed taxes somewhat deferentially, the Foreign and Colonial offices worried lest such demands should result in bloodshed. Likewise, the specter of an African uprising greatly exercised the minds of the local white population, particularly after the Southern Rhodesian "rebellions" of 1896. But only after higher taxes, and the introduction of a cash economy, had increased the influence of radical indigenous leaders, could they counsel resistance. Prophets capitalized upon the general unpopularity of taxation and, in a few isolated but portentous instances, tribesmen actually offered physical opposition to tax gatherers.

The Ila (for a time also known as the Mashukulumbwe) were the first to threaten white hegemony in Northern Rhodesia. Respected for their military prowess, the Ila had been studiously avoided by David Livingstone. Some of his more foolhardy successors had ignored his example and had barely escaped alive from Mashukulumbweland.[45] The first missionaries and administrators thus moved cautiously for fear of arousing the Ila unnecessarily. Taxes were eventually imposed in 1906 and collected without any unusual difficulty. But in July 1907, George Heaton Nicholls (then the Collector in charge of the Mumbwa District, and much later a prominent South African Senator) sounded the alarm: "I have recently become convinced of an impending rising amongst the natives of the Kafue District. . . . I believe the natives have not only plotted to refuse payment of tax this year, but they have also plotted to murder all the white population in their beds. . . . I consider the situation very ominous."[46] Missionaries quickly evacuated their stations in the affected district. In nearby farming areas, the govern-

[45] David Livingstone, *Missionary Travels and Researches in South Africa* (London, 1857), 550; Emil Holub, *Von Der Capstadt ins Land der Maschukulumbe,* (Vienna, 1890), ii, 196–225; the diary of George Westbeech, in Edward C. Tabler (ed.), *Trade and Travel in Early Barotseland* (London, 1963), 76–77; Frederick Courteney Selous, *Travel and Adventure in South-East Africa* (London, 1893), 213–224.

[46] A 3/19/6: Heaton Nicholls to the Secretary for Native Affairs, 27 June 1907, Lusaka archives.

ment provisioned garrisons for a conceivably long siege, and at the
Sable Antelope Mine the manager contrived an elaborate system of
blockhouses and land mines to protect himself and his workers.
Troops armed with machine guns were dispatched to Broken Hill
and to Mumbwa, the *bomas* closest to the disturbed area. Reinforcements were even readied as far away as Bulawayo and Johannesburg. The Administrator of Northern Rhodesia and the High
Commissioner for South Africa personally took charge of defensive
strategy against what they called the Mashukulumbwe Rebellion.[47]

Such frenzied mobilization went for naught. Whether or not a
revolt had in fact been planned, the Ila made no threatening moves.
Yet the time was ripe. Remunerative employment in the rural areas
had almost been impossible to obtain in the midst of Northern
Rhodesia's recession of 1906/07, and, to make matters worse, the
local market for African-grown grain had recently become unmistak-
ably bearish. The Ila had little ready cash with which to pay the
government and, in any case, they would almost certainly have
been receptive to any suggested resistance. Indeed, the government accused a Lozi *induna* (or chief's councilor), who acted
as Lewanika's agent in Mashukulumbweland, of encouraging the
Ila to pay tribute to Lewanika, as in times past, rather than taxes to
the British South Africa Company.[48] He may also have counseled
revolt; in any case, Nicholls and W. E. N. Fowler, his assistant,
claimed to have overheard African discussions about the likelihood
of a violent uprising and to have received authoritative corroborative
reports from their African messengers. They knew that the Tonga
of the Buni-Kariba District had already demonstrated their unwillingness to pay taxes and that, in 1906, the Zulu had risen to defy
the tax collectors of Natal. This time, however, the Africans involved
paid their taxes, enabling the government to withdraw its waiting

---

[47] See the full account in the Chapman Papers, Methodist Missionary Society
archives. The only non-derivative published references that refer to the "rebellion" are Henry and Walter Masters, *In Wild Rhodesia* (London, 1920), 157–
165; E. Knowles Jordan, "Namwala in 1906," *The Northern Rhodesia Journal*,
ii (1953), 34–35. The second combines events that took place in years other
than 1906 with those that did.

[48] Price Papers: Nicholls to Handley, 8 July 1907; Jordan to Price, 24 July
1907, Methodist archives. See aso A 1/1/6: Lewanika to the High Commissioner, 11 December 1907; the High Commissioner to Lewanika, 24 February
1908, Lusaka archives.

troops in late August. In the Administrator's eyes, "there had been no cause for alarm"; the "hysterical" Nicholls and Fowler were asked to resign from the Northern Rhodesian colonial service and the missionaries were chastised for leaving their stations.[49] But the Mashukulumbwe Rebellion that never was demonstrated the fearful light in which colonial governments and white settlers ambivalently regarded the Africans that they ruled so contemptuously.

Over all, the imposition of taxes, like the earlier occupation, met only token opposition. Where the European forces were obviously superior, it seemed foolish to resist. Even so, the remote western Lunda are said to have rioted when the principles of taxation were initially explained to them in 1907–08.[50] At about the same time, anti-tax agitation among the Gwembe Tonga came to a head. The Gwembe or Valley Tonga lived in the isolated gorge of the Zambezi River (Lake Kariba subsequently flooded their homeland), generally cut off from contact with European settlement. They were thus deprived of any easy method—short of emigration—by which they could obtain cash sufficient for the payment of taxes. From about 1904, Patrick Macnamara, the Native Commissioner in charge of the Buni-Kariba District, tried with much difficulty to collect taxes from the Gwembe Tonga. Despite floggings administered to all those who were unable or unwilling to pay, resistance was widespread.[51] At first, defaulters simply evaded Macnamara however they could. But the cold war finally boiled over in 1907 (one year, not necessarily by coincidence, after the Zulu of Natal had rebelled). Maluma, an important "witchdoctor," encouraged the Tonga to stiffen their resistance. In 1909, he even urged a violent overthrow of the colonial regime:

The time has come for us to fight the white people, we will start now and fight through the [1909–10] rainy season. The black people [will] rise . . . and drive all the white people out of the country. We must go

[49] A 3/19/6: Codrington to Selborne, 18 September 1907, Lusaka archives. But see Heaton Nicholls, *South Africa in My Time* (London, 1961), 64–67, and the unpublished part of his original typescript autobiographical narrative, 87–97, privately held.

[50] A 4/2/1: Reports from the Balunda District, Lusaka archives.

[51] A 2/1/3: The Administrator to the High Commissioner, 10 November 1909 and 12 February 1910; Reports from the Buni-Kariba District; the Gwembe (Quimbi) District Notebook—all Lusaka archives.

and burn the camp of the *Nkosi* [chief—i.e., Macnamara] . . . and if we find the *Nkosi* . . . we will fight him. All the white people must be driven out of the country. The tax must not be paid.[52]

The Tonga rose against the government, and Maluma personally led an unsuccessful attack upon Macnamara; but British-led troops arrested him, restored order to the Zambezi Valley, and accomplished the collection of outstanding taxes. Thereafter, the Gwembe Tonga paid, if irregularly and reluctantly, and expressed their opposition without resort to violence.[53]

THE NYASALAND RISING OF 1915

All that had gone before—the government's imposition of increasingly onerous hut-tax obligations and its stricter administration of African activities, the increase of African pressure upon available acreage in the Shire Highlands, and the tendency of many white planters to use their indigenous labor as cruelly as possible—provided an atmosphere conducive to the preaching of Booth, Kamwana, Domingo and, in time, of Chilembwe. Like Maluma (and perhaps the anonymous Lozi *induna*), Chilembwe conspired with others of similar mind to protest violently, to defy constituted authority, and, conceivably, to set up an African government. Although a full study of his rising has been published,[54] the recent discovery of added information, and the importance of Chilembwe's actions in the historical mainstream of Central African nationalism, justify another narration. Brief, bloody, and wholly unsuccessful in its immediate context, the rising of 1915 was the most dramatic of the early indigenous attempts to oppose colonial rule, and must be understood as more than an isolated manifestation of discontent. Moreover, it strikingly colored the reactions of Central Africa's

[52] A 2/1/3: Testimony in Rex v. Maluma, Lusaka archives.

[53] Macnamara was subsequently suspended from his post for flogging Africans illegally and for maintaining a concubine. To keep a concubine was, in the Administrator's eyes, "most degrading . . . and incompatible with the maintenance of the prestige of the British Government." A 2/1/3: The Administrator to the High Commissioner, 11 April 1910, Lusaka archives. With regard to concubinage, cf. Lewis H. Gann, *A History of Northern Rhodesia: Early Days to 1953* (London, 1964), 151.

[54] Shepperson and Price, *African*, 218–319.

white ruling class toward African aspirations and encouraged administrators to make of every subsequent expression of African dismay the dangerous conspiracy of revolt.

Somehow—for a variety of reasons that are not wholly clear—changed personal and political circumstances, or a new awareness of the nature of white rule, eroded Chilembwe's apparent willingness to work within the colonial framework of early Nyasaland. Before 1914, he was regarded in a favorable light by those officials or missionaries who paid any attention to the Providence Industrial Mission. Dr. Alexander Hetherwick, for one, in 1912 regarded Chilembwe "as above the ordinary type of mission native."[55] Unlike Kamwana and Domingo, he eschewed millennial teachings and, as far as is known, disseminated rather orthodox Baptist views to his stable, but still small, congregation. Before 1914, he concerned himself primarily with the promotion and financing of his own affairs (he owned a store for a time), the activities of the mission and its schools, and the Natives' Industrial Union, an African Chamber of Commerce that was formed and held meetings in 1909 and, apparently, under another name in 1911.[56] Throughout, he hoped to improve the lot of Africans generally, to instill in them a sense of self-respect by achieving success on European lines, and to make Africans conscious of their economic and social power. His activities undoubtedly demonstrated a growing national awareness.[57] But this was also a period when he was heavily in debt to Haya Edward Peters, a local African trader (whose provenance and background are unknown) and a sometime secretary of the Natives' Industrial Union, who, in 1908, lent Chilembwe at least £50 to start the store and hounded him regularly for the principal and for simple interest amounting to 100 percent per annum.[58] Frequent debilitating attacks of asthma may also have helped to prepare him psycho-

[55] Quoted in *ibid.*, 176.

[56] Peters Papers, 1909, privately held. But see also Shepperson and Price, *African*, 166.

[57] *Ibid.*, 170.

[58] The Chilembwe-Peters correspondence covers the period between 1908 and 1914. The National Baptist Convention gave Chilembwe much of the money needed to repay "Bro. Peters," but Chilembwe's creditor always wanted more. The possibility of blackmail (if Chilembwe in fact harbored seditious thoughts at this time) cannot be ruled out completely, but there is little evidence of such a relationship.

logically for the possibility of rebellion. "As usual," he wrote to Peters in 1911, "I am suffering with the Asthma and being on heaviest weather and atmosphere being so high has caused a dreadful pain in my system. . . . I am almost too weak but in the spirit there is hope of long living."[59] A daughter died, the condition of his eyes may have caused anxiety, and, a host of personal difficulties, each by itself inconclusive, might well have deepened Chilembwe's disenchantment and warped his view of the future.

The increasingly unsatisfactory social situation that pervaded the Shire Highlands could only have enhanced this disenchantment, which the severe famine of 1913 brought sharply into focus. A flood of Nguru immigrants into the Protectorate from Moçambique had decreased the availability of arable acreage, and the widespread alienation of good land to Europeans had forced numerous African villagers to accept what for them were burdensome conditions of residence and employment. The hut tax, the collection of which they could not then evade easily, added to their discomforts. Nowhere was this discontent expressed more frequently than upon the A. Livingstone Bruce estate that bordered the Providence mission. Bruce, a son-in-law of David Livingstone, delegated the routine management of his three-hundred-square-mile holdings to William Jervis Livingstone, no direct relation of the explorer. Unfortunately, this Livingstone dealt harshly with his tenants and laborers and burned the churches that Chilembwe's followers built upon Bruce property; he compelled them to work long hours, paid them less than the standard wage, and even collected hut-tax revenues directly from employees without the intercession of a government official. In general, the Chiradzulu Resident later told the Chief Secretary, the conditions of employment upon the Bruce estates were "illegal and oppressive."[60] After alluding particularly to difficulties that the Livingstone Bruce estate was having with its labor, Francis Barrow Pearce, the then Acting Governor, concluded a dispatch to the Secretary of State for the Colonies: "I cannot conceive of any real prog-

---

[59] Peters Papers: Chilembwe to Peters, 9 February 1911.

[60] S 1/172¹/19: The Resident (Chiradzulu) to the Chief Secretary, 2 April 1915, Zomba archives. See also *Report of the Commission . . . to Inquire into . . . the Native Rising within the Nyasaland Protectorate,* 6819 (Zomba, 1916), 5.

ress in this country which does not take the natives into account for they are the only fixed and permanent element, while the white man in their midst is a migrant whose ultimate hopes are fixed elsewhere."[61] Chilembwe would have agreed.

Is it sufficient to adumbrate such economic and social prerequisites for revolution? George Simeon Mwase, an educated African clerk who evidently knew and later interviewed Africans who participated in the events that preceded the rising, has fortunately written a graphic, seemingly genuine account that lends vivid support to conclusions already advanced.[62] Chilembwe told his followers that the white planters, traders, and other settlers were not treating their labour well. They paid them poorly, and often in kind (according to testimony taken from an African arrested three days after the rising, William Jervis Livingstone had been killed "because he did not pay us well for our work"[63]), whipped them without reason, and usurped the power of the government by holding their own courts. If an African "asks why, he is . . . beaten and . . . told *choka* [scram]." Furthermore, "a native often met shouts of *chotsa chipewa* [take off your hat] in every corner he could go." He was "often times beaten by a whiteman if he did not take off his hat off his head some thousands yards away, even a mile away of a whiteman."

Africans were "very much astonished" when estate owners moved them arbitrarily. The planters said that they had purchased the land in question from the *boma*. As a result, Africans "kn[e]w not what to do or where to go and live comfortable." Additionally, Mwase explained, "John [Chilembwe] was excited when his prayer houses were totally burnt up by a Planter after allowing them to be built at the first place." But significantly, "he did not threaten them, he only sighed and said 'see the evil doing of these white Planters

[61] CO 525/49: Pearce to the Secretary of State, 14 June 1913.

[62] Mwase, "A Dialogue of Nyasaland." A Tonga from Chinteche, Mwase entered the government service as a postal clerk in Chiromo in 1905. After being employed by the Northern Rhodesia and Nyasaland governments in various capacities, he opened a store of his own in the Dedza district. He re-entered government employ, and later settled in a village near Lilongwe. He was known to the Nyasaland Police as an "irresponsible agitator," and apparently played no major role in the rise of nationalism in Nyasaland. He died in 1962.

[63] S 10/1/2: Testimony of Lupiya Zalela (alias Kettlo), 26 January 1915, Zomba archives.

. . . in the country.' He said if he did not like our prayer houses to be built on his land he would have stopped that at the first request, rather than to allow them [to be] built up and then destroy them by setting fire on them . . . without any . . . reason." This occurrence, Mwase reported, grieved Chilembwe's heart. Later, when white settlers bought goats and chickens from Africans without paying properly for them—"also throwing [the money] when giving it to the native"—Chilembwe was distressed further. As Mwase says, "that was . . . r[i]diculous." Or, as "John said," the government "was biased to white Planters and others."[64]

Every indication points to the growing alienation of Chilembwe and his lieutenants during the crucial two years before the rising of 1915. Some would even read into a murky letter from Chilembwe to Peters in 1908 the veiled signs of conspiracy.[65] The Governor of Nyasaland later put forth the official view, that "the movement had been in the course of preparation for some years."[66] But its gestation period could hardly have been long. If it had, the rising might have appeared to be better planned and less a hasty, headlong rush into desperate martyrdom. Furthermore, in a private letter to his creditor dated 26 March 1914, Chilembwe wrote firmly of leaving Nyasaland in the near future for Europe and America, presumably to raise new funds for his mission and schools.[67]

Almost every shred of available new evidence tends to substantiate Shepperson and Price's hypothesis that the rising was precipitated by the outbreak of World War I on 1 August 1914, and by the almost immediate participation of Nyasas in a phase of the war fought on the soil of Nyasaland.[68] Earlier, Chilembwe had protested against the loss of Nyasa lives in the Ashanti and Somali campaigns. In a sense, he was outraged not only at the unnecessary loss of kinsmen, and at the government's refusal to compensate surviving relatives, but also at the injustice of demanding hut taxes of people who later died for the British government. As Mwase explained Chilembwe's stand: "Their old mothers and fathers were asked, say, forced to pay the tax, although their sons, who were giving

64 Mwase, "Dialogue," 17–18.
65 Peters Papers: Chilembwe to Peters, 20 October 1908.
66 S 1/946/19: Governor George Smith's draft contribution to Charles Lucas (ed.), *The Empire at War* (London, 1924), iv.
67 Peters Papers: Chilembwe to Peters, 26 March 1914.
68 Shepperson and Price, *African*, 238.

them money for tax, were killed at the war, which war was nothing to do with them."[69]

Even so, these relatively isolated campaigns did not of themselves turn Chilembwe into a revolutionary. Only when the Anglo-German phase of the World War threatened again to embroil Nyasaland was Chilembwe's concern aroused to fever pitch. When news of the war reached Chilembwe, he "waited [to see] what will happen again to his country men in regard recruiting more *askari*, for the fresh war, or else they will be left alone."[70] Public expression of this real anxiety about the welfare of his countrymen (he had to some extent imbibed Booth's fundamental pacifism), coupled with veiled threats "to deal with the whites" if they once again sent Africans off to war, may explain the warnings about Chilembwe passed to the government in August 1914, by the Roman Catholic Marist Fathers.[71] A few servants and evangelists attached to their Nguludi Mission, which was situated within a few miles of Mbombwe, averred that Chilembwe was preaching sedition. Government and mission officials sent to investigate were unable to verify these reports, but Chilembwe may have already moved from the plains of criticism to the brink of conspiracy.

Africans quickly understood the part that they were to play in the war. With the Germans attacking Nyasaland by lake and land from the north, they were recruited into the King's African Rifles. A large force of porters was also mobilized to carry munitions and other supplies on their heads in lieu of more sophisticated means of transport and communication. A few of these conscripts were killed in the battle of Karonga, in northern Nyasaland, on 9 September 1914. News of the combat no doubt plunged the already disturbed Chilembwe deeper into his study of gloom. And, as the government accelerated its recruitment of Nyasas, so Chilembwe may have moved even closer to the precipice of action. Nevertheless, he possibly still had not decided firmly upon a violent solution. Sometime in late October or early November, he assembled a number of his followers and several tribal headmen in order to discuss the war. They probably asked him to write a letter of protest, the major

[69] Mwase, "Dialogue," 19.
[70] *Ibid.*
[71] GOA 2/4/14, Zomba archives. But Shepperson and Price, *African*, 238, say that the Marist Fathers warned the government in July 1914.

portion of which was contained in the remarkable *cri de coeur* that he submitted for publication in the settler-owned *Nyasaland Times*.[72]

This letter, paraphrased by Mwase, printed in full in *Independent African* and contained in the Zomba archives, is Chilembwe's eloquent testament.[73] With some reluctance the white editor of the *Times* decided to print it in his issue of 26 November.[74] It read in part:

We understand that we have been invited to shed our innocent blood in this world's war which is now in progress throughout the wide world. . . . A number of our people have already shed their blood, while some are crippled for life. . . . Police are marching in various villages persuading well built natives to join in the war. . . . [But] will there be any good prospects for the natives after the end of the war? Shall we be recognised as anybody in the best interests of civilisation and Christianity after the great struggle is ended?

. . . we are imposed upon more than any other nationality under the sun. [We] . . . have been loyal since the commencement of this government. . . . And no time have we been ever known to betray any trust, national or otherwise, confided to us. . . . For our part we . . . have unreservedly stepped to the firing line in every conflict and played a patriot's part with the Spirit of true gallantry. But in time of peace the Government failed to help the underdog. In time of peace everything for Europeans only. . . . But in time of war it has been found that we are needed to share hardships and shed our blood in equality. It is even true that there is a spot of our blood in the cross of the Nyasaland Government.

. . . we understand that this . . . is a war of free nations against a devilish system of imperial domination and national spoilation. . . . Let the rich men, bankers, titled men, storekeepers, farmers and landlords go to war and get shot. Instead the poor Africans who have nothing to own in this present world, who in death, leave only a long line of widows and orphans in utter want and dire distress are invited to die for a cause which is not theirs. . . . We are invited to [die] for Nyasaland. We leave all for the consideration of the Government [and] we hope in the mercy of Almighty God, that some day things will turn out well and that Government will recognise our indispensability, and that justice will prevail.

[72] Mwase, "Dialogue," 20. The *Central African Times* had changed its name.
[73] GOA 2/4/14; Shepperson and Price, *African*, 234–235.
[74] Professor Shepperson carefully deduced the date of publication from fragmentary evidence. His reconstruction was confirmed by material contained in GOA 2/4/14.

A man earlier accustomed to sign his name, "Yours for Africa," this time signed it simply, "John Chilembwe, in behalf of his countrymen."

Most of his countrymen never saw the letter. The government censor, who had been appointed as a wartime measure, excised it from the first run of the *Nyasaland Times* of 26 November; that morning Chilembwe supposedly received a message from the editor of the *Nyasaland Times* telling him to hide the original letter lest he be arrested. As a result, he and those who had encouraged him to write the letter were understandably aggrieved. They cast about after 26 November, conceivably for the first time, for new ways in which to make their protest known. Until then there may well have been no thought of a rising. As far as the government was concerned, constant checking throughout October and November had provided no evidence of conspiracy.[75] Admittedly, the government's perception of imminent danger was dim. For, even after Chilembwe's letter had been brought to the Governor's attention by the censor, the Blantyre Resident's authoritative view was that Chilembwe's influence would remain limited. "There is little," he said, "to be feared from this man."[76]

Already, on 3 December 1914, Chilembwe and his followers had met again to plan a way of coping with the government's refusal to heed their protest. They conspired frequently during December and, according to Mwase, "they all came to the conclusion that by not answering us on our request, means death on us. They all said that 'It was better for all of us to die, than to live and see all these troubles.'"[77] In other words, the unwillingness of the Nyasaland government to reassure the Africans of Mbombwe and of the Protectorate generally that the war was not merely a means by which they would be exterminated, moved them to militancy. There were also overtones suggestive of millenarian eschatology—that Africans would be dragged by the white governments willy-nilly into the fires of Armageddon, or even sacrificed in their masters' stead. Finally, with Chilembwe probably in the chair, the conspirators

[75] GOA 2/4/14: Moggridge to the Chief Secretary, 3 November 1914; Moggridge to Milthorp, 24 October 1914, Zomba archives.

[76] GOA 2/4/14: The Resident (Blantyre) to the Chief Secretary, 11 December 1914, Zomba archives.

[77] Mwase, "Dialogue," 20–24.

held a meeting on 3 January 1915, to decide to "do the deed, or else [to] leave it for good."

They decided "to strike a blow" or else to be "buried alive alternately." At this meeting, Chilembwe may have had to persuade the timorous and to argue forcefully for "a final solution." In this, his moment of triumph, he evidently drew parallels from histories of the struggle of the American Negro that he may well have read long before in Lynchburg, Virginia. To a perhaps frightened group of headmen and African clerks and teachers who naturally respected his superior academic attainments, he spoke of the inspiration of John Brown, who, on the eve of the Civil War, led a small band of ardent abolitionists in a forlorn attempt to liberate the slaves of Virginia. Like Brown, Chilembwe may have considered himself an instrument in the hands of God. He, too, may have recklessly sought martyrdom. Mwase's circumstantial account can hardly have been manufactured:

John [Chilembwe] referred to . . . a Mr. John Brown of America, who after loosing his hope, in succeeding *the request in writing*, to the authority concerned, in regard slave trading he determinate [sic] to strike a blow and loose his own life, than, as he said, was too good for him and was out of sight and reach. John said, this case stands the same, as that of a Mr John Brown. . . . "Let us then strike a blow and die," for our blood, will, surely mean something at last.[78]

They all agreed to "strike a blow and die."

This moving refrain is the key to a further understanding of the riddle of Chilembwe's revolt. Like John Brown, John Chilembwe almost certainly knew that his chances of worldly success were negligible. He knew that, despite their preoccupation with the German threat, the Protectorate's forces could eventually if not immediately subdue any military adventure that Africans could contemplate or arrange. Why then did he rise? Why did he organize and direct a movement that led to three European deaths? If he did not aspire—in the Resident of Blantyre's words—to be "King of Nyasaland," and if he did not seek a massacre of all of the whites in the Shire Highlands and "the suppression of white rule"— to quote the Governor—why did he study a military manual and

---

[78] *Ibid.,* 21 (italics mine). Cf. Shepperson and Price, *African,* 239.

plan a coordinated attack on white-owned property?[79] Why conspire with others from districts as distant as Ncheu and Mlanje? In short, what were his motives?

After the deliberations of 3 January 1915, Chilembwe apparently informed Filipo Chinyama, a Seventh Day Baptist preacher who had promised to lead a rising in the Ncheu District, and others in the Zomba, Blantyre, and Mlanje districts, that the caucus had decided to attack according to their previously discussed plan.[80] (Chinyama had spent three weeks with Chilembwe in November and December; he may even have been on hand when the editor's runner brought news of the censored letter.) If the tasks were accomplished without meeting strong opposition, Chilembwe might conceivably have hoped temporarily to set up an independent government in the Shire Highlands. But it seems more likely that he simply tried to make the most effective of protests. With such an aim in mind, he therefore sent the "battalions" to Magomero, Mwanje, and Blantyre on the night of 23 January 1915 to obtain guns and ammunition and to bring back the head of William J. Livingstone. If this analysis is correct, he hoped that the symbolic taking of Livingstone's head would at last persuade the government and the planting community that African grievances were real. A supply of guns and ammunition would enable him to make a last stand at Mbombwe or on a nearby hill called Chilimangwanje. In this way Chilembwe could martyr himself for his people.

The course of the rising and the testimony of witnesses supports such a conclusion. Sometime during the third week of January 1915, Chilembwe may have decided that the evening of Saturday, the 23rd, suited his purposes. Many whites would be making merry at the annual festivities of the Blantyre Sports Club and, as Africans knew from experience, they would be in no shape to deal efficiently with a rising.[81] His decision to attack was also influenced, perhaps decisively, by what Chilembwe read into the Governor's proclamation of a state of emergency in the North Nyasa District. (In addition, he may possibly have learned of the Governor's decision to

[79] S 1/946/19: Governor Smith's contribution to Lucas; GOA 2/4/14: Report of the Resident (Blantyre), 31 March 1915, Zomba archives. Cf. *Rising Commission Report*, 6.

[80] Much of the following is from Mwase, "Dialogue," 21–31. It corresponds substantially with the account in Shepperson and Price, *African*.

[81] *Ibid.*, 260.

deport him to the Seychelles.) According to the testimony of one of his battalion commanders, he learned that the whites had planned to kill all Africans.[82] According to another member of the cabal, on Friday or Saturday, Chilembwe unexpectedly sent a messenger to the various Providence Industrial Mission churches to tell his followers that "the Europeans planned to kill the natives on Monday, and that they must rise."[83] At the same time, he sent a messenger (who arrived too late) to Chinyama, telling him to act according to previous arrangements at 7 P.M. on the Saturday. A few days before, he had dispatched Yotam Bango with a letter probably inviting assistance from the German government in East Africa.[84]

On Saturday morning, Chilembwe gathered his followers together in the Mbombwe church for the last time. According to Mwase, he offered a prayer and then carefully explained that they were to die bravely for their country. They could not hope to be victorious, but they were to sacrifice their lives in order to obtain a better future for their fellow Nyasas. In the manner of John Brown, Chilembwe's logic was dramatically simple:

You are all patriots as you sit. . . . This very night you are to go and strike the blow and then die. I do not say that you are going to win the war at all. You have no weapons with you and you are not at all trained military even. . . . I now encourage you to go and strike a blow bravely and die. This is [the] only way to show the whiteman, that the treatment they are treating our men and women was most bad and we have determined to strike a first and a last blow, and then all die by the heavy storm of the white men's army. The whitemen will then think, after we are dead, that the treatment they are treating our people is almost bad, and they might change. . . . You must not think that with that blow, you are going to defeat whitemen and then become Kings of your own country, no. If one of you has such an idea in his head, "God forbid" . . . for it will lead him astray.[85]

---

[82] S 2/18/22: Statement of Duncan Njilima, 17 February 1915, Zomba archives. For the deportation, see GOA 2/4/15: The Governor to the Secretary of State, 3 February 1915, Zomba archives. See also *The Nyasaland Government Gazette,* xxii (22 January 1915), 2.

[83] S 10/1/2: Statement of Lupiya Zalela, 26 January 1915, Zomba archives.

[84] The Germans replied sympathetically, but only on 17 March 1915. S 2/8/19: Zomba archives, contains the fullest account.

[85] Mwase, "Dialogue," 29.

Chilembwe warned his followers to refrain from seizing property, to avoid molesting white women—"You are patriots and not Lechers" —an order they obeyed without fault. He is reputed to have said specifically that, *if* some of the white men were killed during the assault, their heads only should be brought back to Mbombwe. Finally, and significantly for a strongly religious individual who had originally been influenced by Booth, he chose to spend Saturday night and the succeeding evenings meditating on Chilimangwanje hill, where he awaited the white retaliation and, perhaps, his own end.

From Mbombwe two of the relatively small "battalions"—one estimate puts Chilembwe's army at two hundred men—marched north eight miles to the Bruce estates while the others went south fifteen miles to Blantyre.[86] At Magomero, the headquarters of the main estate, the William J. Livingstones were entertaining Mrs. Ranald MacDonald, the wife of the Director of Customs at Chiromo. In a house nearby, Mrs. Emily Stanton, of Zomba, was visiting her sister-in-law, Mrs. Alyce Roach, whose husband was the estate engineer and the custodian of a large arsenal. He spent the weekend in Blantyre. Duncan MacCormick, another employee, lived alone in yet a third house. Five young children were also involved. Dependent upon light from flickering kerosene lamps, the adults tended to retire early. It was during the final stages of this preparation for sleep that the "battalion" led by Wilson Zimba, to whom Chilembwe had given the rank of "major," launched its attack.

The battalion evidently had encircled the house and waited calmly for the whites to conclude their dinner and to dismiss the servants. Both Katherine Livingstone and Agnes MacDonald later agreed that they left the sitting room at 8:50 P.M.[87] Mrs. MacDonald undressed, noticed that the time was 8:55 P.M., and then went into her bathroom. Opening the window, she saw "seven or eight natives close to it, looking in." Others were hiding behind a tree and all were holding bundles of sticks. She assumed that the sticks were

[86] This discussion of the events of the rising does not attempt to supersede that contained in Shepperson and Price, *African*, 269–319. It does, however, contain new information.

[87] GOA 2/4/14: Statements of Katherine Livingstone and Agnes MacDonald, both made on 2 February 1915, Zomba archives.

firewood. She asked who they were; and received no answer. "I went back to my room and just then heard screams."

In the main bathroom, Mrs. Livingstone had been disturbed by a cat. She called her husband to put it out. "He came," said Mrs. Livingstone, "and opened the outside bathroom door and just then five or six natives with spears broke in." The Livingstones quickly retreated to their bedroom, for when Mrs. MacDonald ran to their aid she saw "Mr. Livingstone holding his service rifle by the muzzle and striking with the butt at some natives who were trying to force their way into the bedroom from the bathroom."

The final scenes are confused. "I have no distinct recollection," said Mrs. Livingstone, "of what occurred . . . until I saw my husband fall down in the bathroom of the spare bedroom," some rooms away from the original breach by Zimba's men.

He did not appear to be dead. He fell on his side and I tried to turn him over on his back but did not succeed in doing so. I went into the dining room for a stimulant to give him and found a bottle of Port wine, part of the contents of which I poured into his mouth. The bottle was snatched out of my hand by a native and just then another . . . came in with an axe and proceeded to cut off my husband's head . . . in my presence.

MacCormick, whose house had not been surrounded, had meanwhile been informed by his servants of the attack on Livingstone. Without bothering to gather a rifle, he rushed across the intervening darkness only to have the thrust of spears arrest his gallantry. Mrs. Livingstone said that MacCormick suddenly "rushed in through the bathroom door, covered with blood and fell down beside my husband, apparently dead." The women and children, however, were unscathed. Throughout the melee, the attackers had worked around them, even when Mrs. MacDonald purposely placed herself in their path. Moreover, aside from the arsenal that had perhaps prompted their attack, they looted no European property.

The motivation for the one other assault on European planters is less obvious. At Mwanje, the section of the Bruce estates nearest to Mbombwe, members of a battalion led by "Major" Jonathan Chigwinya entered the unlocked house of Robert Ferguson, the stock manager, at about 8 P.M. Speared on his bed, where he had been reading the week's mail, Ferguson was somehow permitted to stagger to the house of John Robertson, the section manager. There

John and his wife Charlotte were preparing for bed. They heard a dog barking and, according to Mrs. Robertson's testimony, "My husband got up to see what was happening and was met at the door by a crowd of boys [African men] all armed with spears. Just then Mr. Ferguson staggered in. He had been fatally stabbed in the breast. My husband ran out of the bedroom into the dining room and got his rifle . . . and fired his rifle into the crowd until his magazine was empty, then reloaded and ran around the inside of the house firing out of every window. At last he scattered them."[88] But he had been speared, Ferguson was dying, and the house was on fire. From the detached grass hut that served as a kitchen, Robertson continued to "blaze away at them" until he and his wife were able to escape into a nearby cotton field. "We crept into the bush and waited but tho' they passed us they did not seem to see us." Why had they been attacked? Did this battalion also hope to find a cache of arms, was its action simply meant to safeguard Zimba's line of retreat from Magomero, or was a personal vendetta involved?

Aside from an abortive attempt to break into the African Lakes Corporation's ammunition store in Blantyre—foiled partially because John Gray Kufa, Duncan Njilima, and the supposedly loyal watchman and *boma askari* all "shrinked" from their appointed tasks[89]— there were no further attempts to attack white property or the many isolated planters who would certainly have been on Chilembwe's list if a wholesale massacre had indeed been planned. After the engagements of Saturday night and Sunday morning, the rebels refrained from destroying the untended *boma* at Chiradzulu, only five miles from Mbombwe, and evidently spent a large part of their time praying and talking. In the Ncheu district, where Chilembwe's message arrived late on Saturday, the attack of Chinyama and his fellow conspirators on the Ncheu *boma* had been averted by an alert Resident, who managed to intercept them before any assaults could be mounted.[90] But Chilembwe was not to know that Chinyama had failed until Monday or Tuesday, so the extent of the rising's collapse would not necessarily have persuaded him to cancel any further

[88] S 10/1/2: Statement of Charlotte Robertson, made shortly after the rising, Zomba archives.

[89] Mwase, "Dialogue," 24.

[90] GOA 2/4/15, Zomba archives. C. A. Cardew, the Resident (Ncheu), was evidently warned of the conspiracy by a friendly chief; Ian Nance, letter to the author, 3 July 1963.

plans to strike against Europeans on Sunday and Monday. Moreover, Chilembwe had not planned to go underground with his followers in the event that the rebellion failed. He may simply have intended to make a last, dramatic stand on Chilimangwanje Hill—to die symbolically for his people and his country.

The testimony of the Magomero women does not discredit such a conclusion. After the deaths of Livingstone and MacCormick, and Agnes MacDonald's escape through an open window ("My boy came through . . . and whispered 'war—we must go.' . . . I followed him"),[91] Mrs. Roach, Mrs. Stanton, the dazed Mrs. Livingstone, and their children, were escorted with great tact and surprising kindness to a hut on the road south to Mbombwe.[92] They rested between about two and six A.M., and then continued their march. At first it appears that they were being shown the way to Chiradzulu *boma;* later Mbombwe may have been the objective.[93] In any event, the route that they followed was circuitous; they walked all Sunday morning and afternoon, and spent Sunday evening in a village where they were given green mangoes for supper and were left unguarded. Despite the conflicting testimony contained in government files and summarized in *Independent African,* there is every reason to suppose that Chilembwe sent the women and children to the Chiradzulu *boma* on Monday, 25 January, so that they might testify to his deed, and to his readiness to accept his fate.[94]

The attack early the following morning upon Nguludi Mission—Father Swelsen was severely wounded and the mission buildings were set on fire—probably occurred after Chilembwe had lost control of his followers. Whether escaping or on patrol, a group fired the mission buildings and left Father Swelsen for dead. Only after this incident, and the attack on Mbombwe by a detachment of the white Mikalongwe Volunteers, was Chilembwe, perhaps reluctantly, persuaded to leave his hill and his church. Instead of making an orderly retreat in the fashion of disciplined guerrillas, the rebels split up. John Chilembwe and his nephew Morris Chilembwe then fled

[91] GOA 2/4/14: Testimony of Agnes MacDonald.

[92] GOA 2/4/14: Testimony of Katherine Livingstone.

[93] Cf. Shepperson and Price, *African,* 272, 285.

[94] The new gloss is derived from the evidence of Alyce [*sic*] Roach, 30 January 1915, in S 10/1/2, Zomba archives. See also Shepperson and Price, *African,* 285.

toward Portuguese territory beyond the northern side of Mlanje mountain.

Although the whites maintained their *laagers* until 4 February, the rising was really over on 26 January. For the next few days, European patrols and "native friendlies" tracked down the leading conspirators, and hanged them after summary trials. The prospects of financial reward resulted in a number of arrests, but Chilembwe himself carefully eluded the various search parties until 2 February. On that day Garnet Kaduya, a Church of Scotland teacher, "came on the track in the bush which I followed . . . till the evening and being afraid to go on I . . . sent a boy . . . to call the Mlanje Police."[95] In the morning, five policemen came and together they followed Chilembwe's trail around Bankala Hill and across the Migowi stream, about seven miles from Moçambique. At about noon on 3 February 1915, near the modern Kelinde village, they came upon John and Morris Chilembwe and two children. Morris Chilembwe fired two shots but he himself was killed by the policemen. Unarmed, and then wearing a dark blue coat, a striped pyjama jacket over a colored shirt, and gray flannel trousers, John Chilembwe ran for about a mile, "and then Private Naluso fired and we saw that he had wounded the man as he turned round and round and then stood still, then Sergeant Useni fired and hit him again, he still stood, then I fired with Morris' gun and hit him through the head and he fell dead."[96] A pair of gold spectacles and a pair of pince-nez, the right lens missing in each case, were found next to his emaciated body.

The immediately favorable results of the rising were few. Suspected followers of Chilembwe either lost their lives, languished in prison, or spent their remaining days in enforced exile. The government imposed severe restrictions upon the activities of the fringe churches and their leaders. When the official commission of inquiry recommended a number of ways of ameliorating the harsh conditions under which Africans lived and labored in the Shire Highlands, the government refused to make the necessary reforms.[97] Chilembwe

[95] J 2/9/3: Testimony of Garnet Kaduya.
[96] *Ibid.*
[97] GOA 2/4/15: Smith to the Secretary of State, 6 March 1916, Zomba archives.

nevertheless had shattered the widesprad aura of white compla-
cency. He had destroyed the notion that "the natives were happy"
under British domination. Unfortunately, the government learned
this lesson imperfectly, and the rising of 1915 failed to change the
course of colonial rule in Central Africa. The forlorn example of
John Chilembwe only later—during a more propitious era—provided the text for a genuine movement of independence.

Chapter IV

THE ATTEMPT TO ACHIEVE MINORITY RULE

It does not appear to us that amalgamation will unfairly affect any portion of the community of the two territories.

—The statement of a delegation of settlers from Mazabuka and Lusaka, 1927

The Chilembwe rising constituted the opening salvo of the battle between white and black for hegemony in Central Africa. During the succeeding forty-four years, although resort to arms was infrequent, the two sides struggled incessantly, especially in Northern Rhodesia, in order to achieve a lasting ascendancy. For several generations, while Africans protested vainly and responded to white rule in ways that will be described presently, the settlers attempted to increase their own influence locally. Only with the inauguration of a federal government in 1953, however, were their efforts to join Nyasaland and Northern Rhodesia to Southern Rhodesia successful. Before then, they had tried to obtain a larger measure of control over their own destiny by ridding themselves first of Chartered Company, and then of Colonial Office government. In order to do so, they sought to incorporate their own territories within an enlarged Southern Rhodesia—a colony where white settlers had ruled in fact, although not in name, since 1898. Many of the leading white residents of the northern protectorates had immigrated from beyond the Zambezi River, and they not unnaturally attempted to introduce into Northern Rhodesia and Nyasaland a pattern of home rule that was modeled upon the southern example—both for its own sake and in order to negate the comparatively benevolent, and therefore, to them, distasteful British regard for African rights. In the period between the two world wars, white settlers north of the Zambezi had but one major political preoccupation: they tried desperately to free themselves from overseas-imposed restrictions in order to secure their own way of life for the future, and in order to prevent Africans from ever challenging that way of life. But, as the settlers

agitated, so Africans took fright. This adverse African reaction increased settler anxieties and invested their struggle for home rule
with a particular urgency.

THE SEARCH FOR SECURITY

After the end of World War I, the leaders of the small white communities of Northern Rhodesia and Nyasaland reluctantly came to
accept some form of amalgamation—whether with each other or
with Southern Rhodesia—as a potential answer to their perennial
anxieties about the white man's future in Africa. At first, despite the
evident wishes of Cecil Rhodes to make the three Central African
territories one, the settlers had attempted to look instead to increased immigration of whites, and to a subsequent grant of home
rule to a settler government, for the protection of their interests. In
1915–16, they greeted the British South Africa Company's proposal
to amalgamate Northern and Southern Rhodesia with a distinct lack
of enthusiasm. For reasons of administrative economy, the Company
wanted to establish "a single unified administration for the whole of
Rhodesia." It suggested that "amalgamation" would permit the
people of Northern Rhodesia—"too few to have a Legislative Council of their own"—to obtain a "voice in all legislation affecting them,"
that the attraction of postwar immigrants would be assisted, and
that affluence could be more readily obtained by the elimination of
the artificial customs barrier at the Zambezi River. "If . . . Rhodesia
is to have her due weight in the councils which will follow the
War," a Company statement read, "it is desirable that the amalgamation of the two territories should be effected without delay. . . ."[1]
But, in meetings during 1916, many of the settlers of Northern Rhodesia expressed a distaste for amalgamation with Southern Rhodesia
(those who lived in the eastern districts advocated a merger with
Nyasaland) and, in 1917, the representative members of the Southern Rhodesian legislative assembly rejected the Company's plan because they were unwilling to saddle their constituents with the racial

---

[1] B 1/2/270: Memorandum of the British South Africa Company, 24 December 1915, Lusaka archives. See also Lewis H. Gann, *A History of Northern
Rhodesia: Early Days to 1953* (London, 1964), 174–179. Portions of this
chapter originally appeared in Robert I. Rotberg, "The Federation Movement
in British East and Central Africa, 1889–1953," *Journal of Commonwealth
Political Studies,* ii (1964), 141–160. This material is used herein by permission
of the editors of the journal and its publisher, the Leicester University Press.

problems and the debts of the largely unproductive "black north."
To the territory's leading settler, the Company's scheme "meant the
giving up for all time of the ideals of democracy and a free self-
governing country, because in that part of the world [Northern
Rhodesia] . . . representative institutions could never flourish. . . .
It would render impossible the attainment of [complete] self-government."[2]

Settler politics and politicians achieved significance during this
lengthy Northern Rhodesian debate over "amalgamation." Two
long-established pressure groups, the North-Western Rhodesia Farmers' Association and the North-Eastern Rhodesia Agricultural and
Commercial Association, became political institutions—even parties,
and for the first time the Chartered Company faced an aroused
white public opinion. After the Privy Council had ruled against the
Company in a suit brought to determine the ownership of Rhodesian land, this aroused public became increasingly difficult to
mollify. Led by the strident druggist and editor Leopold Frank
Moore, and by a number of farmers, the settlers actively urged the
British government to end the rule of the Company. Moore promised his supporters to do his "best to carry on a sort of guerrilla
warfare . . . keeping always in view the ultimate object to be attained—getting rid of the Chartered Company."[3] He and his colleagues wanted representation—what Moore called "self-determination." They confidently expected that the achievement of local
self-government would eliminate the necessity of amalgamation.
Finally, in 1918—eleven years after the settlers of Nyasaland had
begun their mild debates within a colonial governor's Legislative
Council—the Company agreed to placate settler opinion in Northern Rhodesia by the formation of an Advisory Council, the members
of which could "discuss with the administration any question affecting the white inhabitants of the territory, and draft legislation, the
promulgation of which was not urgent in point of time, could be
submitted to it for observation."[4] Although the European population
had wanted a more powerful forum, its leaders accepted representation on an Advisory Council whose five "unofficial" members were

[2] Charles Coghlan, in Southern Rhodesia, *Proceedings of the Legislative Assembly*, 26 April 1917.
[3] *The Livingstone Mail*, 4 January 1918.
[4] B 1/2/270: Millar to the Administrator of Northern Rhodesia, 2 June 1917.

elected only by white male adults (then fewer than 1000) possessing sufficiently high income or property qualifications, and which met in brief, unproductive yearly sessions. The Company's Administrator controlled the Council; it therefore proved to be a most unsatisfactory instrument for the redress of settler discontent.

The settlers of Northern Rhodesia began seriously to discuss amalgamation in 1919, and the farmers of Kafue and Mazabuka, who hoped to benefit by a new railway between Kafue and Sinoia, in Southern Rhodesia, became its leading supporters. But the settlers of Northeastern Rhodesia preferred to strengthen their ties to Nyasaland, the commercial interests of Northwestern Rhodesia were lukewarm, and Moore was obsessed by the prior need to scuttle the Company's Rhodesian ship of state. By strenuous campaigning he successfully made "amalgamation" a minority plank in the settler platform and, with the fifty or sixty active members of the North-Western Rhodesia Political Association (formed from among the ranks of the Farmers' Association), he advocated a type of government under which the settlers would possess a broad measure of internal autonomy that could be exercised by a popular Legislative Council under a Crown Colonial administration. Thus, in 1921, the settlers opposed the appointment of a joint administrator for both Rhodesias, demanded "real representation" as the price of increased taxation, and voted strongly against any absorption of Northern by Southern Rhodesia. For Moore, the appropriate strategy seemed simple: "The people of this country desire to build up a self-governing state . . . within the empire, which . . . seems to be possible only if Crown Colonial government is established first."[5]

The settlers wanted what Southern Rhodesia was about to obtain —a large measure of responsible government.[6] But, in 1924, although the settlers received some representation in a new Legislative Council, Britain transformed Northern Rhodesia into an Imperial Protectorate. The British government furthermore indicated that it could not possibly make any grant of internal autonomy to such a small

[5] *Proceedings of the Advisory Council,* third session, first meeting, 15–21 June 1922.

[6] See *Second Report of the Committee Appointed . . . to Consider Certain Questions Relating to Rhodesia,* Cmd. 1471 (1921); *Agreement . . . for the Settlement of Outstanding Questions Relating to Southern and Northern Rhodesia,* Cmd. 1984 (1923).

group of settlers in the foreseeable future. The white Northern Rhodesians consequently were compelled to consider new answers to their deeply felt dilemma.

To white Northern Rhodesians, amalgamation or some other form of closer association with Southern Rhodesia, with Nyasaland or with the British territories of East Africa, constituted the reasonable political alternatives. The occupation of Tanganyika by British and South African forces had made the possibility of an East African union real; Alexander Hetherwick, the Scottish missionary and Legislative Council member from Blantyre, and Frederick Melland, a Northern Rhodesian administrative officer with a flair for the dramatic, both argued in favor of this wider grouping during 1917 and 1918.[7] After the British government had officially dampened their hopes for home rule, the settlers of Northern Rhodesia and, to some extent, those of Nyasaland welcomed an exploration of the feasibility of ties to the northern dependencies. They were encouraged by Lord Delamere, the leader of the white East Africans, and by the adoption of common forthright pro-settler policies at the Tukuyu and Livingstone conferences of 1925 and 1926.[8] But the parliamentary commission sent to investigate, *inter alia*, the closer integration of the East and Central African territories, learned that the governments of Northern Rhodesia and Nyasaland were opposed to closer political ties to Tanganyika, Uganda, and Kenya, and that the two Central African territories were economically and strategically oriented toward the south, rather than the north. The commission, chaired by William G. A. Ormsby-Gore, therefore recommended that the provision of better communication facilities and other common services was a necessary prelude to the formation of a broad federation of the five British dependencies.[9]

The movement in favor of an East African, if not an East and Central African closer union, nevertheless was encouraged by Leopold S. Amery, the new Secretary of State for the Colonies, and

[7] Alexander Hetherwick, "Nyasaland Today and Tomorrow," *Journal of the African Society*, xvii (1917), 11–19; Frederick H. Melland (using the pseudonym "Africanus"), "A Central African Confederation," *ibid.*, xvii (1918), 276–306.

[8] S 1/1609/25: Zomba archives; B 1/1/806: Lusaka archives, Elspeth Huxley, *White Man's Country* (London, 1953), ii, 200–216.

[9] *Report of the East African Commission*, Cmd. 2387 (1925).

by Sir Edward Grigg (later the first Lord Altrincham), his governor of Kenya.[10] In 1927, Amery and his influential supporters persuaded the British government to announce that "some form of closer union between the territories of Central and Eastern Africa appears desirable."[11] But the Colonial Secretary was unable, partially because of strong opposition from the influential "African rights" lobby that had been mobilized by Dr. Joseph Houldsworth Oldham and Lord Lugard, to persuade the Cabinet to sponsor the immediate formation of an East African federation. Instead, another commission, under the chairmanship of Sir Edward Hilton Young (later Lord Kennet of Dene) was appointed to investigate and to report, bearing in mind the "Imperial duty" of safeguarding the welfare and interests of the indigenous populations.

Politically representative, the Hilton Young delegation was a suitable forerunner to the British commissions that later went so laboriously over much of the same verbal ground. It toured Northern Rhodesia and Nyasaland, listened to a variety of petitioners, and opened up all of the old political wounds by seeking "responsible opinion" on the virtue either of a closer union with East Africa, or a closer association between two or more of the three Central African territories. By that time, Northern Rhodesia's most outspoken settlers had retreated from any thought of permanent ties to East Africa. They had begun to look south instead, and to welcome a new Southern Rhodesian sentiment in favor of amalgamation. The extent of Northern Rhodesia's copper resources was known, if approximately, and the government of Southern Rhodesia gave every indication of being anxious that the Hilton Young Commission should not, by its conclusions, prejudice the amalgamation of the two Rhodesias.[12]

The threat of an African-dominated confederation with the north had driven white Northern Rhodesians into the arms of their brethren to the south. The Northern Rhodesians told the Commission that they were "totally opposed to any federation with the north [East Africa] until amalgamation with Southern Rhodesia was accomplished." For them, Southern Rhodesia had the "right tradition." In sentiment and ideals, they said, the two Rhodesias were

---

[10] For a further discussion, see Rotberg, "Federation Movement," 141–160.
[11] *Future Policy in Regard to Eastern Africa,* Cmd. 2904 (1927).
[12] B 1/3/37: Governor Chancellor to Governor Maxwell, 12 December 1927.

one. They felt that its similarity of climate, of white population, and of economic circumstances made amalgamation feasible. The southern settlers had evolved a form of government and civil service "adapted to these conditions"; their form of government would attract immigrants and, by relieving the British government of financial liability for Northern Rhodesia, the development of the resources of the protectorates would no longer "be at the mercy of politics at home."[13] For all of these reasons the settlers of Central Africa favored the formation of a new state composed of the two Rhodesias and, in order to placate the farmers of Northeastern Rhodesia, Nyasaland.

In Nyasaland, most of the leading settlers advocated some form of closer association with both Rhodesias. The Anglican Bishop became the moving force in a pro-federation committee that included delegates from the Chamber of Agriculture and Commerce, the Nyasaland and Cholo Planters' Associations, and the Nyasaland Merchants' Association. The Chamber of Commerce, however, joined the Namwera Planters' Association in wanting an amalgamation only with Northern Rhodesia. At this time there were fewer than 1500 whites resident in Nyasaland.

The Hilton Young Commission—in particular the commissioners Sir Reginald Mant (in effect representing the India Office), Sir George Schuster (the economic advisor to the Colonial Office), and Oldham (the secretary of the International Missionary Council)— remained unimpressed by these contentions. They preferred to sympathize with African fears of white domination and, throughout the body of their long report, they argued for a type of closer union that, by entrenching Imperial control, would be of benefit to Africans. The commissioners wrote: "The chief need in Eastern and Central Africa today is that there should be applied throughout the territories as a whole, continuously and without vacillation, a 'native policy' which, while adapted to the varying conditions of different tribes and different localities, is consistent in its main principles."[14]

They proposed to give a British high commissioner (ultimately a governor-general) executive powers to direct African affairs within the three territories of East Africa. At the same time, they hoped to give the European community, especially in Kenya, definite political

[13] B 1/3/35: Lusaka archives.
[14] *Report of the Commission on Closer Union*, Cmd. 3234 (1929), 7.

prerogatives within prescribed spheres, thereby creating a peaceful "mixed state" wherein each of the main ethnic groups would be allowed to develop along its own communal lines. The commissioners, led by Oldham and Schuster, defended their conclusions at length:

Our idea is that, while each [race] pursues its own distinctive and natural line of development, they may be able to settle down together in a single state without the fear of a struggle for domination, provided that there is available an impartial arbiter to decided issues in which there is a conflict of racial interests. It can be the destiny of the Imperial Government to fill this role.[15]

A corollary was that, while the white settlers might be trusted partners of the British government, they could never claim to be the dominant element.

With regard specifically to Central Africa, the Commission reported that Rhodesian communications were still too inadequate, and its racial policies too dissimilar, to justify any form of union with East Africa. It next divided upon the question of establishing a smaller federal unit that would encompass the two Rhodesias and Nyasaland. The chairman, like some of the settlers, favored the partitioning of Northern Rhodesia in such a way that the predominantly "European" and industrial areas would alone be amalgamated with Southern Rhodesia. (Northeastern Rhodesia would join Nyasaland—although it would retain a loose federal association with Southern Rhodesia through the agency of a high commissioner, who would also be the governor of Southern Rhodesia—the central railway strip in which whites had settled would become part of Southern Rhodesia, and Barotseland and the African areas of Northwestern Rhodesia would be transformed into an inalienable reserve administered by the new Rhodesian government.) His colleagues, however, agreed with the Bishop of Northern Rhodesia that Africans of the two protectorates were British wards, and that a Rhodesian government responsive to settler whims would have "the strongest possible temptation to exploit the [natives] for the purposes of personal gain." He testified that "The average settler does not regard the native as an equal. . . . He repudiates them. To him the native

[15] *Ibid.*, 235.

is neither a fellow-worker, a fellow citizen, nor even . . . a fellow man; and the idea of any sort of trusteeship or responsibility is either foreign to him or laughable."[16]

The commissioners rejected any proposals which would "place any further tracts with large native population under the Government of Southern Rhodesia until that Government has demonstrated its ability to cope with the extensive native problems that already confront it."[17] They felt that there were "many reasons for eventually linking Nyasaland and a part at least of Northern Rhodesia with the Northern Territories" and urged the British government to avoid "the forging of any fetters which might bind [the protectorates] permanently to the south."[18]

THE SETTLER CHALLENGE

The investigations of the Hilton Young Commission, and a temporary upsurge in settler economic prospects, stimulated white (and, in turn, African) political awareness and activity. In Nyasaland, where respective colonial secretaries had previously refused to allow the settlers to elect, or the Chamber of Commerce to appoint the white "unofficial" representatives to the Legislative Council, the settlers' Convention of Associations began in 1929/30 to select all of the non-government nominees to the Council with the exception of the missionary chosen to represent "native interests."[19] (Earlier, Governor George Smith had assured the Colonial Secretary that "the interests of the Natives [apart from the voicing they may receive from the mission member] may be, at least . . . for some time yet to come, best left in the hands of the Governor and the official members of the Council.")[20]

The Convention was modeled upon Kenya's successful organization of the same name. It was the successor to a long line of settler pressure groups, the first of which had been the Shire Highlands Planters' Association, which was formed in 1892 and immediately opposed by the Nyasaland Planters' Association. In 1895, these two antagonistic bodies merged to form the British Central Africa

[16] B 1/3/36: Containing the testimony of Bishop May, Lusaka archives.
[17] Cmd. 3234, 90–92.
[18] *Ibid.*, 261.
[19] S 1/1926/19: Milner to the Governor of Nyasaland, 3 October 1920 (telegram); Churchill to the Governor, 2 November 1921, Zomba archives.
[20] S 1/1926/19: Smith to the Secretary of State, 21 February 1921.

Chamber of Agriculture and Commerce. For thirty years, under different labels, it remained the most important pressure group for European interests in the Protectorate, but, dissension having developed between the farmers and the businessmen, a new Nyasaland Planters' Association was organized in 1925. These two organizations, and the numerous local associations that had sprung up after World War I, made such conflicting representations to the Nyasaland Government that Governor Sir Charles Bowring, who had served in Kenya, finally persuaded the businessmen and farmers to express themselves politically through a Convention of Associations.[21] Later governors accorded it a considerable role in the formulation of official policy and encouraged it to represent vigorously the narrow social and economic interests of Nyasaland's European residents.

Northern Rhodesians had already won the battle for representation. But, in the aftermath of the Hilton Young report, their leaders and the white government of Southern Rhodesia still feared that the Central African protectorates would be included within an East African federation (Amery had continued to support the scheme). They struggled to obtain Colonial Office sanction for exploratory maneuvers, but the unfavorable opinion of Governor Sir James Crawford Maxwell was, at the time, probably decisive. "I do not," he said, "regard amalgamation with Southern Rhodesia as being in the interests of the people of this territory, European or Native."[22] A new colonial secretary, Lord Passfield (earlier Sidney Webb), further increased the anxieties of the white settlers and, in 1930, stirred them to renewed action by the issue of his *Memorandum on Native Policy in East Africa*.[23] It reaffirmed the doctrine of trusteeship and paramountcy of African interests that had been enunciated in different circumstances by the Duke of Devonshire in 1923.[24] The *Memorandum* made it abundantly clear that African interests would prevail should they and those of the immigrant races conflict.

[21] File 14334: Correspondence, Zomba archives.
[22] Sec/Ea/9: Maxwell to the Secretary of State, 2 December 1929, Lusaka archives.
[23] *Memorandum on Native Policy in East Africa*, Cmd. 3573 (1930); it was published simultaneously with the *Statement of the Conclusions of His Majesty's Government in the United Kingdom as Regards Closer Union in East Africa*, Cmd. 3574 (1930).
[24] See *Indians in Kenya*, Cmd. 1922 (1923).

This was the declared policy for Kenya, and Lord Passfield had both explicitly extended the Duke of Devonshire's declaration to Northern Rhodesia and Nyasaland and indicated that immediate steps "to ensure strict conformity" were to be taken.[25] Equality of opportunity in the purchase of Crown lands was to be afforded and Africans henceforth were to be encouraged by the granting of easy credit and leases on terms similar to those afforded to Europeans. Taxation was to be limited to a sum that would not upset customary life. African development was expected to be the keystone of colonial policy.

Alarmed, the settlers reacted with alacrity. The unofficial members of the Northern Rhodesian Legislative Council demanded an immediate conference in London and expressed their feelings with some force:

To subordinate the interests of civilized Britons to the development of alien races, whose capability of substantial further advancement has not been demonstrated, appears to be contrary to natural law. . . . [Thus] faced with the declared determination of the Imperial Government to prefer the interests of barbarous races to those of their own, [we] may seek and find sympathy and aid . . . from neighbouring colonies enjoying freer institutions and more equitable opportunities.[26]

Nevertheless, Lord Passfield refused to see them. To him, their views were "wholly irreconcilable with the considered policy of His Majesty's Government."[27] The Secretary of State also informed the House of Lords and Governor Maxwell that, as far as he was concerned, amalgamation between the two Rhodesias was absolutely out of the question. He wrote:

Her Majesty's Government . . . are not prepared to agree to the amalgamation of Northern and Southern Rhodesia. . . . They consider that a substantially greater advance should be made in the development of Northern Rhodesia before any final opinion can be formed as to its future. . . . The European population is small and scattered . . . while problems of

---

[25] Cmd. 3573, 6; S 1/913/30: Passfield to Governors, 20 May 1930, Zomba archives.

[26] *Correspondence with Regard to Native Policy in Northern Rhodesia*, Cmd. 3731 (1930), 5.

[27] *Ibid.*, 10.

native development are in a stage which makes it inevitable that Her Majesty's Government should hesitate to let them pass even partially out of their responsibility.[28]

Lord Passfield inadvertently encouraged a fatal liaison between three states of Central Africa in differential states of development. His rejection of the settlers' feelings of priority increased an insecurity fundamental to Europeans in tropical Africa and, long after the Labour government in which Lord Passfield had served as Colonial Secretary had been replaced by another, white Rhodesians and Nyasalanders continued to clamor for self-government or closer association in order to ensure "the subject" more control over "his destiny and that of posterity."[29] Moore feared that the Colonial Office would turn Northern Rhodesia into a "Native Reserve." He explained: "We White people have not come to this country solely and even mainly to raise the native in the scale of civilization. Our main object is to survive ourselves, to improve our conditions if we can, and . . . to raise a family and perpetuate our race."[30] There were, the Governor of Northern Rhodesia wrote to the Governor of Nyasaland, "too many Europeans here who go even further than Southern Rhodesians and would like the Union of South Africa's policy introduced as regards natives." Both governors were opposed to amalgamation of their protectorates with Southern Rhodesia; similarly, neither wanted his protectorate to play any part in an East African union although, albeit reluctantly, the Governor of Nyasaland expressed his willingness to have Northern Rhodesia absorb Nyasaland.[31]

The onset of the depression ended local hopes for self-government in Northern Rhodesia and transformed the previously skeptical settlers into active proponents of amalgamation with Southern Rhodesia. In 1933, the unofficial members voted in the Legislative Council overwhelmingly in favor of "amalgamation." Together with those of Nyasaland and Southern Rhodesia, their representatives

[28] Sec/Ea/9: Passfield to Maxwell, 1 July 1931 (telegram); Lord Passfield's statement was read in both houses of Parliament, 2 July 1931.

[29] Leopold Moore, in the Legislative Council, 6 April 1933, quoted in J. W. Davidson, *The Northern Rhodesian Legislative Council* (London, 1948), 95.

[30] Moore, in Legislative Council, 29 May 1933, quoted in *ibid.*, 94. But see a contrary statement by Moore in *The Livingstone Mail*, 13 October 1921.

[31] S 1/34/32: Thomas to Maxwell, 30 January 1932; Maxwell to Thomas, 4 February 1932, Zomba archives.

suggested that the three Central African territories should be federated in order to forward economic development, in order to economize upon research expenditures and the provision of facilities for European education, and in order to promote a customs union. To some extent they also wanted to "prevent the infiltration of the Dutch and Dutch ideas northwards from the Union."[32] Two years later, after the Copperbelt riots,[33] they again expressed themselves strongly in favor of ending Colonial Office control of Northern Rhodesia. Moore, their leader, feared that Hitler would soon repossess Tanganyika and that Northern Rhodesia might therefore cease to remain British. He told the Prime Minister of Southern Rhodesia that the white residents of Northern Rhodesia wanted to integrate immediately: "[We want] to come in with you, not as partners and certainly not as rivals, but as an integral part of your country. We want what you have."[34]

By this time Godfrey Huggins, Southern Rhodesia's prime minister, and a large segment of settler opinion in the Colony favored the absorption of Northern Rhodesia and, if necessary, Nyasaland. The Southern Rhodesians thereby sought to ensure a duty-free market for southern goods, a continued supply of African labor, and a similarity of racial policy. They also reacted to the unfavorable conditions imposed upon the Colony by the government of the Union of South Africa in the course of customs negotiations. In London and Salisbury, Huggins publicly espoused the formation of a large Central African dominion wherein whites would rule for the benefit of Africans as well as themselves.[35] But Africans were quick to note that the prevalent Southern Rhodesian practices made apparent mockery of such proposals. Huggins himself explained that "in Southern Rhodesia we do not intend to train natives to replace Europeans, but we do intend to train natives for use in the native area, and the height to which they can rise is only limited by native requirements."[36]

The settlers of Nyasaland ranged themselves firmly on the side of the amalgamationists. They formed a "Greater Rhodesia League" in

[32] S 2/19/35: Memorandum by C. E. Posonby, managing director of the British Central Africa Company Ltd., Zomba archives.
[33] See Chapter VII.
[34] Sec/Ea/9: Lusaka archives.
[35] *Rand Daily Mail*, 10 July 1935.
[36] S 1/145/35: Huggins to Stanley, 21 September 1935, Zomba archives.

order to further "by constitutional means the federation of Nyasa-land with Northern Rhodesia and Southern Rhodesia into a British Central African Dominion."[37] The alternatives, the League's secretary said, were federation or economic stagnation. Similarly, the settlers' local newspaper, *The Nyasaland Times*, argued that the fact that Africans outnumbered whites in the Protectorate by one thousand to one made a Greater Rhodesia that much more desirable. With some form of closer association, it prophesied, "this disproportion would disappear, for the stubborn policy of opposition to white settlement would be replaced by European development schemes."[38]

The new Governor of Nyasaland was sympathetic. In the first of many forceful letters to the Secretary of State for the Colonies, he urged that serious consideration should be given to the proposals of the Greater Rhodesia League. "The underlying principle is," he wrote, ". . . not only right but inevitable." In particular, the governor wanted a merger to be effected between the two protectorates:

His Majesty's Government has already accepted the policy of economic cooperation between the Central African territories but I cannot see how this cooperation can be made fully effective without some form of inter-locked administration. [Nyasaland] should never have been allowed to grow up as a separate entity, though looking back . . . one can appreciate that it was perhaps inevitable. But it does not mean that no re-arrangement is possible. It seems to me that the first step should be to merge the administration of this protectorate in that of Northern Rhodesia. Over a large extent of both areas the problems are similar, and it should be possible by such a merger to reduce materially the overhead expenses of government.[39]

This proposal was supported by Sir Hubert Young, the then governor of Northern Rhodesia and a former governor of Nyasaland. Like many others at this time, Governor Young was particularly anxious lest the Rhodesian governments separately should adopt the racial policies of South Africa or that Southern Rhodesia should, because of its economic plight, be absorbed into the Union. Instead, he

[37] S 1/175/35; Memorandum by F. M. Withers, secretary of the Nyasaland branch of the Greater Rhodesia League, (?) May 1935, Zomba archives.
[38] *The Nyasaland Times*, 20 June 1935.
[39] S 1/7/35: Governor Harold Kittermaster to Secretary of State MacDonald, 27 June 1935, Zomba archives.

wanted to place many administrative services under common control. "In the territories that are still under the control of His Majesty's Government," he wrote, "we have a clean slate upon which to write, and I earnestly recommend that we should not let the opportunity be lost."[40]

But Malcolm MacDonald, the Secretary of State, was unwilling to approve the amalgamation of the two protectorates as an initial step toward federation. Nyasaland remained heavily in debt, and her finances closely supervised by the British Treasury; Northern Rhodesia was comparatively prosperous. Like later secretaries of state, he feared that any form of closer association among the Rhodesias and Nyasaland would be detrimental to the interests of the Africans of the protectorates. "No obstacles," he wrote, "to the future advancement of the natives should be imposed in the interests of any non-native minority, and there may be cases in which the interests of the native majority have to be preferred to those of the non-native community."

It would be premature to make any decision as to the future of Northern Rhodesia and Nyasaland until further development, both economically and in the sphere of native administration, has clarified the lines of development of the different communities in the two protectorates. Until such development has taken place it is my opinion that no steps should be taken towards the administrative union of Northern Rhodesia and Nyasaland with Southern Rhodesia, and the federation of the two protectorates with that colony or any form of high commissionership or central authority for the three territories should not therefore be considered.[41]

The settlers meanwhile continued to demand some form of "closer association." The government of Southern Rhodesia welcomed the prospective annexation of Northern Rhodesia's copper resources and, in order to ensure its farmers a steady supply of labor, was now more than willing to absorb Nyasaland as well. In Northern Rhodesia, the farmers and the business community generally favored amalgamation for economic and racial reasons. Moore, in particular, had begun to despise Colonial Office control for no more significant reason than that the governor had decided to move the territorial capital from Livingstone, where Moore was in business, to Lusaka.

[40] S 1/7/35: Governor Young to MacDonald, 6 August 1935.
[41] S 1/7/35: MacDonald to Young, 21 September 1935.

In late 1935, Moore therefore wrote to Huggins and asked whether the Southern Rhodesians were still interested in amalgamation. Huggins replied affirmatively, and suggested a conference—the first of many—at the Victoria Falls.[42]

Early in 1936, all seven unofficial members of the Legislative Council of Northern Rhodesia and thirty representatives of the Southern Rhodesian political parties met at the Falls and resolved unanimously that amalgamation under the constitution of Southern Rhodesia "is in the best interests of all the inhabitants of both colonies."[43] With amalgamation, the delegates agreed, should also come dominion status. They foresaw a joint legislative assembly composed of partly nominated and partly elected members, of whom three would represent African interests. Separate laws would be maintained until altered by the new government of "Rhodesia." In time, there would be a single high court, sitting in the joint capital of Salisbury.

The Southern Rhodesian legislature supported this first outline for a new government. But it did so only because the plan called for self-government and for dominion status—for greater powers, in fact, than that which the Colony already possessed. In the north, Africans immediately grew alarmed. Colonel Stewart Gore-Browne, a leading unofficial member of the Legislative Council who had voted in favor of amalgamation at the Falls, discovered that African opinion had been aroused. He addressed an African club on the Copperbelt and later wrote to England of his experience: "I admitted at once that white men were here for their own good and they meant to stay, but I said that white and black prosperity was interdependent. . . . They asked many questions, all good ones—and evidently they are very scared at the possibility of Amalgamation with S. Rhodesia.[44] Governor Young and the Colonial Secretary, by now Ormsby-Gore, both also recognized African fears. The latter refused to encourage the amalgamationists in any way. In his formal reply, he simply restated Lord Passfield's earlier refusal to counte-

---

[42] Sec/Ea/9: Moore to Huggins, 14 October 1935; Huggins to Moore, 6 November 1935.

[43] Sec/Ea/9; but see Colin Leys and R. Cranford Pratt (eds.), *A New Deal in Central Africa* (London, 1960), 9.

[44] Gore-Browne Papers: Stewart Gore-Browne to Dame Ethel Locke-King, 23 March 1936, privately held.

nance closer association. "I do not feel," wrote Ormsby-Gore, "that during the period of five years which has elapsed there has been such a material change in conditions as would justify reconsideration of the decision reached after so much thought in 1931."[45]

Northern Rhodesia's elected representatives immediately sought greater political power for themselves. They threatened to resign *en bloc* from the Legislative Council if they were not granted as many seats (and votes) as the official members. In short, since His Majesty's Government was unwilling to acknowledge their spirit of amalgamation, they wanted to manage their own affairs under the Governor's formal aegis: "The ideal form of government," wrote Gore-Browne, "should provide for the efficient representation of all these various European interests [and] for the representation of native interests, not forgetting the fact that while the Europeans can speak for themselves, the natives are and will remain for a long time totally inarticulate as regards anything beyond purely local affairs." If the Government is to be popular, he continued, "it must give the people governed some share in the management of their own affairs. Autocracy, however benevolent, will in time defeat its own ends."[46] His was the moderate expression of settler views. A secretariat minute offered another perspective.

As regards the people managing their own affairs, those who argue thus invariably include in their own affairs the affairs of the natives who outnumber them by 100:1 and who, when they accepted the protection of the British Crown, had no idea that they might find themselves governed by a handful of European immigrants: not all of British nationality or stock.[47]

Even so, Governor Young was in favor of acceding to the request of the settlers. He would, after all, retain a veto and, he argued, their majority in the Legislative Council would in fact be no more than a "pretence." Moreover, he thought that some concession was indicated in view of the intense dissatisfaction felt by the settlers about the rejection of their resolutions supporting amalgamation.[48]

[45] Sec/Ea/9: Ormsby-Gore to Young, 20 August 1936; MacDonald to Huggins, 31 July 1936.
[46] Sec/Misc/10: Gore-Browne to Young, May, 1936, Lusaka archives.
[47] Secretariat minute upon *ibid.*
[48] Sec/Misc/10: Young to the Secretary of State, 14 October 1936.

Once again Ormsby-Gore patiently indicated that His Majesty's Government preferred to continue its role as a protector of Africans. No concessions could be given to settlers that would endanger the security of the indigenous population. Ormsby-Gore wrote in the style of his predecessor:

It is imperative that no change should be made without fully safeguarding the interests of the native inhabitants, who form the vast majority of the population of the Protectorate. I realize that the elected members are concerned for the maintenance and promotion of native interests, but until such time as the native community are themselves in a position to secure the expression of their views, by the participation of elected representatives in the Legislature, it is essential that the power of the Governor and his officers . . . to promote their interests should not be impaired.[49]

The white leaders of Rhodesian opinion felt that they had again been treated badly by unimaginative British ministers. Huggins, in particular, refused to accept a negative answer. Time was important: the north was gaining economic strength and, under the tutelage of the Colonial Office, "creeping blackness" might spread to Southern Rhodesia from the north. "If the territories are ever to be united," he told a public meeting, "it will have to be in the very near future. Otherwise they will draw so far apart in different ways that it will become absolutely impossible."[50] Thereafter, Huggins, still the Prime Minister of Southern Rhodesia, spoke convincingly of new overtures toward a union with South Africa and steadily applied pressure upon the British government.

At a meeting held in London during the Coronation celebrations for King George VI, Huggins, Moore, and Gore-Browne put their various arguments for closer association to the Secretaries of State for the Dominions and the Colonies and, to intensify the pressure, Moore and Gore-Browne demanded that membership of the Northern Rhodesian Executive Council—hitherto exclusively restricted to civil servants—should henceforth include elected settler representatives. The governors of Northern Rhodesia and Nyasaland—despite

---

[49] Sec/Misc/10: Ormsby-Gore to Young, 15 September 1937.

[50] *East Africa and Rhodesia*, 3 June 1937, quoted in Richard Gray, *The Two Nations* (London, 1960), 189.

opposition from the permanent officials in the Colonial Office—generally were sympathetic to settler thinking on these subjects. As a result, the British government appointed a Royal Commission, chaired by Viscount Bledisloe, a former governor-general of New Zealand, to inquire "whether any . . . closer co-operation or association between Southern Rhodesia, Northern Rhodesia and Nyasaland is desirable and feasible, with due regard to the interests of all the inhabitants, irrespective of race . . . and to the special responsibility of Our Government . . . for the interests of the Native inhabitants."[51] The Governor of Northern Rhodesia also promised to consult his unofficial members more fully whenever the Legislative Council was not sitting and, in late 1937, he began meeting them informally before each session of the Council in order to obviate any public debate which might prove "embarrassing."[52]

The Bledisloe Commission spent three months in Central Africa, where it interviewed Rhodesians and Nyasas of all races, classes, and backgrounds. White settlers naturally asked for that racial security which, they said, only amalgamation could ensure. Africans in the northern territories were, however, unanimous in opposing any ties to Southern Rhodesia. Africans had worked there, and they compared the treatment of Africans in the colony unfavorably with that in the protectorates. A Cewa chief told the commission that Southern Rhodesians had no respect for Africans. An African giving evidence in Mongu explained that Southern Rhodesians "do not look upon the black man as a person, they just treat them as dogs. The only time they look after them, is when they want money from them. . . . I am a person, not a dog." On the Copperbelt, clerks and *capitãos* said: "We know Southern Rhodesia and it is not good. . . . They do not speak to you properly, just get hold of you and push you about, and it is not pleasant."[53] "There is no contesting the fact," Governor John Maybin of Northern Rhodesia later wrote, "that a very large number of the natives of this territory have worked in Southern Rhodesia and have an intimate knowledge of conditions there, and that though their views may not have been formed with the clarity of a jurist or the profundity of a political

---

[51] *Rhodesia—Nyasaland Royal Commission Report,* Cmd. 5949 (1939), 4.
[52] Sec/Misc/10: Young to the Secretary of State, 16 July 1937.
[53] Evidence to the Bledisloe Commission, quoted in Gray, *Two Nations,* 192.

philosopher, they were held none the less stoutly and they were unanimously opposed to amalgamation with Southern Rhodesia."[54]

After taking African evidence seriously into consideration, the Commission, in a labored, ambiguous way, brought forth an inclusive compromise. The Central African territories would probably "become more closely interdependent in all their activities," and "identity of interests" would "lead them sooner or later to political unity. If this view should commend itself also to Your Majesty's Government in the United Kingdom, we recommend that it should take an early opportunity of stating its acceptance of the principle."[55] Nevertheless, the Commission understood that Africans in the protectorates were opposed overwhelmingly to any withdrawal of the Crown's traditional oversight. Its members also appreciated that these fears were well founded upon an appreciation of the restrictive racial policies of Southern Rhodesia. Their report said: "It is the fear that the balance is not fairly held between the two races in Southern Rhodesia that alone prevents a recommendation being made for immediate amalgamation; the avowed policy of segregation, under the name of 'Parallel Development,' and the institution of the colour bar stand in the way."[56] The Commission therefore refused to suggest any swift development of the admittedly substantial identity of interest that existed among the three dependencies. It deferred the real implementation of unity indefinitely. Instead, as an interim measure, it proposed that the British government should amalgamate Nyasaland and Northern Rhodesia, and that some kind of an inter-territorial council should be established to co-ordinate governmental services without executive authority. "I asked for a loaf," Huggins later said, "and was given a crumb."[57]

[54] Sec/Ea/14: Maybin to the Secretary of State, 13 July 1939, Lusaka archives.

[55] Cmd. 5949, 214. Governor Maybin commented (Sec/Ea/14: Maybin to the Secretary of State, 13 July 1939) that he did not understand what was meant by "the principle" of amalgamation. If the British government had concluded that divergent "native policies" made amalgamation impossible, he wrote, then there could be "no question of accepting amalgamation in principle." He suggested that a statement should be issued stipulating that only if and when the "native policies" were reconciled in a manner amenable to the British government would further consideration be given to the concept of amalgamation.

[56] Cmd. 5949, 252. See also Gore-Browne Papers: Gore-Browne to Locke-King, 25 March 1939.

[57] The Bulawayo Chronicle, 25 November 1948.

Racial discrimination was once again the main, if not the only, barrier to some form of closer association in Central Africa. The whites had wanted to increase the prospects of perpetuating their own way of life indefinitely. Africans, on the other hand, had wanted at the very least, to maintain the *status quo*. Out of this confrontation emerged the struggle of the late 1940's and early 1950's. Its tone, however, had been foreshadowed by the activity of the months immediately succeeding the publication of the Bledisloe Commission's *Report*. During that period, the dialogue between spokesmen for settler demands and British reservations continued: Huggins stormed to London and again presented the case for the amalgamation directly to the Colonial and Dominions Offices. In Lusaka, Moore resigned his seat in the Legislative Council in order to obtain a new mandate from his constituents. (They obediently returned him in the resulting by-election.) On the Copperbelt, various local European political associations, and the so-called European Protection League, condemned the *Report* and the evidence on which it was based:

. . . the time when the native can express an opinion with an intelligent appreciation of the issues involved is too distant to allow the question of his agreement or disagreement to affect the question of amalgamation.

The Southern Rhodesian [native policy] is both wiser and juster. The native's interests are protected and he is being educated to become a good agriculturalist.

. . . the report of the Royal Commission appears to be based on the conclusion that the colonial settler is not to be trusted to administer a fair and just native policy and the report is therefore unacceptable.[58]

Even the governor of Nyasaland felt that the Commission had been misguided. Like the local settler community, he felt that only in the distant future, "when the native community can express an opinion with an intelligent appreciation of the issues involved, [could] the question of agreement or disagreement . . . be allowed to affect the question."[59] He thought that the differences between

[58] Sec/Ea/14: Resolutions of the Luanshya branch of the European Protection League, 11 April 1939 and 23 August 1939.

[59] 1a/45: Governor Donald Mackenzie-Kennedy to MacDonald, 23 June 1939, Zomba archives. Mackenzie-Kennedy was apparently not influenced by the Luanshya resolutions.

the policies of "parallel development" and Colonial administration were negligible, and that, in any event, it was desirable to tie Nyasaland to Southern Rhodesia in order to obtain the development funds that the Protectorate needed so urgently.

The onset of World War II ended these discussions. But, before British and colonial energies had been directed completely against the Axis, Sir Cosmo Parkinson, the Permanent Under Secretary of State for the Colonies, summed up his discussions with Huggins for the benefit of the governors of Nyasaland and Northern Rhodesia. His remarks constituted a valedictory to the interwar years and sounded an unintended keynote to subsequent discussions about a Central African federation:

The only point which has clearly emerged is . . . that native policy is the crux of the whole question and that, if it should be desired to take any further steps in the direction of closer political association between the three territories, it will be essential for Her Majesty's Government to be able to show that a real attempt is being made to face up to the difficulties in this respect.[60]

Neither he, the bureaucracy that he served, nor his official representatives in Central Africa realized, however, that the white struggle to achieve minority rule in Northern Rhodesia and Nyasaland already had made a lasting impact upon the indigenous population. It had encouraged, perhaps even stimulated, the parallel rise of African nationalism. For, during the period of gestation, this upsurge of nationalist feeling fed upon the fears aroused by settler political agitation as much as it did upon a more diffuse, but just as real, indigenous dissatisfaction with the conditions of colonial rule.

[60] Sec/Ea/14: Parkinson to Maybin, 8 August 1939.

Chapter V

AFRICAN VOLUNTARY ASSOCIATIONS AND THE EXPRESSION OF INCIPIENT NATIONALISM

The white people cannot fool the black man all the time, they can . . . forbid people to speak their English language, but it is clear that they are only blind forgetting human history. What is desired [is] that you get on going there and [organize] . . . and we shall be able therefore to open the eyes of the people, who are today living in darkness. The sun of righteousness, it seems to me is rapidly springing upon the sons and daughters of Africa and who knows that sooner or later we may hail the dawn of freedom. To accomplish this fact we must act in unionism, breaking all our tribal prejudices. . . .

—Clements Kadalie to Isa Macdonald Lawrence,
4 April 1925

During the years between the two World Wars, Africans in Nyasaland and Northern Rhodesia sought in every conceivable constitutional way to better the political, social, and economic order to which they had been subjected. Chilembwe's abortive rising signified the end of a defensive era; thereafter, Africans recognized that the colonial governments had come to stay and that the imposed codes of law were not to be removed easily. Africans tried to work within the colonial context. Using the political concepts and language of their rulers, they unsuccessfully claimed a democratic right to participate in the governing process. At first they wanted no more than to have their collective voice heard in those matters directly affecting the lives and actions of the indigenous population. To this end, those Africans (for the most part clerks, evangelists, and teachers) to whom the white man's ways had become most familiar imitated the settler example by forming associations through which their pleas for reform, and for consideration, could best be expressed.

Among the several widespread manifestations of indigenous protest, the establishment of voluntary associations played the most significant role in the development and the eventual emergence of the avowedly nationalist movements of the 1940's. For more than twenty years the associations sought redress for grievances suffered or allegedly endured by Africans. They urged reform upon hostile or amused governments. They countered every public move made by the settler associations to entrench white privilege at the expense of Africans. They reacted strongly against the settler agitation in favor of amalgamation and closer union. They concerned themselves continually with matters of immediate, even parochial, consequence to the otherwise unrepresented people of the protectorates. Perhaps unintentionally, these gentle skirmishes with authority represented an intermediate phase in the history of Central African nationalism during which the indigenous leadership, like its counterpart in West Africa, gradually came to appreciate the essential futility of a strictly constitutional, *ad hoc*, and basically elitist approach to the problems posed for subject peoples by colonial rule.[1] In Nyasaland and Northern Rhodesia specifically, the part played by the voluntary associations during the intermediate period differed somewhat in accord with the varying designs of the respective white-led pressure groups and governments.

NYASALAND: THE PROLIFERATION OF "NATIVE ASSOCIATIONS"

Even before Chilembwe rose, members of the indigenous intelligentsia had, in 1912, organized Nyasaland's first "native association" with branches in the northern centers of Chinteche, Karonga, and Mzimba.[2] Its leaders, Tonga and Ngoni educated by the Livingstonia Mission, had adopted a European organizational form, of which there were abundant local examples, as a direct response to the imposition by the Protectorate Government of the District Administration Ordinance of 1912.[3] This measure had stipulated, *inter*

---

[1] Some of these matters have already been summarized in Robert I. Rotberg, "The Rise of African Nationalism: The Case of East and Central Africa," *World Politics,* xv (1962), 78–83.

[2] The Central Government records of this association probably perished in the Zomba Secretariat fire of 1919. A. Simon Muhango was a founder and R. Peter Mwakasungula was its first president.

[3] The establishment of the South African Native National Congress also dates from 1912, and may well have influenced the Nyasas.

alia, that an assembly of gazetted principal headmen should, in each district, be regarded as the only authentic voice of the people of that district.[4] Denied by the ordinance a role that they felt themselves qualified to play, and deprived more generally of any particular place in a European-run colonial society, these educated Africans formed their own association and, in time, personally established similar vehicles of protest in central and southern Nyasaland.

The battles of World War I and the Chilembwe scare interrupted the development of African associations. But educated Africans returned from military service with a new confidence and a renewed determination to right the wrongs that had been inflicted upon their indigenous compatriots. At the same time, they wanted reform rather than radical change. Then, and for many years, they acted according to well-defined constitutional formulas. Indeed, when the North Nyasa Native Association resumed its meetings in 1919, the passage of numerous resolutions amply demonstrated such a point of view. Levi Mumba, a Senga who may have been its guiding spirit in 1912, and who later became the first president of the Nyasaland African Congress, urged and persuaded his colleagues to add their belated opinion to the discussion of the Chilembwe rising. They decided that: "The Association regretted exceedingly the rising of John Chilembwe and others inasmuch as they knew that a High Court exists to which appeal could have been made, the decision of which after sympathetic hearing, no doubt, could have prevented such mischief from happening. The rising being a black mark on the natives of the Protectorate in general."[5]

This same group also asked the government to grant Africans permission to approach District Residents with their grievances. The association's subsequent debate indicated that Africans not infrequently suffered imprisonment or flogging when attempting to put their complaints before government officials. "Natives," the association wrote, "should have free access to the Residents . . . without threats of *cikoti* [a hippopotamus-hide whip] or imprisonment before the man states what he has come for. This will greatly foster mutual trust."[6] Finally, the association demanded "universal repre-

[4] See also Chapter II.
[5] S 1/1481/19: Minutes of a Meeting of the North Nyasa Native Association, 17–20 June 1919, Zomba archives.
[6] *Ibid.*

sentation" in the Legislative Council. But, what Mumba and his friends wanted turned out to be far less revolutionary than it might have seemed. They indicated that the association would settle for increased representation in the form of a European specifically appointed by the Governor to "look after native interests."[7] They hoped that such a European would tour the Protectorate in order to obtain a firsthand appreciation of indigenous dissatisfaction.

In these, as in other instances, they hoped vainly. But they and others of like mind continued to meet periodically in order to pass resolutions on kindred subjects and to seek the betterment of their people solely by employing the weapons of persuasion, persistence, and petition. From 1920, for example, the North Nyasa Native Association continually urged the Government to spend more money on education and, indeed, to raise hut taxes in order to do so. It asked for alterations in the postal regulations so that Africans might not have to apply directly to Zomba for the delivery of parcel post packages. In 1929, it explained knowledgeably that Africans emigrated to Rhodesia and South Africa because the British Government had spent almost no money developing Nyasaland. The association demanded that the government should provide Nyasaland with a good road network in order that Africans might thereby be enabled to export their agricultural produce. If the government refused to provide a decent infrastructure, the members of the association thought that Nyasaland could never hope to develop economically. In another vein, they later tried to persuade the government of the iniquity of a law that penalized intercourse between black men and white women only. But to all these and to other requests the administration turned a deaf ear. And, with regard to the last iniquity, Karonga's district commissioner showed a complete disregard for, or lack of appreciation of, the problem. He wrote: "It is a peculiar thing that almost every highly educated native of the Livingstonia Mission is politically minded and race conscious and always on the look out for some stigma. At the back of their minds is an intolerance of the Europeans and their creed is 'Africa for the Africans'."[8]

[7] Actually, the Government of Nyasaland already regarded the missionary member of the Legislative Council as an unofficial representative of African interests, but not of the Africans as such.

[8] S 1/1481/19: The District Commissioner, Karonga to the Northern Provincial Commissioner, 27 January 1931.

After 1920, Nyasas elsewhere in the Protectorate followed the example of their brothers in the north and established a number of independent bodies to serve ends similar to those espoused by the first association. At Mumba's suggestion, in 1923, forty Africans organized the Southern Province Native Association with headquarters in Zomba. The main original object of what was to become the most articulate of the many associations was ostensibly "to assist the Government in every way, especially by keeping it informed of Native public opinion." Like other associations, it expected "to assist the Native by representing him in all political matters, [and] by keeping him informed of and explaining the objects of legislation . . . to organize public meetings for the discussion of subjects of general or special interest, and to keep in touch with other similar native associations."[9]

The activities of the Southern Province Association began innocuously; but, as its members gained confidence in their undertaking, their proposals grew more aggressive. In 1924, at a time when the Phelps-Stokes educational commission was visiting the Protectorate, they urged the government to improve the quality of the educational instruction available to Nyasas. Frederick Gresham Njilima, a son of Duncan Njilima, one of the Africans executed for his part in the Chilembwe rising, wrote to the Chief Secretary on behalf of the association: "[We are] aware of the fact that education in Nyasaland is in a lower stage than that of any other British possession. [We take] this opportunity of assuring [you] that every member of this body is ready to support and to follow [you] to better this condition."[10]

He also asked the Chief Secretary to charge Dr. James Kwegyir Aggrey, the prominent Gold Coast educator who was then a member of the visiting commission, with overseeing Nyasaland's educational system. The government conveniently ignored the association's letter. When the association later complained about the iniquitous way in which white estate owners abused their African labor, evicted Afri-

[9] S 1/3263/23: Rules of the Nyasaland (Southern Province) Native Association, 23 December 1923, Zomba archives.

[10] S 1/3263/23: Frederick Gresham Njilima to Ranald MacDonald, 13 May 1924. Gresham had spent the years between 1909 and 1919 in the United States and in Europe. He attended Natchez (Mississippi) College High School, Lincoln Ridge (Kentucky) College, and Kentucky State Industrial University. He served with the British army in France, where he was wounded.

can tenants without cause, and took unfair advantage of African women resident on the estates, it likewise turned a deaf ear. The association, undaunted, continued its campaign against the settlers. In 1926, for example, the Southern Province Association forwarded a list of its conclusions to the Governor:

With regard to the fears always indulged in by the planting and commercial communities, the native fails to see why these communities are always against the welfare of the natives of the country. It would appear that this part of the community does not practise justice, good order and peace amongst the natives of this country and they know themselves that they are not treating the natives fairly and well and this causes their fears. If they were treating the natives properly they would not have been filled with such alarm. When Government wishes to do any good to the native this community quickly runs forward with obstruction.[11]

The government remained unimpressed.

The Administration of Nyasaland demonstrated its disregard for African opinion and, incidentally, for Africans generally, in the so-called affair of the white solar topee. In 1929, the secretary of the Blantyre Native Association forwarded to the Provincial Commissioner a specific complaint made by one of its prominent members. Wesley Mwachande reported that Nelson, his nephew, had purchased a white topee in Limbe. One day, while returning from Chiradzulu to Limbe, "the boy put on the helmet . . . and on the main . . . road he met District Commissioner Parker . . . [for whom] he removed his helmet." Parker evidently failed to observe Nelson's respectful behavior. The District Commissioner, in the words of the complainant, felt himself "treated lightly." He refused to believe that Nelson had removed his hat and demanded the topee. "To the boy's great amazement," Mwachande continued, "he saw the district commissioner placing the helmet in his car and off he went with it."[12] Parker later admitted that he had taken Nelson's hat. He told the Provincial Commissioner: "When proceeding to Blantyre by car . . . I passed a native, wearing a white helmet [who was] walking in a swaggering manner and who made not the slightest movement to raise his hat. On my suggesting to him that he had

[11] S 1/3263/23: Minutes of the meeting of 14 August 1926.
[12] NS 1/3/2: The Secretary of the Blantyre Native Association to the Provincial Commissioner, Southern Province, 26 September 1929, Zomba archives.

omitted this small courtesy, his manner was insolent. I therefore told him that I considered he required a lesson in manners, and took his helmet."[13]

The Provincial Commissioner naturally supported his subordinate. He gave to the aggrieved parties and the members of the Blantyre association absolutely no satisfaction. They continued to "wonder . . . at the action of the district commissioner . . . seeing he is the officer who administers the laws of justice, and yet he starts playing the bad game and what is to be expected of the public?"[14]

The essentially rural Mombera Native Association had, to no avail, previously raised the same general point. In 1921, a year after its foundation, members of the association had explained their dilemma. "We have been taught to wear cloths, not skins," they said. "Now do Europeans want us to wear cloths [only]?" ". . . if a person is asked to show marks of honour or respect through fear . . . this is no real honour at all. A gentleman is not really honoured by a native simply keeping off his hat from his head, as long as he is near a European, because this is done, not out of good will, but by terror. This gives the same European indignity instead of dignity."[15]

Using similar methods of argument, this small but active association raised issues of importance throughout the period between 1920 and 1935. It wanted the government to protect African women from the lascivious advances of Europeans. It wanted the government to concern itself with the care and treatment of lepers, with village sanitary arrangements, with the high prices prevalent in rural stores, with the discouragement of early marriages, with the incidence of African alcoholism, with the provision of postal services, improved roads, and new bridges, and with a wide variety of matters affecting the people of the Mombera district particularly and Nyasaland generally. Its members—the important chiefs, teachers, and clerks of the district—acted deliberately and with due deference to government. They put their opinions forward politely, if forcefully, and returned again and again to the same

[13] NS 1/3/2: Parker to the Provincial Commissioner, 5 October 1929.
[14] NS 1/3/2: In above letter of 26 September 1929.
[15] Mombera Minute Book: Minutes of the 26–27 September 1921 meeting of the Mombera Native Association. The Rev. Mr. Charles C. Chinula kindly lent the Minute Book to the author and generously discussed its contents (21 September 1962).

themes. But the Government of Nyasaland steadfastly ignored even these pillars of educated, in some cases conservative respectability.

The Government of Nyasaland preferred by and large to regard members of the traditional hierarchy of authority—all of whom owed their appointments to the Governor—as the only authentic indigenous voices. By 1930, the administration had further begun to think that the various native associations were more of a nuisance than they were worth. The Chief Secretary preferred to "pour cold water on the associations [rather] than try to regulate or suppress them." The Governor said that, while "he wished always to be kept informed of native opinion . . . the opinion he valued most was that expressed by tribal chiefs who in the course of time would be given a more responsible share in the governance of the Protectorate."

It was the duty of the more educated natives, such as members of the associations, to help their less enlightened chiefs with advice on the conduct of native administration. The true voice of the people expressed by the chiefs through their own institutions will in this way be heard by the Governor and his responsible officers and the need for native association for the expression of native opinion on public affairs will come to an end.[16]

Thereafter, the government refused even to read the resolutions of various associations unless they had been endorsed by the district councils of chiefs. After the administration introduced Native Authorities in 1933, district commissioners attempted to eliminate the associations. The government explicitly denied Mumba's contention that the Native Authorities tended to be too conservative and totally out of touch with African opinion. It refused to regard the associations as serious vehicles of protest.

By 1933, educated Nyasas had formed fifteen different associations. Their memberships occasionally overlapped, and a number of individuals each helped both to organize and to administer several groups as adjuncts of their own professional careers. Each association had its obvious leader, whether the Rev. Mr. Yesaya Zerenji Mwasi in West Nyasa, The Rev. Mr. Charles C. Chinula and the Rev. Mr. Yesaya Mlonyeni Chibambo in Mombera, George Simeon Mwase

---

[16] NC 1/3/5: Minutes of 3 March and 6 August 1930, Zomba archives.

and James Ralph Chinyama in Lilongwe, Mumba in North Nyasa, Zomba, and later Lilongwe, Andrew Jonathan Mponda and Charles Jameson Matinga in Blantyre, or, in Chiradzulu, the American-educated Rev. Dr. Daniel Sharpe Malekebu, leader of Chilembwe's Providence Industrial Mission. Educated men all, they sought concessions, compromises, and recognition from the government. They argued according to the British conventions of the day or, on occasion, of an earlier era, and contentedly turned their associations into debating societies. They purposely limited the membership of their associations to the new elite of Nyasaland, shunned the masses, and refused to make of their constitutional approach a genuine popular movement of political change. They patiently awaited the happy day when the government would begin to deal justly with Africans and their self-appointed representatives.

The happy day failed to arrive. The governor appointed Mumba to the advisory Native Education Board in 1933, but, despite associational protest and agitation, the governor and his successors refused to permit educated Africans to circulate freely in the townships after dark, to encourage owners of stores and cinemas to allow educated Africans into their establishments, to spend more money than before on education, to construct a proper government hospital, or to appoint an African representative to such statutory bodies as the Native Tobacco Board.[17] In 1936, although the Blantyre association protested forcefully, the governor even introduced legislation to compel urban Africans to register their thumbprints and to obtain the hated passes. On the other hand, collective opposition by various associations may conceivably have helped to prevent the amalgamation of Nyasaland and Northern and Southern Rhodesia during the late 1930's. In 1935, the Blantyre association presented a petition (drafted by Matinga) to the British Government. It stated unequivocally that any form of closer union was anathema to the Africans of Nyasaland.[18] Similarly, the Blantyre association reiterated its views to the Bledisloe Commission. To its members, "Southern Rhodesia simply [was] anti-native."[19]

[17] S 1/3263/23: The Chief Secretary to the Blantyre Native Association, 31 July 1937.
[18] The text is contained in S 1/175/35, Zomba archives. It is dated 10 August 1935.
[19] LB 2/21: Memorandum dated 28 May 1938, Zomba archives.

By the outbreak of World War II, Nyasaland's many separately-run associations could claim few concessions from the government of the Protectorate. The government still failed to regard African opinion in a serious light. The administration had refused to accept the logic of Mumba's simple, if eloquent, plea that "the natives of the country should be taken into the confidence of the government as His Majesty's subjects like all others." Mumba continued: "[We] are aware that natives are considered as children in these matters, and so they are, but it is as children when they can better be initiated into what is demanded of them when they grow up."[20]

WELFARE ASSOCIATIONS: THE RHODESIAN PATTERN

Before World War II, associations played a more immediate role in the highly charged racial atmosphere of Northern Rhodesia than they did in Nyasaland. In Northern Rhodesia the conditions of urban life and the pressure and political ambitions of a comparatively large white settler population openly and significantly disadvantaged educated Africans. The latter possessed abundant sources of grievance and, in absolute terms, probably were discriminated against more persistently than were their fellow Africans in Nyasaland. In time, therefore, Africans resident in Northern Rhodesia—many of whom had lived elsewhere—imitated the example of Nyasas, Southern Rhodesians, and South Africans and formed political organizations.

In Northern Rhodesia, Africans established what were ostensibly welfare societies. The first owed its inspiration directly to Nyasaland. In 1923, Levi Mumba sent a copy of the constitution of the North Nyasa Native Association to Donald Siwale, then a clerk. Together with David Kaunda (the father of the president of Zambia) and Hezekiya Kawosa, he organized the Mwenzo Welfare Association in order to provide a forum where Africans could express their political and social views. A year later, they protested against the heavy tax burden that the government had forced rural Africans to bear. But complaints availed them little and, after Siwale and Kawosa had both been transferred elsewhere, the Mwenzo association became defunct.

[20] 1a/1380: Mumba to the Chief Secretary 10 April, 1935, Zomba archives.

The first permanent African political body originated in the minds of four or five Nyasa civil servants (at least one of whom had been in communication with Marcus Garvey and had been a member of the Lilongwe Native Association) working in Livingstone, the capital of the Protectorate. In 1928, Isaac Rankin Nyirenda later recalled, the people of Maramba, Livingstone's main African township, expressed little interest in the possible formation of an association. But in 1929, Nyirenda and Edward Franklin Tembo asked the government if they and their friends might form the tentatively entitled "Northern Rhodesia Native Welfare Association" in order both to "help the Government to improve the country" and to "deal with matters and grievances affecting the native people."[21]

Early in 1930, the Secretary for Native Affairs gave Nyirenda and Tembo permission to form what members of the government obviously envisaged as no more than a social club. Through George Sharrat-Horne, his district representative, the Secretary, then the influential James Moffat Thomson, forbade them, however, to name or to envisage more than a "Livingstone" society. At the same time, Sharrat-Horne and Geoffrey C. Latham, the Director of Native Education, assured Nyirenda and Tembo that, "if the association [did] well, no doubt other associations will start to work . . . [elsewhere] . . . [and you can] join them all into one large association with a headquarters staff and a central committee."[22] These two comparatively sympathetic European officers helped Nyirenda and Tembo to devise a constitution for the association.

With Nyirenda in the chair, the Livingstone Native Welfare Association held its inaugural meeting in the autumn of 1930. To about three hundred and fifty Africans, few of whom joined immediately, he explained the purpose and the value of the new organization in terms that reflected the temper of the times:

There are many amongst us who say that we are little children and that we cannot do anything at present for our people; those who say so are fools. You must take an example from children. If a boy of eight years cannot behave himself like a human being he grows up as a bad man.

[21] ZA 1/9/45/1: Minutes of meetings of the Livingstone Native Welfare Association, 9 June 1929, 19 April 1930, Lusaka archives. See also Sec/Nat/321, Lusaka archives; *Central African Mail* (24 October 1964), 38.

[22] ZA 1/9/45/1: Sharrat-Horne and Latham to Tembo, 11 February 1930.

It is just the same with us, if at this age we cannot practice new ideas of building up brotherhood amongst ourselves and try the best we can to pave the way for our children, we shall be young till the end of the world. . . . the white man brought in liberty and abolished the slave trade . . . [but] it is now surprising to see that the white man is ignoring his first duty.[23]

The vice-chairman of the association, J. Ernest C. Mattako, raised an additional, rather novel concept: "We can get freedom through pulling together in this movement." Six weeks later, the association held a second meeting that was attended by three local chiefs, Sakasipa, Mkuni, and Musokotwani. The last chief aired a number of complaints against individual European officials and then told the crowd that the white man was "chasing us from our lands where our forefathers died to lands which are strange to us where we are not allowed to cut down trees." They also chase us, he continues, "out of the [district] like dogs."[24]

The government of the Protectorate reacted sharply to such outspoken opposition. The governor, Sir James Crawford Maxwell, demanded that his subordinates forbid criticism. Moffat Thomson further regretted that chiefs had seen fit to act through an association when they possessed their own, quite distinct, channels of communication. He reprimanded them orally, and cautioned the secretary of the association: "His Excellency does not want government officials to be criticized again. The tone of . . . the speeches is noted with regret. Many of the statements were irresponsible, ill-worded and unsupported by facts."[25] But, if the chiefs desisted, the leaders of the association continued to air grievances. In successive meetings, they protested the arrest of Africans for walking on the pavements (sidewalks) or the footpaths of Livingstone, asked the Administration to provide the African community with a market in Maramba, condemned the taking of black concubines by white men, decried the denial to African passengers of the right to buy tea or food on the railways, wanted the education of African children to be made compulsory, sought improved agricultural advisory services

[23] ZA 1/9/45/1: Minutes of the meeting of 19 April 1930. The succeeding quotation may be found in the same report.

[24] ZA 1/9/45/1: Minutes of the meeting of 9 June 1930.

[25] ZA 1/9/45/1: James Moffat Thomson to James Nkata, 18 July 1930; the Chief Secretary of Moffat Thomson, 16 July 1930.

for African farmers, and urged the government to appoint attorneys to defend African prisoners in the local courts. To every proposal and complaint, even those occasionally supported in private by younger officials, the government gave no satisfaction. The Governor suggested that his subordinates should ridicule the members of the association and "treat them as errant children."[26]

By this time, however, Africans elsewhere in Northern Rhodesia had begun to form welfare associations. Mattako, a court interpreter, had been transferred to Ndola. There, in the winter of 1930, he joined with Ernest Alexander Muwamba, the trusted head clerk at the Ndola *boma* and a Tonga from Nyasaland (he was also a close relative of Clements Kadalie, the founder of the Industrial and Commercial Workers Union of South Africa[27]) and Elijah Herbert Chunga, another civil servant, to organize an association along lines constitutionally similar to those of Livingstone.

Their initiative worried the officials responsible. Moffat Thomson did not want civil servants to hold office or to participate vocally at meetings. He worried about the reaction of mine owners to the existence and the activities of the proposed welfare society. "The conduct of the Livingstone association," he wrote, urging Mackenzie-Kennedy to deny the Ndola group permission to meet, "fails to show any promise of being helpful."[28] Finally, after considerable debate in the highest official circles, the governor and his Executive Council sanctioned the formation of both the Ndola and the newly proposed Mazabuka associations. They placed no restrictions on the roles to be played therein by African civil servants.

Ernest Alexander Muwamba opened the first meeting of the Ndola Native Welfare Association, as many fellow chairmen did, with a prayer. Taking his text from the Epistle of Paul to the Ephesians (iv:29), he asked his colleagues to let no corrupt communication proceed out of their mouths "but that which is good

[26] Sec/Nat/321: The Chief Secretary (Donald Mackenzie-Kennedy) to Moffat Thomson, 24 February 1931.

[27] Unbeknown to Muwamba, the Government of Northern Rhodesia frequently intercepted and inspected his correspondence with Kadalie and with his brother I. Clements Muwamba, a Lusaka clerk. Even so, during World War II, Muwamba for a time ran the Serenje *boma* singlehanded and, after leaving Northern Rhodesia, sat in Nyasaland's Legislative Council and served as a member of its Public Service Commission.

[28] Sec/Nat/322: Moffat Thomson to Mackenzie-Kennedy, 21 July 1930, Lusaka archives.

to the use of edifying, that it may minister grace unto the hearers." He went on to proclaim that the association was no more than "a mouthpiece between the Native Community and the Government in all matters affecting the natives—thus creating peace and prosperity."[29] Mattako counseled his colleagues to be circumspect. "We must," he said, "prohibit foolish words so the government will not stop us." For if it did, "there would remain no other way of getting our grievances heard and settled." We ought, he continued, to "honour Europeans [and] if we conform with this procedure the Europeans will treat us philanthropically."[30] In subsequent meetings, the Ndola association complained about the high African death rate, the poor, crowded housing, the coarseness of the local mealie meal, the contaminated meat and fish, the inadequacy of the African hospital, inadequate supplies of water in the compounds, and the need for public latrines in the main town "so that Africans won't be arrested for creating a nuisance."[31] The government agreed to build a new hospital for the Africans of Ndola.

During the next two years educated Africans formed five other welfare associations along the line of rail. In Broken Hill, P. J. Silawe, a civil servant transferred there from the capital, attempted to organize a branch of the Livingstone association, but the Protectorate authorities distrusted moves that would encourage African unity, and Silawe contented himself with the establishment of an unaffiliated society. The Broken Hill Native Welfare Association aimed to stimulate "cooperation and brotherly feeling, to interpret to the government native opinion on matters of importance, to encourage the spread of civilization, and to protect and further native interests in general."[32] Later it requested a "proper" school, better treatment in the hospital, the closing of the local beer hall on Sundays, a market, and that the African compounds should be kept clean.

Tonga from Nyasaland organized both the Mazabuka and Lusaka welfare associations. During the first months of their formal existence, both associations condemned the conditions under which

---

[29] ZA 1/9/45/2: Minutes of the meeting of 7 November 1930.
[30] *Ibid.*
[31] ZA 1/9/45/2: Minutes of the meeting of 22 January 1931.
[32] Sec/Nat/324: P. J. Silawe to Moffat Thomson, 29 September 1930, Lusaka archives.

Africans were compelled to purchase meat. I. Clements Katongo Muwamba and Henry Mashwa Sangandu, chairman and secretary respectively of the Lusaka Native Welfare Association, averred that the local European butcher refused to sell decent meat to Africans. He either threw it on the floor or refused to allow Africans to see what they were purchasing before they paid for pre-wrapped items. Sangandu wrote that the butcher treated Africans "as though the native was a dog whereas as a human being the natives know what is good to eat."[33] Members of the Mazabuka association likewise reported that they were permitted to buy only intestines and other offal and that the staff of the municipal abattoir trampled on whatever Africans finally purchased.[34] District officers wrote that the African complaints were well-grounded in fact, but the Administration continually refused to intercede. Indeed, Africans throughout the Protectorate failed to obtain what they considered to be fair treatment from European butchers until 1956, when the African National Congress led a successful boycott against those butchers who habitually discriminated against their darker-skinned customers.[35]

Members of the Choma and Lusaka associations separately requested the right to farm plots of agricultural land outside the confines of their urban townships. Africans who already called themselves "detribalized" wanted these allotments both in order to grow food for themselves and for sale. They thought that a partial return to the land, and an admittedly compromise marriage of urban and rural ideals, would contribute to the mental and physical "uplift" of town-dwellers. But, a member of the Choma association asked, "do you think the government will ever agree for a black man to have a piece of land near the township?"[36] The questioner doubted correctly, for Moffat Thomson quickly warned the Chief Secretary that Europeans and Africans should not have the opportunity of mingling. "The African," he wrote, "must build up his civilization in accordance with his needs and not mixed with Europeans."[37]

[33] Sec/Nat/332: Minutes of the meeting of 3 June 1931, Lusaka archives.
[34] Sec/Nat/330: Minutes of the meeting of 31 July 1931, Lusaka archives.
[35] See Chapter X.
[36] Sec/Nat/333: Minutes of the meeting of 15 August 1931, Lusaka archives.
[37] Sec/Nat/333: Moffat Thomson to the Chief Secretary, 7 November 1931.

In 1932, the Lusaka and Luanshya associations began a concerted attack upon the mass of discriminatory legislation to which Africans were subjected by the alien white government. They wanted responsible Africans, like all whites, to be permitted to carry guns. Of even greater moment to their members, the associations asked "Why only Africans need to carry passes in their own country?"[38] They referred to the identification certificates that the government had, since 1927, compelled all Africans to carry when they resided in the towns, and the passes necessary if they wanted to leave their housing compounds after dark. Both associations requested that "Africans of good character" should be exempted from the need to carry identification certificates. In a subsequent meeting with representatives of the Lusaka association, Mackenzie-Kennedy, the acting governor of the Protectorate, agreed that Africans must find it difficult to understand why they carry passes and are "subject to certain inconveniences which do not appear in the case of Europeans." Despite such inconveniences, he said, "there was no such thing as a colour bar in Northern Rhodesia and I trust that there never will be." But he could not yet advise the repeal of the relevant Native Registration Ordinance.[39] And Moffat Thomson, his Secretary for Native Affairs, later urged the governor to remove troublesome Africans from urban compounds. "Compounds are private places," he wrote, "and when natives are more advanced and crimes of larceny . . . shew some signs of decreasing, the matter [of passes] may be considered but in my view the time is not yet ripe."[40]

Africans organized themselves into associations even in the rural areas. Abercorn, Kasama, and Fort Jameson each boasted a welfare society before 1933, although the government strictly defined their functions. "It must be clearly understood," the Chief Secretary wrote to the provincial commissioner responsible, "that membership of the association must be confined solely to natives who, though residing in Abercorn, owe no kind of allegiance to any Native Authority there, and who engage in no sort of political activity. The association can act as the mouthpiece of natives who are not within the ordinary

[38] Sec/Nat/325: Minutes of the Luanshya meeting, 16 September 1932, Lusaka archives.

[39] Sec/Nat/332: Report of an interview between Mackenzie-Kennedy and the Lusaka Native Welfare Association, 8 October 1932. See also S 1/52/35, Zomba archives.

[40] Sec/Nat/332: Moffat Thomson to the Governor, 6 December 1932.

organisation of native society, but there must be no question or possibility of the association becoming either a rival to or a "cell" within the Native Authority."[41] Moffat Thomson tried to limit the membership of the Kasama association to "alien or detribalised natives" only. These rural groups instead sought to imitate the initiative of their urban counterparts. But their members were few and, in the face of administrative disinterest, only a very small number of educated Africans devoted themselves to endless rounds of debate in the rural meetings. Their associations became social societies and football and recreation clubs and, before World War II at least, contributed little to the political ferment of Northern Rhodesia.

In the urban areas, meanwhile, the momentum of the associations had carried them from complaint to combination. In 1933, after the Lusaka and Ndola associations (both chaired by the brothers Muwamba) had together protested against the possible amalgamation of the two Rhodesias, and the Lusaka group had altered its name from "Native Association" to "African Association" (Moffat Thomson characteristically declared that welfare associations should not be permitted to discuss amalgamation, that the use of the name "African Association" could not be condoned," and that the Nyasas were "professional agitators"[42]), the urban organizations decided to resurrect the earlier idea of a single association for the entire Protectorate. To this end their leaders, under the chairmanship of Clements Muwamba, met publicly at Kafue in the winter of 1933 in order to organize a national association of associations.

The participants included Nyirenda, Godwin Mbikusita Lewanika, and Nelson Nalumango of Livingstone, Blair William Mhone of Mazabuka, and William B. Konie of Lusaka. Clements Muwamba opened the meeting with a prayer and then advised his colleagues to think carefully about their position: "We are here to make a recognition that should cement the existing friendship between the government, the settlers, and the Africans. Whatever we are going to discuss must be in line with the government because they are our fathers upon whom we should rely for our progress and welfare."[43]

41 Sec/Nat/327: R. S. W. Dickenson (the Chief Secretary) to the Provincial Commissioner (Abercorn), 9 March 1933, Lusaka archives.

42 Sec/Nat/332: Moffat Thomson to the Chief Secretary, 19 June 1933.

43 Sec/Nat/311: Minutes of the Kafue Meeting, 10–11 July 1933.

Although Mbikusita Lewanika urged his colleagues to remember that Europeans were their masters and that it was "foolish to desire oneself to be in the same category with a white man,"[44] they demanded a number of improvements in the status and treatment received by educated Africans. They also asked the governor to persuade the editor of Northern Rhodesia's only newspaper, *The Livingstone Mail,* to accept their letters. Finally, Nalumango advocated that they should carry their cause into the villages. He also underlined the importance of unity and, following his lead, the assembly of leaders voted overwhelmingly in favor of the immediate amalgamation of all of the various Northern Rhodesian native welfare associations.

The Secretary of Native Affairs and other members of the government of Northern Rhodesia moved quickly to eliminate such open subversion. Moffat Thomson opined that the object of the local associations should be simply to look after the general welfare of "alien and detribalised natives" resident in the urban areas; they should not discuss politics. In his view, the "bulk of the members of welfare associations are detribalised or alien natives and such are not entitled to speak on behalf of natives living in the tribal areas."

I recommend that the welfare associations be told definitely once and for all that they are not permitted to carry on their activities in the villages, that native authorities under district officers are much more capable of attending to their own affairs than any group of alien or detribalised natives and that disciplinary action will be taken against members in government employment of any association that ignores this warning.[45]

Mackenzie-Kennedy, again the Chief Secretary, embodied Moffat Thomson's suggestions in a circular minute to all provincial commissioners. It instructed them to limit the native welfare associations to the pursuit of non-political interests. "In future," he declared, "the activities of welfare associations must be confined to matters strictly pertaining to the township in which they function. . . . African employees . . . are debarred from becoming members of any political organization. . . . Native employees must not address public meeting

[44] *Ibid.*
[45] Sec/Nat/311: Moffat Thomson to Mackenzie-Kennedy, 25 August 1933.

on any but academic subjects; neither should they write letters to the papers."[46]

For the next ten years, these constraints effectively curbed the activities of the various associations. African civil servants tried to keep in the good graces of their employer; many continued to participate in meetings but, for the most part, they confined themselves to the expression of innocuous grievances and to the furtherance of social and cultural ends. While others held office, the usually more articulate, often better-educated former leaders played a conspicuously less prominent part in the political life of the associations. The flame flickered. Although several continued to meet regularly and, despite the public inactivity of some of their best members, to demand redress anew for many of their old grievances, they accomplished little, and again and again forlornly aired matters that had already met with an unfavorable official response. A few associations grew moribund; others followed bursts of action with periods of indifference. In 1937, a group of Mazabuka chiefs and civil servants tried to resuscitate the old idea of a territorial united association. They held two "illegal" meetings in Chief Chongo's village and drafted a constitution of what, following a Southern Rhodesian example, they wanted to call the Northern Rhodesia African Congress. However, Rowland S. Hudson, then in charge of native affairs, refused to approve the establishment of such a society because its members wanted to consult with similar associations elsewhere and because they would interfere with the work of the Native Authorities.[47] Thus, although they were subsequently to play a major role in the representation and expression of African disaffection, Northern Rhodesia's voluntary welfare associations were, on the eve of World War II, playing a role of little immediate importance to the nationalist cause.

Despite numerous rebuffs, the various African voluntary associations of Northern Rhodesia and Nyasaland refrained from speaking publicly of self-government and, by 1939, they had alluded only

[46] Sec/Nat/332: Circular minute of 4 September 1933. The use of the word "African" was idiosyncratic, and did not really imply any disagreement between Mackenzie-Kennedy and Moffat Thomson.

[47] Sec/Nat/348: Rowland S. Hudson to the Chief Secretary, 5 August 1937, Lusaka archives. The Rev. Mr. Thompson Samkange had already formed a Bantu Congress of Southern Rhodesia.

in the most tangential manner to the possibility that Africans might one day be represented in the Legislative Council by persons of their own choice. Their leaders spoke rarely of "freedom" and of the stratagems that might ultimately return the two protectorates to indigenous control. At the onset of the war, they wanted equality of opportunity more than power, and status within the existing society more than its wholesale transformation. Yet, if timidly, their actions kept alive the fires of protest. Associational activity also provided training for future politicians. Through such channels Africans could harmlessly vent their frustrations and exhaust many of the ordinary British methods of effecting change. Although they accomplished little thereby, their formation of and participation in associations filled large, unsatisfied needs. At the time, Central Africans may have lacked the experience or the desire to organize themselves in ways from which they might have derived greater and more lasting benefit. Their associations were, nonetheless, the logical progenitors of the more "modernist," nationalist-minded congresses of a later day.

Chapter VI

THE RELIGIOUS EXPRESSION
OF DISSATISFACTION

There they are, they who over burden us with loads, and beat us like slaves, but a day will come when they will be the slaves. . . . God only is to be respected and obeyed, nobody else on earth has any right to it; no more the European than the native chiefs. The English have no right whatsoever in the country, they are committing injustice against the natives in pretending to have rights.

—Hanoc Sindano, Watch Tower preacher,
1923

In Nyasaland and Northern Rhodesia Africans continued to express their opposition to colonial rule in a religious fashion throughout the interwar years. During this period, despite the enforced exile of Kenan Kamwana, the execution of John Chilembwe and his followers, and widespread governmental antagonism, separatist and chiliastic sects increased in number and in influence. For many, they provided the only means by which aggrieved Africans might reject foreign domination, voice aspirations displeasing to their rulers, and achieve prominence outside of the colonial context. Although the sects and the voluntary associations existed side by side, and religious leaders occasionally filled important positions within the associations, their premises, and the resultant ways in which each attacked the problems of colonial rule, were dissimilar. The religious rejection took many forms, and the sects represented a seemingly infinite variety of possible responses to colonial, spiritual, and temporal stimuli. In both Nyasaland and Northern Rhodesia, Africans accepted the prophets, seceded from orthodox white-run mission churches and, in endless ways, followed the particular paths first illuminated by Chilembwe, Kamwana, Domingo, and Mokalapa.

THE WATCH TOWER MOVEMENT

In Northern Rhodesia, religious separatism erupted into violence for the first time immediately after the end of World War I in 1918. Late in the previous year, the government of Southern Rhodesia had deported six adherents of the African Watch Tower or Kitawala (from the sound of the English name) movement to their homes in Northern Rhodesia.[1] On their return journey from Salisbury they passed through the Mkushi and Serenje districts, where they preached a millenarian message. At home, in the Abercorn, Fife and Chinsali districts, these converts found that their fellow Iwa, Namwanga, Mambwe, and Bemba were aggrieved by the treatment that they had received during the war, and that they were receptive to the new doctrines of disobedience. The Kitawalans spoke persuasively of the imminent end of the world, when "the last [i.e., the oppressed Africans] would be first," and of the end of the then prevalent system of colonial government. Since the Apocalypse was at hand, they argued, Africans should prepare themselves for the coming of the new age by accepting baptism, by severing polygynous bonds, by forsaking their huts for the forests, and by vigilantly praying and waiting there for Judgment Day. Cultivation and care of livestock was unnecessary. Preachers urged their followers to refuse either to labor for or to obey chiefs and European officials. They accused white missionaries of preaching deceitfully and of expounding only half-truths.[2]

By late 1918, the movement had gained several thousand supporters, primarily in the Iwa and Bemba areas of the Fife and Chinsali districts. In September of that year, the local administrators tried to curtail the spread of such religious disaffection by charging two of the leading Watch Tower "prophets" with offenses under an ordinance that made unlicensed preaching illegal. But a magistrate

[1] Nyasa Tonga followers of Kamwana had evidently converted the deportees in Que Que and Shamva. See RC/9/29: The Administrator of Northern Rhodesia to the High Commissioner for South Africa, 6 February 1919; N 3/5/8: Statement by Hanoc Sindano enclosed in the Secretary of Native Affairs of Northern Rhodesia to the Chief Native Commissioner of Southern Rhodesia, 23 March 1920, both Salisbury archives.

[2] ZA 9/2/2/2: Memorandum prepared by Hugh Charles Marshall, 15 August 1919, Lusaka archives; Donald R. Siwale, letter to the author, 6 October 1963.

acquitted the defendants for want of evidence and, capitalizing upon the disruption caused by the German invasion of Northeastern Rhodesia during the last two weeks of World War I, the influence of the Watch Tower movement grew appreciably. Its leaders assaulted and insulted chiefs and headmen (they said, for example, that the important chief Kafwimbi was not, as everyone believed, a man, but that he was in fact a woman pregnant with child) and baptized numberless new converts. Finally, in late December 1918, the district commissioners responsible for Fife and Chinsali sought to counter the Watch Tower doctrines directly. At a large village in the Fife district, Charles Richard Eardley Draper told four hundred staunch believers that they must cease spreading "irresponsible teachings." By way of reply, the recalcitrant congregation sang messianic hymns lustily. Members shouted prayers of defiance and "indulged in wild frenzy, rolling [their] eyes . . . contort[ing] their bodies, [and] making unintelligible ejaculations."[3] Outnumbered, Draper failed to make any arrests.

Early in 1919, Draper and several African policemen visited the village of Terefya, a minor Iwa chief strongly opposed to the Watch Tower movement. In the evening, Draper later reported, "hymn singing commenced, and I walked over."

After the singing a youth got up and commenced to preach in an excited manner, which became more pronounced as he proceeded. One of his companions would read out a Bible text, and he would dilate upon it. The congregation consisted mostly of young women and children. . . . From what I could gather there was no harm in the actual words used, but the preacher becoming more and more excited, appeared to work on his audience, and soon three youngsters started shivering and groaning, one getting up and staggering about the place in a stupid and hysterical manner. . . . [Later] a lad was heard shouting loudly on the outskirts of the village [in imitation of John the Baptist]. . . . We found a lad in the bush shouting out more or less incoherent passages of scripture, and calling upon *lesa* [God] . . . continuously but what it was all about . . . was most hard to determine. We got hold of this lad, who at once called out he had been caught, and another immediately took his place and started the same game. Both were arrested for making an infernal noise.[4]

[3] RC 3/9/5/29: Draper to Charles A. Wallace, the Administrator of Northern Rhodesia, telegram, 30 December 1918, Lusaka archives.
[4] RC 3/9/5/29: Draper to Wallace, 19 January 1919.

This type of behavior, Terefya explained, was common among Watch Tower adherents. They preached that the European was "deceiving the blacks and retaining all good things to himself, [but] by constant prayer all [would] be changed." They prayed over wild animals and took African medicines to counteract the influence of Satan. In the Abercorn district, Hanoc Sindano, the leading local Kitawalan, spoke often of the white man's sins. His phrases, like those of a Melanesian "cargo cult" prophet, promised much:

God made [Europeans] know [Africans] and sent them with goods and many things we see to come and give us free, and teach us about God, and when they get into this country, they hide everything, and teach us very little about God, they teach us how to write but they did not tell us what God sent them here for, and they could not give us the things free what God gave them to give us. They make us work very very hard and give us little for the work we have done to them, and therefore if we pray very hard with all our hearts, God will hear our prayer and will clear all the Europeans back home to England and everything will be ours, and we will be rich as they are.[5]

Draper and his fellow district commissioners soon acted decisively. In the vicinity of Fife, Draper arrested several African believers accused of showing disrespect to the Iwa headman Musamansi, and tried and convicted them "on the spot." In the charge of a police escort, he then sent them to the provincial jail in distant Kasama. But the local villagers forcibly released the prisoners, obstructed Draper, and swore that they would not allow Kitawalans to be taken "to another country; we will be killed in our own country." "Talk," they said, "will not move us."[6] Fearful of the growth of a general lawlessness and aware that dissension inspired by Watch Tower preachers had already infected the nearby Chinsali district, Draper wired for troops and machine guns and, during the last week of January, arrested one hundred thirty-eight of the movement's most influential members at a village near the border between the Fife and Chinsali districts. Another official arrested Sindano at Jordan, his prophetically named village in the Saisi valley. In the High Court of Northern Rhodesia, Justice Philip Macdonnell later sen-

[5] ZA 1/10: Testimony of an African detective, Lusaka archives.
[6] RC 3/9/5/29: Draper to Wallace, 19 January 1919.

tenced most of these preachers to short terms of imprisonment. He and other members of the government confidently anticipated that such a demonstration of authority would rapidly halt the spread of Watch Tower doctrines. "There is every reason to believe," one sanguine administrator wrote, "that the sentences awarded in the High Court will check the Watch Tower movement for a long time."[7]

But neither the sentences, nor Nyasaland's continued restriction of Kamwana in the Seychelles, halted a widespread African search for religious means of political expression. The Watch Tower gospel remained popular. In its name, itinerant Africans baptized and held revivals, taunted chiefs, flaunted white authority, and preached what governments considered sedition. They offered a millenarian remedy —despite the frequent postponement of judgment day—for the economic and political ills of which Africans were only too conscious. And, at least during the years between the two World Wars, this was a solution that owed only its inspiration to Francis Taze Russell and the United States.[8] Variously called Kitawala in Northern Rhodesia and the Congo, and Choonadi ("truth") or Mpatuka ("those apart") in Nyasaland, the African Watch Tower movement had its own prophets—of whom Kamwana was pre-eminent—its own distinctive means of expression, its own forms of ritual, and its own peculiar interpretations of scriptural revelation. Confusingly, however, its members often purchased Watch Tower tracts distributed from Cape Town. In Central Africa, individual preachers at times even claimed to be affiliated to the American organization. But they invariably acted independently, and the Americans eventually disavowed their actions and addressed themselves more and more to the needs of the European residents of Central Africa.

In Nyasaland, Kamwana's followers increased in number and in influence. Particularly in Tongaland, they perpetuated and embellished upon his teachings and maintained a special spirit of revival. At the same time, they continued to preach a message which the government heard with suspicion. In the Neno district, for example, Africans of Watch Tower persuasion proclaimed in 1923 that "the chieftainship of the Europeans is nearing the end. God will punish

[7] ZA 9/2/2/2: Memorandum by Marshall, 15 August 1919.

[8] See George Shepperson, "Nyasaland and the Millennium," in Sylvia L. Thrupp (ed.), *Millennial Dreams in Action* (The Hague, 1962), 156.

the Christians of Babylon. All the Europeans of the Boma, together with the Europeans of the missions, are greatly ashamed because they were hiding 'the path' of God, but now it is visible to us black people that all the Europeans are sorry."[9] The District Resident responsible for Neno furthermore reported that Watch Tower believers failed to show respect for Europeans by "raising their hats and saluting." "I should imagine," he added, "that this was a bad sign."[10]

During the next sixteen years, administrators throughout the Protectorate viewed Watch Tower activities and evangelical successes with similar alarm. After about 1925, American agents of the Watch Tower Bible and Tract Society likewise sought unsuccessfully to curb their nominal, often antagonistic, African brethren. To every attempt to make them conform, however, African Watch Tower adherents responded negatively. They believed themselves to be of the Elect, and reacted in ways that tended to reaffirm such beliefs. They also maintained their assemblies and meetings as centers of opposition to every form of established authority.

In the neighboring Protectorate of Northern Rhodesia, Africans of every tribal and socio-economic background gratefully accepted Watch Tower teachings.[11] Many of their number became active preachers rather than passive members. These who did so, and who achieved a certain notoriety, often gave to the standard message and the usual texts a decidedly political twist. In 1929, Jeremiah Gondwe (a Henga from Nyasaland) thus appealed to a large following of discontented Africans in the Ndola district:

The white people have now no power and they will come to be the last people and the black people will be first. . . . These white people who are here now came to our country and did not deliver the things they were told to deliver to us. Some of them have returned to our elder brothers [American Negroes] and told them that we are monkeys and have tails.

[9] S 2/51/23: Criminal Investigation Department report of 11 August 1923, Zomba archives.

[10] S 2/51/23: Resident (Neno), to the Chief Secretary, 8 May 1923.

[11] Nonetheless, white representatives of the Watch Tower Bible and Tract Society sought to disavow the traditional connection and to forbid African congregations to use its name. ZA 1/10: Thomas Walder to all Watch Tower churches, 10 September 1924; Sec/Nat/314: Llewellyn Phillips to G. R. Phillips, 3 November 1943, Lusaka archives.

Our elder brothers have made aeroplanes and have come to see if the white people are telling them the truth.[12]

Three years later, after Gondwe had fled to the Congo in order to escape arrest, Joseph Sibakwe (a Namwanga from Fife) told an audience in the Broken Hill area that "the present government [of Northern Rhodesia] was no good and that during the [coming] year a new one was coming from America, and would be made up of natives only. . . . Next year all the trains will be stopped and all the Europeans will leave the country to the natives who will then be able to live their own life."[13] In Barotseland, Mulemwa—who wore his hair long and carried a gold-topped cane—said that he had come "to abolish everything. There will be no more taxation, nor carrying work, no more arrests, no more dying. Everybody will be baptised at the Jordan River. . . . The missionaries are thieves."[14] Thereafter, both Sibakwe and Mulemwa languished in prison.

The Kitawala movement nonetheless swept Northern Rhodesia during the 1930's. In centers as separated from each other as Abercorn and Mwinilunga, it found a receptive audience of eager Africans. The Gospel varied. Near Fort Jameson, Africans expected that "Europeans will soon eat from the same plate as the natives . . . when Jesus comes."[15] In Luanshya in 1935, African believers "read in the Bible that the Wise Men came from the East, following a great star which led them to the birth of Jesus Christ. They did not go with gifts but they went to destroy Him in the same way as the government or *boma* is doing in these days."[16] Throughout the Ndola and Nchanga districts, where Kitawalans later advocated and practiced free love and ritual intercourse in order to cleanse their souls (their text was Rom. 12.1: "I beseech you therefore, brethren, by the mercies of God, that ye present your bodies a living sacrifice, holy, acceptable unto God, which is your reasonable service"), and almost everywhere else in Northern Rhodesia, the Watch Tower

---

[12] Sec/Nat/393: Report of a speech by Jeremiah Gondwe, n.d., Lusaka archives.

[13] *Ibid.*, report of the trial of Joseph Sibakwe. See also Sec/Nat/312, Lusaka archives.

[14] Sec/Nat/393: Report of the trial of Mulemwa in the Mongu District.

[15] Sec/Nat/314: A statement attributed to John Kayo, 4 August 1934.

[16] *Ibid.*, statement of 13 September 1935.

movement thus seduced Africans away from all of the institutions to which they had previously given allegiance.

At first, in the absence of violent manifestations of their faith, the government of Northern Rhodesia tried to deal severely only with those Kitawalans who actually preached sedition.[17] It also refrained from tampering with the distribution of Watch Tower propaganda and with the sale of tracts. But, after the Copperbelt riots of 1935, in the stimulation of which Watch Tower preachers were supposedly implicated,[18] the Governor of Northern Rhodesia barred the import or sale of any Watch Tower literature within the Protectorate. Nyasaland followed suit, and both territories maintained their bans until 1946. But the African Watch Tower Church, independent as it was of support from the United States or South Africa, continued to gain militant followers who willingly awaited the coming of a new dawn and the creation of a black-run Jerusalem. They believed in the efficacy of their symbols and in the good life that would be theirs in the aftermath of Armageddon. Happily content in their sublimation, their beliefs offered an escape from the realities of colonial rule and an alternative path leading to the political, as well as spiritual, salvation of a subject people.

MWANA LESA AND THE FINDING OF WITCHES

Associated with the growth of chiliastic separatism in Central Africa was the spread of messianic movements that had as their object the finding and exorcism of witchcraft. They represent a recurring theme common to both protectorates and to other areas of Africa. Prophets frequently proclaimed a magic method by which witches might be found and human suffering eliminated.[19] They offered their adherents an easy eschatological escape from fearful everyday problems. Theirs was, in sum, the welcome message of speedy salvation.

Of the many recent Rhodesian and Nyasan prophets, none was more destructively successful than Tomo Nyirenda, who styled him-

[17] The government of the Belgian Congo acted more vindictively. It arrested and deported adherents and, between 1932 and 1939, sought vigorously to remove the Watch Tower infection from the mining areas of Katanga.

[18] See Chapter VII.

[19] For the *mcapi*, see Audrey I. Richards, "A Modern Movement of Witch-Finders," *Africa*, viii (1935), 448–460; M. G. Marwick, "Another Modern Anti-Witchcraft Movement in East Central Africa," *ibid.*, xx (1950), 100–112.

self Mwana Lesa. A Henga from Nyasaland, Nyirenda attended classes at Livingstonia and then went to Broken Hill, where he found employment as a cook.[20] In about 1924, a chiefs' court convicted him of molesting a young African girl. After his release from prison, he obtained work at a mine near Mkushi, where he was introduced to Watch Tower beliefs by Gabriel Phiri, a fellow Nyasa.[21] Nyirenda accepted baptism in early 1925, and then began to roam the Mkushi District, everywhere preaching the message of his new faith. By doing so, he created a stir sufficient to arouse the enmity of the local European administrator, who imprisoned Nyirenda for failing to register as an "alien native."[22] Released in April 1925, after a period of weeks in the Mkushi jail, Nyirenda recommenced his evangelical activity.

He declared himself to be Mwana Lesa, the Son of God—a name by which he was thereafter known—and, during the next few months, he urged the Lala of the Mkushi and Serenje districts to prepare themselves for the millennium. He promised his followers immediate entrance into the select circle of believers and a reserved seat in the Garden of Eden. Like others of similar belief, he foretold the arrival of Americans who would divide a great wealth among the baptized African elect. These Americans, he said, would drive away the white men and would help Africans to enslave the remaining white women, all of whom would thereafter serve as porters. The followers of Mwana Lesa would divide the property of Europeans among themselves. They would end taxation and welcome supplies of food that would fall from heaven. In the meanwhile, he directed his followers to refrain from fighting and stealing, to cease abusing people, to renounce the practice of adultery, to be hospitable to strangers, and patiently to anticipate the day when the setting of the evening star would herald the Second Coming. God would come through the trees in the middle of a shining light.[23]

This was in almost every respect no more than an echo of the usual Watch Tower message. But to it Nyirenda added a special

[20] But see Shepperson, "Millennium," 157.
[21] Another, suspect account of Nyirenda's early history may be found in Carl von Hoffman (ed. Eugene Löhrke), *Jungle Gods* (London, 1929), 43–46.
[22] KSM 5/1/1: Memorandum by James Moffat Thomson, 8 June 1926, Lusaka archives.
[23] *Ibid.* But see S 2/4/26: Memorandum by P. E. Hall, 13 March 1926, Zomba archives.

word about baptism: He taught that baptized persons would never die; that baptism would permit Africans to see their dead forefathers; that aged persons who accepted baptism would become young again; and, significantly for the later success of his movement, that the test of baptism would demonstrate whether persons were or were not infected with witchcraft—whether, in fact, they were possessed of spirits.

Among a people persuaded of the existence and the danger of sorcery, Nyirenda's professed ability to divine witches set him apart from the usual apocalyptic advocates. Indeed, although the exact nature of his early evangelical operations is not known, it is clear that Nyirenda quickly won a large following among the Lala. In at least six villages, he baptized converts by immersion and, perhaps tentatively, cleansed supposed witches of their sins by special forms of incantation. Nyirenda's reputation consequently spread. Shaiwila, the local chief, thereupon summoned him to prove that he could in fact outwit a witch. "How," the chief reputedly asked, "do you know that a witch is a witch?" Triumphantly, Nyirenda explained that evil ones gave themselves away during the baptismal ceremony. They simply "could not be completely immersed."[24]

In the popular imagination, God had sent Mwana Lesa to purge Lalaland of evil. Chief Shaiwila, who initially may have used Nyirenda for his own nefarious ends (the chief denounced his enemies as witches), commended the movement to his people who, in turn, anxiously sought to prove themselves innocent of sorcery. At first, those who "remained on the top of the water" were merely ostracized by their fellow villagers. But the number of wizards grew alarmingly, and Chief Shaiwila urged Mwana Lesa to remove them permanently from Lala society.

Among surviving accounts, that of the death of Chinkumbila provides the fullest insight into the operations of Mwana Lesa. At a subsequent inquest, the widow and the son of the deceased, sup-

[24] Sec/Nat/313: Quoted in a memorandum by R. S. Hudson, 23 October 1945. Kathaleen Stevens Rukavina, *Jungle Pathfinder* (London, 1951), 185, contains a completely different account of this confrontation. Baroness Rukavina also claims that Mwana Lesa possessed John Foxe's "Book of Martyrs" (John Foxe, *Actes and Monuments of these latter and Perillous Dayes* [London, 1563]), with its pictures of drowning witches, but the present author has been unable to confirm either this, or a number of her other statements about Mwana Lesa.

ported by a number of witnesses, declared that Nyirenda personally had killed Chinkumbila. His son said:

I remember when Tomo . . . came to the Lukasashi [stream]. He built a shelter . . . [and then] sent a message to the village telling us to come and be "washed." The whole village went together. . . . We found that Luputa's people had washed before our arrival. Four of them floated. After[wards] . . . five of Mulilima's [people] floated [and] only one of Nalongo's . . . namely, my own father. Then Shipekula's people were washed. Ten . . . floated. Then Shenge's . . . but none of them floated. . . . Those who floated were put on one side and the others on another. Tomo was sent for when the washing was finished . . . [and he] said to Mulilima: "I am going to kill your people." Mulilima refused, saying it was the white man's country. . . . Tomo . . . beat the people of Mulilima with a switch and told them to go home. He did this to all those who had floated except Chinkumbila whom he brought to the shelter. I think he seized Chinkumbila because he is partly blind and could not run away and because [some accused him of killing their children]. Tomo said that he would kill him as he had no friends. . . . Tomo asked Chinkumbila why he had killed the children. Chinkumbila said he had *kasenga ka chipato* [literally, the "calabash of the anus"] and perhaps that had killed the children. . . . It was then Tomo seized him and hit him on the neck with a piece of firewood, twice. He then tied him to a tree. Tomo did this himself. Chinkumbila submitted to be tied up in this way. Tomo then got a stick and beat Chinkumbila on the back of the neck five times and afterwards he beat him with a *chikoti*. . . . Then he died.[25]

Nyirenda killed "witches," not people. Indeed, many of his victims appear to have accepted their failure to immerse, and the judgment of Mwana Lesa, as evidence of their own guilt. "I killed those witches," the prophet was reputed to have said, "because God is coming, and before God comes the witches must be killed to keep the villages clean."[26] In any event, the victims seem to have acquiesced in their own executions. During May and June 1925, Nyirenda drowned or otherwise ended the lives of sixteen Lala. Moving north into the Ndola district, he claimed six further victims during the last weeks of June. Later in Katanga he aroused great interest, made innumerable converts, and killed about one hundred

---

[25] KSM 5/1/3: Testimony of Mushitu before J. Gordon Read, 6 October 1925, Lusaka archives.
[26] *The Rhodesia Herald*, 22 January 1926.

and seventy "witches," some of whom he herded into cages before subjecting them to gradual starvation. Eventually, however, he over-played his hand. His excessive zeal or, perhaps, excessive success, brought his movement to the attention of the Belgian authorities, who promptly sought his arrest. Pursued, he escaped back into Northern Rhodesia where, after receiving food and shelter from innumerable villagers, he was finally arrested in September in the Petauke district. After a two-day trial, Justice Macdonnell sentenced Nyirenda and Chief Shaiwila to hang, thereby removing from the scene a serious threat to the ordered nature of colonial society.[27]

THE SCHISMATIC SECTS

More prosaic in the expression of discontent than the millenarians, numerous Nyasas and Rhodesians demonstrated their equally vehement rejection of colonial society by the establishment of a variety of separatist churches.[28] These took innumerable forms, particularly in Nyasaland, but each emphasized the control by Africans of the religious present and offered their adherents an avenue of advancement that rivaled that of the European mission churches. For the most part, they resembled religious versions of the secular protest movements common to both protectorates during the years between the two world wars. In many cases, the leadership of associations and separatist churches corresponded; to educated men, most of whom had received their instruction from European missionaries and had worked, in one capacity or another, for the missionaries, it seemed as appropriate and necessary for them to establish "break-away" churches in opposition to the missions as it did for them to organize associations in opposition to the settlers. In both cases, theirs was a bitter response to the ways in which Europeans discriminated against and hindered Africans from sharing the cultural and material riches of the new colonial society by which they had been caught up.

[27] B 1/2/234: The records of Rex v. Nyirenda, Lusaka archives. Sir Kenneth Bradley kindly shared his memories of Nyirenda after the trial. (London, 13 September 1963).

[28] While the use of the terms "Ethiopian" and "Zionist" in order to categorize African religious movements may originally have served a useful, if limited, function, it no longer seems appropriate either to label them in such a misleading fashion or to draw a sharp line between the two supposed divisions.

During the interwar years, Northern Rhodesia's African-led churches were few. No successors to Willie Mokalapa[29] alarmed the government until 1921/22, when Bernard Kumwembe, a Nyasa Yao employed by the Dutch Reformed Church Mission in Lusaka, founded a short-lived Church of Zion. Influenced evidently by what he had learned of a similar organization in South Africa, he said that his was the only "true church." He urged his followers to believe only in the Bible, to reject the ministrations of white medical doctors—who were "agents of the Devil"—and to pray for the end of European rule.[30] Later, the New Apostolic Church and the Seventh-day Adventist Reform Movement both gained converts in widely separated parts of the Protectorate. To their initiative, however, the government reacted adversely. Yet, dangerous though he thought their existence as foci of discontent, Moffat Thomson, the Northern Rhodesian Secretary for Native Affairs, understood at least some of the causes that contributed to the movement in favor of separatism. "Natives," he wrote, "are becoming wider in their outlook and more independent and have reached the point where they want to try and do things for themselves." Moreover, "there is a feeling amongst natives that they have not been treated in the true spirit of Christianity in religious matters."[31] But, despite the extent to which Northern Rhodesians harbored grievances that could be expressed religiously, these churches, unlike those of similar provenance in Nyasaland, played a role of secondary significance in the rise of nationalism.

The Nyasa churches owed a part of their inspiration to Joseph Booth and John Chilembwe. But South African precedents, and a growing awareness that missionaries refused to practice what they preached, equally stimulated the proliferation of new indigenous sects. Jordan Msuma, a Tonga, became the first of the important postwar separatists in 1925, when he broke away from the Livingstonia mission to establish the Last Church of God and His Christ.[32] He and his followers (most of whom lived in the Karonga district)

[29] See Chapter III.
[30] B 1/1/499: Report of the Magistrate, Chilanga, 16 December 1921, Lusaka archives.
[31] Sec/Nat/288: Moffat Thomson to the Chief Secretary, 2 February 1932, Lusaka archives.
[32] In 1923, Genesis Mbedza, an Ngoni, introduced into Nyasaland the doctrines of the (American) Christian Catholic Apostolic Church in Zion.

believed only in the authority of the New Testament; during their services they sang hymns of their own invention and read particular, selected extracts from the Gospels. In direct opposition to the missionaries of the United Free Church of Scotland, they baptized immediately upon a sinner's confession of faith (they prescribed no "waiting period" of instruction) and sanctioned, even commended, the practice of polygynous marriage. The constitution of the Last Church justified this departure from the Christian custom in terms of interest to students of African reactions to European rule:

. . . man should live according to his religion and not merely be a nominal member of a church whose rules he cannot carry out. Like other countries, Africa is in need of a church that would correspond with her God-given customs and manners. We believe the commission of the Christian church to Africa was to impart Christ and education in such a way as to fit in with the manners and the customs of the people and not that it should impose on the Africans the unnecessary and impracticable methods of European countries, such as having one wife . . . which have no biblical authority.

We believe that the immoralities now prevailing among us are the direct result of the unnatural position into which the African has been driven coupled by the false and misleading theory that outside one's own church beliefs, others can do no good. We believe in the fatherhood of God and the brotherhood of man regardless of colour and creed and that the African religion with its traditions, laws, and customs was instituted by Him so that the African may realize Him by their observance.

The aim of this church is the uplifting of the African . . . as well as winning those who are considered bad because of polygamy and drink and are [said to have no] latent qualities for doing good any more . . . and [to] restore an atmosphere of a deep . . . naturally religious life as prevailed in the day of long ago.[33]

In the next year, after consistently refusing to do so since 1920, the government of Nyasaland reluctantly allowed adherents of Chilembwe's church, the Providence Industrial Mission, openly to worship together and to revive the use of their corporate name. This action coincided with and was influenced by the return to Nyasaland of the Rev. Dr. Daniel Sharpe Malekebu, a Yao from Chirad-

---

[33] NN 1/20/3: Constitution of the Last Church of God and His Christ, Zomba archives. Msuma himself presumably drafted this document.

zulu who had originally accompanied Emma B. DeLany to the United States in 1908. (Miss DeLany, an American Negro, had assisted Chilembwe by teaching singing and sewing to members of the mission in Chiradzulu.) Since that time, Malekebu had obtained degrees from Selma (Alabama) College, from what was then called the National Training School at Durham (now North Carolina College), and from Meharry Medical College in Nashville, Tennessee. Ordained a Baptist minister, he had married a Congolese student who had attended Selma College and, for three years prior to his return home, had served with the American Baptist mission in Liberia. Under his leadership, and with the support of the National Baptist Convention of the United States, the Providence mission tried carefully to continue Chilembwe's evangelical work without incurring the displeasure of the government. Both through the activities of the mission and the Chiradzulu Native Association, Malekebu voiced the grievances of his parishioners and strove, by setting a personally respectable example, to persuade whites to alter their prejudiced image of Africans. Unspectacular though his actions may have been, they played a small, significant part in the Nyasan response to colonial rule before World War II.

Of the influential sects that apparently organized openly in the wake of the re-establishment of the Providence mission, several sprung from the folds of the Livingstonia mission. In 1929, three graduates of Livingstonia—Levi Mumba, the associationist, Isaac Mkondowe, a teacher, and Paddy Nyasula, a government clerk—formed the African National Church with congregations initially at Deep Bay and Florence Bay, and later at Chinteche and Mzimba.[34] This church modeled itself closely upon the Presbyterians. It refused to condone polygyny or to baptize by immersion. It conducted its services in the Scottish manner, held regular communion, and demanded of its members a strict obedience to an array of fundamentalist injunctions. It also gave strong support to the proposals advanced on behalf of Africans by the various northern Nyasa native associations. Above all else, the church sought to make good its national claims and to provide, by the opening of churches and

[34] Robert Sambo, a Henga from the Karonga district and a colleague of Clements Kadalie in South Africa before being deported to Nyasaland in 1929, later organized branches of the African National Church in Ncheu and Lilongwe.

schools, a meaningful alternative to the worldly success offered to its members by the Livingstonia mission.

Three African ministers ordained at Livingstonia and Loudon by the United Free Church of Scotland established yet another African variation of Presbyterianism. In 1932, Yafet Mkandawire of Deep Bay organized the African Reformed Presbyterian Church. In 1933, Yesaya Zerenji Mwasi, who was related to Kadalie and the brothers Muwamba, and who had earlier engaged in a long correspondence with Marcus Garvey of the Universal Negro Improvement Association, founded the Blackman's Church of God Which is in Tongaland; and, in 1934, Charles C. Chinula formed the Eklesia Lanangwa (The Church of the Christianity of Freedom) in Mzimba.[35] In 1935, the leaders of these three churches joined forces in order to inaugurate the Mpingo wa Afipa wa Africa, the Church of the Black People of Africa. Under its aegis, they started separate school systems and gathered a reasonably large following in the Northern Province of Nyasaland. There it competed for African attention with the older mission and separatist churches, with the Chipangano, or Messenger of the Covenant Church—the members of which practiced polygyny—after 1935 with Lameck Hara's rather vaguely defined Zion Prophecy Church and, after Kamwana's release from exile in 1937, with his Watchman's Society, a distinctive version of the usual African Watch Tower Church.

If the content of the Watchman's message indicated the aggressiveness of its leader, Kamwana had changed little. The church said:

We are the children of God and must therefore pay no attention to the laws of the *boma*. The time is at hand, do not respect the *boma*, that is earthly, if we obey the laws on earth made by the *boma*, then we are worshipping the Devil. We know today there are government present at our meetings who plot against us. We are being hated by government

---

[35] Mwasi, who himself claimed the relationship with Kadalie, also organized the short-lived West Nyasa Blackman's Educational Society in order to promote the establishment of a university in Nyasaland. George Simeon Mwase [*sic*] was his brother. See also Chapter III. Chinula, an Ngoni, had "slipped from grace" on two occasions before his final break with the Livingstonia mission. He reported that he left the mission church because it punished sinners too harshly and because it "lacked the forgiveness of Christ" in its dealings with "fallen" converts. (Interview with the author, 20 September 1962, Edingeni.) Mkandawire, the first African ever ordained at Livingstonia, likewise was under a moral cloud at the time of his break with the European church.

for no reason. Be of courage for the time of trouble is near. People must not be afraid to break government laws. Nobody should remove his hat to the Provincial Commissioner or the District Commissioner. These gentlemen . . . are pretenders.[36]

To the south, in these years, the other main separatist sects included the very anti-establishment African Seventh-day Baptists of Dedza and Chiradzulu, the Full Gospel Mission of Ncheu and Mlanje, a Nyasa variation of the African Methodist Episcopal Church administered by the Rev. Mr. Hanock Msokera Phiri (a relative of Dr. H. Kamuzu Banda) in the Kasungu District, the African Church of Christ, near Zomba, and a schism from the last-named group, George Massangano's Church of God in Africa, the members of which left the African Church of Christ because they wanted to grow and to smoke tobacco. At one time or another, each of these schismatic sects challenged the authority of the government, but, although the Criminal Investigation Department of the Nyasaland Police compiled periodic reports on their activities, their protests and pleas were invariably turned aside. Only on the eve of World War II did a separatist church leader activate the defensive machinery of official power.

WILFRED GOOD AND THE ANA A MULUNGU

"Look here Government," wrote Wilfred Good in 1938, "I and my Christian followers, starting from today we shall never pay tax for the British Kingdom."[37] Good, a Mang'anja who had been born more than fifty years before in the Cholo district of Nyasaland, joined the Seventh-day Adventist mission at Malamulo in 1906 and taught and preached in its employ from 1911 to 1918/19, when he supposedly underwent a brief period of mental derangement. The mission re-employed him in 1921; shortly thereafter, Good tried and failed to oust the Ngoni who had obtained prominent places in the Adventist organization and, in 1925, he again incurred the displeasure of the European-led church. Finally, in 1935, Good evidently questioned the way in which an adultery case had been decided by the missionaries of Malamulo. He later testified:

[36] 1a/1339: Report of the Criminal Investigation Department, Chinteche, 1940, Zomba archives.
[37] 1a/1413: Good to "the Government, Cholo," 2 February 1938, Zomba archives.

. . . there was a case of adultery at Malamulo. I said publicly that it ought to be settled with justice, against the boy responsible. He was not suspended, but I was because of what I had said. I told the mission that I would not attend Holy Communion until six months had passed. After about five months the mission wrote saying I was no longer a member. I asked what had I done. I was told I had been dismissed because of my disagreement with adultery.[38]

At this juncture, Good decided to start a church of his own, the Ana a Mulungu Church, or the Church of the Children of God. He gathered a following without difficulty: many later explained that they had each dreamed in 1935 that Good was calling them. "I believe," one said, "that Wilfred Good talks to God and God talks to him and because of this I would do anything that [he] told me to do."[39] Together they lived in the area of the Cholo district governed by Native Authority (Chief) Ntondeza. Good built a brick house on the top of a small hill, from whence the houses of his followers radiated in neat lines. They planned to support themselves by growing maize for sale to the nearby tea plantations. But Good and Ntondeza quarreled over the land upon which the members of the Ana a Mulungu Church had sown their crops: the chief claimed that Good and his disciples had usurped gardens belonging to others; Good, in turn, declared that the acreage in question had been assigned to him by a previous chief. Denied a hearing by the local district commissioner, who sent a police detachment to support Ntondeza, the Ana a Mulungu in 1937 were ousted from the land on which their crops were ripening. "Then I wrote to the District Commissioner," Good affirmed, "that do not trouble me for the hut tax along with my Christian followers, and the answer from the District Commissioner made me to think that we have agreed, and we kept on with our work of the house of God."[40]

From its point of view, the government obviously could not refrain from collecting taxes from Good. On 2 February 1938, a constable therefore cycled from Cholo to Ntondeza's area. He tried unsuccessfully to arrest Good, who refused and thereupon penned a revealing letter, the first part of which has already been quoted. He also wrote:

[38] *Ibid.*, statement by Good, 1938. The mission offered a different version of the events leading up to Good's suspension.
[39] *Ibid.*, statement by an African named Gideon, 1938.
[40] *Ibid.*, Good to "the Bwana Superintendent" of Prisons, 18 March 1938.

I thought you [the government] were servants of God as the Bible says; that is why I was paying taxes, but now I realise that you are not the servants of God. Since from 1935–37 I had three serious cases which I had believed that the government could help, but you . . . refused to hear my cases nor to see my face whilst . . . Village Headman Kaponda and his boys . . . [could] reap all my maize, ha! it's a pity! Is it lawful to decide a case privately without hearing one's evidence? Is there a law to quit a person from his own home without judging his case? Is there a law to seize a person's food or to kill him before his case is settled? All right, since you have refused, God will judge it. But do not ask me for Hut Tax. This will never be repaired. (Signed) The Servant of God, Wilfred Good.[41]

After another constable had failed to arrest him, a European police inspector arrived with reinforcements to take him into Cholo. Several weeks later the District Commissioner of Cholo sentenced Good and twenty-nine of his male followers to three months in jail for refusing to pay taxes. Subsequently, in the Zomba prison, they all refused to wear the usual uniforms and to obey rules—they only "obeyed the orders of God."[42]

The Governor wanted to deport Good to Karonga. "I should make it clear," he wrote to London, "that [Good's] refusal to obey the orders of Government as well as his wild and subversive statements that he recognized no Government, but only the will of God, have created a certain amount of political excitement."[43] But the Secretary of State for the Colonies urged the Governor to give Good a chance to reform, and upon his release from prison, the government of Nyasaland reluctantly did so. The members of the Ana a Mulungu Church continued, however, to refuse to pay their taxes. In late October 1938, a magistrate therefore issued another warrant for Good's arrest and, early in November, several European police officers and a troop of African police tried to capture Good and the twenty-nine of his followers for whom warrants had been sworn. The deposition of the officer in charge of the operations provides a summary of the succeeding events from the point of view of the attackers and, incidentally, provides a harbinger of later, analogous interchanges between Africans and colonial authority:

[41] *Ibid.*, Good to "the Government, Cholo," 2 February 1938.
[42] *Ibid.*, the Chief Inspector of Prisons to the Chief Secretary, 11 March 1938.
[43] *Ibid.*, Harold Kittermaster to W. G. A. Ormsby-Gore, 13 May 1938.

When I arrived I found Good and his followers in an open air enclosure. He was addressing them from a central stand. I told him to come quietly. His manner at once became insolent and truculent. He said that he would not go to the *boma* for me, for the District Commissioner, or for anyone. He then went on about his gardens. I ordered the constables to take him. His followers closed in around us. Their manner was aggressive and insolent. They assaulted the police who tried to take him, many of whom were tripped up. Someone ripped my sleeve. Smith was bitten on the hand. It was becoming a riot . . . and [they were hurling remarks at us] as follows: "If you attempt to arrest me we will cut your throat and also the throat of that dog from Blantyre. . . . You, and the rest of you are in this country to steal the wealth of the natives. . . . If you want to send me away, send me to a country where there are no Europeans."[44]

Eventually, after further skirmishing, during which stones were thrown, and after the arrival of reinforcements, the police charged the Children of God with batons and arrested Good and many of his followers. Sentenced to six months in prison, the Governor thereafter detained Good in the Zomba district for a further period of three years.

Good returned home in 1942 and tried forlornly to revive the fortunes of the Ana a Mulungu Church. He also reiterated his opposition to European rule. In 1944, for example, he excoriated Europeans anew:

The Europeans came with the word of God but they are selling it with money, when a child goes to school they are charged school fees, that is why I say they are selling the word of God. When we work for the Europeans they give us little money but they themselves get £90 or £100 every year. When I preach the word of God I do not wear cloth made in England but I wear that which I have made my self.[45]

Nevertheless, Good paid his taxes and, somewhat ostentatiously, stayed on the right side of the law. His day, in fact, had passed. But he and all of the other leaders of indigenous religious movements had earlier provided an alternative means for the expression of dissatisfaction and disagreement. Although they had avoided the dramatic confrontation experienced by Good, they had been no less

[44] *Ibid.*, Inspector Tate to the Superintendent of Police, 8 November 1938.
[45] 1a/1339: Report on Wilfred Good. His echo of Gandhi may have been coincidental. See also the similar comments by Joseph Booth in Chapter III.

opposed to the established order and to the hegemony of the white man. They too had sought change, whether by successful organization for the pursuit of present-day glory or by the assurance of their presence, after Judgment Day, among the Elect of God. They rejected colonial rule outright, and sought in a variety of ways to prepare for and to hasten the arrival of the New Jerusalem.

Chapter VII

INDUSTRIALIZATION AND THE EXPRESSION OF URBAN DISCONTENT

Whatever you get for us it will be less than the white man gets. Has not a black man blood in his veins too? In any case we don't want to hear about compensation now. We want 5/- a day.

—An African striker to Stewart Gore-Browne,
11 April 1940

The pressures of industrial life intensified the prejudice and discrimination to which Nyasas and Rhodesians were subject during the years before World War II. Their experiences on the Copperbelt added significantly to the ferment of discontent that, perhaps more directly than elsewhere in the protectorates, ultimately sought to express itself aggressively. In time, workers with experience on the Copperbelt or in the mines of Southern Rhodesia or South Africa lent their services to the nationalist cause, but they participated equally in associational and religious forms of protest and, on important early occasions, in violent demonstrations against the white man's rule.

Africans smelted the copper of Rhodesia and Katanga long before the arrival of Europeans. David Livingstone and several of the other nineteenth-century explorers sought to confirm its presence and, between 1895 and 1899, Britons discovered reasonably large lodes in the Hook of the Kafue region and at Kansanshi, near Solwezi.[1] The copper ore found there proved insufficiently rich, however, to justify large-scale mining. During the next decade, prospectors and government officials located new outcrops of ore, several of which comprised the nucleus of the urban complex later known as the Copperbelt. Farther south, the Broken Hill lead, zinc, and

[1] David Livingstone (ed. Horace Waller), *Last Journals* (London, 1874), ii, 120; Verney Lovett Cameron, *Across Africa* (London, 1877), 298, 353, 358, 475.

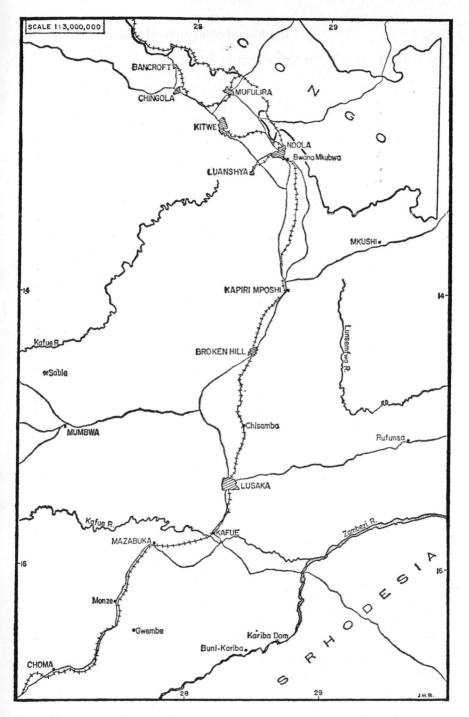

Central Northern Rhodesia, showing major urban areas, railways, rivers, and roads.

vanadium mine began operations in 1906, when the railway from Cape Town and Livingstone extended its tracks thither. In 1909, the railway reached the site of modern Ndola and, in 1910, Elisabeth-ville, the Katangan mining center. It permitted the import of coal and machines and the economic export of concentrates that Africans had previously carried on their heads. But the Rhodesian surface ores were oxidized, and of poor quality compared to those of similar composition found in Katanga. The former therefore lay dormant from about 1913 to 1923, when a rising world demand encouraged British and American financiers carefully to investigate the potential value of the Northern Rhodesian deposits. Shortly thereafter, an American mining engineer demonstrated that a zone of sulphide copper lay at moderate depths below the Rhodesian surface ores and the ground-water level, and others invented the so-called flota-tion method of concentration, which permitted its profitable ex-ploitation.[2] These two discoveries rapidly altered the economic future of Northern Rhodesia.

The Copperbelt experienced its first boom in 1929–30: white and black labor flocked to the mines from all over southern Africa. The companies responsible built new towns, sunk shafts underground, and, in 1930, employed about 30,000 Africans on the Copperbelt.[3] But the world-wide slump in demand soon affected Northern Rhodesia. During the early years of the Depression several of the mines shut down and the others retrenched their labor, thereby add-ing to the unease already experienced by Africans unaccustomed either to industrial or to urban life. Nevertheless, the Rhodesian com-panies weathered the crisis more easily than their competitors. They emerged as low-cost producers dependent upon abundant supplies of African labor and ores that were technically easy to treat.[4] By early 1935, they had begun to re-employ Africans in sizable numbers.

---

[2] In Katanga, the deposits of copper remained oxidized to the lowest depth mined. See E. A. G. Robinson, "The Economic Problem," in J. Merle Davis (ed.), *Modern Industry and the African* (London, 1933), 142; Kenneth Brad-ley, *Copper Venture* (London, 1952), 78–81; Lewis H. Gann, "The Northern Rhodesian Copper Industry and the World of Copper: 1923–1952," *The Rhodes-Livingstone Journal*, xviii (1955), 4–5.

[3] A. W. Pim and S. Milligan, *Report of the Commission Appointed to En-quire into the Financial and Economic Position of Northern Rhodesia*, col. no. 145 (1938), 19.

[4] See Robert E. Baldwin, "Wage Policy in a Dual Economy—The Case of Northern Rhodesia," *Race*, iv (1962), 75–77.

The mining companies stood *in loco parentis* to their African workers. With the assistance of organizations established for the purpose, they initially recruited prospective employees in the rural areas of Northern Rhodesia and Nyasaland and transported them from their homes to the mines. They also conveyed their families and, at the conclusion of a contracted period, returned to their rural homes those Africans who wanted to leave the mines. While two of the three major producers also tried to encourage the growth of a stable resident working force, the management of the Nkana mine believed that Africans should not be employed longer than two consecutive years, after which it feared that they might become "detribalized." Nkana favored the employment of single Africans; the others saw virtue in family life and went a small way toward supplying the schools necessary for a youthful population.[5] On all of the mines, Africans lived either with their families in small huts supplied by the Company or singly in communal barracks. The single men at Nkana fed at a common kitchen; elsewhere families and bachelors all received weekly rations of meal, meat, salt, and vegetables from the commissaries of their respective companies. They attended their own medical clinics, saw free movies, shopped at their own stores or market stalls, and looked to their employers for every kind of service. As the authoritative report said, "considered as labour camps, the conditions in the compounds of these mines [were] good in many ways."[6]

But Africans greeted such paternalism uneasily. They believed themselves to be badly paid, particularly in comparison to the wages received by the Europeans with whom they worked. African miners drew compensation at an average rate of 23/- a month, out of which they purchased all of the necessities demanded by urban conditions. For them, "any mode of living above a purely animal existence demanded considerable sums of money."[7] Africans disliked the supposedly inferior houses to which they were assigned, and complained of primitive sanitary arrangements in the townships. In their eyes, conditions of employment, particularly underground, were con-

[5] Nkana in this chapter is meant to refer both to the Nkana and the Mindolo shafts of the Rhokana Corporation's mining complex in what is now Kitwe. Compared to the need, however, the contribution of the mining companies to educational development was negligible.

[6] Pim, and Milligan, *Report*, 41.

[7] Richard Gray, *The Two Nations* (London, 1960), 117.

siderably less than ideal. More than anything else, however, Africans resident on the Copperbelt endured virulent expressions of white prejudice. A young miner thus queried the nature of European bigotry. "I do not know," he said, "why [Europeans] despise us. . . ."

Even though the African is educated [he] is . . . like a monkey to the Europeans. All the Africans who are at work at [the] mines are treated like this: when an African is carrying a very heavy load, [and] a European is coming behind him without the notice of an African, the European kicks him. When the African says "What's the matter Bwana?" now the Bwana says, "shut up, get away," and gives the African a very hard blow. When an African wants to know the reason why he is beaten, the Bwana takes [his] number . . . so an African will have to be fined . . . for nothing. . . . Englishmen are thrifty like a python which swallows the animal without leaving anything out.[8]

At Mufulira, the compound manager customarily boxed the ears of Africans, a punishment which occasionally caused his victims permanently to lose their ability to hear. The commissioners investigating the subsequent strike at Mufulira recorded:

This boxing of the ears was by no means a casual cuff on the side of the head, but was a deliberate punishment. The offending native was made to stand and hold his head sideways in a stiff position, and then blows with the open hand on the side of the head were administered. . . . [One] boy said he had been struck on the ear; there was a little blood and the drum was ruptured.[9]

Whites insulted Africans and demonstrated the depths of their contempt (some would call it fear) in innumerable harsh ways. They erected a color bar which effectively prevented the promotion of Africans to better paying positions. At the same time, they allowed Africans in practice to perform the very "skilled" work for which they themselves received handsome remuneration. The management at Nkana, an official wrote, simply wanted "to get two shillings worth of work for one shillings wage out of the 'bloody nigger.'"[10] In sum, the mine managements and the white miners,

[8] Sec/Lab/136: Kwafya Kombe, letter of May, 1940, Lusaka archives. Unless stated otherwise, files cited in this chapter may be found in the Lusaka archives.

[9] *Report of the Commission Appointed to Enquire into the Disturbances in the Copperbelt, Northern Rhodesia* (Lusaka, 1935), 15.

[10] Sec/Lab/16: R. S. W. Dickenson to Harold Francis Cartmel-Robinson, 6 October 1933.

many of whom had earlier lived in South Africa, together compelled Africans individually and collectively to appreciate the extent of their inferiority. "I have the impression," a British official reflected, "that the attitude of Europeans to natives at Nkana is neither politic nor in the best interests of the Mine."[11] The subsequent unrest on the Copperbelt thus expressed a discontent generated as much by instances of discrimination as by sharply felt grievances of a narrowly economic kind. In a microcosm, they displayed the problems besetting Northern Rhodesia's African population.

THE FIRST MASS PROTEST: 1935

Early in April 1935, a notice mysteriously appeared in the Nkana beer hall exhorting African mine workers to strike because of bad conditions. Written in Cibemba, it summed up an accumulation of grievances. But, to the Europeans responsible, it seemed an isolated murmur. The notice read:

Listen to this all you who live in the country, think well how they treat us and to ask for a land. Do we live in good treatment, no; therefore let us ask one another and remember this treatment. Because we wish on the day 29th April every person not to go to work, he who would go to work, and you see him it will be a serious case. Know how they cause us to suffer, they cheat us for money, they arrest us for loafing, they prosecute and put us in gaol for tax. What reason have we done? Secondly do you not wish to hear these words, well, listen this year 1935, if they will not increase us more money stop paying tax, do you think they can kill you, no. Let us encourage surely you will see that will be with us. See how we suffer with the work and how we are continually reviled and beaten underground.

Many brothers of ours die for 22/6. Is this money that we should lose our lives for [?] He who cannot read should tell his companion that on the 29th April not to go to work. These words do not come from here, they come from the wisers who are far away and able to encourage us. That's all. Hear well if it is right let us do so. We are all of the Nkana Africans men and women—I am Glad.[12]

---

[11] *Ibid.*, Cartmel-Robinson to Dickenson, 11 October 1933.

[12] Sec/Lab/67: Translation by an African policeman of a notice posted on 5 April 1935. A slightly different version is contained in *Evidence Taken by the Commission Appointed to Enquire into the Disturbances in the Copperbelt, Northern Rhodesia* (Lusaka, 1935), 416–417.

A "G. Loveday" or "Lovewey" signed the warning, but the district officer in charge at Nkana was unable to locate any such person. Yet, because of the way in which the warning was phrased, he and his superiors attributed its provenance—probably incorrectly—to the Watch Tower movement. In any event, 29 April 1935 passed by uneventfully. Smoldering grievances there undoubtedly were, however, and they subsequently received further expression.

The government's decision to raise the tax rate sparked off the actual disturbances. Toward the end of May 1935, the Secretary for Native Affairs formally notified his administrative officers that Africans employed on the Copperbelt would henceforth be required to pay several shillings more than previously. At the same time, he reduced the tax obligations for residents of a number of rural districts. Far from being designed to raise additional revenue, the new tax schedule in fact sought an equitable sharing of revenue needs among Africans. At the Mufulira mine, John Smith Moffat, the officer in charge, evidently intended personally to explain the changes involved to an assembly of mine workers. Before he could do so, however, the African clerks and mine police (whom he had briefed privately) spread the somewhat inflammatory word that Africans would be required, from that moment, to pay higher taxes.[13] The next day, about six hundred of the three thousand Africans employed at Mufulira complained about the tax increase and refused to go to work. At a meeting on the soccer field, they aired their grievances, most of which concerned pay, and sought a further clarification of the tax arrangements from Moffat. By that evening, the leading strikers (the government forbade the unionization of Africans until after 1940) had removed from their jobs those Africans who had gone underground on the afternoon shift. "We have been down to the mine," they told Moffat, and have taken everybody away from there and no one is left."[14] Later that evening, Moffat arrested eight of the leading troublemakers. Otherwise, neither the strikers nor the government acted provocatively on the first day.

[13] The testimony of John Smith (later Sir John) Moffat (a great-grandson of the pioneer missionary), Mateyo Musiska, the head clerk at Mufulira, and Benjamin Schaefer, the Mufulira compound manager, conflicted. See Sec/Lab/ 67, and *Evidence Taken*, 250, 257–258, 289–290, 303. Ironically, the new rates of tax were not then legal, the relevant *Gazette* not having been issued. *Report of the Commission*, 33.

[14] Moffat's testimony. *Evidence Taken*, 264.

At Mufulira, the strikers specifically wanted better wages, lower taxes, more abundant rations, an end to the system whereby they paid for certain items of safety equipment, and better treatment from Europeans who had previously boxed them on the ears or otherwise subjected them to physical and mental maltreatment. On the morning of the second day of the strike, some of the demonstrating Africans told Moffat that "You have to make our tax 7/6 and we want free boots, and free other things."[15] The strikers were, in general, dissatisfied with their life at Mufulira, and the tax announcement had provided a catalyst sufficient to occasion Northern Rhodesia's first important industrial unrest. But, at Mufulira, Moffat refrained from displaying his police force in a hostile posture, and most of the miners returned to work on the afternoon of 23 May 1935, the second of the strike. "The conduct of the natives," the Commission of Inquiry later concluded, "was remarkably restrained."[16] The following days proved quiet.

Meanwhile, trouble brewed at Nkana. There the first threat of a strike had not been followed by any overt signs of unrest. Alexander Thomas Williams, the district officer in charge, had begun collecting the new, higher tax without opposition. Then, on 24 May, Empire Day, notices, probably composed by some of the Nyasa clerks in the compound office, appeared on the main road to the shaft-head.[17] Again written in Cibemba—which many of the Nyasas knew—the notices demanded a wage increase, threatened violence to persons who refused to strike on 27 May, and appeared to have been influenced in their content by the occurrences at Mufulira. A number of Africans later testified that miners from Mufulira had brought word of the strike there, and that they had urged the men at Nkana to demonstrate for higher pay.[18] The leaders of the Bemba semi-secret Mbeni dancing society, many of whom played a suspicious, if tertiary, role in the strikes both at Mufulira and Nkana, may also have contributed to the atmosphere of agitation, but the district officer and the compound manager blamed the unrest pri-

---

[15] *Ibid.*, 265.

[16] *Report of the Commission*, 17.

[17] Testimony of Alimoni Juli, Muleta Jonothan, and Yamikani Phiri, *Evidence Taken*, 530–531, 536–537, 550. But see the testimony of Reuben Jele, *ibid.*, 528.

[18] Paulos Mulenga said that Mateyo Musiska, the head clerk at Mufulira, had sent a letter urging his friends at Nkana to strike. *Evidence Taken*, 549. See also the testimony of Alamu Bwalia, *ibid.*, 529.

marily upon the Nyasa clerks.[19] In any event, on 25 May, two Africans preached violence at a secret meeting held in the Nkana compound. On the afternoon of the next day, a Sunday, the miners decided to go on strike immediately after the ostentatious arrival of police reinforcements. They forcibly removed about two hundred workers from the concentrator, and at dusk began to throw stones and broken bottles at European officials massed near the main compound office. Detonators sounded in the compound itself. Despite such evident hostility, the European mine and government officials sent truckloads of Africans willing to work the evening shift through the massed crowds of stone-throwing strikers. The police escorted others to the shaft-head on foot through a hail of stones and sundry missiles. Strikers threw stones at strikebreakers (but not at Europeans) again the following morning, and white officials tried to escort the latter to work. At one point a white miner, perhaps provoked, beat a number of Africans with a sjambok, a rhinoceros-hide whip. Throughout the next few days, a number of Africans continued to attempt to prevent others from working. But most reported for their shifts, and the presence of police and military troops prevented any serious outbreaks of violence. The arrival by train from Southern Rhodesia on 31 May of a troop of the British South Africa Police intimidated the remaining recalcitrants.

By then, the scene of action had shifted to the Roan Antelope mine at Luanshya. On 28 May, after visitors had related the Nkana and Mufulira experiences and had conceivably urged their friends to act, Africans at the Roan Antelope mine began to talk openly of a strike that had been called for the following day. That evening large groups of Bemba met in the compound and on the soccer field, presumably in order to agree to enforce a stoppage. A notice appeared that read: "Nobody must go to work. . . . All tribes and people. We shall die. They will kill us."[20] The next morning a few of the 4400 Africans reported for work, but the majority refrained from doing so, and some among them sought successfully to prevent their fellow employees from going underground. They assaulted several African guards. At this juncture, two truck-loads of African police arrived, some of whom evidently took the law into their own hands

---

[19] Testimony of A. T. Williams and William John Scrivener, *Evidence Taken,* 436–437, 441, 449, 457.

[20] Quoted in the *Report of the Commission,* 21.

and, without provocation, attacked African bystanders and strikers —who retaliated by hurling stones—before European officials managed to restore order.[21] Police trucks were then used to convey some Africans to their places of employment. Although the strikers then stoned the concentrator and the smelter, they did not attempt sabotage. Shortly thereafter, the district officers in charge and the compound manager tried to hold a meeting on the soccer field, but "there was so much shouting and waving of sticks that it was practically impossible . . . [for the Africans] even to hear." Asked "what the trouble was," the massed strikers "let out a big shout of 'tax' and 'more money.' " But the district commissioner "pointed out to them that it was absolutely impossible to do anything for them in view of the attitude they had adopted in presenting their complaint." He asked them to select spokesmen, who could present grievances through the proper channels in due course. "But they shouted that they wanted all to talk together." And the district commissioner and his party withdrew; they refused to listen further until the Africans had "decided otherwise."[22]

The whites and their African police contingents reassembled at the compound office which, although it was earlier surrounded reputedly by groups of "perfectly orderly" Africans, by mid-morning had assumed the appearance of a redoubt. A number of whites and African clerks, elders, and other "friendlies" attempted to find shelter there, while the police, some of whom "seemed to have lost their heads," charged the by now threatening strikers.[23] The latter began to retaliate by throwing stones, sticks, bottles, iron grinding balls, and miscellaneous paraphernalia at the police and the compound office. The stoning grew intense, creating an infernal din on the corrugated iron roof of the office. The police and their white supervisors ran about wildly, and many of the police tried to crowd into the office. In the midst of this noise and confusion, a white police officer tried to throw stones back at the strikers. Soon he, and possibly some of the African policemen, opened fire, first above the heads of the strikers, and then at their bodies. They killed six

---

[21] Testimony of Cecil Francis Spearpoint, *Evidence Taken*, 586.

[22] *Ibid.*, 587. See also the testimony of Arthur William Bonfield, *ibid.*, 734–735.

[23] *Report of the Commission*, 24. See also the testimony of Police Inspector John Cavan Maxwell, *Evidence Taken*, 4–5.

of the strikers and wounded twenty-two. This circumstance caused the line of strikers to withdraw; shortly thereafter, two platoons of the Northern Rhodesia Regiment arrived from Nkana. They faced the rioters in close lines, "sometimes literally belly to belly," and for about two hours received from them insults and threats. At some point, a district commissioner went out into the crowd of strikers; distressed and angry, they shouted "against the Government and [said] that it had killed them; they were trying to talk with the Government, and the Government had killed them like cattle." They complained about bad food, the tax, about low wages—"if you want us to pay this tax you must tell the Mines to give us more money"—and about the abuse that they had suffered at the hands of the police.[24] Finally, after the soldiers fixed their bayonets and fired over the heads of the strikers, they gradually dispersed.

Although the strikers later looted the grain store and hurled stones at it and at other targets, there were no other major clashes between white and black. The army made its strength known, and several district officers encouraged the strikers to air their grievances. At an assembly on the soccer pitch, Joseph Kazembe, a Ngoni from the Fort Jameson district of Northern Rhodesia, and a number of Bemba said that, since the government had asked for more money, "the Government must tell the mine to give [Africans] more pay." They averred that the Roan Antelope management provided inferior housing, paid underground workers far too little, gave to injured miners or the relatives of workers killed while working underground the smallest of pittances, supplied poor quality food in insufficient amounts, and, on top of every other indignity, forced African employees to buy their own boots, lamps, and coats—the cost of which was deducted from their pay.[25] Later, in testimony before the Commission of Inquiry, a number of African workers reiterated and amplified these grievances. Eliti Tuli Phili, a Tonga from Nyasaland and a clerk in the compound at Luanshya added:

The first thing I wish to speak about as being the cause of the disturbances is the natives' wages on the mines. The natives have seen that they started work at the same time as the European and the European at

[24] Testimony of John Lucien Keith, *Evidence Taken*, 144–146.
[25] *Ibid.*, 148. See also the testimony of Glyn Smallwood (later Sir Glyn) Jones, Shienga Mwepa, and Joseph Kazembe, *ibid.*, 569, 782, 811.

once is able to buy a motor car and he gets a lot of food at the hotel. The natives complain about this. They compare the wages of the Europeans with the wages of the natives. They do the same kind of work, for instance, the natives working underground are supervised by a European who only points out to them the places where they should drill holes. After doing this the European sits down and the natives drill the holes. The natives know where the holes should be drilled, they have been doing that work for some time and they know and understand the work.[26]

It seems abundantly clear that Africans believed themselves "hard done by," and that this feeling expressed itself with comparative mildness at Mutulira, Nkana, and Luanshya. The strikers limited their manifestations of discontent to the throwing of missiles, the hurling of abuse, and the loud voicing of grievances. They complained about the way in which the *bwanas* treated them, but refrained almost completely from attacking whites or from destroying valuable mine property. Yet mild though the disturbances were, they constituted the first mass protest by urban Northern Rhodesians against the established order. They alerted the government to the existence of discontent and, in a very real sense, they were harbingers of future trouble.

The government took note. It strengthened its defenses and supplemented the white manpower available on the Copperbelt for administrative duties. The Commission of Inquiry had, without much evidence, called the Watch Tower teachings "dangerously subversive" and "an important predisposing cause of the recent disturbances"; the government promptly banned a number of Watch Tower publications and sought to curtail the activities of its local leaders.[27] But both the government and the commission refused to admit as irritants, less causes, the grievances voiced by the strikers. In the eyes of the commissioners and the governor, the wages on the mines compared favorably with wages paid in other forms of employment—"that the wages are considered to be good is shown by the numbers of natives who are ready to accept employment on the mines"—the rations on the mines provided adequately for the support of the workers, and "complaints about the deductions from

[26] Testimony of Eliti Tuli Phili, *ibid.*, 757. These complaints, particularly the last, recurred as alleged causes of the 1940 strike and riots.
[27] *Report of the Commission,* 49.

wages [were] without foundation."[28] In other words, the government of Northern Rhodesia took few positive steps to improve the conditions under which Africans worked. They refrained from advising the mining companies to remedy the causes of African displeasure. The mine managements therefore did little and, for the most part, life on the mines and in the mine compounds continued as before. Fred Kabanga, supposedly a Watch Tower preacher, supplied the *leitmotiv* of the post-strike period. "You natives on the mines are still receiving little pay, this is the fault of the white men who are making all the money—the natives are suffering still. What," he asked, "are you going to do about it?"[29]

A SECOND ROUND OF HOSTILITY: 1940

By 1940, the production of copper had once again proved profitable. The Rhodesian producers were amassing handsome returns; in 1940, a ton of Northern Rhodesian copper cost about £27 to mine and to export to London, where it fetched about £43 on the world market. Since 1929, the total revenues of the Protectorate, 70 percent of which were due directly to copper, had increased fourfold because of the demand.

White workers had shared significantly in the prosperity of the times. African wages had, however, remained at their 1934/35 level. Africans, although they drove trucks, blasted, or "lashed," earned less in a month or two than a white worker—whose physical exertions were minimal—earned in a day. No matter how skilled, they could never hope to advance into the job categories occupied by Europeans. Although they willingly labored overtime and on Sundays, Africans, unlike whites, received straight-time rather than time-and-a-half pay. Everywhere they met discrimination. Europeans continued to abuse them physically and verbally. For example, one African complained that a European underground worker "had called him a monkey and had further stated that all natives were monkeys and had to have their tails removed at the hospital on recruitment and that the native police were only fit to superintend

---

[28] *Ibid.*, 35–37; Sec/Lab/69: Governor Sir Hubert Young to Malcolm MacDonald, Secretary of State for the Colonies, 23 October 1935.

[29] Sec/Lab/69: Enclosure in a communication from John Moffat, 18 July 1935.

the removal of excrement from European houses."[30] In sum, the grievances voiced to and rejected by the first commission of inquiry continued to serve as breeding grounds of unrest. Rightly or wrongly, African miners generally believed themselves to be underpaid, poorly fed, and in every respect underprivileged compared to the whites with whom they worked, and for whom they had little respect.

The white miners precipitated the African strike and riots of 1940 by striking themselves. Displeased with their rates of pay and their conditions of service, they struck the Mufulira and Nkana mines (Europeans at Roan and Nchanga, the new mine, refused to follow suit) during the third week of March 1940.[31] After ten days, during which mining operations ceased, the government intervened and the companies reluctantly promised to boost the average pay of their European employees by about 5 percent. They also granted them a number of other concessions, including one that increased overtime earnings and another that conceded the "closed shop." Both sides submitted additional issues to arbitration.

Meanwhile, even before the conclusion of the European strike, African discontent had roiled the prevailing calm at Nchanga. There, on the morning of the fourth day after the beginning of the white walkout at Mufulira, an African woman argued violently with an African *capitão* in charge of issuing rations from the grain store. The *capitão* assaulted the woman—the wife of a miner—and, in order to put her in her place, the white assistant compound manager subsequently handcuffed and flogged the woman and her husband in public for "causing a disturbance." According to African witnesses,

Which cause us to be angry is this: We came here to work from home with our wives with us. . . . Now we saw that the feeding store *capitão* was beating a woman and took her to the compound manager's office, the *capitão* then made a statement to the European who listened to him, but the woman was never asked to make a statement, but she was merely being beaten without her statement [and] she was handcuffed.

[30] Sec/Lab/58: Quoted in Cartmel-Robinson to the Chief Secretary, 19 November 1940.

[31] The strike was a clear breach of an agreement made in 1937 between the European mineworkers union, which had been established the previous year, and the companies. By that accord the union had agreed to submit grievances to conciliation before calling a strike. See *Report of the Commission Appointed to Inquire into the Disturbances in the Copperbelt, Northern Rhodesia* (Lusaka, 1940), 12.

The husband came and was instantly handcuffed, then the compound manager . . . started beating them with a sjambok without reasons. He made both the husband and wife lay down, this made us very angry . . . because he said "come here you all and see what we are doing to your friends." Seeing this, we were very, very angry. We said these people despise us and also our wives, then see these Europeans, the meal they give us . . . does not fill our stomach, yet they make us suffer for it.[32]

Nchanga Africans struck the mine and demanded that the management alter its unfair method of issuing rations. They also urged the district commissioner to flog a white man and a white woman: "Now before we go to work, a European must handcuff his wife and be beaten, both the European lady and her husband together. If you refuse to do this, then do to us things you like. We have finished. We are all Africans."[33] They stayed out for two days, stoned several policemen, broke the arm of a white police officer, and threatened the white compound staff until officials of the government assured them that the assistant compound manager would be prosecuted and that the company would reform its food distribution arrangements. The miners thereafter returned to work, their actions having heightened significantly the atmosphere of tension in which the Copperbelt was then immersed.

In the aftermath of the Nchanga strike, African miners at Mufulira and Nkana had nursed their grievances and had informally made known their intention to stage a walkout if the European demonstrators extracted concessions from the mine managements. Three days before the whites resumed work, notices counseling a strike appeared in the Nkana African compound. Signed by "Katwishi," the Cibemba equivalent of "I don't know," in a translation by an African clerk they read:

My friends, listen to me my fellow workers. I say to you, are our grievances many in number? In what respect do we differ from the police because we are working men and the police are very overbearing towards us. This annoys me greatly and I say, all who feel like me should attack the police. Moreover, this fact embitters my mind. The Europeans left their work without any trouble falling upon them. Cannot a slave, too, speak to the master?

[32] Sec/Lab/132: Elders from Abercorn and Isoka to the District Commissioner, Nchanga, 23 March 1940. The assistant compound manager spent fourteen days in jail and lost his job.

[33] *Ibid.*, letter of 22 March 1940 to the District Commissioner (Nchanga).

See what we did in 1935 without any result . . . because in fact we are their slaves. So if the Europeans receive an increase by leaving their work then we should cease working too. We should not fight or cause disturbances because, if we do, they will bring many machine guns and aeroplanes. In this matter we are in God's care. He really loves us. . . . If you fail in this you are only women. You have defiled your mothers. If you think that they will kill you, not at all. They are only human beings like ourselves.[34]

In light of these occurrences, the governor and the labor commissioner urged the companies to give to their 15,000 African employees a monthly pay increase equal in value to that obtained by the 1,700 Europeans.[35] Instead, on the day that the Europeans returned to work, the four mine managements offered Africans a flat 7 percent temporary wartime cost-of-living bonus that added only 2/6 to their average monthly earnings. The companies refused to alter existing overtime arrangements or to entertain other concessions put forward on behalf of Africans by the commissioner of labor. At Roan and Nchanga, where the whites had not gone on strike, African miners apparently accepted these terms without much thought. At Mufulira and Nkana, however, they derisively rejected the proferred increase and sought by other means to emulate the whites. "We asked for [more] money," a miner later explained, "because we saw Europeans . . . who do not work very hard asking [and getting] . . . an increment."[36] Another African offered a fuller indication of his feelings: "At this time when our King George VI is in the trouble of war, we were very surprised to see the Europeans refuse their work. We know the Europeans are responsible people and we have seen what they have done. To-day they came back to their work very happy and we know they have got what they wanted by refusing to work. We want more money too, and if we do not get it, we too will refuse to work."[37]

In meetings with officials, *ad hoc* representatives of the miners asked to be paid 2/6, 5/-, or even 10/- a day instead of the then

[34] Sec/Lab/136: Diary entries of 24 March 1940.

[35] *Ibid.*, minute by Governor Sir John Maybin, 26 March 1940.

[36] *Ibid.*, letter from Kwafya Kombe, May, 1940.

[37] Quoted in A. T. Williams, "Report on the Strike of African Employees of Rhokana Corporation, Limited, at Nkana and Mindolo. . . ." in *Confidential Reports . . . Concerning the Copperbelt Disturbances of March–April 1940* (Lusaka, 1940), 127.

average of 9d. "Their argument," a white legislator wrote, "was that incompetent white men got paid never less than £30 a month while the black men did all the work—a line of reasoning which had more than a little truth in it."[38] The African representatives resented being insulted by Europeans who "were lazy, did not know the work, and whose presence on the mine was unnecessary." They even offered to demonstrate, by undertaking all of the responsibilities of one shift, that they could produce more ore than Europeans working on a comparable face during the same shift.[39] Expressed in another way, "the feeling [was] that the African [was] doing the European's work and not receiving fair treatment from the Europeans that they have put over them. Their demands are that they should be given more opportunity of showing what they can do with selected supervision." Furthermore, a district commissioner wrote with approval, "they strongly object to the low class and unexperienced Europeans who are put over them underground."[40] The basic issue—which was resolved only in 1963/64—was that of African advancement. All other issues stemmed from it or were, like complaints about the inadequacy of compensation payments for injuries and the rations provided for the wives and families of married workers, subsidiary to it.

Africans successfully struck the Mufulira and Nkana mines on 28–29 March 1940, the two days following the end of the European walkout. Without an overt display of force, the more militant strikers managed effectively to prevent their less-determined colleagues from reporting for work and to call out the non-mine laborers of Kitwe. They also persuaded the district commissioner and the mine manager concerned to close the smelter at Nkana. Yet, although they organized themselves and the strike with dramatic success, they refused to discuss their grievances until the mine managements agreed to raise wages. On 30 March, at a mass meeting on the Mufulira football field, numerous Africans demanded 10/- a day and described how they did all the work for which the Europeans were paid. The district commissioner noted in his diary: "Graphic

[38] Gore-Browne Papers: Stewart Gore-Browne to Dame Ethel Locke-King, 11 April 1940, privately held.
[39] Sec/Lab/137: Report of meetings of 27–28 March 1940. See also W. F. Stubbs, "Report in Diary Form on Native Strike at Mufulira," in *Confidential Reports*, 31; Williams, in *ibid.*, 128.
[40] Sec/Lab/139: W. F. Stubbs, minute of 5 April 1940.

description of the European ganger at work. His abuse of his natives and his laziness and inefficiency. Parables used."[41]

At both mines, the situation reached an early impasse. Africans continued to withhold their labor and, it seems clear, feared that the government would forcefully compel them to return to their jobs. At Mufulira, 7000 Africans even began to sleep out at night on the soccer field because they preferred to "die sitting down and offering no resistance."[42] For their part, Europeans feared that the Africans would attack the white residential areas or would sabotage the mines. The two sides appeared no closer to a resolution of their differences on 2 April, when a number of European officials addressed a large crowd of Africans at Nkana. After an abortive early morning encounter, Colonel Stewart Gore-Browne, the Legislative Council member nominated to represent "native interests," organized another meeting between Africans and Europeans in order to ascertain, once and for all, whether any room for negotiation remained. The more vocal members of the crowd reiterated their demands for 10/- or 5/- a day. One speaker, who dared to suggest that he might accept 3/- a day, was not only shouted down but forced to leave the meeting. After about two hours of what the district commissioner called "unprofitable wrangling," the Europeans agreed that negotiations were impossible.[43] The meeting was, Gore-Browne wrote, "a complete failure." He reported that "A few of the speakers were reasonable, but were howled down. The crowd were not violent but they were certainly not polite, and it would surprise people who only know the obsequious Government employee or house-boy to see what a tough crowd of Bantu, fired by a long-felt grievance, really can be like."[44]

At this point, William John Scrivener, the Nkana compound manager, threatened the strikers. After promising them that the Rhokana Corporation had no intention of increasing its offer of an additional 2/6 a month, he urged them to "decide for themselves" what they wanted to do. But, under no circumstances, he continued, could the Corporation feed the strikers indefinitely. The compound manager proposed to cease the issue of meat and relish at once,

[41] Stubbs in *Confidential Reports,* 33.
[42] *Ibid.,* 35.
[43] Williams in *Confidential Reports,* 140.
[44] Gore-Browne Papers: Gore-Browne to Locke-King, 11 April 1940.

and to halt the distribution of meal two days hence. Thereafter, the Corporation would refuse to provide rations for miners who failed either to return to work or to apply for their discharge. "Mr. Scrivener made it clear," the district commissioner recorded, "that he did not want to force the natives to return to work by stopping their food. He emphasized the fact that they were free to make their own decision."[45] The crowd of strikers received this news in silence. Later that day, however, they stuffed their identity certificates into three large metal drums and carried them to Scrivener's office. Their answer was eloquent; only by presenting his identity certificate could an employee obtain his discharge. That night a majority of the strikers evidently slept on the soccer ground. The compound remained quiet.

The strikers rioted on 3 April. Provoked early that morning by police patrols in the compound and by the stationing of military reinforcements nearby, they were antagonized further by the Corporation's willingness to hold the usual pay-out at the compound office. Although many of those who lined up for their pay were strikers, others no doubt viewed the pay-out suspiciously, and associated it with Scrivener's earlier announcement. They may also have suspected that the Corporation was paying "blacklegs." In any event, after about fifty men had lined up to receive their wages, a large crowd streamed out of the soccer enclosure (one of their leaders supposedly encouraged them in the millennial fashion by shouting that they were leaving Egypt for Canaan, the promised land[46]) and raced toward the compound office. The waiting troops moved to head them off and the police dealt with others who had approached the offices from another direction. The strikers then began indiscriminately to stone the offices, the troops, and the police. The police retaliated by hurling tear-gas bombs at the rioters, but such action by police inexperienced in the use of tear gas served only to infuriate the crowd. It hurled a profusion of bottles, iron bars, bricks, and stones at the defenders and the offices. A number of police retired because of injuries and the defenders retreated toward and onto the verandah of the office. Inside, the noise of falling missiles and shattered glass created a confusion equal to that ex-

[45] Williams in *Confidential Reports*, 140.
[46] Williams in *Confidential Reports*, 159.

perienced at Luanshya in 1935. Finally, after about a half-hour of rioting, Captain Ronald Francis-Jones, the Commander of the Second Northern Rhodesia Regiment, and a European police officer, fired into the crowd when its leaders were within eight yards of the verandah.

After a momentary lull, the crowd of strikers went mad, biting at barbed wire with their teeth. In a mass, they charged the soldiers and hurled rocks as they came. One among them silenced a machine gun with a well-placed brick, and another knocked out the sergeant in charge of the other machine gun. Nevertheless, before Francis-Jones ordered his troops to cease fire, thirteen rioters had been killed (four more died later) and sixty-nine lay wounded.[47] The rioters had, in turn, injured twenty African soldiers. Gore-Browne described the scene: "The place was just a shambles—bandaged and wounded soldiers, broken glass everywhere, shattered doors and windows, huge stones lying about everywhere, white-faced Europeans, and stolid African soldiers standing and sitting about with their rifles in their hands, cartridge cases everywhere, and blood—outside the barbed wire a sullen, angry mob, cursing, cursing, cursing, and shaking their fists."[48]

Once again, only bloodshed had halted the riotous actions of African strikers. On this occasion, however, the miners continued to demonstrate against white authority. On the evening after the shooting, Africans at Nkana continued to stone mine property. They looted and burned the huts of African mine policemen and, early on 4 April, they armed themselves with axes, knives, and spears and pillaged a cafe in the compound. Thereafter, partially because Gore-Browne sensibly prevented troops from being sent into the compound, they began to bury their dead peacefully, and neither at Nkana nor at Mufulira were there further violent demonstrations. The miners began going back to work at Nkana on 6 April and at

[47] See the "Report of Captain Ronald Francis-Jones" and "Minutes of Proceedings of Kitwe Inquest," both in *Confidential Reports*, 7–8, 51–52, 54, 65–66, 75; Sec/Lab/79: Report of Police Superintendent Henry Michael Wilkinson. When the European miners in Mufulira heard that the troops had killed Africans at Nkana, they cheered. "This," said the district commissioner, "would give His Excellency [the Governor] an idea of the type of European miner that we have there." Sec/Lab/79: Letter by Stubbs, 5 April 1940.

[48] Gore-Browne Papers: Gore-Browne to Locke-King, 30 April 1940.

Mufulira two days later. At that point they had obtained no concessions whatsoever.

In order to ensure an impartial assessment of the causes of the riots, the Colonial Secretary compelled a reluctant governor to appoint a commission of inquiry composed of Britons with no previous connection with the Protectorate.[49] With the help of three local assessors, they heard testimony from a variety of knowledgeable African and European witnesses and, at the end of July 1940, recommended a number of measures to ameliorate the conditions under which Africans mined copper. They suggested that the companies boost the wages of their African workers by 2/6 a month in addition to the temporary 2/6 increase already granted, freely issue clothes essential for employment underground, pay overtime rates identical to those enjoyed by whites, periodically revise the cost-of-living bonus, provide a more satisfying diet, build new, more adequate houses for married miners, and devise some form of workable industrial conciliation machinery.[50]

These advances the mine managements and the government by and large implemented. But the companies managed to persuade the Secretary of State and the governor largely to ignore the commission's most important, if delicately phrased, recommendation that African advancement should be encouraged with all deliberate speed.[51] The opponents of advancement argued that the urgent need to produce copper for the war effort outweighed every other consideration, and that the European miners would no doubt refuse to work if dilution of their reservoir of scheduled occupations was threatened. Quite genuinely, the companies also feared that the demand for copper would slacken at the conclusion of hostilities, and that, if they advanced Africans, the mines would then be faced with the difficult task of absorbing returning whites whose jobs had been usurped by miners of another color. The government of Northern Rhodesia therefore decided magisterially that the "revised wage scales to which the Companies have agreed afford very considerable

[49] Sec/Lab/78: The Secretary of State for the Colonies to the Governor, 5 April 1940.

[50] *Commission Report, 1940,* 30–33.

[51] *Ibid.,* 46–47; Sec/Lab/139: Lord Moyne to Governor Maybin, 28 April 1941; Sec/Lab/79: the Secretary of State for the Colonies to Maybin, 22 November 1940, 25 January 1941.

advancement on present limits and offer to Africans reasonable satisfaction during the next few years of their aspirations towards higher remuneration."[52]

Predictably, during the next few years African mineworkers— and industrial laborers generally (in 1943, they struck the Mulobezi Sawmills in Livingstone)—remained dissatisfied. They continued to complain, with abundant justification, that they were often supervised by inefficient whites who received higher rates of pay because of their color. The mine managements still paid bonuses to European miners (who were really supervisors) on the basis of the initiative shown by their African "gangs." Moreover, Africans actually drove locomotives, tapped smelter furnaces, ran casting machines, fitted pipes, blasted underground, and did numerous other jobs for which whites received the credit.[53] In 1942, for example, when the Roan Antelope mine installed its third reverbatory furnace, it placed whites in charge of the African workers who had previously been responsible for operations of the previous two. This departure from an earlier practice suited the European mineworkers, who regarded Africans "as a step below" themselves.[54] It was the type of attitude that caused white officials otherwise sensitive to the needs of Africans to shrink away from the implementation of the recommendations made by the second commission of inquiry. Indeed, the Colonial Office reluctantly permitted the government of Northern Rhodesia, "in view of the overriding need for maximum output of copper during the war," to impose "a standstill arrangement in so far as [African] advancement towards obtaining skilled employment is concerned."[55]

The government of Northern Rhodesia nonetheless sought to stabilize labor relations on the Copperbelt. Rowland S. Hudson, the labor commissioner, gently tried to introduce the concept of collective bargaining into the relations between the mine managements and some of their African employees. He formed and obtained recognition for associations of "boss boys," the African "gang"

---

[52] *Statement by the Government of Northern Rhodesia on the Recommendations of the Report of the Copperbelt Commission, 1940* (Lusaka, 1941), 5.

[53] Sec/Lab/58: See a memorandum by R. S. Hudson, 10 November 1941.

[54] *Ibid.*, Spires to Sir John Waddington, 12 June 1943. Many of the miners had previously been employed in South Africa.

[55] Sec/Lab/58: Oliver Stanley to Sir John Waddington, 28 April 1943.

leaders, but refused to extend the same organizational principle to the mass of workers.[56] Throughout the war, he and the government continued to believe that Africans were not yet "ready" for straightforward unionization. They also resisted attempts on the part of the European union to form a subsidiary in which it could enroll Africans. By so doing, the European unionists thought that they could control the rate of African advancement and, *inter alia*, exercise an all-pervasive influence on postwar mine policies.[57]

By 1945, African mineworkers had noticed few improvements in the conditions surrounding the employment on the mines. Despite the two earlier strikes and a generally heightened appreciation of the crucial role played by Africans in industrial life, neither the mine managements nor the government had acted decisively. The causes of discontent remained largely untouched. They later assisted the rise of a nationalist spirit on the Copperbelt and in Central Africa generally. No one, in fact, expressed the dilemma of the mid-forties better than a British administrator: "It is no use blinking our eyes," he wrote, "to the fact that a strong and efficient colour bar exists at present and to the probability that the Europeans will do their best to preserve it." "Africans," he continued, "are becoming increasingly conscious of it and everything is set for a struggle between the races, which is certain to come eventually, unless an unexpected change in the European attitude takes place or the managements are in a position to resist pressure from the European union."[58]

[56] In late 1943, Henry Malenga meanwhile organized the first Kitwe African Shop Assistants and Tailors Committee.

[57] The discussions are contained in Acc/52/20. See also Baldwin, "Wage Policy," 78–79.

[58] Sec/Lab/71: Cartmel-Robinson to George Beresford Stooke, 2 February 1944.

Chapter VIII

DISCOVERING THEIR VOICE:
THE FORMATION OF
NATIONAL POLITICAL MOVEMENTS

When is Africa going to be freed? Where is that freedom promised to the world, when is it going to come to be enjoyed by everyone living on this earth?

—Charles Wesley Mlanga, during the first meeting of the Nyasaland African Protectorate Council, 28 January 1946

During the early years of World War II, white officials and indigenous leaders both, but for different reasons, sought to involve Africans more intimately than hitherto in the political processes of Nyasaland and Northern Rhodesia. Agitation in India and Palestine influenced many. The spirit of the Atlantic Charter infected the African air, and the promise of the "Four Freedoms" obviously gave hope. Moreover, influential humanitarians and parliamentarians in Britain, and the members of both the permanent and the political staffs of the Colonial Office recognized the possibility that the subject peoples of the empire deserved to obtain a betterment of the conditions to which they had been accustomed. Lord Hailey's investigations into the discharge of Britain's colonial responsibilities, and the passage of the Colonial Development and Welfare Act, echoed Lord Passfield's earlier concerns and indicated a widespread sensitivity to the overseas climate of opinion. Such sentiments helped to shape the report of the Bledisloe Commission and permeated the governmental corridors of Lusaka and Zomba. The lessons of the Copperbelt strikes of 1935 and 1940 also influenced the official mind.

Although Africans wanted political rights and the means of expression for their own sake, Britons hoped to give them no more than the sense of participation in national affairs. At this time few thought of training Africans so that they might some day rule. Instead, the recognition of African frustrations led British officials to create organizational safety valves that would embody the shadow rather than the substance of power. On the Copperbelt, the government of Northern Rhodesia established Urban Advisory Councils as early as 1938. But it allowed them to meet only four times a year. It regarded these councils as the "eyes, ears and mouth" of the district commissioners; their existence would, a provincial commissioner believed, help to check the pace of detribalization.[1] They would "keep the District Commissioner in touch with African opinion . . . act as the mouthpiece between the Government and the Africans . . . advise on matters of African welfare [and] in general . . . discuss administrative, political, economic and social problems and difficulties in so far as they affect the African population . . . outside of the mine compounds."[2]

In practice, the members of the Urban Advisory Councils—all of whom were at first nominees of the Administration—exerted little influence. They accomplished nothing material, failed understandably to represent the interests of their fellows, and, in the end, were bypassed by the mainstream of political change. In Lusaka and Broken Hill, where the government established Urban Advisory Councils in 1943, the composition of their membership remained (except for the district commissioners) the same for five years, during which period the African representatives tediously debated the same kind of petty problems in meeting after meeting. But the governments of Northern Rhodesia and Nyasaland welcomed this absence of real representation. They sincerely believed that the Urban Council system marked a safe forward step along the path of political evolution and that councils designed to direct the current of African grievance down accepted bureaucratic channels would satisfy indigenous aspirations. As late as 1948, a prominent Northern Rhodesian official mistakenly assured his superiors that the formation of councils had prevented the development of a national African

---

[1] Sec/Nat/75: Minutes of the first meeting of the Nkana Native Advisory Committee, 11 November 1938, Lusaka archives.

[2] *Ibid.*, memorandum dated 1 August 1941. See also Gervas Clay, "African Urban Advisory Councils in the Northern Rhodesia Copperbelt," *The Journal of African Administration,* i (1949), 37.

political consciousness. In fact, by then Africans themselves had already begun to organize the movements with which they would eventually grasp the nettle of independence.

THE CREATION OF THE NYASALAND AFRICAN CONGRESS

Several Africans and at least two whites inspired the establishment of the Nyasaland African Congress—the organization that deserves pride of place in the Central African lexicon of modern nationalism. Of its begetters, James Frederick "Piagusi" Sangala remains the most important. A Mang'anja, Sangala was born near the Domasi Presbyterian mission in about 1900. He completed Standard Six (equivalent roughly to an American eighth grade) at Blantyre in about 1921 and, for at least the next five years, taught at Domasi. Thereafter, until about 1930, he earned between 30/- and 75/-a month as a bookkeeper, clerk, and *capitão* for a succession of businessmen. Then, and for the better part of the next twelve years, Sangala typed for and otherwise assisted a succession of provincial and district commissioners in Blantyre. In 1942, he joined the High Court as an interpreter. Throughout this long period of government service, he also participated prominently in the affairs of the Blantyre Native Association and endeavored, as he later wrote, "to struggle for freedom and peace of all."

My first duty was to do such things [that would] . . . cause people to be happy. Due to this aim I do not fear to speak to any person providing it is the truth and this always does not please my friends who suggest that I am a difficult person . . . I am quite experienced in native affairs, I give advices to peoples who seek such advices and do help them whenever possible.[3]

Sangala passionately defended the natural rights of his fellow Africans. He cherished the attributes of dignity, and personally refused either to acknowledge or to accept the air of inferiority that pervaded colonial Nyasaland. Earlier than other nationalists, he recognized that, while they remained disunited and continued to speak in many voices, Nyasas could never hope to claim their independence. In early 1943, after President Roosevelt and Prime

[3] Misc/SA 15: James Sangala, "A Brief History of James Frederick S/O Sangala" (c. 1946), 2, Salisbury archives. Mr. Sangala graciously granted the author a number of interviews in August 1961, and September 1962.

Minister Churchill had enunciated the principles of the Atlantic Charter and the Allies had effectively eliminated the threat of an Axis conquest of Africa, Sangala apparently began to find new organizational ways in which to express his political thoughts. To this end, he either sought or, without soliciting it, received detailed advice from W. H. Timcke, a British South African who had settled in Nyasaland after World War I. Timcke managed the white farmers' cooperative organization in Cholo until it failed in 1929, and for a few years thereafter he grew tobacco on a small farm nearby. During the 1930's, he supposedly built and rented to Asian shopkeepers the unsightly row of *dukas,* or corrugated iron-roofed stores, near Cholo that still carry his name. Later, the Growers' Association permitted him to plant three hundred acres of tea. Nevertheless, financial success continued to elude him.[4] During the 1930's Timcke had established himself as a voluble, cantankerous critic of the government of Nyasaland. On occasion, he accused officials of being unnecessarily cruel to Africans. Contemporaneously, he played a fairly important part in the activities of the settler-dominated Convention of Associations, and for two years he sat in the Legislative Council. There he harried the representatives of the government and campaigned vigorously, if idiosyncratically, for a number of projects dear to the hearts of the European residents of Nyasaland.

The events of World War II, and Timcke's own changing personal fortunes, appear to have turned his intellectual energies in directions that, for him at least, seem to have been new. He sympathized with the Russian defenders against Germany and, in 1943, if not before, Timcke openly championed what he understood to be the Soviet system of government.[5] At about the same time, he evidently began to encourage Sangala's search for new means whereby Africans could collectively express their grievances. During their frequent encounters, Timcke seemingly represented only himself. There is equally no evidence that he either manipulated

[4] A. R. Westrop, letter to the author, 30 August 1962. Westrop was Timcke's neighbor for many years. An interview with G. G. S. J. Hadlow (Cholo, 4 September 1962) corroborated Westrop's report. Timcke, who died with his family when the M.S. *Vipya* capsized on Lake Nyasa in 1946, apparently left no personal papers.

[5] 1a/1449: W. H. Timcke to Mrs. L. Byart, 10 May 1943; Timcke to Mrs. P. Mundy, 11 February 1944, Zomba archives.

Sangala or used him as a front for the advancement of his own increasingly radical views. However, Timcke clearly influenced Sangala, and conceivably may have persuaded him to accelerate the pace of political emergence in Nyasaland.

In August and September 1943, Sangala summoned at least two meetings of the African leaders of Blantyre and Limbe. Although a complete list of those who attended these conferences is unavailable, it seems clear that Sangala consulted Charles Jameson Matinga, Ellerton Mposa, Andrew Jonathan Mponda, Harry R. Tung'-ande, and Sydney B. Somanje—all of whom had been active in the Blantyre Native Association. He also discussed his plans with K. T. Motsete, a Tswana-speaking teacher employed by the Blantyre Secondary School who wrote that Nyasaland was "a bluff [and] indirect rule a farce,"[6] and with Isa Macdonald Lawrence, a Mang'-anja who had long associated himself with African and American Negro freedom movements (in the 1920's the Government of Nyasaland prosecuted Lawrence for receiving copies of Clements Kadalie's *Workers' Herald* and Marcus Garvey's *Negro World*).[7] As a result of these discussions, on 1 October 1943 Sangala penned a "circular letter to all Africans resident in Nyasaland." It proposed the organization of an "association" that would seek effectively to represent their interests. The letter, which was published in two local newspapers, the *Nyasaland Times* and *Nkhani za Nyasaland*, and in the *Bantu Mirror*, a South African periodical, explained that the "chief reason" for forming an association "is because experience has taught that unity is strength."

In the past grievances and other vital matters affecting the country and people have been presented to the government and/or other authorities by local organizations who were interested only in their local worries. It is considered that the time is ripe now for the Africans in this country to strive for unity so as to obtain the greater development of the peoples and country of Nyasaland.

In sum, Sangala appealed to "all Africans and leaders of this country to give their support . . . so that our race should have a place among the civilized."[8]

---

[6] 1a/1449: K. T. Motsete to Margaret H. Ballinger, 29 November 1943.

[7] S 2/50/23: Rex v. Lawrence, 22 September 1926 and S 2/28/21, Zomba archives. Lawrence had also corresponded with Kadalie.

[8] 1a/1423: Circular letter of 1 October, 1943, Zomba archives.

Sangala and his colleagues envisaged the creation of a new representative body, to be called the Nyasaland African Council, "which should be the mouthpiece of the Africans." They presumed that the proposed Council would meet once or twice each year in order to deal with matters affecting "the Protectorate generally." In the reassuring style of the earlier voluntary associations, these leaders also promised that the council would cooperate with the government, with commercial, planter, and missionary bodies, and with Native Authorities "in any matters necessary to speed up the progress of Nyasaland."[9] Perhaps at the urging of Motsete, they specifically welcomed the participation in their affairs of Africans who resided in, but had not been born in Nyasaland. At the same time, they modeled the structure of their proposed council on that of the local Convention of Associations. Sangala and others expected that the various African interest groups already in existence separately would adhere to the Council; it would not, as a matter of principle, enroll individual members. Like the nearly contemporaneous Nigeria National Council (later the National Council for Nigeria and the Cameroons), the Nyasaland Council was designed organizationally as an umbrella under which different constituent bodies could find shelter. Sangala specifically reserved a seat on the executive committee of the Council for representatives of each of these groups.

In the months that followed the publication of the proposals, Sangala and Timcke grew more intimate. Whenever Sangala wrote an important letter destined to be read by European eyes, he sent a draft to Timcke beforehand. A standard refrain, with appropriate word substitutions by Timcke, dates from this period and demonstrates the extent of Timcke's identification with Sangala's cause:

> Men of Nyasa, Unite! Unite!
> You have nothing to lose but your chains.
> Join up, Join up and Fight the Good Fight
> And Freedom shall be [the] least of your gains.
> Bees of Nyasa, wherefore toil?
> For Honey, for Drones to eat?
> Organize, ye sons of the soil,
> Ye will find the honey sweet.

[9] *Ibid.*

Men of Nyasa, why groan and groan?
When the dawn is coming near!
When African Manhood will *act,* not moan,
Yes, act like men without fear.
Africans, Africans, 'tis time to end
The Filth, Poverty, and Misery!
Combine, Combine and let us rend this modern Slavery
Africans, Africans, join and unite!
You've nothing to lose but your chains.
Act all together and defend your right
To be free and use your brains.[10]

Timcke urged Sangala to try to obtain admission to the meetings of the Convention of Associations in order "to hear what is going on." A refusal, he reasoned, would strengthen any case that Sangala might later make to the government on the need for an organization to represent African interests. Timcke suggested that Sangala should protest loudly whenever government officials publicly advertised job vacancies "for Europeans and Asians only." Such advertisements, he felt, "should really ask for applicants as such, and racial discrimination should be avoided."[11] With regard to both immediate and long-range strategies, Timcke urged Sangala to ask Arthur Creech Jones, later the Colonial Secretary in Britain's postwar Labour government, to raise questions in Parliament. Timcke himself even wrote to Creech Jones, expressing his own fears that the British government had secretly decided to amalgamate Nyasaland and the two Rhodesias at the end of the world war. Such a decision, he prophesied, would have disastrous consequences for the African population of Nyasaland.

During these formative months, Sangala also received advice from several other outside sources. On his own initiative, or conceivably as a result of a suggestion by Timcke or Motsete, he wrote to William G. Ballinger, a trade unionist who was then the South African representative of the Friends of Africa, an organization chaired by Creech Jones. Ballinger later became a South African Senator. His wife, Margaret Hodgson Ballinger, who had taught history at the University of the Witwatersrand, represented the indigenous inhabitants of the Eastern Cape Province in the South

[10] 1a/1449: Enclosed in Timcke to Sangala, 29 November 1943.
[11] *Ibid.,* Timcke to Sangala, 2 December 1943.

African House of Assembly. Sangala also corresponded with her. From William Ballinger, Sangala obtained copies of the Constitution of the Friends of Africa, a pamphlet called "The Political Representation of Africans in the Union," the reports of the Friends, their "model rules for unions," their pamphlet on African cooperatives, and the first of several letters of encouragement. "Quite clearly," said Ballinger, "your country is in many respects even more reactionary than the reactionary Union."[12]

James Kanyema, a Nyasa employed in the Brakpan, Transvaal, Native Hospital, exhorted Sangala to follow the principles of "Scientific Socialism" in order to redress the wrongs so long endured by their fellow countrymen. He recommended that the proposed council should meet regularly and that it should agitate for improved educational facilities and a removal of the color bar. He urged it to campaign against any form of miscegenation. Nevertheless, whatever "Scientific Socialism" (the educational slogan of the South African Communist Party) meant in practice, it seems that Sangala paid little attention to the letters from Kanyema. They came unsolicited, and Sangala may not even have possessed any prior knowledge of his new correspondent. On the other hand, although Sangala could claim no previous personal acquaintance with Dr. H. Kamuzu Banda, he welcomed the encouragement and financial support that the latter transmitted to him.[13]

At the time, Dr. Banda practiced medicine in North Shields, England, where he had been living for about a year.[14] As far as can be ascertained, he was born about 1902, near Kasungu in what was then Nyasaland. In late 1915 or early 1916, Banda left his home and joined Hanock Msokera Phiri, an "uncle" who had previously taught at the Livingstonia mission school near Kasungu and had since found employment in Hartley, Southern Rhodesia. In January 1917, both Phiri and Banda moved south to Johannesburg.[15]

[12] *Ibid.*, W. G. Ballinger to Sangala, 19 November 1943. Mrs. Ballinger does not remember Sangala. Letter to the author, 19 August 1964.

[13] See also Richard Gray, *The Two Nations* (London, 1960), 340.

[14] In 1942, Dr. Banda became an assistant medical officer in the Preston Hospital, North Shields. In 1959, after his arrest in Nyasaland, residents of North Shields who had known Dr. Banda rallied to his side, and wrote letters on his behalf to the local newspapers.

[15] Dr. Banda, in a letter to the author, 8 February 1965, says that the 1902 birthdate is "more or less correct." According to the Rev. Mr. Msokera Phiri,

For the next seven or eight years, Banda labored first as an engine-room oiler and later as a clerk and interpreter in the compound manager's office of the Witwatersrand Deep Mine near Boksburg on the Transvaal Reef. Phiri left the same mine in 1918 to teach in a Paris Evangelical Mission school in Livingstone, Northern Rhodesia. In 1922, Banda became a member of the American-run African Methodist Episcopal Church. After Phiri had returned to Nyasaland in order to preach on behalf of the same African Methodist Episcopal Church, Banda evidently made plans to further his own education in the United States. Bishop W. T. Vernon of the African Methodists sponsored Banda's journey to New York in 1925.

In the United States, Banda enrolled in the high school section of Wilberforce Institute, now Central State University in Wilberforce, Ohio. In 1928, after graduating from Wilberforce, where he apparently studied Latin and Spanish and participated in the activities of the debate society, Banda enrolled as a premedical student in Indiana University. On his personnel blank he listed Bishop Vernon as his guardian, and admitted that his health had

---

whose complete testimony Dr. Banda rejects totally, Banda was born in February 1898. Phiri, then a teacher at the Livingstonia mission school near Kasungu, instructed his "nephew" in Standards II and III. From Dr. George Prentice, a Scottish missionary, Phiri says that he had also learned the rudiments of first aid. At the beginning of World War I, he left the mission and found employment near Hartley, Southern Rhodesia. Banda joined his uncle there in late 1915 or early 1916; and, in January 1917, both Phiri and Banda—according to Phiri's account—moved south to a coal mine near Dundee, Natal. Banda pumped water and Phiri worked underground. But they both, says Phiri, soon tired of these occupations and began to travel north to Johannesburg. On their way they stopped in Charlestown, a small settlement on the railway between Natal and the Transvaal. There they met an eccentric retired Scot named MacArthur who claimed to have lived in Blantyre, David Livingstone's birthplace. MacArthur evidently took a fancy to Phiri and Banda. When he learned that both could read the Bible, he provided them with room and board. He also paid their railway fares to Johannesburg and, when Phiri and Banda took leave of their benefactor, MacArthur evidently urged Banda to educate himself and then return home to help his own people. Hanock Msokera Phiri, interview with the author, 14 September 1962. Mr. Phiri was born about 1884 and, sometime thereafter, baptized by the Rev. Dr. Robert Laws. See also NN 1/20/3, Zomba archives. For additional, conflicting accounts, see T. Cullen Young and H. Kamuzu Banda (trans. and eds.) *Our African Way of Life* (London, 1946), 7–8; Clyde Sanger, *Central African Emergency* (London, 1960), 186–187; Interview with John Freeman (B.B.C., unpub. transcript, 22 April 1960).

suffered "due to change of climate."[16] According to the University transcript, Banda performed creditably in all his courses. Mrs. W. N. Culmer, over whose garage Banda lived for a semester, recalled that young Banda "was very smart," but that he "didn't have a great deal of personality." She explained that he "wasn't unfriendly, he just had nothing to say."[17] Several of his teachers remembered Banda as a serious, intense student who sat in the front row of the Indiana classrooms in order not to miss any part of the lectures.[18] In any event, after spending four semesters and a summer-school session at Indiana, Banda transferred to the University of Chicago, where he majored in history and obtained a Bachelor of Philosophy degree in late 1931. He remained at its graduate school in order to study chemistry for an additional three months. Thereafter, he attended Meharry Medical College in Nashville, Tennessee, a leading Negro institution which granted him a doctorate of medicine in 1937. He graduated with an over-all average of 82.24 percent, including final year grades of 99.45 in surgery, 90 in obstetrics and medical jurisprudence, 89 in orthopedics, 88.5 in applied anatomy, and 88 in pathology and preventive medicine. He was least proficient in "tuberculosis."[19]

After receiving his medical degree, Dr. Banda determined to obtain the appropriate British medical cachet. In due course, and with financial support from three Scottish ladies, he enrolled in the Edinburgh Royal College Medical School, where, in 1941, he obtained the medical qualifications L.R.C.P. (Edin.), L.R.C.S. (Edin.), and L.R.F.P.S. (Glasg.). He later studied tropical medicine at the University of Liverpool.

Throughout these student years, Banda attempted to remain abreast of events in his homeland. He corresponded with relatives and many leading African spokesmen. In Edinburgh, he also moved in church circles. Scottish missionaries who had served in Nyasaland

[16] The author is indebted to Dr. George Brooks for information derived from Dr. Banda's files in the Records Office of Indiana University.

[17] Quoted in John McAuliff, "Fiery African Leader Seemed 'Quiet, Retiring' to Local Woman," *Indianapolis Times,* 11 September 1961.

[18] See Daniel James, "Little Did One Realize Student Would Become African Leader," *Indiana Alumni Magazine* (October 1960), 12–13.

[19] Data from official transcript. When he was at Meharry College, Banda received some financial support from Walter B. Stephenson, then the president of the Delta Electric Company of Marion, Indiana.

sought his company; a few befriended him. In 1939, this happy combination of circumstances again brought him to the attention of the government of Nyasaland. Before the outbreak of World War II, it agreed to send Chief Mwase Kasungu to England so that he might help the faculty of the London University School of Oriental and African Studies to analyse the Nyanja language. The Rev. Mr. T. Cullen Young, who had served the Livingstonia mission, recommended that Dr. Banda should become the chief's advisor. "He . . . is not only acquainted with London," Young wrote, "but is a very sound fellow of good judgement and character."[20] Mwase later said that he owed his favorable impression of England to Dr. Banda. "In two or three of his letters to me before I came here, Dr. Banda told how kind and friendly the Europeans were to him in Britain. I did not quite believe then, as I did not then think a European could be so as kind and respectful to an African as the letters suggested. But I can now see that Dr. Banda was quite right."[21] And Young explained that Mwase had been well received due to "his own natural wisdom and poise [as well as] the guidance he has received . . . from Dr. . . . Banda."[22] Politically, the months with Mwase later proved important both to Dr. Banda and to Nyasaland. The experience also helped to turn Banda's own immediate attentions thither. From about this time, he exerted an influence of some importance to the pace of political emergence in his homeland.

These various streams of somewhat divergent influence converged to form the first modern Central African political organization. In January 1944, Sangala convened and presided over a major session of the *ad hoc* executive committee of what was now called the Nyasaland African Association. (The government, which had been thinking about the need for African political representation, preempted the use of the word "council" for its own undertaking, and forced Sangala and his colleagues to use the traditional appellation.) Matinga, Lawrence, Tung'ande, and Somanje again joined Sangala. R. J. Kabambe, G. Ndovi, C. B. Kachingwe, G. G. Makon-

[20] 1a/468: T. Cullen Young to Dr. Bargery (SOAS), 11 July 1939, Zomba archives.
[21] *Ibid.*, Mwase to the Provincial Commissioner (Northern Province), 18 August 1939.
[22] *Ibid.*, T. Cullen Young to the Chief Secretary (Nyasaland), 22 January 1940.

yola, L. K. Mkomba, and K. Matupa also took part in the discussions. Together they ratified Sangala's conception of the role that would be played by the association. In a significant policy pronouncement that owed some of its inspiration to Timcke, the committee demanded that the government should provide Nyasas with the best possible educational facilities, and employ qualified teachers (they rejected the "usual evangelists"), offer opportunities for advancement to responsible positions in the civil service, and pay salaries commensurate with those "at present enjoyed by Europeans." They wanted the government to build modern houses and to sponsor the kind of recreational experiences that would prevent young Nyasas from spending their free hours in community beer halls. They demanded the right to organize trade unions. They asked that the lands that Europeans had "taken from us," and that still remained undeveloped, should be restored. "We starve," they said, "because of the unwillingness and selfishness on the part of those responsible."

In a forward-looking departure from the traditional search for economic betterment, the committee forthrightly decided that Africans should henceforth occupy the majority of the seats on all of the bodies that advised the Government. They totally rejected the continued representation of "African interests" in the Legislative Council by a nominated missionary. They condemned missionaries in general for their prejudice and their unwillingness to share power and authority with African clergy and laymen. For such reasons they declared their inability to accept anything short of direct African participation in the Legislative Council. "We feel," they wrote, that "the policy of the missionaries as lately demonstrated does not justify us to accept that our interests should continue to be represented by [missionaries who] have introduced colour prejudice because of our ignorance. . . . There are many Africans in our ranks and files capable of representing us."

The committee, like earlier African bodies, stood unequivocally against either the amalgamation or the federation of Nyasaland with any of the other British dependencies in Central and East Africa. "We totally refuse to amalgamate," they wrote, "until we have been given at least 99% of the rights we are entitled to enjoy in the administration of our own country."

Sangala and his fellow nationalists wanted "whatever is good for Europeans and Asians. . . ." They unconsciously echoed Chilembwe:

In conclusion, we beg to state that we have served loyally in any war which His Majesty . . . has asked our boys to serve and we think this is the time that we should ask for justice [so] that our boys and girls may enjoy the freedom of being part and parcel . . . of a British empire. . . . We cannot go on allowing our country becoming a labour centre for the neighbouring territories. We must have justice done. . . . We ask you to give us the right to speak for our people be it in the mission councils or in the bodies that govern our country. . . . We have paid the price and we must be compensated accordingly. . . . It is not a question of being ungrateful but seventy years of patience is a very long time to wait.[23]

A few weeks after the committee had issued its manifesto and had met publicly, if abortively, with Bishop Frank Thorne of the Universities' Mission—their ostensible representative on the Legislative Council—Sangala realized that police detectives had placed him and his colleagues under surveillance. He may also have suspected that his incoming and outgoing mail was being read. He therefore tried to remove whatever anxieties the administration might have entertained. "We have the honour," he wrote to the Chief Secretary, "to assure the Government that it will have nothing to fear from us."[24] But the government collectively was not so much fearful as uncertain whether or not the time had come to crush the new association. Fortunately, Sangala had worked for a number of influential administrators, many of whom described him either as a "nice type" or as a "peculiar, however, charming," fellow.[25] They refused to believe that the Blantyre intelligentsia was exclusively responsible for the apparent agitation. Moreover, M. E. Leslie, who had then attained a position of administrative prominence, wrote vigorously in defense of African aspirations and echoed many of the sentiments that he shared with such imperial figures as Lord Hailey.[26] Of even greater significance, the acting

[23] 1a/1423: Minutes of a meeting of a committee of the Nyasaland African Association, 21 January 1944.
[24] 1a/1423: Sangala to the Chief Secretary, 24 February 1944.
[25] Ibid., Cecil Barker, minute, 5 March 1944; W. L. Jennings, quoted in "Brief History of James Frederick S/O Sangala."
[26] 1a/1394: Leslie to the Chief Secretary, 5 February 1940, Zomba archives.

governor tended to agree that repression would serve no lasting purpose. Instead, he thought that it would still be possible to "train" the educated Africans "the way we want them." He thought the "best way out" would lie in the establishment of provincial councils composed of chiefs, tribal elders, and the more mature members of the intelligentsia. Like Leslie, he sincerely believed that the root of the trouble was simply "the lack of contact between Europeans and educated natives."[27] The government had, however, already lost the initiative to Sangala and Timcke.

In May 1944, before the administration could even select the members of the provincial councils, Sangala convened a meeting of what had now become the Nyasaland African Congress. Perhaps at Lawrence's insistence, the executive committee had meanwhile adopted the name "Congress" because it implied an organization of importance greater than another "association." Lawrence may also have appreciated the implicit connection with the South African and Indian congresses. To an audience of about ninety chiefs and commoners he, as the chairman *pro tem*, and Sangala, the acting secretary, explained that the Congress would stand in respect to other African organizations as the Convention of Associations stood with respect to the various settler groups. It would be the "mother body." On the other hand, they continued to assume that the various African district associations and societies would function on a local basis. "The Congress," Lawrence told the meeting, "will only be concerned with major problems which affect the Protectorate generally. The first duty it has to do is to bring up unity between the chiefs and their people and break down the present differences [between them]. To do such things will mean to remove away misunderstandings between the black and white so that the two races should cooperate in doing things that are for the uplift and development of the country."[28]

Lawrence, who delivered the keynote speech, feared that his listeners insufficiently appreciated the reasons why a new national organization would prove beneficial to their interests. He recognized that many leading Africans were conservatives at heart. He knew that the Congress, if it were to make an early impact on the

---

[27] *Ibid.*, the Acting Governor to the Acting Chief Secretary, 18 April 1944.
[28] 1a/1423: Minutes of a meeting held in Blantyre, 20 May 1944.

government, would necessarily need to win the overwhelming support of traditional-thinking Nyasas as well as their intellectual counterparts. In appealing to them both, he neatly captured the tone and the spirit of the political times:

You will see that we are now coming to one union which is always strength. Without unity we cannot do anything better, neither can we have a word to our government and other authorities; and we cannot even lay good foundations for our future generations. All the Africans now should take the responsibility to see that we must keep in store something better and valuable for our coming generations; so we must not be selfish; in all our undertakings let us hold on [to the] one good thing which will be the heir of our children hereafter. . . .

Our soldiers have fought with the King's men all over chasing away enemies. When the enemies shall be defeated, we feel certain that whatever privileges will be given to the victorious big nations of the world, the Africans will also have a share, and once the peace is won, we shall all look forward to fight the daily war of ignorance, suspicion, poverty and disease. . . .

We should defeat these things and not put off for tomorrow what we can claim today . . . the time is flying so we must also learn to fly.[29]

Lawrence, Sangala, and the other founders of Congress believed that unity automatically would mean strength. Implicitly they jumped to the understandable, facile conclusion that the government would respect the voice of a national African movement more readily than it would listen to the complaints of the older, fragmented associations. In response to Lawrence's speech, Village Headman Musa, of Michiru, reiterated the expressed views of Chiefs Kadewere and Nchema. Congress, they thought, would soon "be regarded as a lake where various streams flow in."[30] But these proved unwarranted assumptions. The gradual formation of the Congress widened rather than narrowed the gap of sympathy between the Government of Nyasaland and its politically conscious subjects.

Throughout the African winter months of 1944, a steering committee prepared for what came to be regarded as the inaugural meeting of the Congress. During July and August, Timcke cor-

29 *Ibid.*
30 *Ibid.*

responded frequently with Sangala and Matinga. To both he urged "the absolute necessity for Africans to be on all public bodies that affect native interests." Kenya, he pointed out, had already appointed Eliud Mathu, an African, to its Legislative Council. "You must press," he wrote to Sangala, "for direct representation on the Legislative Council" and for promotion by merit.[31] He also deprecated the new provincial councils and advised Sangala to regard their members, most of whom were chiefs, as paid agents of the administration.

At the October 1944 inaugural meeting, the speeches and resolutions generally followed the lines suggested by Timcke, Banda, Sangala, and Lawrence. After delegates from the seventeen associations that had already affiliated to the Congress (they thereafter regarded themselves as branches) had elected as president-general Levi Mumba, the founder and leader of a number of early associations, he opened the meeting with a long address on the heritage and future importance of Congress.[32] Two hundred fifty Africans heard him say little that was novel. Yet, the tenor of the era emboldened his efforts. In terms more strident than ever before, he denounced the continued "exploitation" of Africans by Europeans. Africans desired, he said, all of the attributes of full citizenship and, in a perhaps conscious echo of Roosevelt, "opportunities for all regardless of race, colour, or creed." In words that almost exactly matched those used by Timcke, he demanded the representation of Africans in the Legislative Council by Africans. And together, he

[31] 1a/1449: Timcke to Sangala, 15 and 25 July 1944.

[32] Charles Matinga became vice-president general; Charles Wesley Mlanga, editor of the local newspaper *Zo-Ona*, secretary-general; James Dixon Phiri, clerk in the Public Works Department, assistant secretary-general; H. R. Tung'ande, second assistant secretary-general; Isa M. Lawrence, treasurer-general; and H. B. Dallah, assistant treasurer-general. Sangala, whom the Government had transferred away from Blantyre, was unable to attend the meeting. The executive committee of the Congress included A. D. Mbebuwa, of Blantyre; George Simeon Mwase, the politician and biographer of Chilembwe, Lilongwe; B. R. K. Namboyah, Mlanje; Rafael B. Mbwana, Likoma; Charles Chinula, the separatist sect and association leader, Mzimba; M. I. Chowe, Fort Johnston; A. R. Gondwe, Karonga; Garnett Chenyama, Malimba; I. C. Ndiwo, Dowa; J. C. C. Chirwa, Zomba; G. N. Ndovi, Livingstonia; T. W. Grant, Limbe; Chakuwama Mlolo, Chiromo; and Alexander Phambala, Cholo. In addition, other delegates represented the Mombera Dairies Co-operative Society, the Mlanje Foodstuff Growers' Association, the Nyasaland Railways Social and Recreation Association, and the Southern Rhodesia Bantu Congress.

and the many delegates expressed the hope that the Governor would, on their behalf, inform the Secretary of State for the Colonies of their overwhelming opposition to amalgamation.

In a major enunciation of policy, they condemned the color bar. They deplored the restrictions which reduced Africans to a state of social inferiority and humbly requested the government to permit Africans to enter movie theaters, either to distill their own liquor or to buy European-produced spirits, to purchase goods from European-owned stores without being forced to ask for them through a hatchway, and to wear shoes and hats in the presence of whites. They also wanted to be paid according to their ability and not exclusively in terms of their color.[33]

By the time of the next meeting of the executive committee, in April 1945, the leading members of Congress had realized that their efforts of the previous year had accomplished little. What irritated and dismayed them most was the government's refusal either to answer their many requests or even to note their various resolutions. By then, too, the settlers had for the first time begun electing representatives to the Legislative Council. Distraught, and saddened considerably by the recent deaths of both Mumba and Lawrence, the members of Congress resolved, at Matinga's suggestion, to redouble their efforts to obtain a place in the Legislative Council. They also drew up a constitution, which formally listed the aims of the Congress, the short name of which was to be Nacre—or mother of pearl —because if associations were precious, then "the one which mothers them all may rightly be NACre."

To work for the unity of the aborigines of Nyasaland, to secure mutual understanding between tribes and the several independent organizations or associations . . . to air native opinion . . . in order that a well-digested native opinion may be . . . ascertainable by the government . . . to encourage thrift and cleanliness . . . to record all grievances . . . to lift up the race spiritually and morally . . . to agitate and advocate by just and constitutional means against any discriminatory legislation.[34]

Like the earlier associations, the Congress had not yet found a modern political voice. It still felt constrained to seek official bless-

[33] Minutes printed in a pamphlet entitled *African Congress: First Annual Meeting* (Blantyre, 1944), 16.
[34] 1a/1423: Minutes of meeting of 1 April 1945 and printed constitution.

ing for its proposals. For the accomplishment of social and political change, it looked to the government; in general, it continued to operate openly within the colonial frame of reference. It eschewed subversion. In May 1945, for example, the Congress submitted a long and detailed memorandum to the Chief Secretary. Imaginatively phrased, it suggested that the government should assume from the missions the entire responsibility for the provision of African education, that the government should pay higher salaries to teachers and, in general, that the government should use every means at its disposal to improve the quality and scope of the existing school system. Once again, the Congress demanded the direct representation of Africans in the Legislative Council. How, it asked, could the government understand the wishes of two million of its subjects without deigning to consult them? "Sir," the memorandum continued, "is it not in the interest of the government that the views of the African people should be known and their problems interpreted in the Legislative Council?"[35]

Matinga, who had become the acting president-general of the Congress, requested a formal discussion of these matters with the governor. With some reluctance, the latter agreed to receive a delegation. But when it arrived, he gave the Congressmen little satisfaction. He dismissed their educational suggestions on financial grounds. In detail, however, he made a few concessions. He also indicated that he would soon create an African Protectorate Council to which the members of the three provincial councils could send representatives. He also implied that in time he might include a member of the Protectorate Council in the Legislative Council. In the meanwhile, it remained his own responsibility, he said, to safeguard the interests of the indigenous inhabitants of the Protectorate.

The leaders of the Congress gradually grew both disillusioned with the pace of change and more outspoken in their criticism of a wide range of racial iniquities. The Rev. Mr. Charles Chinula, who became its vice-president general, drew attention to the dangers of miscegenation. He wanted the government to protect African women. "Europeans call Africans 'boy,'" he said, "but have not given any name to an African woman . . . although they are taken

[35] Ibid., memorandum of 15 May 1945.

to bed to stay with them."[36] Others observed with alarm that Europeans had removed Africans from the shores of Monkey Bay so that they could build a hotel there, and that they had acquired a monopoly of the local commercial fishing rights. They noted, again with some consternation, that, although Africans had repeatedly reiterated their opposition to any form of amalgamation, the British government had recently created a Central African Council to deal with matters of technical interest to the two Rhodesias and Nyasaland. They were frightened that the Council might lead to a variation of "closer association" by which Nyasas would "lose what few privileges [they] have." For these several reasons, and because of their continuing irritation over the color bar (Sangala spoke forcefully to this point), they reluctantly decided to send a delegate to the Fifth Pan-African Congress, then meeting in Manchester, and to strengthen their ties to the British Labour Party and the Fabian Colonial Bureau. In these circumstances, the leaders of the Nyasaland Congress (of whom Chief Mwase was now one) naturally turned to Dr. Banda, then practicing medicine in Harlesden, London. Perhaps at his own suggestion, they officially appointed him their overseas representative, and charged him with the advancement of the interests of his fellow countrymen.[37]

Dr. Banda took an increasingly active interest in the affairs of the Congress. He began regularly to advise its leaders from afar, and to contribute small but useful sums of money toward the cost of its activities. Early in 1946, he persuaded Matinga to reconsider the way in which the Congress was then organized. He suggested that it should begin to centralize the collection and expenditure of dues and other revenues. If not, he said, Congress would remain privy to the whims of its various branches. Dr. Banda had, in fact, appreciated the Congress' main source of weakness. It possessed no central exchequer; in order to cover costs, each of the individual branches contributed a small fraction of its own revenues to the governing executive. Each branch spent its own funds without

[36] 1a/1424: Minutes of the Second Annual Conference at Lilongwe, 16–19 October 1945, Zomba archives.

[37] *Ibid.*, cablegram from Charles Matinga to Kamuzu Banda, 16 October 1945. See also George Padmore (ed.), *History of the Pan-African Congress* (London, 1963), 10, 71. At this time, Dr. Banda was a member of the Willesden branch of the British Labour Party.

reference to the needs or obligations of the Congress as a whole. And, in the past, the Blantyre branch had alone supported most of the activities of the Congress. These financial arrangements clearly clouded the independence of the Congress, but it was only with great reluctance that the executive committee finally agreed to accept Dr. Banda's suggestion that the treasurer-general should "keep all the Congress money in one bag" and thereby give their association an important measure of control over its diverse, practically autonomous affiliates.[38] In April 1946, at the same meeting of the executive committee, a number of the delegates praised Dr. Banda for his efforts on their behalf. B. R. K. Namboyah, the representative of the Mlanje Foodstuff Growers' Association, warned Dr. Banda to "try his best to take great care of his life that he must live long for the good of our country." McKinley Qabaniso Y. Chibambo, then representing Lilongwe and later, after independence, a Member of Parliament from Mzuzu, indicated how grateful he and his Lilongwe association were to Dr. Banda.

During the next six months, Matinga and Banda, in their separate spheres, acted to further the aims of the Congress. Matinga traveled to South Africa, where he tried to persuade Dr. A. B. Xuma of the South African National Congress to sponsor a Pan-African Congress. But the latter refused.[39] Matinga also visited Nyasas in Cape Town, Johannesburg, and Bulawayo, and encouraged his fellow countrymen to increase their financial and spiritual support for their Congress at home. Meanwhile Banda, with assistance from the Fabian Bureau, lobbied Members of Parliament and persuaded several of their number to raise questions about Nyasaland in the House of Commons. He also submitted a memorandum to the Colonial Secretary that set out at some length the position that the executive committee of the Congress had taken in Lilongwe. After the governor of Nyasaland had refused to appoint a commission to investigate the African educational system, Banda raised this issue in London. In order to bolster his efforts,

[38] *Ibid.*, minutes of the Second Annual Executive Committee Conference, 20 April 1946. At this time, the total expenditure of the Congress amounted to little more than £ 100 a year.

[39] In his negotiations with Dr. Xuma, Matinga received important assistance from Martin Kaunda and Champion Ngoma, two Nyasas then studying at Fort Hare Native College, and from J. G. Scott Chingattie, a student at the Jan Hofmeyr School of Social Work.

Matinga tried to obtain the funds with which to send a deputation to London. But, even though the Congress inherited £200 from Timcke's estate, it could not immediately afford such representations.

The annual Congress meeting of September 1946, at Salima, largely concerned itself with administrative reorganization. Dr. Banda had suggested that the Congress should employ a full-time organizer, for whose salary he would be responsible. George Simeon Mwase agreed to build an office in Lilongwe. A committee of the Congress accepted these offers, and urged that such a person be appointed forthwith. The committee recommended that the organizer should earn a total yearly salary of £63. But the delegates to the general meeting voted overwhelmingly against such an appointment. Unlike the United Gold Coast Convention, which only a few months later would agree to employ Kwame Nkrumah as its first full-time paid secretary, the Nyasas evidently feared such a professional, indeed radical, departure from their usual political round. Instead, they resolved to ask Dr. Banda merely to buy a typewriter for the use of the part-time secretaries. At Salima, the Congress had not yet reached the point of political "take-off." Their leaders still hoped, albeit with somewhat less confidence, that patient nagging of the government, and the careful drafting of memorials and petitions, would ultimately provide them with their rightful share of the political kingdom. They were not yet in a position to appreciate the future extent of their struggle; nor could they realize the need for professional efficiency if they were ever to achieve the political freedom that, however vaguely, they had begun to seek. They lacked the necessary vision. Of even greater importance, they lacked both vigorous personal leadership and the necessary political catalyst of events. These prerequisites appeared later. In the interim, the Congress continued to affect the course of Nyasan life only marginally.

THE REPRESENTATION OF AFRICAN INTERESTS IN NORTHERN RHODESIA

In Northern Rhodesia, the government seized the political initiative from Africans before they themselves had begun to organize nationally. On the one hand, Colonel (later Sir) Stewart Gore-Browne, the Legislative Council member nominated to represent African interests, took his role seriously, He spoke Cibemba and

traveled incessantly, everywhere seeking to understand what his
African constituents wanted and cared about. Formally, in meetings
of the Legislative Council, and informally, in private sessions with
the governor and other officials, he voiced and sought redress for
African grievances. Long before others appreciated the extent of
their aspirations, he urged the government to give Africans a
greater sense of participation in the affairs of their country. He realized that the views of educated Africans deserved equal recognition
with those of the chiefs and elders who generally accepted the
maintenance of the colonial *status quo*. And to some extent, Africans understood how well—within the context of European overrule—Gore-Browne cared for their interests during the early 1940's.
On the other hand, in order to provide a further institutional safety
valve, the Secretary for Native Affairs, as a direct result of a suggestion persuasively made by Gore-Browne, created new regional
councils.[40] After 1943, these new councils, and the pre-existing
Urban Advisory Councils, together comprised a system that permitted a number of African leaders to feel a sense of involvement,
however marginal, in the management of their own country. While
members of similar councils in Nyasaland could discuss only those
items placed on their agenda by European provincial commissioners
in consultation with the Secretariat in Zomba, Northern Rhodesians
could and did publicly raise embarrassing questions, many of
which were later omitted from the *Proceedings* published at the
conclusion of each council session.

In official eyes, the provincial councils (as the regional councils
came to be called) consciously constituted a form of insurance
against the growth of indigenous nationalism. By creating such
councils and giving their members a measure of verbal freedom,
the Government of Northern Rhodesia believed that, together with
the urban assemblies, they would provide an alternative sufficiently
meaningful to satisfy the political passions of refractory Africans.
At first these assumptions proved superficially correct. A number of
the more articulate educated Africans, many of whom had earlier
played such important roles in the welfare associations, accepted
nomination to the provincial councils and for a time gave its mechanism a fair trial. Unlike the Nyasas—some of whom also partici-

[40] Gore-Browne, in Northern Rhodesia, *Legislative Council Debates,* 43
(1942), cc. 150–154.

pated in the provincial councils of their own protectorate—Northern Rhodesians refrained from immediately creating their own new vehicle of political expression.

The provincial councils, of which there were at first six in Northern Rhodesia, began to meet in 1943–44. Their memberships included a majority of chiefs and other rural personalities of importance, and purposely over-represented country interests while devaluating the opinions of those who dwelled in towns. Provincial commissioners presided, and the Secretary for Native Affairs, district commissioners, and Gore-Browne often attended. According to the official pronouncements read at the first meeting of each of the councils, the government expected members to inform Gore-Browne of the matters to which Africans thought he should pay attention. A provincial commissioner also thought that the councils had been devised in order "to enable the representatives of the various Native Authorities to hear . . . what the younger and more educated people [were] thinking."[41] The government did not, however, envisage that it would ever regard the deliberations of these councils as other than advisory. They performed no statutory or administrative functions, and remained forums for the expression of feelings and grievances only.

Africans welcomed any opportunity to criticize the policies of the government and the machinery of the color bar. They complained about European proprietors who refused to permit Africans to enter their stores. They demanded that the government should prohibit the common European use of the word "boy" to describe a mature African. Headman Chitulika claimed that Europeans refused to regard Africans as human: "Africans are asking when they will stop smelling in the nostrils of Europeans. When an African asks a European for a lift in his car he is made to sit in the back and not in front with the driver."[42] At a Western Provincial Council meeting, Dauti Yamba, a schoolteacher from Luanshya, and Ashton M. Kabalika, from Chingola, denounced David Welensky, whose brother Roy later became the Prime Minister of the Federation of Rhodesia and Nyasaland, for publicly referring to Africans by the

[41] Sec/Nat/103: Minutes of the meeting of the Northern Province (Northern Areas) Regional Council, 22 May 1944, Lusaka archives.

[42] *Ibid.*, minutes of the first meeting of the Northern Province (Central Areas) Regional Council, 19 May 1944.

pejorative sobriquet "Jim Fish." "Could a fish open a door," Kabalika asked, "could he be sent to fetch a cup, could he be asked to
do any work that a human being could?" Yamba said that "members
of the ruling race should show Africans a little honour, to recognise
that they were human beings and, in fact, equal in creation."[43]
Later, Isaac Potiphara, of Ndola, summed up the feelings of his
many fellow councilors throughout Northern Rhodesia: "We have
seen that there is only one great thing and that is the colour bar."[44]
Councilors also spoke deprecatingly of fishing regulations, of laws
framed to control land usage, of urgently required schools and hospitals, of divorce laws, and of a number of other matters on which
they thought that the government should take note of their views.
The members of the various councils constantly raised their voices
in one other major refrain: we want no part, they said, of amalgamation with Southern Rhodesia in any form. Each of the councils
voted yearly against amalgamation. Chief Nkolemfumu early expressed their faith in the British system: "If we constantly say we
do not want amalgamation we shall not have it thrust upon us."[45]

The government of Northern Rhodesia paid little official attention
to the sentiments expressed by the members of provincial councils.
Neither with regard to the major issues—like "amalgamation"—nor
the many minor ones—like forestry regulations—did it try to understand or deal sympathetically with African fears and complaints. The
attitude of its own representatives toward criticisms of the color bar
manifested an over-all inability to appreciate the African point of
view. With regard to African objections about the use of the word
"boy," the Secretary for Native Affairs opined that "many Africans
worr[ied] too much about these things."[46]

Unable to obtain any appreciable amelioration of their grievances
through the agency of provincial councils, educated Africans re-
vived the urban and rural welfare associations that had played such
a major part in their previous political life. During the years im-

[43] Sec/Nat/102: Minutes of the Fourth Meeting of the Western Province
Regional Council, 8 October 1945, Lusaka archives. David Welensky was a
prominent trade unionist.
[44] Ibid., minutes of the Sixth Meeting, 9–10 July 1947.
[45] Sec/Nat/103: Minutes of the First Meeting of the Northern Province
(Central Areas) Regional Council, 19 May 1944.
[46] Ibid., minutes of the Fourth Meeting of the Northern Province (Central
Areas) Council, 20–21 April 1947.

mediately after the 1940 strike, these organizations provided an alternative channel of communication for those who found themselves either frustrated or disillusioned by the limited opportunities for expression available through the different advisory councils.[47] The Lusaka African Welfare Association, for example, began once again to meet frequently in 1943. Its members accused the compound manager, a man named Nichols, of introducing the racial practices of South Africa into Northern Rhodesia. They said that he had cut down their clotheslines, grazed his cattle on their maize fields, and mistreated Africans at the town beer hall. They sought service without reference to color from butchers, banks, the local mill, and the railways. At one meeting, they urged the town of Lusaka to provide, with its profits from the municipal beer hall, a daily ration of hot soup to children of impoverished parents. They asked for the services of a full-time welfare officer. In sum, the amended constitution of the Lusaka association affirmed that its aims were "to protect and further African interests generally."[48]

By this time the several associations regarded themselves, and not the provincial councils, as the legitimate voices of the African community of Northern Rhodesia. "I would like this association to make it clear to the authorities," a Lusaka spokesman said, "that it is the mouthpiece of the people in the whole of the Lusaka district and that it does not represent individuals, but the community as a whole."[49] After meeting with a number of these societies and listening to their arguments, Gore-Browne had reported that thinking Africans throughout the towns wanted to form a Congress on Southern Rhodesian and Nyasaland lines. He annoyed the administration by suggesting that the members of the so-called welfare societies were really more progressive than their counterparts who sat on the urban and provincial councils. At a conference of provincial commissioners, he even proposed the merger of the urban advisory councils and the town associations. He reasoned that the latter represented the opinion of educated, dissatisfied Africans more accurately than the former, and that officials dominated the proceed-

---

[47] A. L. Epstein, *Politics in an Urban African Community* (Manchester, 1958), 67–68, makes this point with reference to Luanshya.

[48] ACC/65/1/1: Amended constitution of the Lusaka African Welfare Association, 1945, Lusaka archives.

[49] *Ibid.*, Joseph Y. Mumba, quoted in the minutes of a committee meeting of 10 February 1946.

ings of the former.[50] But neither the assembled provincial commissioners—who nevertheless decided that they should not define the functions of the welfare societies because the societies had been privately constituted—the Secretary for Native Affairs, nor the Chief Secretary could agree. Instead, they decided to try to eliminate the renewed influence of the voluntary associations.

The "Elwell Incident" provided a convenient pretext for such action. In 1944, the Colonial Office arranged for the British National Assistance Board to second Archibald H. Elwell, a mature, forthright member of its administrative establishment, to the Government of Northern Rhodesia. The Colonial Office posted Elwell to Kitwe, on the Copperbelt. He became Northern Rhodesia's first official social welfare officer. Elwell soon demonstrated a warm sympathy for Africans individually and for African aspirations generally. In particular, he befriended Jason Achiume, who then worked for the Kitwe Township Management Board as a "welfare assistant" and, in his own time, helped to run the Kitwe African Society, a typical urban voluntary association. Early in January 1946, Achiume —a Tonga from Nyasaland—asked Elwell to inform members of the Society of the possible ways in which their organization might forward the interests of Africans more effectively than hitherto. Elwell knew that he would be treading a treacherous path, but he believed that the Colonial Office had expected that he would discuss such subjects with Africans and that it was high time that they received a public exposure.[51]

One evening during mid-January, Elwell addressed the annual general meeting of the Kitwe African Society. He spoke briefly and confined his remarks to a survey of the three main ways in which welfare associations could increase their effectiveness. He said that they might further the aims of the existing, officially sponsored wel-

[50] Sec/Nat/311: Gore-Browne to the Secretary for Native Affairs, 21 November 1945; Sec/Nat/75: Minutes of a meeting of the Administrative Conference, 25 September 1945, Lusaka archives.

[51] Elwell Papers: A. H. Elwell to A. L. Saffery (Organizing Secretary of the South African Campaign for Right and Justice), 10 January 1946, privately held. Saffery had earlier investigated African living conditions on the Copperbelt. For a fuller discussion of the Elwell Incident, see Robert I. Rotberg, "Race Relations and Politics in Colonial Zambia: the Elwell Incident," *Race,* vii (1965), 17–29.

fare centers, form a congress and seek the political kingdom thereby, or organize trade unions as a means to improve their standard of living. He also alluded to the benefits which Africans might obtain from a well-conducted strike. He refused to speak in detail about either of the last two alternatives, but instead offered to answer questions and to explain procedures subsequently to a small group of the leading members of the Society.

Elwell's performance angered both the manager of the local mine and the local district commissioner. One of the members of the Society informed the district commissioner of the substance of Elwell's suggestions, and the former reported immediately to his provincial commissioner: "The mere fact of [Elwell] addressing a welfare society on politics is undesirable. It is not his business. . . . The chief compound manager is annoyed . . . Mr. Elwell is upsetting the administration of this district and should be transferred."[52] In any event, Achiume lost his job as a welfare assistant and his position as secretary of the Society,[53] and Elwell was first transferred to Livingstone and, a few months later, relieved of his position and sent home to London.

But Elwell's appearance and subsequent actions had raised larger issues that the government could not ignore. Were Africans prohibited from discussing politics? Should administrative officers supervise the private affairs of an African society? Early in February 1946, the acting chief secretary circulated new instructions to his various commissioners that tended to overlook their collective decision of the previous September. While the government did not disapprove of Africans talking politics, he wrote in a manner that consciously recalled a similar official stand in 1933,[54] the government had recognized African welfare associations solely in order "to look after the non-political interests of Africans resident in town-

---

[52] Sec/Nat/311: J. B. Hall (Kitwe) to G. S. Fane Smith (Ndola), 19 January 1946.

[53] The district commissioner evidently ordered both the Kitwe management board and the officers of the Society to discharge Achiume. The members of the former were, for the most part, at one with this request. And, according to the district commissioner, Godwin Mbikusita Lewanika, the president of the Society, knew on "which side his bread [was] buttered." Sec/Nat/311: Hall to Fane Smith, 25 January 1946.

[54] See Chapter V.

ships," and they should remain "strictly non-political" in their activities. Furthermore, commissioners should prevent African civil servants from discussing politics in public (i.e., as members of the private societies).[55] In Elwell's own words, the government thereby refused to acknowledge "the very great importance of the rights of freedom of speech and freedom of association in the development of any society towards responsible citizenship."[56]

Despite the evident antipathy of Rhodesian officials, Africans enlarged upon the suggestions made to them by Elwell and others. The comparable South African, Southern Rhodesian, and Nyasan examples also impressed the leaders of the more active welfare societies. Elwell, who had corresponded with the Rev. Mr. Percy Ibbotson, the secretary of the church-sponsored Southern Rhodesian Federation of African Welfare Societies, may further have suggested to his Northern Rhodesian acquaintances that they should give to their own proposed organization its rather innocuous form and name. Whatever the precise inspiration, in May 1946, representatives of fourteen welfare associations met at Broken Hill and decided to create the Federation of African Societies of Northern Rhodesia. As its name implies, the Federation, like the Nyasaland Congress, was merely a body to which local organizations could affiliate in order to achieve the objectives for which their progenitors had unsuccessfully met at Kafue in 1933.[57] Among the delegates, Dauti Yamba, of Luanshya; Godwin Mbikusita Lewanika, of Kitwe; Nelson Nalumango, of Livingstone; N. S. Liyanda, of Mongu; Sykes Ndilila, of Broken Hill; Joseph Y. Mumba, of Lusaka; and George W. Charles Kaluwa, of Mazabuka, played major roles. Kaluwa, a storekeeper who became the organizing secretary of the Federation, had much earlier attempted to establish an African National Congress in Mazabuka.

Yamba became the president of the Federation, and Mumba acted as its assistant secretary. The welfare associations of Kasama, Abercorn, Shiwa Ngandu, Mufulira, Chingola, Monze, and Fort Jameson also participated. Together, the delegates subscribed to a constitu-

---

[55] Nat/M/1: Rowland S. Hudson to all provincial and district commissioners, 13 and 26 February 1946, Lusaka archives.
[56] Elwell Papers: Elwell to the Secretary for Native Affairs, 28 March 1946.
[57] See Chapter V.

tion which declared that the Federation had been established in order

to create cooperation and mutual understanding between constituent societies of rural and urban areas in Northern Rhodesia, . . . to speak for and on behalf of Africans . . . and . . . to cooperate as much as possible with the Government of Northern Rhodesia with a view to the continuance of good government . . . to promote and support any work which is calculated to ensure good feeling between Europeans and Africans in general.[58]

For the next two years the Federation competed for the attention of the government, and the allegiance of Africans, with its own constituent associations—many of which continued independently active—and with the African Representative Council. The government decided to create the latter council in 1946 (Nyasaland kept in step by establishing a council of its own in the same year) as a logical third rung in the already existing ladder of councils. The steady deterioration in race relations and the quickening pace of African politics had apparently hastened the actual decision to do so. "We had been warned," the Secretary for Native Affairs later wrote, "by what was happening in the south."[59] He presided at Council sessions, and the six provincial councils, from their own ranks, and the paramount chief of Barotseland, from among his *indunas*, each supplied a proportion of the members of the Representative Council. Among the first twenty-nine, only six resided in urban areas.

When he opened its first session, the acting governor of Northern Rhodesia explained that the members of the African Representative Council should seek primarily to advise the governor of the Protectorate on matters directly affecting their constituents. He spoke grandly of their responsibilities:

It is not your function to make the laws of the land . . . nor is it your function to administer those laws . . . but you will have a hand in the shaping of those laws which affect Africans and it is for that reason that certain draft legislation will be submitted to you . . . for any comments and advice you wish to give . . . The Governor is not bound to accept

[58] Sec/Nat/353: Minutes of the meeting of the executive committee of the Federation of African Societies, 18–19 May 1946, Lusaka archives.
[59] Sec/Nat/113ii: Minute of 24 December 1948, Lusaka archives.

your advice but I wish to give you this assurance that any recommendations coming from this Council will always receive the full consideration which you as the supreme representative body of the African community have the right to expect.[60]

The members of the council took these views at their face value and proceeded, during the next three days, to criticize existing policies and to suggest a number of ways in which the government could improve the lot of its subjects. In sharp terms they unanimously condemned the idea of amalgamation with Southern Rhodesia under any circumstances whatsoever. They demanded equal pay for equal work and the return of lands taken by Europeans from Africans, and advised the establishment of a homecraft school for girls. With support from Gore-Browne, they also urged the governor to permit Africans to buy European-type beer and wine.[61]

A year later, when the then governor opened the second session of the Representative Council, he warned its members primarily to "give voice to what you honestly believe the people you represent think and believe."[62] Certain types of criticism, he implied, might be disloyal or unwise (the presiding officer later began to rule certain subjects out of order). Nevertheless, members of the council persisted in tabling awkward motions. They urged the governor to appoint Africans to commissions of inquiry, particularly where those inquiries affected Africans. They spoke at length about "a matter of grave concern . . . a subject which is as bad as a chronic disease" —the practice of serving Africans only from hatches opening onto the outside of a European-owned store.[63] They denounced miscegenation and the unwillingness of European fathers to support their coloured offspring. Finally, some thought that the members of their own Council should elect the three Europeans then representing African interests in the Legislative Council.

The decisions, suggestions, and questions offered and the motions debated during the first two sessions of the Representative Council

[60] Northern Rhodesia, *African Representative Council Proceedings*, 1 (1946), cc. 3–4.

[61] Edward Clegg, *Race and Politics: Partnership in the Federation of Rhodesia and Nyasaland* (London, 1960), 122, wrongly implies that the African Representative Council dealt with trivial or non-political matters only.

[62] *Representative Council Proceedings*, 2 (1947), c. 4.

[63] Nelson Nalumango, quoted in *ibid.*, c. 43.

provided the Administration with a large file of matters of interest to Africans. But, despite the acting governor's original assurance that the recommendations of the Council would carry weight, there is little evidence to show that officials in the Secretariat considered those recommendations seriously. In official eyes the activities of the Council merely provided another escape mechanism for African frustrations. Certainly the Africans involved never experienced a meaningful participation in the affairs of the state in which they lived. Furthermore, although their number included several outspoken, indeed radical, educated Africans, most of the members of the Council represented interests that were primarily rural and parochial. The leaders of the Federation of African Societies, and others of a similar background, consequently believed that their own interests were decidedly undervalued. At one point, the Federation suggested that five of its own members should receive seats on the Council. But the government refused to do so because it felt that it "could not afford" to recognize the Federation officially.[64]

Early in 1948, Africans became aware that their political needs urgently required a new means of expression. In January of that year, Gore-Browne, their trusted friend, alarmed Africans by demanding "responsible government" for the unofficial (settler) majority of the Legislative Council. "The point at issue is simple enough . . . we mean to have . . . neither more nor less than responsible government. We are one and all [the unofficial members] convinced that government by bureaucracy . . . is no longer good enough for Northern Rhodesia."[65] Gore-Browne and Roy Welensky, who had replaced the former as the leader of the unofficial members of the Council, sought by these proposals to make the executive branch of government subject to the legislature, which would, according to the Gore-Browne proposals, henceforth be dominated by a coalition of elected whites, elected Africans, and others nominated to represent African interests. Welensky and his fellow elected unofficials saw "responsible government" as a prelude to settler control and "amalgamation." At the same time, Gore-Browne, who had

---

[64] Sec/Nat/353: Minutes of a meeting with the Secretary for Native Affairs, 19 December 1946.

[65] Gore-Browne in Northern Rhodesia, *Legislative Council Debates*, 59 (1948), c. 839; misquoted in Clegg, *Race*, 133.

on many public and private occasions denounced any form of "amalgamation" with Southern Rhodesia, apparently felt that his proposals would place Africans in a position sufficiently strong for them to resist white domination and the "closer association" favored by Welensky. "My plan," he wrote to an intimate of long standing, "is the only thing that can save [Africans] from amalgamation, or anyhow put them in such a position that when it does come they will be able to claim their own terms."[66]

Africans nevertheless believed themselves betrayed. Nothing Gore-Browne could say persuaded them otherwise. In special meetings called by the various welfare societies, speaker after speaker denounced "responsible government" as a sly scheme designed to deprive Africans of their natural rights as protected persons. The Kitwe African Society, for one, withdrew its support of Gore-Browne. Mbikusita Lewanika indicated that the "responsible government" proposals demonstrated that the settlers were "determined to disregard the rights of others and to deny [Africans] true partnership [in a] serious and flagrant violation of the fundamental principles of real and true British statesmanship."[67] In the many provincial councils and the Representative Council, other Africans similarly condemned their betrayers. Chief Ishinde, of the Western Lunda, explained that his people did not "wish self government yet, we wish the Colonial Office to continue, we fear being ruled by people who are against African interests. We do not want a government like Southern Rhodesia, where the Africans are little better than slaves."[68] At a meeting of the Western Provincial Council, Ashton Musonda, of Chingola, spoke for many: "I am suspicious that the unofficial members will put the Africans in an envelope or a ditch. What I am afraid of is amalgamation."[69] In the Representative Council, the Rev. Mr. Paul Mushindo, of Chinsali, went so

[66] Gore-Browne Papers: Sir Stewart Gore-Browne to Dame Ethel Locke-King, 15 February 1948. See also Sec/Misc/72: Gore-Browne and Welensky to Governor Sir Gilbert Rennie, 19 February 1948, Lusaka archives; *Mutende*, 264, 4 March 1948.

[67] Sec/Nat/96: Address of Welcome to the Secretary for Native Affairs, 10 May 1948, Lusaka archives.

[68] *Ibid.*, Ishinde to the president of the African Representative Council, 12 July 1948.

[69] In minutes of the Seventh Meeting of the Western Provincial Council, 28–29 April 1948.

far as to demand partition as a substitute for "responsible govern-ment" and the inevitable "amalgamation."[70]

Gore-Browne's constitutional proposals frightened the leaders of the Federation of African Societies. In June 1948, they asked that one of their number be included in the protest deputation that the government had agreed to send to London. The Secretary for Native Affairs declined to entertain such a request. He preferred to treat the Federation "as just another of many societies."[71] Shortly thereafter, the Federation held its third annual general meeting in Lusaka. The various delegates refused any longer to consider Gore-Browne as their representative. They condemned "responsible government," "amalgamation," and "federation," and insisted that Northern Rhodesia should "be declared a Protectorate in the truest sense of the word and that the misleading name 'Northern Rhodesia' be changed to 'Queen Victoria's Protectorate.'" They drafted a memorandum:

As the policy of the Colonial Office rule is to educate and civilise Africans and then let them rule themselves, *it is earnestly hoped that this sacred promise will be fulfilled.*

As no English blood was shed by Africans when the English first entered . . . Northern Rhodesia, it is hoped that the Colonial Office will, as before, protect the interests of Northern Rhodesian Africans from the oppression of European settlers.

As Northern Rhodesia is ruled by the Colonial Office on behalf of the Africans who have not yet come to the stage of representing themselves directly on the United Nations Organization, it is hoped that their interests will remain paramount in Northern Rhodesia.

As Africans are the sons of Northern Rhodesian Soil and as their number is greater than that of Europeans, it is hoped that their say on anything in Northern Rhodesia will not be outweighed by any demand from the European settlers, such as responsible government, amalgamation, or Federation.[72]

---

[70] In Northern Rhodesia, *African Representative Council Proceedings,* 3 (1948), c. 35.

[71] Sec/Nat/353: Minutes of a meeting between the Secretary for Native Affairs and the officers of the Federation of African Societies, 29 June 1948.

[72] *Ibid.,* memorandum dated 15 July 1948. Original italics.

At this time the leaders of the Federation of African Societies felt that they could best further the interests of indigenous Northern Rhodesians by transforming their organization into the Northern Rhodesian African Congress. According to the constitution that they adopted, the new Congress expected to "promote the educational, political, economic, and social advancement of the Africans." Apart from the government, Congress would "be a mouthpiece of the Africans." It would "only do its best to interpret truly and faithfully the real African opinion in order to cooperate with the Central government in the building up of a satisfied, peaceful, and progressive Northern Rhodesia."[73] With the exception of "political advancement," these pious generalizations echoed the safe sentiments of the Federation and the earlier welfare associations. Robinson M. Nabulyato, a teacher at the Kafue Training Institute and the vice-president of Congress, took pains to assure the Secretary for Native Affairs that he and his fellow officers would always refrain from "encouraging fantastic and impractical politics."[74] Yet a new aggressiveness appeared to infect their actions. The Secretary for Native Affairs urged the Governor neither to snub the leaders of Congress nor to grant them or their organization any kind of official recognition. "Unless carefully handled," he warned, Congress "will be a focus for political agitation. . . . It might become an embarrassment."[75]

By the end of 1948, African nationalists had discovered their voice. They had created congresses in Nyasaland and Northern Rhodesia and had begun, albeit hesitantly, to demand a wide range of social and political rights. The Nyasas, with encouragement from Dr. Banda in London, sought to strengthen their own organization and to develop a movement that could truly claim the loyalties of the entire Protectorate. In early 1948, the Congress sent Matinga and Mponda to Britain, where they joined Banda in protesting against the inadequate educational facilities available in their own

[73] Constitution in *ibid.*

[74] *Ibid.*, Robinson Nabulyato to the Secretary for Native Affairs, 17 September 1948. The other officers were Godwin Mbikusita Lewanika, president; L. Mufana Lipalile, vice-president; Mateyo Kakumbi, treasurer; John Richmond, assistant secretary; and George Kaluwa, assistant treasurer.

[75] *Ibid.*, R. S. Hudson to the Governor, 25 September 1948.

country.[76] Northern Rhodesians meanwhile protested vigorously against "responsible government" and girded themselves for a struggle against the possibility of "federation." At this stage, both congresses primarily sought to improve the benevolent exercise of Colonial Office overrule. They did not plot or want its overthrow. Impressed by what they conceived to be the horrors of settler rule, they desperately desired to retain their positions as protected persons and gradually to obtain the home rule that protection had, in their eyes, always implied. Both congresses acted submissively until the specter of white domination cast a newly ominous shadow over Central Africa.

[76] At the last minute, Mponda and Matinga personally conspired to prevent Chinula, who had been selected to go by the Congress, from making the trip to London. A district commissioner later accused Matinga of embezzling £162 from the funds of the Congress. See 10120: Minutes of the Fourth Congress of the Nyasaland African Congress, 22–26 September 1947, Zomba archives.

PARAMOUNTCY VERSUS PARTNERSHIP: THE BATTLE OVER FEDERATION

Some people may think that the African does not see clearly the meaning of Federation. We see its meaning and it means to enslave the African.

—Confidential memorandum of the Northern Rhodesian African Congress, 28 December 1948

The catalyst of settler aspirations altered the political character of the African reaction to white overrule. In the 1920's and 1930's, when settlers had talked loudly of the need to amalgamate the Rhodesias and Nyasaland, Africans had voiced a militant opposition. In 1939, the Bledisloe Commission also responded unfavorably to the idea. Its report underscored the differences in "native policy" that militated against any hasty devolution of Imperial responsibilities for African interests from the Colonial Office to a new Central African government dominated by white Rhodesians. The Commission implied that African interests should remain paramount in the two protectorates for the "foreseeable future." Yet, in seeming contradiction, the report also recognized the general relevance of "closer association" to Central Africa and envisaged a time when such arrangements might prove possible.[1]

World War II intervened, but, in the territories concerned, institutional and political pressures once again propelled the issue of "closer association" to the surface of debate. The governors of the three territories had hitherto conferred periodically. From 1941, they and their representatives met frequently in order ostensibly to

[1] See Chapter IV.

discuss and coordinate matters pertaining to the war against the Axis. The British government intended this so-called Inter-territorial Conference, which had its own secretariat, to confine its deliberations to non-political matters. But the officials and settlers concerned nevertheless sought to use the Conference and its mechanism to advance the cause of "closer association." In 1941/42, Sir Godfrey Huggins, the prime minister of Southern Rhodesia, and Sir Herbert Stanley, the governor of the same colony, consciously tried to guide the Conference along such lines.[2] At about this same time, Northern Rhodesian politicians renewed their agitation in favor of amalgamation with Southern Rhodesia. In the Legislative Council, Roy Welensky, then the president of the Northern Rhodesian Labour Party, moved that "Northern and Southern Rhodesia be amalgamated under a constitution similar to that now enjoyed by Southern Rhodesia."[3] Others capably represented the many European groups that had favored amalgamation so overwhelmingly in 1939.

Africans reacted immediately to these different threats. Ever alert for utterances that might foreshadow the "great betrayal" of their interests, they once again condemned Welensky and "amalgamation" in no uncertain terms. Harry Nkumbula, then a schoolteacher on the Copperbelt, aptly expressed African concern in a meeting of the Western Province Regional Council. "Africans," he said, "dread the very idea of amalgamating this country with Southern Rhodesia."

When the Royal [Bledisloe] Commission came . . . very strong and reasonable objections were pronounced by the Africans of this country. . . . These strong and reasonable objections have remained unchanged in the minds of Africans. . . . The Prime Minister of Southern Rhodesia has made it clear to everybody that his country is a white man's country and that the black man shall always remain a servant of the white man, if not a slave. . . . If His Majesty's Government would sign an agreement . . . with Southern Rhodesia . . . that the now existing Native Policy in Northern Rhodesia will not be altered, then the Africans in this country will speak in favour of the question. If no agreement of the kind is made and the Dominions Office decided to hand over Northern Rhodesia and

[2] 1a/355: Dominions Office to the Governor of Southern Rhodesia, 20 February 1942; 1a/360, *passim*, Zomba archives.
[3] Northern Rhodesia, *Legislative Council Debates*, 46 (1943), c. 76.

Nyasaland to . . . Huggins, the black peoples in the entire British East Africa will fast lose confidence in the British Imperial Government.[4]

In 1944, the British government concluded that "under existing circumstances" (i.e., because of divergent "native policies"), it could not regard amalgamation "as practicable."[5] Nonetheless, it chose to keep the issue alive for the future. It replaced the Inter-territorial Conference with a formal body, the Central African Council, and thereby bound the three dependencies more closely than before. Huggins called the creation of the Council "nothing more than a sop," and agreed to its formation reluctantly.[6] But Welensky apparently realized that the formation of the Council left "the door slightly ajar towards amalgamation." "If we can make a success of it," he continued, "I believe it is a lead towards amalgamation."[7]

The Central African Council,[8] an advisory body with no executive powers, coordinated research activities and the medical, educational, and economic policies of the three territories. It attempted to further the sharing of transport and communications systems. At its second meeting, in October 1945, the Council discussed the advisability of establishing a jointly controlled air service, the damming of the Zambezi River at the Kariba Gorge and the consequent production of power, the development of an archives service, the hospitalization of mentally ill patients, the need for a customs union, the creation of one currency for the three territories, soil conservation, the pro-

[4] *Proceedings* of the Western Province Regional Council, 20 December 1943. Nkumbula addressed harsher letters along these lines to the *Bantu Mirror* and *Mutende*, two newspapers. The Government of Northern Rhodesia suppressed their publication.

[5] Quoted in A. J. Hanna, *The Story of the Rhodesias and Nyasaland* (London, 1960), 248.

[6] Quoted in *ibid.*, 249; Lewis H. Gann, *A History of Northern Rhodesia: Early Days to 1953* (London, 1964), 358. The British government considered the creation of such a council as early as 1939.

[7] Northern Rhodesia, *Legislative Council Debates*, 49 (1945), 16 January 1945, c. 192. See also Roy Welensky, *Welensky's 4000 Days: The Life and Death of the Federation of Rhodesia and Nyasaland* (London, 1964), 25.

[8] Gore-Browne objected to the name "Central African." The Council, complained Gore-Browne, was neither "Central" nor "African" because no Africans were represented. The Governor of Southern Rhodesia chaired the sessions of the Council, the other two governors attended, and each territory sent three delegates, at least two of whom were usually unofficials. See 1a/336: Minutes of the first meeting of the Council, 24 April 1945, Zomba archives.

vision of educational facilities for Europeans, the problems of tsetse fly clearance, and a number of other matters of common concern. Three years later, the seventh session of the Council contemplated similar subjects: mutual broadcasting arrangements, the future of the by then established Central African Airways, a statistical sampling program prepared by the Council's director of research, the Kariba project, the establishment of an agricultural college in Southern Rhodesia, and coordination of railway policy.[9]

In short, the Council concerned itself with a variety of "technical" problems which both affected the economic and social development of the region and advanced the cause of political "closer association" by demonstrating the advantages of cooperation in other spheres of activity. The Council also provided a forum for the sharing of amalgamationist sentiment; Huggins and Welensky joined (later Sir) Malcolm Barrow and G. G. S. J. Hadlow of Nyasaland at its meetings. The three governors—Sir John Kennedy of Southern Rhodesia, Sir Gilbert Rennie of Northern Rhodesia, and (later Sir) Geoffrey Colby of Nyasaland—shared the views of the unofficials. Moreover, W. A. W. Clark and Hugh Parry, the principal administrators of the Council's small permanent secretariat, individually supported amalgamation and, informally at least, added to the subtle pressures in its favor.

In 1948, settlers again searched for the means of controlling their own destinies. By then the economic climate of Central Africa favored their quest. Only together, it seemed, could the three territories realize their potential for growth. Many interested parties, including the British government, believed that a single, unified administration could attract capital and implement the necessary development program more easily than could three dependencies. African agitation and the reality of Indian independence also frightened some persons of influence. At the same time, the British government—then controlled by the Labour Party—reiterated its refusal to amalgamate the Rhodesias. In these circumstances, Gore-Browne, whose opposition to amalgamation was well known, publicly suggested that a federation of the Rhodesias and Nyasaland might provide the organizational medium which could both preserve African rights and promote the benefits of economic interdependence.

---

[9] 1a/338 and 1b/1: Verbatim Records of the Second and Seventh Meeting of the Central African Council, Zomba archives.

Speaking in the Legislative Council, he explained that "many people, myself amongst them, came out here to lead a patriarchal kind of life in some quiet part of the country, surrounded by contented, happy-go-lucky Africans, and enjoying a certain amount of big-game shooting. That was what many of us hoped for. But it has all gone. . . . Instead, we have to go ahead with the rest of the world, and progress—whatever that means." In the same debate, he suggested that the two protectorates should be federated with Southern Rhodesia. "I said federation, and I want to make it perfectly clear that I mean federation and not amalgamation. . . . [To] my mind [federation] would entail all the advantages of amalgamation without any of its disadvantages. Above all it would ensure the rights of Africans."[10]

A few months later, in May 1948, Dr. Daniel F. Malan led his Afrikaner Nationalist Party to an unexpected victory over Jan Christian Smuts' United Party in the South African general election. The fear that Afrikaner racial and political ideas might spread north to engulf the Rhodesias thereafter dominated thinking in some influential circles in Central Africa. It also troubled several prominent permanent officials in the Colonial Office. In Northern Rhodesia, Rennie appointed a committee to consider federal suggestions. Meanwhile, Welensky had made the idea of "federation" his own. When he went to London, in July 1948, to discuss "responsible government," the Secretary of State for the Colonies, who opposed "amalgamation," evidently promised to examine the advantages and disadvantages of a federal union of the Rhodesias and Nyasaland.[11]

When Welensky returned home to Broken Hill in August, he assured his constituents that such an approach to the British government would succeed. "I am convinced," he reported, "that the stage has arrived when the dream of a great British Central African dominion can become a reality. It is something that we can now settle ourselves."[12] It is apparent that Welensky realized that he and his fellow

[10] Gore-Browne, 24 March 1948, in Northern Rhodesia, *Legislative Council Debates*, 60 (1948), cc. 439–441. Gore-Browne had first suggested "federation" in 1936.

[11] Colonel Oliver Stanley, a former Conservative Party Secretary of State for the Colonies, also urged that a federal scheme might win support where the idea of amalgamation would not. See Don Taylor, *The Rhodesian: The Life of Sir Roy Welensky* (London, 1955), 105; Welensky, *4000 Days*, 22–26.

[12] *Bulawayo Chronicle*, 19 August 1948.

white settlers could, by federating with Southern Rhodesia, at last obtain complete control over their own affairs and, by implication, the affairs of the African population of Northern Rhodesia as well. In October 1948, Welensky and Huggins attended a Commonwealth African conference in London. There Welensky persuaded Huggins that they should both consider federation an excellent substitute for amalgamation. Welensky approached the problem realistically.

Like Sir Godfrey [Huggins], I am also a believer in the amalgamation of the two territories, but I am afraid that "straight out" amalgamation of the Rhodesias would meet with considerable opposition from the African peoples—whereas the varying political privileges and rights now enjoyed by the natives can most definitely be ensured under federation. Under a federal system the chances of the three territories getting dominion status must be immediately immensely improved.[13]

Africans viewed these proposals, like "responsible government" earlier, as cynical attempts to deprive them of their natural rights. They reacted particularly to Welensky's speeches and to the reports of an interview with him in *The African Weekly*.[14] "Mr. Welensky," the leaders of the Northern Rhodesian Congress wrote, "is likely to bring the miseries of civil war to Northern Rhodesia." They advised their followers to "be cool and . . . nonviolent," and promised to seek Welensky's resignation from the Legislative Council. "We can see," they added, "that amalgamation is the same thing as Federation . . . [and] . . . he wants to enslave Africans by bringing in Federation." Their "strictly confidential" memorandum articulated African objections perspicaciously. Gore-Browne, it read, had advised the Congress to demand a treaty of some kind from the British government.

What guarantee shall we have from the Colonial Office for the preservation of our interests? When we think of Native Policy, the Colonial Office . . . has failed to wield its influence in Southern Rhodesia. . . . How much more of the failure of the Colonial Office shall be experienced under the Central African dominion of the Federated States? The secret of Federation is to subordinate African interests. . . . All these proposals come from the European community based on fear which the European

---

[13] *Ibid.*, 29 October 1948; Welensky, 12 November 1948, in Northern Rhodesia, *Legislative Council Debates*, 62 (1948), cc. 55–59.

[14] Printed on 3 November 1948.

has about the African. . . . Under Federation it is said that rights "NOW" enjoyed will be safeguarded, this shows no African progress because the "NOW" word implies that the position is neither commensurate nor elastic enough to allow development. Federation will bring us segregation and oppression. Thus, any proposal in connection with Southern Rhodesia, especially when it does not come from us, shall be rejected. . . . We are . . . not prepared to alter our present colonial rule to that of the Federal government. We are the people to claim for things, and we now claim that Colonial Office rule is better for us at present than any other form of government. . . . We like other forms of government but as we are not developed yet we must keep to a bird in hand which is worth two in the bush.

. . . we know our needs and any persuasions from other people . . . shall be regarded as snakes [in the grass]. . . . Partnership . . . is a ladder for Europeans in Northern Rhodesia to climb on us.[15]

By the beginning of 1949, both sides had drawn their battle lines. Although their preparations and plans of attack recalled the bitter confrontations of the 1930's, the historic conflict had at last entered a conclusive phase. Welensky and Huggins realized that economic needs and recent events in South Africa assisted their cause; Africans, who saw no important differences between the old "amalgamation" and the new "federation," sensed that these white opportunists hoped to deprive them forever of the possibility that they might someday rule themselves. The events of 1948 had caused them to distrust anew the designs of whites.

FROM THE VICTORIA FALLS TO BRONDESBURY PARK

In 1949, at a time when Kwame Nkrumah was leading his supporters to the brink of political power in the Gold Coast, Huggins and Welensky, with the knowledge of the governments concerned, convened a private conference of settlers, like that of 1936, at the Victoria Falls. Under the chairmanship of Sir Miles Thomas, a director of the Colonial Development Corporation who advocated some form of "closer association," and who had earlier advised the Government of Southern Rhodesia on economic matters (he later became the chairman of the British Overseas Airways Corporation),

---

[15] Sec/Nat/353: Strictly Confidential Memorandum drawn up at a meeting of a committee of the Northern Rhodesia Congress on 28 December 1948 and written by Robinson Nabulyato, Lusaka archives.

1. John Chilembwe and family, circa 1905

2. Charles C. Chinula in his ministerial robes, Edingeni, 1962

3. Dauti Yamba, 1951

4. Harry Mwaanga Nkumbula, 1958

6. H. Masauko Chipembere, Washington, D.C., 1963

5. Dr. H. Kamuzu Banda addressing a rally at Liwonde, 1962

8. W. Kanyama Chiume, Accra, 1958

7. John Msonthi, Zomba, 1962

9. Yatuta Chisiza, Washington, D.C., 1962

10. Chief Mwase Kasungu and Native Authority messenger, at Kasungu, 1962

11. Augustine Bwanausi (l.) and Aleke Banda (r.), with Colin Cameron obscured in the upper left, at Liwonde, 1962

12. Sewing class at Lumezi mission, near Lundazi, 1959

13. Contrasting African high-density housing near Ndola, 1959

14. Kenneth David Kaunda, Chilenje, 1960

15. Orton Chirwa, Dr. Banda, and Dunduzu Chisiza (l. to r.) at a conference in London, 1960

16. Malawi Youth League marching near Chinteche, 1962

17. Political rally of the United National Independence Party, Lusaka, October 1962

18. Simon Mwansa Kapwepwe speaking to the October 1962 rally

19. Sikota Wina, after addressing the rally

20. Kenneth Kaunda leaving the October 1962 meeting;
behind him is Justin Chimba

four white delegates each from the Rhodesias—Huggins refused to
include Africans—and three white Nyasas—whose invitations to attend had arrived belatedly—met to consider the future of the white
man in Central Africa. Each had previously expressed himself in
favor of amalgamation or some other form of mutual cooperation.
It remained for them collectively to decide how they might best
achieve the unified control over their own destinies that had eluded
them for so long.

During the better part of two days in February, the delegates
sought to formulate a plan that would enable them speedily to
accomplish their primary objectives. In their opening speeches,
Huggins and Welensky suggested "federation" as the best possible
alternative to amalgamation. Welensky and the representatives from
Nyasaland recognized that the extent of African antipathy would
prevent the British government from ever agreeing to the outright
amalgamation of the Central African dependencies. Otherwise, they
refused to let African needs and fears stand in their way. While
they expressed contempt for Africans and African opinion generally
—Huggins said that the "Native African [had done] nothing for
Africa and very little for his own good before the Europeans took
charge [and that] Africa [could] not be left to waste in the hands
of the Bantu"[16]—the more influential delegates approached the
problem with the realism that was so typical of Welensky. He reminded the delegates that he remained an amalgamationist.

. . . but I am also a realist. . . . I feel that whether one likes to accept the
idea that African opinion amounts to anything or not, it is useless to
deny that as far as Northern Rhodesia is concerned . . . we would be
unlikely to carry much weight with the Home Government otherwise.
I am not suggesting that African opinion is well informed, but . . . African
opinion in Northern Rhodesia is . . . solidly against amalgamation; therefore I believe that is out of the question.[17]

Welensky then proposed, and the delegates unanimously advocated,
the unification of the two Rhodesias and Nyasaland under a federal
type of constitution.

[16] Report of a Conference of Delegates from Northern and Southern Rhodesia and Nyasaland, 16–17 February 1949 (unpublished typescript), 6, privately held.
[17] Ibid., 8, 55. Later (58) he said: "There is no one more than I who
realises how little the African thinks."

Welensky and the other settlers from Northern Rhodesia and Nyasaland saw the accomplishment of federation as a means whereby they might rid themselves of further supervision by the British Colonial Office. Welensky said: "As far as the Colonial Office is concerned you realise, and I am certain that everyone must, that we detest the Colonial Office government, but that is not sufficient. . . . I look upon this first step towards the formation of a Federal Government as the original step to getting rid of the Colonial Office."[18] They also assumed that the federal solution would allow them eventually to create an independent dominion. Its institutions they modeled generally upon the decentralized Australian example, although they referred frequently to Canadian and American practices as well. Huggins preferred a completely centralized federation —really a greater Southern Rhodesia. He proposed to run Northern Rhodesia and Nyasaland from Salisbury, leaving little power and initiative to what he called the "county council" governments in Lusaka and Zomba. Others sought to preserve local initiative, but the conference, after a cursory examination of the problems involved, agreed that the central legislature should discharge nearly all of the accepted functions of government.

In order to appease African opinion, they proposed to affirm existing land rights and to make the three state governments responsible for African education and agriculture, and for "native administration" generally. "It is necessary," said Barrow, "to put something across that will convince the Africans."[19] Welensky explained:

I want a clear statement which we can put to the African peoples in Nyasaland and Northern Rhodesia on native rights. . . . I want to take the Africans all the way with us if we possibly can. If they don't come, it is just too bad but I want to be reasonable and if it is possible to bring them along with us I want to do so. It would help tremendously.[20]

On the other hand, the delegates planned to deny Africans effective representation in the proposed bicameral federal parliament. The upper house, or senate, would play an advisory role; in it, the delegates from Northern Rhodesia and Nyasaland (where Africans at last participated in both legislative councils) thought that one or two nominated Africans might conceivably sit. While the delegates

18 *Ibid.*, 56.
19 *Ibid.*, 35.
20 *Ibid.*, 33.

agreed that the number of members of the lower house should be "chosen . . . in proportion to the respective numbers of their people," they equated "people" with "whites" and both denied Nyasaland— which possessed the largest population—more than a small token proportion of the total number of places. Neither Huggins nor many of the other delegates could envisage Africans sitting therein. No one spoke of "partnership." Thus, as Barrow admitted, the settlers in the conference supposed that they could "hand over" about five million Africans to Southern Rhodesia. "That is, in fact," he said, "what will be happening."[21]

The leaders of European opinion had backed Welensky's federal scheme. But no formal demands issued from the conference. Instead, the delegates expected that the substance of their decisions would serve as the basis for the actual drafting of a federal constitution, and ancillary protocols, by committees of experts supplied by the governments involved. Thereafter, they thought, the delegates would reassemble at the Victoria Falls to ratify the instruments of federation, the entire European population of the three territories would vote by postal ballot, and, if the referendum were favorable, Huggins and Welensky would ask the British Parliament to ratify the arrangements agreed upon in Central Africa. Even pessimists, like (later Sir) Edgar Whitehead, the Southern Rhodesian Minister of Finance, presumed that federation could be accomplished, if all went well, before a year had elapsed. But neither the British nor, therefore, the Northern Rhodesian and Nyasaland governments, at first played their expected roles. With them, African opposition initially mattered.

At home and abroad, Nyasas and Northern Rhodesians reacted anxiously to press reports of the Victoria Falls conference. They did not want to be "handed over" to Southern Rhodesia. Dr. Banda, in particular, realized immediately that, despite the absence of detailed information about the federal scheme, Africans needed to make their opposition known without delay; if not, he feared the loss of the African case by default. "All talk of waiting for full details," Banda reasoned, "was simply falling into the trap, which was being well set for us. And I for one was not going to fall into that trap."[22]

[21] *Ibid.*, 45.
[22] Gore-Browne Papers: H. Kamuzu Banda to Sir Stewart Gore-Browne, 9 July 1950. See also Banda to Gore-Browne, 27 June 1949.

Eleven days after the whites had adjourned their conference, a small group of Central Africans then studying in Britain met in Banda's house in Brondesbury Park, London (where he was then practicing medicine) to counter the threat of "federation." The detailed rejection of the European proposals, which Banda drafted in the form of a memorandum to the Colonial Office, and both Banda and Harry Nkumbula (then at the London School of Economics after two years at Makerere College and a year at the London University Institute of Education) signed on behalf of their colleagues, contained a point-by-point rebuttal of federationist arguments as well as the first comprehensive statement of political objectives ever made by Nyasas and Rhodesians.

The memorandum recognized federation as the "thin end of the wedge of amalgamation"—the "same old pill of amalgamation, coated with the sugar of federation to make it easier for the Africans and the Imperial Government to swallow." It declared that federation would not be in the best interests of the peoples of Central Africa because such a plan would extend to the two protectorates the policy of segregation and discrimination under which their "fellow Africans in Southern Rhodesia . . . legally suffer[ed] social indignities and civil and political disabilities." The authors observed that Southern Rhodesia, because of its large white population, would dominate the proposed federal government and deprive "protected" Africans of their traditional rights. Their appraisal echoed earlier assessments:

. . . of all the Europeans of Central Africa, those of Southern Rhodesia have the worst antipathy towards Africans. . . . They look upon the Africans as inferior beings, with no right to a dignified and refined existence and fit only as hewers of wood and drawers of water for Europeans. . . . They do not even pretend that they are in Africa to help the Africans, but blatantly declare that they are in Africa to live and to rule. In all their dealings with the Africans they always assume the attitude of conquerors . . . [and] it is these Europeans . . . who will rule and govern the federation. . . . The cardinal principle in [Colonial Office] administration is guidance or guardianship. But under the Government provided by Southern Rhodesia, the relationship between us and the authorities will be one of slaves and masters, and the cardinal principle . . . domination.[23]

[23] Hastings Kamuzu Banda and Harry Mwaanga Nkumbula, "Federation in Central Africa" (unpublished typescript), 1 May 1949, privately held.

The authors of the memorandum explained that they feared the spread of the Southern Rhodesian color bar—which they equated to that of South Africa—into trans-Zambezia. For them, the racial climate of the two protectorates seemed relatively less objectionable than that of Southern Rhodesia because in the protectorates the authorities had not yet made of the color bar a political philosophy or an instrument of administrative policy. For these and many other reasons, Banda and Nkumbula affirmed that under present circumstances the Africans whom they represented not only rejected federation but were unwilling "even to discuss it, guarantees or no guarantees." They refused uncompromisingly to trust promises made by Europeans because of the many that had previously been made to Africans and subsequently ignored by the governments of South Africa and Southern Rhodesia. "What reason," they asked, "have we for supposing that we . . . under . . . federation . . . will fare any better?" To accept the proffered guarantees, they declared, would both jeopardize their own political future and that of their fellow Africans in Southern Rhodesia. They believed that federation would reduce all Africans to the same servitude. At the same time, their memorandum indicated that Nyasas and Northern Rhodesians would willingly enter into a federal union with Southern Rhodesia when and if Africans in all three dependencies possessed universal suffrage, and each territory the right to secede whenever a majority of its people regarded federation as harmful to their interests. As a corollary, they specifically rejected the notion that, because of the supposed backwardness and ignorance of their people, "any group of self-appointed aristocrats, benevolent or malevolent, has any right to deny us a voice in the affairs of the country we call our own and our home." Had Europeans then heeded Banda's political dicta, the history of federation might have been altered substantially. He wrote: "We too desire partnership between Africans and Europeans in Central Africa. But this partnership must be a real and genuine partnership, and not a façade, which conceals domination of the African group of partners, by the European group. We, too, must be on the board of directors and in the inner councils of the affairs of the firm."[24]

In the two protectorates, African opinion, if less articulate than

[24] *Ibid.*

that of Brondesbury Park, equally regarded the Victoria Falls proposals in the same light. In Northern Rhodesia, the Congress, the African Representative Council, and the various provincial councils all recorded their opposition to federation. Mbikusita Lewanika, then the Congress president and a white-collar employee at the Nkana mine, presented a petition that detailed these objections to Arthur Creech Jones, the Secretary of State for the Colonies, when he visited Central Africa in the wake of the 1949 Victoria Falls conference. In the neighboring protectorate, Creech Jones discovered that Nyasas differed in the response to "federation" only to the extent that they were even more vehemently antagonistic than the Northern Rhodesians.

As a result of the expression of these sentiments, Creech Jones assured a meeting of its Central Provincial Council that the British government would not join Nyasaland to Southern Rhodesia or Northern Rhodesia without consulting all of the peoples of the countries concerned. "His Majesty's Government," the Colonial Secretary said, "has entered into a very solemn obligation towards you, and they will not be transferred or entrusted to anyone else. We shall honour the responsibilities we have entered into and shall not transfer our responsibilities or abrogate them." In short, he urged Africans "not to be anxious."[25] Elsewhere he indicated that white settlement in Northern Rhodesia needed to be "controlled."[26]

For a few months Africans breathed more easily. Statements made by and attributed to Creech Jones reassured them; the fact that Europeans believed that the Colonial Secretary had sold white stock short pleased them even more. "As I can see it," Dr. Banda wrote, "the Europeans are angry with [Creech Jones] . . . not because he said anything that favoured Africans . . . to any newer extent, but because he refused to reverse the British traditional policy in Central Africa."[27] Then, in November, after Huggins had once again attacked the Central African Council, Welensky tabled a motion

[25] Minutes of the Eleventh meeting of the Central Provincial Council, 21 April 1949. Creech Jones only reiterated promises earlier made by himself, by George Hall, his predecessor as Colonial Secretary, and Labour Party pronouncements dating from 1944 and 1945.

[26] *Bulawayo Chronicle*, 22 April 1949.

[27] Gore-Browne Papers: Banda to Gore-Browne, 27 June 1949. See also *The Economist*, 6 August 1949; Edward Clegg, *Race and Politics: Partnership in the Federation of Rhodesia and Nyasaland* (London, 1960), 156.

in the Legislative Council that asked the British government to devise and establish a federal government in Central Africa. To the alarm of Africans, the elected white members supported the motion while the official members, on the orders of Governor Sir Gilbert Rennie, abstained. They indicated that the Northern Rhodesian government did not want to vote "yes" and thus signify its acceptance of the action suggested; nor could its representatives vote against a motion on which the government both maintained an open mind and wanted to elicit an official response in London. Only Gore-Browne, the Rev. Mr. Edward G. Nightingale—a missionary who represented African interests—the Rev. Mr. Henry Kasokolo and Nelson Nalumango, the two African delegates themselves, and J. F. Morris of Chingola opposed the motion.[28]

BACK TO THE VICTORIA FALLS

Welensky, ever realistic, knew that no Labour-controlled government in Britain would now back a federation of the kind outlined at the Victoria Falls. On the other hand, he probably appreciated that the tide of imperial opinion had begun to run in his favor. The mining companies and the British South Africa Company, which, since 1924, had retained a massive financial interest in the affairs of the Rhodesias, had begun to support "federation" as a means of rationalizing the economic structure of, and attracting new developmental capital to, Central Africa. Moreover they, and one or more senior officials in the Colonial Office, had come to view the creation of a federation as the only alternative to the gradual spread northward of the increasingly harsh Afrikaner racial policies that they distrusted.[29] For strategic and, in the case of the Colonial Office civil servants, economic and humanitarian reasons, they wanted to construct an ideological buffer state wherein multiracial partnership would offer an alternative to the extremes of black nationalism and white apartheid.

In 1950, the debate over federation assumed new urgency. Perhaps at the instigation of Welensky, and certainly in response to the favorable climate of overseas business opinion, Huggins de-

[28] Northern Rhodesia, *Legislative Council Debates,* 66 (1949), 24 and 28 November 1949, cc. 346, 404.

[29] The Colonial Office even attempted unsuccessfully to persuade the Government of Northern Rhodesia to limit Afrikaner immigration.

manded action from a British government that clearly preferred drift to decision. In January, he indicated that if the British government failed to give some such federal body as the Central African Council—which he had never liked—greater powers before the end of the year, his government would terminate its membership therein.[30] Huggins thus threatened to destroy the many cooperative ventures (such as airways, broadcasting, and customs) that had proved so successful and so beneficial to the economic development of Nyasaland and Northern Rhodesia. Thereafter, both in the Northern Rhodesian Legislative Council and in the local press, Welensky and his colleagues added to the chorus of voices that demanded a federal solution. They spoke enthusiastically of partnership, and gave further gloss to the spindly frame of federation.

Overseas, "partnership" beguiled a wide variety of persons interested in the welfare and future political advancement of Africans. At the same time, they assumed that white Rhodesian settlers could voluntarily bring themselves to share real power with Africans. Even the most liberal among this amorphous pressure group—which included a number of highly placed British civil servants—supposed that they had time sufficient to permit the construction of a truly multiracial state. Few saw the speed with which the winds of revolution would overtake Africa. Fewer still appreciated the extent to which the indigenous leaders of Nyasaland and Northern Rhodesia already sought the political kingdom, and would bitterly contest any scheme that purported to exchange British protection for settler domination.

If whites had many, Africans possessed few illusions. They early suspected that "partnership" might, in practice, disguise further domination. Then Welensky, speaking for the benefit of a local white audience rather than for Britons and Americans overseas, made it perfectly clear that partnership would not mean equality: "I accept and I think the vast majority of Europeans would accept the policy of partnership between the two races is . . . commonsense . . . [but] as far forward as I can see, the European, with his energy, initiative and capital, will be the senior partner." Furthermore, Welensky remained convinced that "the African" alone could never develop Northern Rhodesia "in the way it should be developed."

[30] Minutes of the Eleventh Meeting of the Central African Council, 25 January 1950.

Therefore, he said, "it is vital to encourage European immigration into the country on a large scale."[31]

Africans could only understand partnership in terms of the known. If Welensky's views were not sufficiently worrying, they knew that whites would not willingly relinquish the advantages that color had apparently given them. They could not immediately see how the creation of a federation could change the attitude of someone, for example, like John Bryson, the white supervisor of the Broken Hill railway camp. In March 1950, the featured columnist of the *Northern Rhodesia Advertiser* complimented Bryson for keeping the camp tidy and particularly for sprinkling chloride of lime in the sanitary buckets. "But what struck me as the most splendid effort of all," the columnist praised, "was that no matter what the weather or sunshine, Mr. Bryson is riding through the streets and lanes [of the camp] on his bicycle with a very handsome whip to dispel any congregation of [African] loafers he may encounter."[32]

While European support for the federal scheme matured, Nyasas and Northern Rhodesians reiterated their implacable opposition to any kind of closer association with whites who lived south of the Zambezi. Banda, who now kept in even closer touch with events and with persons of influence in both of the protectorates, fought federation in London and encouraged the Rhodesian and Nyasaland congresses to do so at home. In Nyasaland, Sangala had temporarily replaced Matinga as president of the Congress; in April 1950, forty delegates from its fifteen branches confirmed their opposition to the federal scheme and promised that Nyasas "have and will still protest at all costs."[33] Their counterparts in Northern Rhodesia followed suit. Mbikusita Lewanika, still the president of Congress, condemned "federation" because it would mean self-government for the senior partners only. He also demanded universal suffrage—"one man, one vote."[34] The Mporokoso Native Welfare Association voted against federation. So did the Luwingu and Mwenzo Welfare asso-

---

[31] Quoted in *Bulawayo Chronicle*, 13 April 1950; *African Weekly*, 22 March 1950. See also Welensky, *4000 Days*, 34.

[32] *Northern Rhodesia Advertiser*, 11 March 1950.

[33] 10120: Minutes of the Executive Committee of the Nyasaland African Congress, 8–9 April 1950, Zomba archives.

[34] N/25521/1, Lusaka archives. This may have been the first use of the slogan in Northern Rhodesia and the initial expression of a demand for universal suffrage.

ciations, the Northern and Western Provincial councils, the African Representative Council, and a number of other official and unofficial forums of African opinion whose minutes have since been lost.

The debates in the Western and Northern Provincial councils illustrate the drift of African dismay. Gabriel Musumbulwa, then a clerk at the Roan Antelope mine and later the Northern Rhodesian Minister of African Education in the white-run government of 1960–62, saw the pitfalls of a partnership that contained senior and junior members. (The Council's presiding officer, the white provincial commissioner L. F. Leversedge, told Musumbulwa that he would always find the world full of senior and junior partners.) Mufana Lipalile, earlier a member of the Federation of African Societies, then analyzed the concept of partnership in terms that seemed to summarize the anxiety of his colleagues:

. . . the word itself has a good sound, but everything, however good it may be, can be turned into a bad thing. Of course we are not as well-educated as the Europeans are, but the meaning of the word "partnership" gives us the feel that there are two oxen, one black and one white, pulling the wagon. . . . But now we look around and see how things are going and we find it is not what we thought, because one bull says "I must go ahead and you must come behind me all the time." In that way I do not see how the plough can go.[35]

In the Northern Provincial Council, Donald R. Siwale, an elderly former Church of Scotland mission teacher who had retired from the government civil service, explained that his fellow Africans wanted the protection of the Colonial Office until they were "ready"; then they would ask for "something else." Despite the sentiments expressed to the meeting by the Secretary for Native Affairs—that Northern Rhodesia would *never* achieve African self-government because of its preponderance of European settlers—Siwale made it clear that educated Africans derived considerable inspiration from events in the Gold Coast and Nigeria. He personally looked forward to the day when Africans would rule Northern Rhodesia. The Rev. Mr. Paul Mushindo of the Chinsali African Welfare Association, Bemba Senior Chief Mwamba, and a number of others agreed. Paul Sikazwe expressed the sense of the meeting in a graphic parable:

[35] Proceedings of the Western Provincial Council, 28–30 March 1950, 12–16.

"Every African in Northern Rhodesia does not want to be federated with Southern Rhodesia. If a man is given food and he vomits it, can he again eat what he has already vomited? And when a man vomits food it means that the food is not good to him. Most of us know that our friends in Southern Rhodesia are slaves."[36]

The movement in favor of federation continued strong. Industrialists and humanitarians alike were convinced that the apparent advantages of closer association outweighed its possible, conceivably temporary, disadvantages for Africans. The British military high command now backed federation on strategic grounds. A major copper producer symbolically moved its main offices from London to Lusaka. Huggins' threat to leave the Central African Council influenced some. Finally, after Welensky and Huggins had again demanded that the British government should convene a conference to discuss the federal question, A. B. (later Sir Andrew) Cohen of the Colonial Office persuaded James Griffiths, who had replaced Creech Jones as Colonial Secretary, and Patrick Gordon-Walker, the Secretary of State for Commonwealth Relations, to permit a committee of theoretically impartial Central African and British civil servants to consider and decide whether or not the Rhodesias and Nyasaland could feasibly and profitably federate.[37] Cohen apparently did not then appreciate the depth of African hostility to any schemes, however benevolently conceived and executed.

Africans received a number of official assurances that the conference of civil servants would not necessarily jeopardize their interests. The governor of Northern Rhodesia said publicly that the decisions of the conference would not commit the three territories in any way. He promised that Africans would have a "full opportunity" to consider such proposals that might emerge from its deliberations. Members of the conference would "keep African interests fully in mind."[38] But Africans had long since lost any faith in prom-

[36] Proceedings of the Northern Provincial Council, 15 April 1950. Also Donald R. Siwale, letter to the author, 6 October 1963.

[37] Gann, *History*, 410, wrongly assumes that George Herbert Baxter, the then Assistant Under-Secretary of State for Commonwealth Relations, originated the idea of a meeting of officials. Similarly, Taylor, *Rhodesian*, 128, supposes that Huggins first suggested such a meeting.

[38] "Notes on Points Raised in Discussion between his Excellency the Governor and Members of African Representative Council in Committee," February 1951 (mimeographed). Reiterated in N/0002/2: James Griffiths to Sir Gilbert Rennie, 5 April 1951, Lusaka archives.

ises made by white men. Both congresses and the Representative and Protectorate councils deprecated the discussion of federation by any conclaves of officials or unofficials. Since the officials had abstained from voting on Welensky's motion in 1949, why, Africans wondered, should they now be any more considerate of African interests? Africans therefore protested vociferously, reiterated their contention that ties to Southern Rhodesia would subject Africans in the protectorates to new forms of segregation and, conceivably, extermination as well (Welensky later ineptly compared the fate of Indians in America to the possible fate of Africans in Northern Rhodesia[39]), and then dilated upon the dilemma in which Africans found themselves. "While appreciating the principle of partnership," a petition read, it should be clearly understood that the Africans' home is in Africa, whereas the Europeans can have access to other parts of the British Commonwealth. If opportunities for advancement of our race are denied in Africa, where else in the whole wide world shall we . . . be found?"[40]

Like so many other white men sitting in judgment upon the future of their subjects, the twenty-seven officials in conference (they represented the governments of the three territories, the Commonwealth Relations and Colonial offices, and the Central African Council), presumed that they knew what would be best for the indigenous inhabitants of Nyasaland and Northern Rhodesia. "Provided," their report read, "that some . . . form of closer association could be designed containing adequate provision for African representation and adequate protection for African interests, and provided that the services more intimately affecting the daily life of Africans were outside the scope of a Central African Government, Africans might well come to realise the very substantial advantages of closer association."[41]

Despite the conclusions of their own study group,[42] the report of the conference minimized the ways in which the existing "native

[39] Quoted in Harry Franklin, *Unholy Wedlock: The Failure of the Central African Federation* (London, 1963), 49. See also Welensky, *4000 Days*, 57.

[40] N/0002/2: Petition of the African Representative Council to the Secretary of State for the Colonies, 22 January 1951.

[41] *Central African Territories: Report of the Conference on Closer Association*, Cmd. 8233 (1951), 10.

[42] *Central African Territories: Comparative Survey of Native Policy*, Cmd. 8235 (1951).

policies" of the three territories diverged. In fact, because most of the officials, for various reasons, wanted to see the British government create a federation in Central Africa, they tended to dismiss African objections as expressions of so much conservative sentimentality. At least, to those who drafted the conference's report, it seemed more urgent and important that they should prevent the introduction of South African racial policies into Central Africa than that they should respect redundant responses of enraged Africans.

"Consistent with the United Kingdom Government's responsibilities towards the African inhabitants" of the three territories, the conference recommended the creation of a federally governed British Central Africa. It proposed to exclude those subjects predominantly involving Africans from the federal purview, to provide for the indirect election of a very few Africans to the proposed unicameral federal legislature, and, by means of a complicated constitutional device—the African Affairs Board—to reserve certain kinds of federal legislation affecting African interests to the ultimate decision of the British government. It also provided for a Minister for African Interests, who would be a type of legislative watchdog. Implicitly the officials thought that legal draftmanship and cleverly designed constitutional formulas could effectively limit the exercise of power by white settlers, and that their federal creation could, in the ripeness of time, offer opportunities for political, economic, and social advance sufficient to compensate Africans for the loss of their previously entrenched rights. This was muddled thought. It mixed the quixotic with the cynical. But the report of the conference of official representatives at least recognized the need to allay African fears.

Influential white persons in and out of government attached great weight to the supposedly impartial recommendations. Creech Jones might conceivably have ignored them; but the federal concepts intrigued Griffiths and Gordon-Walker, both of whom received advice from the very persons who had drafted the report. They proposed to confer publicly with representatives of all shades of Rhodesian and Nyasa opinion after whites and Africans had had time to consider the scheme afresh. Africans reacted predictably. Banda, in London, and James Ralph Nthinda Chinyama, president-general of the Nyasaland Congress and a former president of the Lilongwe

Farmers' Association, denounced what they called a cynical plan to betray African interests. In Northern Rhodesia, the Congress re-enunciated its opposition to any form of federation. The threat of an imposed solution harmful to African interests also instilled a new fire into the nationalist movement. Simon ber Zukas, a white Rhodesian whose parents had emigrated to the Copperbelt before World War II from Lithuania, and Justin Chimba, Reuben Kamanga, Edward Mungoni Liso, and other young, militant Africans helped—the last three beforehand and Zukas at the time—to persuade delegates to the annual meeting of the Congress to replace the rather ineffectual Mbikusita Lewanika, their president, with Nkumbula, who had recently returned home from London.[43]

Zukas actively influenced the course of nationalist history. During his days as a schoolboy, he had been a model settler. He had even achieved the coveted rank of King's Scout. During 1945, Zukas served as a sergeant in the Third Battalion of the King's African Rifles. While stationed in Uganda, his battalion was sent to quell riots in Buganda; only then did he begin to question the validity of colonial rule in Africa. He wondered what "protection" meant. Later, during his student days at the University of Cape Town, he and other former soldiers began to criticize the color bar on moral grounds. Zukas also imbibed the waters of left-wing thought that ran through the academic terrain of Southern Africa. In 1948, with the assistance of James Robert Chikerema—later a leading Southern Rhodesian nationalist—he edited and mimeographed the "Rhodesia Study Club Newsletter." Until 1950, the newsletter circulated clandestinely in the Rhodesias; it displayed anticolonial, often crypto-Marxist sentiments. After receiving an engineering degree, Zukas returned to Ndola where he worked for the municipality and openly preached a message of equal rights for Africans. With Chimba, Kamanga, and Liso he formed the Anti-Federation Action Committee, and published *The Freedom Newsletter*, a broadsheet that dramatically presented the African point of view on a number of political issues. Finally, in 1951, he and his three principal African colleagues,

[43] Nkumbula's supporters capitalized upon Mbikusita Lewanika's failure to take a staunch anti-federal stand. Chimba and Kamanga subsequently became ministers in the first Zambia cabinet. In early 1951, Mbikusita Lewanika had reported Zukas to the police. He had come to be known as a "stooge" and an informer. Zukas and others also thought that he was in the pay of the government.

with some covert help from Thomas S. L. Fox-Pitt, a distinguished provincial commissioner on the verge of retirement, joined the Congress and voted for Nkumbula.

The delegates elected Nkumbula because he, alone of the possible replacements for Mbikusita Lewanika, possessed a militant mien, an intelligence that expressed itself articulately, and had attended an overseas university. He commanded a widespread reputation among Africans. Yet, at the time of his elevation to the presidency of the Congress, Nkumbula was earning his living by selling cowrie shells to gullible fellow Ila. The Government of Northern Rhodesia had, a year earlier, terminated Nkumbula's scholarship to the London School of Economics after he had failed its intermediate examination. The Government may also have objected to his political activities overseas; his associations with Banda and with the West African Students' Union—then aggressively anticolonial—were well known. He had also taken part in a number of meetings of the Fabian Colonial Bureau. In any event, despite Gore-Browne's activity on his behalf, when Nkumbula returned to Northern Rhodesia the government refused to give him the kind of position to which he thought himself entitled.

With Nkumbula at the helm, the Congress began to steer a more radical course. He and Zukas talked energetically of self-government for Africans. Their influence had already persuaded the Representative Council to replace Kasokolo and Nalumango on the Legislative Council with Yamba and Paskale Sokota, both members of the Congress. But, throughout 1951 and much of 1952, the Congress remained a weak and essentially unorganized collection of thirteen branches and eleven affiliated bodies. Despite its many stands against federation, it failed to halt the onrush of the federal juggernaut.

When they toured Central Africa, Griffiths, Gordon-Walker, and Cohen appreciated, perhaps for the first time, the extent and force of African opposition to federation. In September 1951, at the end of their visit, they convened the third Victoria Falls conference and insisted, despite Huggins' vituperative antagonism, upon the inclusion of Africans in the delegations from Northern Rhodesia and Nyasaland. The two secretaries of state also supported African demands that their traditional protected status should not be diluted. Neither Huggins nor Welensky would give way, however, and, after

Prime Minister Clement Atlee secretly informed Griffiths and Gordon-Walker of the imminent prorogation of Parliament, the conference ended abruptly and abortively. Yet, perhaps foolishly,
Griffiths and Gordon-Walker, with their eyes on the General Election, agreed—although Africans refused to assent—that the conference should publicly declare, and issue a press communiqué to the
effect that it favored federation in principle.[44] Had the Labour government continued in office, the movement for federation might have
died a natural death. At the very least it would have undergone
considerable modification to meet the more pronounced African
criticisms. However, the Labour Party lost the British General Election of October 1951, and the Conservative Party which formed the
government put federation high upon its list of legislative priorities.

THE ROAD TO CARLTON HOUSE TERRACE

The African nationalist movement in Nyasaland and Northern
Rhodesia gained strength from the British government's decision to
impose a federal solution upon the peoples of Central Africa. In
November 1951, Oliver Lyttleton (later Lord Chandos), the Conservative Secretary of State for the Colonies, announced that his
government favored federation unequivocally, that it supported the
conclusions of the conference of officials, and that he would convene a meeting early in the new year to discuss the idea further.
"In the light of the economic and other aspects," he hoped that
Africans would be prepared to accept "the assurances" embodied in
the report of the conference of officials.[45] Such hopes proved unwarranted and, conceivably, disingenuous. Earlier that month,
twenty-one representatives of a number of African organizations
had unquestionably repudiated "partnership" in any political form.
Meeting at Kitwe, they had accused the British government of betraying their protected status, and had rejected federation. "Africans have at heart," their most important resolution read, "the
strong feeling of becoming a nation."[46] In December, a special session of the Northern Rhodesian African Representative Council re-

[44]*The Times*, 22 September 1951. Cf. Gann, *History*, 412; Franklin, *Wedlock*,
59–61.

[45] *Closer Association in Central Africa: Statement by His Majesty's Government in the United Kingdom*, Cmd. 8411 (1951).

[46] *Northern News*, 9 November 1951.

fused even to help the government to define partnership. Yet, when opening the meeting, Rennie had described "partnership" as "a way of life and an attitude of mind" that throve "on honest intention and good will."[47] The next day, in Ndola, Huggins once again defined "partnership" for a European audience: "We do not pretend there is any equality of partnership at the present time, but the Native has joined the firm and has his foot on the lower rungs of the ladder; he will have to learn the wisdom of trying to help himself; we cannot carry the whole of his burden."[48]

As Gore-Browne had predicted in 1948: "The moment the Government at Home [was] convinced that it [was] to the Imperial advantage for Northern Rhodesia and Southern Rhodesia to be amalgamated—whether for purposes of trade, or for purposes of development . . . or more vital still for purposes of defence—then, immediately, . . . a formula [would] be devised and amalgamation [would] become a fact, and nothing [Africans or others] . . . [could] do here either for it or against it [would] make the slightest difference."[49] The moment in question arrived in late 1951; Lyttleton and his fellow Conservatives not surprisingly persuaded themselves that the federal form of amalgamation would benefit the British balance of payments, its world-wide strategic posture, the financial interests of the City of London, the British-backed copper companies of Northern Rhodesia, and the tobacco firms of Southern Rhodesia. With federation Britain would no longer be burdened by Nyasaland's steady drain on the Imperial exchequer. This British government, even more firmly than its predecessor, also sought a way by which it could simultaneously contain both apartheid and black nationalism. More than anything else, however, the Churchill government saw no reason why it should not make Africans the junior partners of whites. If Lyttleton, Lord Salisbury, the then Secretary of State for Commonwealth Relations, and other members of Churchill's cabinet appreciated the fervor of African opposition, they apparently thought it could either be suppressed or mollified. Moreover, Salisbury—who believed that whites should rule subject peoples almost everywhere—understood the importance of speed: We

---

[47] *African Representative Council Proceedings*, 8 (1952), 7.
[48] *Northern News*, 4 December 1951.
[49] Gore-Browne, 12 March 1948, in Northern Rhodesia, *Legislative Council Debates*, 60 (1948), cc. 133–134.

must rush federation forward, he said, because "if nothing is done [Africans] will become more and more averse to it and you might have trouble."[50]

With the odds against them, Africans fought back as the two Congresses grew in stature. "There is now a rising tide of nationalism among our people," Nkumbula aroused an emergency meeting of members of the Northern Rhodesian Congress. "We must have our own parliament," he declared, "in which Europeans and Indians will [only] have reserved seats." At his fiery best, Nkumbula aptly diagnosed the situation. "There existed," he said, "a cold war between the British government and the indigenous peoples of Africa."[51] Early in 1952, Huggins, Welensky, the respective governors, and the secretaries of state met in London and, at the behest of Huggins, emasculated further even those vague constitutional safeguards—particularly the African Affairs Board—that the officials had so carefully devised to allay indigenous suspicion and prevent untrammeled white domination. In an atmosphere of increasing tension, the Northern Rhodesian Congress for the first time threatened to use violence. "In the absence of normal constitutional power to prevent" it otherwise, Congress promised to oppose the imposition of the federation by the use of the "mass protest" weapon that Nkrumah had developed in the Gold Coast. Nkumbula warned Europeans in Northern Rhodesia that Africans would make their lives "intolerable" if the British government sanctioned the federation.[52] At the suggestion of Zukas, who together with Fox-Pitt attended its February 1952 meeting, the Congress also appointed a Supreme Action Council to plan and, if necessary, order a total stoppage of African work. Nkumbula thereafter appointed the Congress' first full-time provincial organizers and set about creating a truly national movement.

Others raised their voices in protest. In the Nyasaland Legislative Council, K. Ellerton Mposa (at one time a member of the Blantyre Native Association), Ernest Alexander Muwamba (the former leader of the Ndola Native Association), and the Rev. Mr. Andrew Doig (a leading Scottish missionary) urged the British government

[50] Quoted in Franklin, *Wedlock*, 65.
[51] Quoted in *Northern News*, 11 January 1952. Nkumbula's complete speech —which *Northern News* refused to publish because of its "inflammatory content"—was delivered on Christmas Day, 1951.
[52] Quoted in *Northern News*, 29 February 1952.

not to default upon its historic promise to transfer authority in the Protectorate only to Africans.[53] In Scotland, Dr. Banda and the Rev. Mr. Kenneth Mackenzie, who had served in both Nyasaland and Northern Rhodesia, persuaded a meeting of the Edinburgh World Church Group to denounce "federation" and to call for the eventual devolution of power in the protectorates to Africans. The Rhodesian coloured community rejected federation. And, in the rural areas of the two dependencies, Africans of many different persuasions added to the din of denunciation. The Chinsali African Welfare Association, for example, rejected federation outright because no one knew what "partnership" would mean in practice.[54]

Kenneth David Kaunda and Simon Mwansa Kapwepwe, two teachers who trained and taught, for a time, under Mackenzie, were then members of the Chinsali association along with Robert Kaunda, Kenneth's brother, and Reuben C. Mulenga, its dynamic secretary. Kaunda, later the first President of Zambia, and Kapwepwe, his first minister of home and foreign affairs, had long been friends. They had both previously taught on the Copperbelt after failing to find satisfactory teaching opportunities in Southern Rhodesia and Tanganyika. Both had participated in the activities of the urban welfare associations and the congress movement. Thereafter they had returned to Chinsali, Kapwepwe to teach and Kaunda to farm and peddle second-hand clothes purchased in and transported from Katanga. The campaign against federation gave them the opportunity to play a major part in nationalist politics.

During the months before the publication by the British government of a draft federal scheme, many Africans hoped unrealistically that the principles of "fair play" which they had come to associate with Britain would somehow prevail over the forces in favor of federation. Instead, Huggins and Salisbury counseled haste. The government of Northern Rhodesia secretly prepared an elaborate plan to meet the threat of African civil disturbances and, at the urging of Welensky, served notice of its intention to deport Zukas because he had supposedly conducted himself in a manner dangerous to peace and good order. It accused him of intriguing against

[53] Nyasaland Protectorate, *Proceedings of the Legislative Council,* 17 December 1951, 49–51.

[54] N/2193/2: Minutes of the meetings of 29 December 1951 and 16 February 1952, Lusaka archives.

constituted authority. The government knew that Zukas had publicly and privately advised the Congress to assume an aggressive posture. But it also suspected him—quite wrongly—of controlling and manipulating the Congress and Nkumbula, its president, for his own nefarious ends. The government and the leading Rhodesian newspapers, one of which Welensky controlled, called Zukas a communist. During the brief court proceedings, the Crown alleged that the defendant had called officials of the government of Northern Rhodesia "agents of imperialism," and that he had urged Africans opposed to "federation" to withhold their tax payments and go on strike. On the basis of such evidence, the presiding judge recommended that Zukas be deported.[55] The government refused to allow bail and Zukas, then twenty-six years old, languished in prison until, having exhausted the period during which he had leave to appeal to the Privy Council, he was deported to Britain in December. In time, he became a prosperous consulting engineer. He returned to Northern Rhodesia in 1964.

Meanwhile, Salisbury and Lyttleton had convened a meeting at Lancaster House, in London, of representatives and advisors from the four countries directly affected by the federal proposals. The settlers participated in force, and Julian Greenfield, a clever Bulawayo lawyer, and Whitehead, Huggins' financial expert, ultimately wrested important constitutional and economic concessions from the British negotiating team. Of the African delegates, only Joshua Nkomo and Jasper Savanhu, two Southern Rhodesians who respectively later occupied important positions in nationalist and governmental circles, took part.

The delegates from the protectorates—Yamba, Sokota, Musumbulwa, and Amos Walubita from Northern Rhodesia, and Mposa, Ernest Muwamba, E. K. Gondwe, and Clement R. Kumbikano from Nyasaland—on the advice of Dr. Banda, boycotted the official proceedings for fear that they might compromise their adamant opposition. The Northern Rhodesians knew the extent to which they had previously damaged their cause by participating in the third Victoria Falls confrontation. Nevertheless, Lyttleton tried on several occasions to persuade them to take part. He promised that "African

[55] *Northern News*, 5 and 8 April 1952. The Rhodesian counsel for the defense, who supported Welensky, seemingly refused to exert himself unduly on Zukas' behalf.

interests would be safeguarded in any federation." But he also told them that the case for federation appeared "unanswerable." "The most urgent reason," he said confidentially, "was the need to counteract the effect of increasing Afrikaner influence."[56] He also advanced the economic rationale—which the Korean war had given greater force—but failed to allay the suspicions of the delegates. They continued to maintain their boycott in the face of considerable pressures. Yamba told a press conference that he and his fellow representatives could not see how Southern Rhodesia, which had "put Africans right down in to the ditch, could come and nurse" the protectorates.[57]

Sessions of the Lancaster House conference occupied part of April and May 1952. Africans of the protectorates played no part, and their arguments accordingly went by default. Instead, Huggins, Welensky, Greenfield, and Whitehead persuaded the British government to meet settler objections on a number of crucial points by altering further the proposals initially advanced by the officials' conference of 1951. In the end they moderated what remained of the real powers of the suggested African Affairs Board, eliminated the position of the Minister for African Interests, gave the federal government important new responsibilities previously left with the states, moved important items from the "territorial list" to the "concurrent list" of subjects on which federal law would ultimately prevail, and, over-all, granted to the settlers a large portion of what Huggins had demanded at the second Victoria Falls meeting in 1949. Only the efforts of Edgar Unsworth, then Northern Rhodesia's Attorney General and later the Chief Justice of Nyasaland, apparently prevented the British government from eroding constitutional safeguards further.[58] In conclusion, the conferees offered a *Draft Federal Scheme,* and appointed three commissions to recommend solutions to outstanding judicial, fiscal, and staffing problems. Their reports would later prove the basis for a decisive conference.[59]

The political decisions had been taken. Yet, pending the final con-

---

[56] N/0002/3: Meeting of 18 April 1952, Lusaka archives.
[57] *Northern News,* 24 April 1952.
[58] Franklin, *Wedlock,* 71.
[59] See Southern Rhodesia, Northern Rhodesia, and Nyasaland: *Draft Federal Scheme,* Cmd. 8573 (1952); *Report of the Judicial Commission,* Cmd. 8671 (1952); *Report of the Fiscal Commission,* Cmd. 8672 (1952); *Report of the Civil Service Preparatory Commission,* Cmd. 8673 (1952).

ference, the issue of federation appeared to remain still in doubt. Both sides therefore unloosed their most potent verbal guns. They blazed away from Zomba and Lusaka to London and Edinburgh, enlivening innumerable platforms and providing the public press with the hot fire of controversy.[60] In a special article in *The Northern News*, Simon Albert Kaluwa, of the Northern Rhodesian Congress and the African Mineworkers' Union, carefully and at some length explained to a hostile white audience the reasons behind the almost universal African dislike of the federal proposals. With considerable prescience he predicted the ways in which the federal scheme, if adopted, would deprive Africans of a considerable part of what they had come to regard as their rights. He also showed how poorly the supposed "safeguards" of the draft scheme would work in practice.[61] At about this time, Nkumbula's various provincial organizers, of whom Kaunda was one, began to increase the influence of the Congress in the rural areas of the Protectorate. Then, in June 1952, Nkumbula continued the attack. Before a large public gathering of members of the Congress in Mapoloto Township, near Lusaka, he harangued and criticized in a style then new, but later, as the campaign against federation increased its intensity, to become common. Nkumbula said that he based his opposition to the federal scheme on the fact that the Europeans of Central Africa and the Conservative Government were patently aiming "at a complete domination and exploitation of the Black people of Central Africa." He condemned Huggins and Welensky personally. Then he moved to his peroration:

Ladies and gentlemen, we are being betrayed by the British government and it is high time that we tell the white people in this country that their support of this plan is not only dangerous to us but to their well being and happiness in this country. This is our country. There is no mistake about that. I have time and time again stated that imposition of this scheme against the wishes of . . . Africans will make life intolerable for the whites in Central Africa. I cannot say anything more about this. . . .

[60] For a select review of the pamphlet war see J. Gus Liebenow and Robert I. Rotberg, "Federalism in Rhodesia and Nyasaland," in William J. Livingston (ed.), *Federalism in the Commonwealth: A Bibliographical Commentary* (London, 1963), 207.
[61] *Northern News*, 20, 22 May 1952. Cf. Gore-Browne, in *ibid.*, 26 June 1952.

I must say one thing that I have always avoided. I cannot help thinking and convincing myself that . . . the best government for the black people is a government fully manned and run by the black people of Africa. That is also true of any race. I shall die a very unhappy man if I shall not see a truly African government in Central Africa. . . . The only safeguard [for] an African is self-government in which the African will play a predominant part in determining the destinies of his fellow men.[62]

The settlers and the governments of both Northern Rhodesia and Nyasaland worked in concert to counteract the effect of such views and to make the federal pill more palatable. The government of Northern Rhodesia even printed a rebuttal to Nkumbula's speech and distributed it to all provincial and district commissioners for further dissemination in African circles. At the behest of the Colonial Office, it also distributed propaganda pamphlets that had been prepared by the United Central Africa Association, a pro-federal British pressure group chaired by Huggins and supported by Lord Altrincham, a former governor of Kenya; Leopold S. Amery, a sometime Conservative Party Colonial Secretary; Sir Alfred Beit, the financier; and Sir Shenton Thomas, an earlier governor of Nyasaland, and backed financially by copper companies and interested parties in the City of London.[63] The government of Nyasaland itself published a pro-federal booklet in vernacular languages. Both governments purposely refrained from summoning meetings of their respective African councils.[64] Their governors ordered administrative officials to use every opportunity to forward the idea of federation. Rennie minuted a report by a district commissioner:

We must keep on explaining the main points of Federation, the main assurances, and this government's and His Majesty's Government's support of the draft Federal scheme. . . . The more widely the District Commissioner's explanations can be given the more chance there is of getting a few intelligent and independently-minded men to realize that some of the Congress' points are not true.[65]

[62] N/0001/2/5: Report of a meeting of 26 June 1952, Lusaka archives.
[63] The pamphlets bore the title: *The Only Way to Partnership between the Races* (London, 1952).
[64] N/0001/2/5: Vivian Fox-Strangways to Ronald Bush, 6 October 1952.
[65] *Ibid.*, minutes of 18 August 1952 on the District Commissioner (Mufulira) to the Provincial Commissioner (Ndola), 9 August 1952. But see Gann, *History*, 427. Significantly, Rennie conceded that "some" points *were* true.

Shortly thereafter, Ronald Bush, the Secretary for Native Affairs, instructed his subordinates to contradict so-called Congress "misstatements" at all costs. He urged them to concentrate their efforts upon the masses and to persuade some "average" people to declare themselves in favor of the federal plan.[66] Welensky subsequently paid Frank Kaluwa, an agent of the Capricorn Africa Society, to "sell" federation to rural Rhodesians.[67]

The settlers meanwhile confirmed the worst fears of the Africans. Welensky urged an audience of Europeans in Livingstone not to trouble their minds with respect to the African Affairs Board. "Time will show," he said, "that the Board's power is more limited than now appears." In Ndola, he reportedly told another meeting that "We do not want to dominate, but, if there is going to be domination, it is going to be my own race that will dominate. The African is unfit . . . to be a full partner."[68] In Southern Rhodesia, Whitehead spoke appreciatively of Northern Rhodesia's prosperity. "If we had Federation," he continued, "it would lighten the taxation problem very much indeed in this country." Later he explained that, when the federal government appeared on the scene, Southern Rhodesia would easily rid itself of more than half of its national debt—"a considerable relief."[69] Huggins, for another, made it abundantly clear that the federation now envisaged would possess powers approximating those of a dominion.[70] Others in the protectorates and overseas played similar refrains.

British parliamentarians toured the protectorates, but Africans found these newcomers also privy to what Africans had come thoroughly to regard as a conspiracy. In August 1952, Yamba, Sokota, Musumbulwa, Dixon Konkola, the chairman of the African Railways Union; Abner Kasunga, of the Ndola Urban Advisory Council; Law-

[66] Ibid., circular memorandum of 28 August 1952; Stubbs to Fox-Strangways, 31 October 1952. See also Governor Colby's address to the Nyasaland Legislative Council of the same date, Nyasaland Protectorate, Proceedings; Northern Rhodesia, Debates, 73 (1952), cc. 234–346; Griff Jones, Britain and Nyasaland (London, 1964), 151, 154.

[67] N/0001/2/4: passim, Lusaka archives. The Capricorn Society espoused multiracial, "moderate" views.

[68] Northern News, 17, 22 July 1952.

[69] Ibid., 12 July, 25 September 1952. See also Michael Faber, "Southern Rhodesia Alone? A Look at the Economic Consequences," South African Journal of Economics, xxviii (1960), 283–303.

[70] See also Northern News, 30 August 1952.

rence Katilungu, the president of the African Mineworkers Union; Lipalile, the headmaster of the Chingola school, chairman of the Chingola Welfare Society, and vice-treasurer of the Congress; and Nkumbula tried to put arguments against federation to Henry Hopkinson (later Lord Colyton), the British Minister of State for Colonial Affairs. But Hopkinson refused to believe that they, or the officers of the Nyasaland Congress, spoke for the mass of Africans.

In Northern Nyasaland, a delegation of five chiefs reiterated what the congressmen had said. Even so, Hopkinson later told the press that Congress' claim that African opinion was "solidly against federation" was untrue. "African opinion on the subject," he decided, "hardly exists."[71] Throughout the area of the proposed federation, Hopkinson addressed seventy-eight formal meetings of Africans. He met chiefs and officials of Congress, Europeans, Asians, and coloureds. To everyone he urged the advantages of federation, and demonstrated over and over again that although the British government still "had an open mind," it was "100% behind Federation."[72] He felt that the federal scheme now contained greater safeguards than before. He echoed the thoughts of many who believed, quite sincerely, that humanity—both black and white—would in time benefit immeasurably from federalism:

In Central Africa we have a field in which to carry out a great social experiment, and we think federation is the proper background against which partnership can flourish. At every opportunity I told Africans that the territories are multi-racial; European settlers have contributed greatly to their development and welfare . . . and they are there to stay.[73]

Attlee, the former British prime minister, followed Hopkinson into the Rhodesias and, to the dismay of Africans, echoed his sentiments. He told Congressmen and chiefs that the Labour Party backed the federal scheme on economic grounds. Attlee even supported Welensky's demand for 500,000 white immigrants.[74]

In desperation, the Congress movement adopted doctrines that it had previously rejected. At a joint meeting of leading chiefs and its

[71] Quoted in *East Africa and Rhodesia*, 4 September 1952.
[72] *Northern News*, 2 August 1952.
[73] *East Africa and Rhodesia*, 4 September 1952.
[74] *Northern News*, 2 September 1952. See also Peter Fraenkel, *Wayaleshi* (London, 1959), 167–169. Attlee later changed his mind.

officers, Congress demanded self-government. It drafted a constitution that provided for a bicameral parliament with a strong lower house elected by British subjects and British-protected persons voting on separate voters' rolls. It further excluded the mass of Africans by suggesting a qualified franchise; voters would need to earn at least £100 a year. The upper house, which would possess limited powers of review, would contain members of the prominent racial communities in equal proportions. This draft scheme also outlined four gradual stages during which the protectorate would shed itself of British oversight and move toward self-government. Only in the final phases would the proposers introduce a universal franchise.[75] This was an imaginative, to some extent realistic, proposal. But its provenance, and the atmosphere in which it was unfolded, prevented whites from paying it due attention. It amused the Secretariat. Moreover, its implications then seemed far too radical.

The Nyasaland Congress fared little better. By this time it too favored a period of accelerated tutelage that would lead the British government to transfer power to Africans and, ultimately, to grant them self-government. Its stand against federation had already become hackneyed. In these circumstances, Governor Colby and Vivian Fox-Strangways, his Secretary for Native Affairs, summoned Chinyama and Chinula, the president and vice-president of Congress respectively, to Government House. The governor tried to persuade them to cease agitating against federation. "Congress," he told Chinyama and Chinula, "was playing with fire, with things that they did not understand and which were likely to get out of their control." With regard to self-government, when that day arrived "it would be a self-government which would take account of the rights of all races" and Congress "must understand this once and for all." The governor further told Chinyama and Chinula that when and if the Nyasaland Government decided that federation was not in the interests of Africans, "they would say so."[76] The governor gave the two leaders of Congress little opportunity to reply or object. They

[75] African National Congress. Northern Rhodesia, "Proposed Constitution for a Self-Governing State of Northern Rhodesia as Adopted by the Chiefs in Conference," 18–25 August 1952 (mimeographed). Congress produced this scheme in response to a suggestion made by the Fabian Colonial Bureau.

[76] 10120: Minutes of a meeting at Government House, 29 October 1952, Zomba archives. See also the address of Governor Rennie to the opening session of the Northern Rhodesian Representative Council, 18 December 1952, *Proceedings*, 9 (1953), cc. 7–9.

understood the meaning of the sermon. Much later, under another governor, its message received a fuller expression.

In January 1953, at Carlton House Terrace, in London, the final intergovernmental conference agreed upon a constitution for the proposed federation. The delegates, none of whom were Africans (they boycotted the meeting), enthusiastically urged the immediate adoption of a scheme that essentially embodied the provisions discussed earlier at Lancaster House. Again, however, the British government agreed to lessen the impact of the African Affairs Board. It now became no more than a standing committee of the federal parliament. Similarly, the federal government added to the extent of its powers *vis-à-vis* the three states. In the last analysis, the British government conveniently obscured the many promises that it had made to Africans. As indicated by Gore-Browne, when circumstances appeared to demand it of them, British officials simply abdicated their responsibilities in Central Africa and, at least in the eyes of Africans, abandoned their faithful subjects to a government of white settlers. "We have reached the moment for decision," the Carlton House Terrace report affirmed.

We are convinced that a Federation . . . is the only practicable means by which the three Central African Territories can achieve security for the future and ensure the well-being and contentment of all their peoples. We believe that this Federal Scheme is a sound and a fair scheme which will promote the essential interests of all the inhabitants of the three Territories, and that it should be carried through.[77]

Africans warned the British government of the consequences that would follow the implementation of the plan formulated at Carlton House Terrace. A week after the conclusion of that confer-

[77] Southern Rhodesia, Northern Rhodesia, and Nyasaland, *Report by the Conference on Federation Held in London in January, 1953,* Cmd. 8753 (1953), 7. See also the text in *The Federal Scheme for Southern Rhodesia, Northern Rhodesia and Nyasaland Prepared by a Conference Held in London, January, 1953,* Cmd. 8754 (1953). Some of the officials on the spot may have "abdicated their responsibilities" in good faith. "As far as Nyasaland was concerned the tragedy was not that officials abdicated their responsibilities but that because of the poverty of the country they persuaded themselves that the extract quoted was in fact true and that though the Africans might not like Federation it was a betrayal of the trusteeship principle *not* to enter the Federation which would, in the long run, be in the best interests of the African population. It was this belief on the part of the bulk of the senior civil servants that vitiated the doubts expressed by the few." Ian Nance, letter to the author, 4 October 1964.

ence, Dr. Banda, Nkomo, and a delegation of important chiefs from Northern Rhodesia and Nyasaland predicted bloodshed. The Ngoni Paramount Chief, Nkosi ya Makosi M'mbelwa II, asserted that the British government could only impose federation by using bombs and guns. Chief Maganga, a Cewa from Central Nyasaland, said that if the British people wanted to federate Central Africa, they could do so. "They are a powerful country. . . . They can come home and kill every child, man and woman, and then they can federate our country." Nkomo promised that Africans would not take the imposition of a federal government "sitting down." Only later did Europeans recall his message: "Africans shall struggle. They will use every power they have to fight against this scheme. Let there be no illusions about this. Let us not be blamed that the Africans resort to savagery again. . . . We refuse to be bound by unjust laws."

Banda approached the problem calmly. Federation, he said, had been designed specifically to deprive Africans of their right to govern themselves. After these many years, he accused the British government of defaulting upon its policy of guardianship by handing Africans over to whites in a "cold, calculated, callous and cynical betrayal of a trusting, loyal people." Then he declaimed:

It is not I, the agitator in London, who is opposing federation. It is my people at home. You cannot bring to Central Africa partnership by force. Partnership between the Europeans and the Africans can only come from their hearts and minds. We, the Africans of Nyasaland and Northern Rhodesia, are people. Some of the clauses of the Atlantic Charter which Mr. Roosevelt and your Mr. Churchill signed guaranteed territorial integrity and the right of any people to choose the form of government under which they would live. We, the Africans of Nyasaland and Northern Rhodesia, are people under the provisions of the charter and this clause that guarantees the rights of the people to choose their own form of government.[78]

A new, legislated "partnership" loomed on the Central African horizon. In the protectorates themselves, however, racial inter-

[78] 2/14: Verbatim report of a public meeting held at Church House, Westminster, London, 23 January 1953, Lusaka archives. For the opposition of a delegation of chiefs then touring Britain and their petition, see the *Nyasaland Times*, 2 February 1953; *East Africa and Rhodesia*, 15 January 1953; G. Michael Scott, *A Time to Speak* (London, 1958), 277–279, 341–342. The Queen was advised to decline to see them.

action continued to follow its traditional course. In February, for example, the former mayor of Ndola and two other white men apparently without provocation assaulted an African at night in a dark alley. The African in question lost the sight of an eye; the local white magistrate fined the three white men only £5 each. He declined to try them on charges that would have carried stiffer punishments. Later in the month, a white railway clerk refused to sell Nkumbula a ticket at Mazabuka, shoved him out of the office, and jammed a door on his fingers. The clerk complained that Nkumbula had used abusive language, and a magistrate fined the latter £1.[79] In the Legislative Council, Yamba tried afresh to make his white colleagues appreciate the way in which discrimination actively vitiated talk of "partnership." He raised a number of specific examples. In Kitwe, the banks refused even to permit Sokota, a member of the Council, to stand in line with whites. When Yamba and other African members of the delegation to Britain returned home, they landed at Ndola airport. There the mayor ordered them out of a facility that had evidently been appropriated for use by whites only.

Suddenly . . . a certain gentleman . . . [told] us that we were not rightful members of the community to walk in a common and a public place of convenience, and that a second place was put aside for people of our type. . . . I told the gentleman how shameful it was that when I leave my own country, . . . I am given that respect which I require, but when I drop in my own home I am told . . . to be careful where to move. . . . That is really a prison, it is not the home.[80]

Before the federal bill could come into being, the British Parliament, the voters of Southern Rhodesia, the two legislative councils, and Queen Elizabeth all needed to approve it. During the last stages of the debate in Parliament, Nkumbula symbolically burned the federal white papers (Cmd. 8573 and 8574) before a Lusaka audience of eight hundred Africans and six prominent chiefs. Self-government had become the Congress' only important objective, and Nkumbula, interpreted from English into Cibemba by Kaunda, once again threatened widespread unrest if the British government continued with its plans to create a Central African federation. Despite

[79] *Northern News*, 18, 24 February 1953. Both magistrates were Britons.
[80] Dauti Yamba, 25 February 1953, Northern Rhodesia, *Debates*, 76 (1953), cc. 281–282.

the firm opposition of the Archbishop of Canterbury, he called for two days of prayer during which no African should work for a white employer. The poorly organized strike failed. The leaders of the African Mineworkers' Union refused to cooperate, and Nkumbula may have acted indecisively after learning that the government had suggested that he be deported to the Seychelles. Only in Mufulira, Lusaka, and Chilanga did Africans abstain from work in any number. Nonetheless, Nkumbula had introduced the boycott weapon into the nationalist arsenal.[81]

Early in April, three thousand Africans crammed the market square in Blantyre to attend an emergency conference of the Nyasaland Congress. They listened to Chinyama, to the chiefs who had visited Britain, to a summary of a letter from Dr. Banda, and to the Rev. Mr. Michael Scott, the director of the Africa Bureau in London, before resolving to meet the imposition of federation by "the strongest non-violent resistance." They threatened a national withdrawal of their labor, the non-payment of taxes, a wholesale boycott of European-owned stores, and appeals to the United Nations and the International Court of Justice. Like Northern Rhodesians, they wanted self-government.[82]

Huggins, Welensky, and a number of Britons still feared that the ship of federation might yet founder on the rocks of white opposition in Southern Rhodesia. They believed that many whites might prefer association with the Union of South Africa to ties, however advantageous, with the protectorates. In mid-April, however, the electorate demonstrated their understanding of the federal scheme. Sixty-two percent, or 25,570 persons, voted in favor of federation (82 percent of the electorate actually cast ballots). A total of 14,729 opposed, and Fort Victoria, the Afrikaans-speaking stronghold of the colony, rejected the proposal overwhelmingly. No more than 380 Africans could participate.[83] Later in the month the two legislative councils overrode vehement African objections and supported motions backing federation. Otherwise, neither Europeans nor Africans living in the protectorates received the opportunity to express

[81] N/0001/2/15, passim. See also A. L. Epstein, Politics in an Urban African Community (Manchester, 1958), 161; Fraenkel, Wayaleshi, 176–179.

[82] 10120: Resolutions of the Emergency General Conference, Blantyre, 5–6 April 1953; Northern News, 23, 26, 30 March, 3, 8 April 1953; Nyasaland Times, 9 April 1953.

[83] Northern News, 10, 11 April 1953.

their feelings with regard to the federal proposals. The oft-repeated official reassurances appeared to have gone for naught.

In desperation the two congresses besieged their own and the British governments with pleas, petitions, and propositions. In Nyasaland, Chief Mwase and twenty-three other tribal leaders asked to be heard before the Bar of the House of Commons. Alternatively, they asked the Commons to follow the precedent of 1931 and to appoint a select committee to ascertain the real feelings of the people concerned.[84] One hundred thirty Northern Rhodesian chiefs petitioned Queen Elizabeth not to erode the protection previously granted to them by Queen Victoria. In desperation Nkumbula even supported Gore-Browne's plan for the partition of Central Africa into separate white- and African-governed areas.[85]

Nyasas meanwhile greeted the rumors that Dr. Banda might return home with great satisfaction; but the rumors proved false, and Banda instead left England for the Gold Coast. Thereafter, their political leaders urged supporters of the Congress to refrain from participating in any activities sponsored by the government. They forbade dancing, because "it was a time of crying." Chief Mwase refused to attend the Queen's coronation (but the Yao Chief Kawinga went in his stead). Chief Phillip Gomani of the Ncheu Ngoni obstinately ordered his people to disregard all agricultural, forestry, and veterinary laws. He suggested that they should refuse to pay taxes. Consequently, the government of Nyasaland deposed him and ordered him out of the Ncheu district. In the course of attempting to effect his arrest, the government precipitated a riot and the chief, his son Willard Gomani—later chief and a member of the first Malawi Parliament—and Michael Scott fled into Moçambique, where they were apprehended and returned to Nyasaland for trial and, in Scott's case, for deportation. Two months later, the government of Nyasaland charged McKinley Qabaniso Y. Chibambo and two other Africans with sedition. Their opposition to federation resulted in prison sentences and, for Chibambo at least, a long enforced exile in humid Port Herald.[86]

[84] *Manchester Guardian*, 23 March 1953, had already suggested the second alternative.

[85] Gore-Browne Papers: Sir Stewart Gore-Browne to Angela Gore-Browne, 28 April 1953; *Northern News*, 29 April 1953.

[86] *Nyasaland Times*, 14, 18, 21, 25 May, 1 June, 6, 30 July 1953. Scott, *Speak*, 282–284.

"We are not protesting blindly," Chief Mwase tried to explain. "We are protesting for our future centuries. We cannot sell our FREEDOM." His letter continued:

I am sorry many officials and some of the Lords feel it as an easy thing to oppress us in this way, forgetting that we are no [longer] slaves [having been] . . . completely saved from all slavery . . . by the Bible where a human being has equal rights [and] by the protection of . . . Queen Victoria who . . . granted to our Grandparents, a full protection from any power outside to attack us. Even today we trust . . . Queen Elizabeth II will carry such protection . . . [and will] not hand us over to a Government which . . . aims to use Africans [as] labourers, and not as partners.[87]

But, a day after this somber protest appeared in print, the House of Lords ratified the federal enabling bill, the House of Commons having done so in June, and Queen Elizabeth gave to it the royal assent. The much-vaunted federal experiment—what a governor later called "the great opportunity, perhaps the last opportunity to create an influential State in Africa where colour and race were to become of no account."[88]—began legally on 1 August 1953, a day which marked the end of the African campaign against what they conceived to be a political betrayal and the beginning of the nationalist struggle for independence from any kind of alien rule whatsoever. Instead of ensuring white domination for the foreseeable future, the federal gambit hastened the day when Nyasas and Northern Rhodesians would govern themselves.

[87] Letter to the editor, *Nyasaland Times*, 13 July 1953.
[88] Sir Arthur Benson, in a letter to the editor of *The Times*, 20 February 1961. The federal government was not formed until September 1953.

Chapter X

THE FEDERAL DREAM AND AFRICAN REALITY

People who are oppressed come to a stage where . . . the people, deprived of expressing themselves by constitutional means, tend to take means that are violent . . . the Government is forcing the African people into that position. . . . African rule will come. We are going to overthrow you one day; you just wait. . . . A minority race can never rule a majority race for ever. That has never been done anywhere.

—Wellington Manoah Chirwa, in the Federal Assembly, 16 December 1957, *Debates*, 1798, 2160

The Federation of Rhodesia and Nyasaland emerged from the crucible of racial antagonism with a mandate to rule about eight million Africans and two hundred thousand whites for the benefit of both. Supposedly, its creed was partnership. Humanitarians expected white Rhodesians to share the attributes and prerogatives of power with Africans. They assumed that the federal government would gradually try to create a truly multiracial society where color would be of no significance. Had the federal government translated these ideals into practice, it would have generated an enthusiastic African response. By so doing, it would probably have undercut the strength of nationalism. But partnership seemed a hollow creed, and Africans continued to view federation as a cynical device designed to perpetuate white domination between the Limpopo River and Lake Tanganyika. Although they may have hoped, only a few believed that the inauguration of the federation could persuade Europeans to change their way of life and their deeply rooted attitudes toward Africans.

Partnership possessed an air of liberal respectability. From the first days of Federal rule, however, Huggins and Welensky abundantly demonstrated their contempt for African sensitivities and aspirations. Within sixty days of taking office in the Federal cabinet, Huggins, the prime minister, and Welensky, his heir-apparent and the minister of transport and development, both made it clear that they still wanted to remove the last vestiges of British control in order to achieve their independence as a dominion. They wanted what Africans had always feared that whites might obtain—absolute control over "native policies." Even without such total mastery of Central Africa, Huggins reassured his white followers that he would never allow Africans to play an equal part in the affairs of the Federation. If and when Africans threatened white hegemony, Huggins promised to alter the Federal constitution. Welensky, speaking in Northern Rhodesia, explained that partnership presumed no more than cooperation between Africans and their European masters. "We do not want social equality," he said, "we mix with our social peers and no one can legislate against that." The Federal government proposed to guide Africans along a white-defined path toward goals that, nonetheless, remained inferior. Welensky explained that Africans would "never" be capable of holding "European" jobs. A few months later, Oliver Lyttleton, the British Secretary of State for the Colonies, visited Lusaka. "It is significant," he remarked, "that what is happening in Africa is occurring in a continent which since the dawn of time has not made any noticeable contribution to civilization."[1] Later he refused to meet the leading African politicians of the two protectorates.

A debate in the first Federal Assembly illustrated the real meaning of multiracial partnership. Dauti Yamba, one of the two indirectly elected African representatives from Northern Rhodesia, moved "that equal treatment be accorded immediately to all races in all public places within the Federation and that such action be enforced by [Federal] legislation." He asked for concrete legislative or administrative expressions of partnership. Instead, he received ridicule from the prime minister. Huggins refused to allow Africans to use "white" entrances to post offices or to expect impartial service on the railways, both federally controlled.

If this motion were carried out . . . it would create so much ill-feeling and so much resentment in the Europeans that we should put back the clock of advancement and cooperation and partnership by at least ten years. It is a very mischievous motion. . . . You cannot expect the Euro-

[1] *Central African Post*, 23 October 1953; 15 January 1954.

pean to form up in a queue with dirty people, possibly an old *mfazi* [African woman] with an infant on her back, mewling and puking and making a mess. . . .

"It is perfectly obvious," Huggins concluded, "that the system we have . . . at . . . present . . . is the most satisfactory to both sides."[2] Later in the debate, Huggins boasted that he could and would make differential laws for different sections and peoples of the Federation. Patently, under the Federal system, Africans in the protectorates could expect to find themselves subjected to "separate development"—the traditional segregationist policy of Southern Rhodesia. Every speech by Huggins and Welensky deepened their fears.

In practice, the first five years of Federal rule saw no important relaxations in the administration of public and private color bars. Post offices retained separate entrances, hospitals separate services and plants, and the railways differential facilities of all kinds. The Central African Airways belatedly began to carry African passengers. Hotels, stores, and private establishments discriminated. An industrial color bar effectively prevented Africans from competing with whites for jobs. Even the federal civil service remained a white preserve. As late as 1962, only nine Africans had obtained administrative or executive positions in it. In that year, when Jasper Savanhu resigned as the parliamentary secretary to the Federal Ministry of Home Affairs, he cited these figures to support a statement of his disillusionment. "I have finally reached the decision," he wrote to Welensky, "that your government, despite strong representation by the African party members . . . has failed or has no intention of fully implementing the policy of partnership. . . . As matters stand today I feel that my presence . . . is only tolerated and I feel . . . a piece of window dressing."[3]

[2] Federation of Rhodesia and Nyasaland, *Debates of the Federal Assembly*, 1 (28 July 1954). Yamba commented that all he had tried to obtain was "a promise by the Federal Government that all races will be given a fair play, but pity the [Prime] Minister went too far out of rail, and instead of trying to catch the Africans' confidence he simply added the insults to the injuries. Sir, I must say that his speech was harmful to the progress of Federation." Gore-Browne Papers: Dauti Yamba to Sir Stewart Gore-Browne, 10 January 1955.

[3] Quoted in Robert I. Rotberg, "Welensky's Last Stand," *The New Republic* (24 September 1962), 10.

Whites consciously deprived Africans of meaningful representation in the Federal Assembly. Until 1956, the Representative and Protectorate councils of Northern Rhodesia and Nyasaland each selected two Africans to sit in the Federal Assembly. Thereafter, however, the size of the Assembly increased and four instead of two Africans sat for each protectorate. But, of the four, Europeans virtually elected two. Moreover, these changes and the increase in European representation diminished African participation in the Assembly. From 1953, the qualified Federal franchise also discriminated against Africans. In 1957, the Assembly altered its provisions in order to disadvantage African voters further. In addition, a complicated dual roll arrangement seriously devalued the votes of the few Africans who cast ballots.

These measures provided the first test for the African Affairs Board. In particular, it termed the Constitution Amendment Bill discriminatory, and urged the British government to disallow it. Unbeknown to the Board, however, the Secretaries of State for the Colonies and Commonwealth Relations had already sanctioned these additional legal entrenchments of white privilege. Their subsequent refusal to support the African Affairs Board thus provided African politicians with additional evidence of the "great betrayal."[4] In these circumstances, Wellington Manoah Chirwa, a "moderate" who sat for Nyasaland in the Assembly, warned that Africans would no longer "look to Britain nor to the Europeans of Central Africa for justice." They must, he said, "look to their own means to get that justice." After all, "people deprived of expressing themselves by constitutional means tend to take means that are violent."

[You] are digging the graves of the Europeans in Central Africa. . . . You can only control people if they have confidence in you. If that is lost you cannot control them. You can smash them, you can destroy them, but you cannot control them. If the Government were to kill or destroy them, the spirit of the African people would never yield.[5]

Yet, if nothing else, many expected the creation of the Federation to profit the inhabitants of the protectorates economically. The re-

[4] See Colin Leys and Cranford Pratt (eds.), *A New Deal in Central Africa* (London, 1960), 113–117; Harry Franklin, *Unholy Wedlock* (London, 1963), 129.

[5] Federation, *Debates*, 8 (16 December 1957), cc. 1778–1779. See also cc. 229–230, 362–364, 390–391, 504–506, 2159–2160.

verse, however, appears to reflect the facts with greater accuracy. Southern Rhodesia drained revenue and revenue-producing industrial and service establishments from Northern Rhodesia. To its clear benefit, Southern Rhodesia tapped about £70 million of taxes that the government of Northern Rhodesia could otherwise have used to better the life of its own citizens. From the pool, Nyasaland gained new medical facilities and improved roads. But, relatively, Nyasaland and Northern Rhodesia shouldered proportionally more of their previous expenses than Southern Rhodesia which, for example, transferred its former responsibilities for European education and agriculture to the Federal exchequer. The Federal government, in turn, spent more absolutely upon European schooling than the three territorial governments together spent to educate Africans. Its decision to build the Kariba rather than the economically and structurally more sensible Kafue dam also limited the economic growth of Northern Rhodesia, while its southern neighbor benefited considerably.[6] Whites in this one dramatic instance did in fact take African land in the way envisaged by those who had fought against the imposition of federation. The decision to construct Kariba furthermore forestalled the development of the Shire Valley hydroelectric project in Nyasaland.

In direct economic terms, the Federation affected Africans adversely. The Federal government spent more, in both proportional and absolute terms, on whites. Admittedly, whites contributed about twice as much in direct taxes to the revenues of the four governments concerned. But, if one compares the levels of personal income (during the ten-year period 1953–1963, annual per capita money incomes were about £700 in the European and £15 in the African sector), Africans felt the impact of direct taxation far more severely than whites. Of even greater moment, Africans apparently bore the major brunt of indirect taxation. In 1955 and 1956, the Federal government deliberately taxed the least expensive brands of cigarettes more heavily. It also raised duties on cheap imported clothing. In 1958, it reduced the subsidy on maize, an African staple, thereby increasing the cost of food to Africans considerably.[7] In these

[6] For "The Great Kariba Swindle," see Franklin, *Wedlock*, 105–120.

[7] William J. Barber, "Federation and the Distribution of Economic Benefits," in Leys and Pratt, *New Deal*, 90–94; Arthur Hazlewood and P. Arthur Henderson, *Nyasaland: The Economics of Federation* (Oxford, 1960), 64–91.

instances, and in innumerable other specific ways, the Federal government heightened the level of African discontent. In African eyes, the actual economic experience failed to support the lavish claims previously made on behalf of the Federal experiment.

THE BITTERNESS

If the struggle against the imposition of the Federation fired the nationalists of Nyasaland and Northern Rhodesia, their failure to forestall its creation and their bitter experiences of partnership after its inception served further to inflame Central Africa. Whereas Africans had hitherto challenged primarily the social and economic disadvantages of colonial rule, the lesson of the federation taught them to distrust British political intentions as well. Africans thereafter appreciated that their own efforts alone would determine the ultimate outcome of the struggle against the real threat of settler domination. And in this struggle, nationalist leaders could for the first time count upon the sympathy of the mass of the indigenous population. Support came later, but initially both Congresses represented rather than deployed popular opinion. Nevertheless, in the early days of the Federation, the Congresses remained weak, poorly organized bodies lacking deep institutional roots. During this period, they also were hindered by the willingness of "moderate" Africans to test the principles of partnership in practice. Throughout, however, nationalists in both protectorates steadfastly sought the right to secede from the Federation and endeavored to promote their own claims upon an independent future.

Both Congress movements employed weapons borrowed from campaigns elsewhere against British rule. They groped ceaselessly for ways in which to exploit the obvious grievances of the day. Petitions and memorials circulated anew, boycotts became common, and *ad hoc* outbreaks of violence testified to the existence of a fast-running current of discontent beneath pools of surface calm. Despite official hostility, nationalist leaders attempted to control this discontent and to divert its flow into constructive channels. Simultaneously, historical enmities between white and black, Federal action inimical to "protected persons," and the failure of Federal statesmen to honor their pledges of partnership fed the springs of African disenchantment. Throughout the first six years of the Federal experiment, the tide of nationalism thus grew until it threatened to inundate the previously sacrosanct islands of white privilege.

Disturbances punctuated the first months of the Federation. In Nyasaland, where the deportation of the Rev. Mr. Michael Scott, the deposition of Chief Phillip Gomani, and the detention of McKinley Qabaniso Chibambo had already dramatized the lack of Anglo-African rapport, widespread unrest expressed the depths of indigenous hostility. In August 1953, the Cholo district, where pressures on the land had always been acute, provided the scene for further demonstrations of discontent. The so-called Cholo riots grew out of a series of non-political incidents that, perhaps at the suggestion of local Congressmen, assumed political significance.

One evening in mid-August, a small group of Europeans apprehended two Africans who had apparently stolen a large quantity of oranges from white-owned citrus groves on the Tennent estate between Cholo and Luchenza. The whites planned to take the thieves to the district commissioner's office in Cholo but, before they were able to do so, a number of armed Africans responded to cries from the thieves; frightened, the European planters released their prisoners and fled, some on foot and some by car—after stuffing the sacks of stolen oranges into its luggage compartment. Confusion corrupted later reports of the melee, but the Africans involved believed that the Europeans had killed the thieves and had put bodies, not oranges, into the car. The pursuing Africans may also have assumed that the planters in question practiced *cifwamba*, the mysterious cannibalistic ritual that Africans often associate with whites. For whatever combination of motives, when daylight came about one thousand Africans attacked nearby European residences and the Tennent estate office despite the intervention of the local district commissioner. They later cut telephone wires, blocked the main road, and refused to accept anything less than the trial and imprisonment of the Europeans who had supposedly killed the two citrus thieves.

Police reinforcements arrived about midday, and the mood of the large crowd grew uglier. The district commissioner read the riot act, which few heard; the police charged the crowd with batons; and then a policeman accidentally discharged his rifle, killing one of the crowd. This event naturally aroused the Africans surrounding the estate office. They stoned the police, injuring two whites, who retaliated by tossing tear-gas grenades. Neither the stones nor the tear gas dissolved the stalemate, and the stoning continued for several hours. But the police arrested Village Headman Ngamwane, who they termed a leading agitator, and other Africans finally persuaded their fellows to disperse pending Ngamwane's hearing in court.

By the morning of 20 August, Africans had come to direct their anger against whites generally. In addition to their earlier complaint against the planters, they resented the arrest of Ngamwane. About six thousand armed Africans surrounded the district office in Cholo and demanded the release of their headman. But the police had already taken him to Limbe, twenty miles away. Africans blocked the nearby roads, and their truculent attitude eventually persuaded the provincial commissioner in charge to obtain the release on bail of Ngamwane. He returned the headman to Cholo in the afternoon, and the crowd gradually dispersed.[8]

During the course of the next week, small gangs of armed Africans moved about the Cholo district encouraging estate laborers to stop work. Africans blocked main and secondary roads throughout the district, cut telephone wires, hindered police patrols, struck the Luchenza Plywood factory and the railways, frightened the staff of the Seventh-day Adventist mission at Malamulo, fired tea plantations, and generally contributed to an atmosphere of disorder. The Government of Nyasaland therefore obtained police reinforcements from Tanganyika and Northern and Southern Rhodesia. These forces saw service on 27 and 28 August, when the Government of Nyasaland tried Ngamwane at Cholo. The magistrate dismissed the case for lack of evidence, but Africans who had crowded around the *boma* refused to disperse until the police used force. For four miles, a Northern Rhodesian newspaper later reported, "one platoon had to blast its way through a road which was blocked every 100 yards with rioters."[9] They used tear gas, injured a number of Africans, and then began to round up tax evaders—many of whom had supposedly swelled the ranks of the rioters—and to try them at a rate of forty cases an hour.

[8] "Report of the Commission of Enquiry . . . on the Recent Disturbances in the Southern Province," in *Nyasaland Times*, 29 October 1953.

[9] *Central African Post,* 23 October 1953.

The spirit of disaffection spread, apparently with the help of the Congress, throughout southern Nyasaland. In the Chikwawa district Africans blocked the main roads and spoke of deposing Chief Katunga, who had refused to oppose the federation openly. In the Chiradzulu district, Africans again blockaded the roads, particularly those leading to the court of Chief Kadewere, and sought to punish that chief for his support of the Federation. Later they fought police detachments sent to free Kadewere, who reached the safety of Limbe only after a pitched battle during which the police opened fire. People living in Chief Ntondeza's section of the Cholo district —where Wilfred Good had earlier disturbed the peace—burned estates, fired Chief Ntondeza's court, destroyed bridges, and felled trees across the roads of their district. Nearby, rioters attacked a tung oil experimental station. On the last evening of August, in yet another section of the Cholo district, armed Africans tried to depose Chief Chitera. They stoned the police, who killed two and wounded two more.

These, and a number of other clashes between Africans and the police, reflected the prevalent malaise. They were sporadic responses of a number of different groups for whom the imposition of the federation proved the final blow. Yet, despite the degree to which the Congress had capitalized upon the original agitation and had later promoted new confrontations between Africans and the government, these disturbances lacked a central coordination. Their character gained confusion during September, when Africans began to drift back to work on the plantations. The police arrested "troublemakers" with little difficulty.

District Commissioners managed to compel Africans almost everywhere to begin paying their taxes for the year. But in rural sections of the Blantyre district, tax collectors met hostility. There, and in the Chikwawa, Mlanje, and Port Herald districts, Africans destroyed property belonging to various Native Authorities, stoned police and, in Port Herald, rioted. Later, at Domasi, two hundred Africans armed with spears, axes, and bows and arrows tried to prevent the district commissioner from trying a village headman who had been accused of transgressing agricultural laws. The police, in attempting to disarm the crowd, riled them, and stoning in turn provoked retaliation in the form of bullets. Two Africans died in this clash, bringing the total number of African dead to eleven during August and September.[10]

The leaders of the Congress refused to take responsibility for the disturbances. Like Joseph Danquah, George Grant, and others in the Gold Coast, Ralph Chinyama, the president of the Congress, claimed that he personally, and the central leadership of the Congress more generally, regretted the outbursts of violence. He believed that the Congress movement should continue to seek the political kingdom only by following constitutional paths. The Congress therefore cancelled its program of "non-cooperation," and instead demanded that the Government of Nyasaland should henceforth grant to Africans the right to elect half of the members of the Legislative and Executive councils. The Council of Chiefs, led by Mwase, joined the Congress in asking the governor for equality on those councils as well as on a number of other representative bodies. Together, they suggested that all literate Africans twenty-one years of age or older should possess the right to vote. They reiterated their opposition to the Federation, condemned the recently formed Nyasaland Progressive Association—an organization of "moderates" led by Charles Matinga, Andrew Mponda, and Orton Ching'oli Chirwa, and urged Africans to observe every September 27 as a day of national prayer in behalf of "all those killed for their resistance against Federation." The chiefs and the leaders of the Congress told the governor that their members hated oppression but that they professed not to be "anti-white." "We aim not to dominate," they wrote, "but to have equality."[11]

In Northern Rhodesia, Africans had meanwhile greeted the formation of a Federal government sullenly on the Copperbelt, and violently in the Luapula and Eastern provinces. In the former area the enforcement of fishing and agricultural regulations, and their dislike of the Federal plan, provoked chiefs and commoners alike to attack representatives of the Government of Northern Rhodesia. In the Eastern Province, Chief Mpeseni of the Ngoni urged his fol-

[10] *Nyasaland Times,* 5 October 1953.

[11] 101020: Statement by Ralph Chinyama, 5 September 1953; cablegram from Chief Mwase and Charles Chinula to the Africa Bureau (London) and the Chief Secretary (Zomba), 13 September 1953; Resolutions of a meeting of the Union of Chiefs of Nyasaland, 11–12 September 1953, Zomba archives.

lowers to shun all official requests from the territorial government. At Samfya, on Lake Bangweulu, at Abercorn, Luwingu, and in the Gwembe Valley, riot police quelled other manifestations of discontent. In the urban areas, what had now become the Northern Rhodesian African National Congress sponsored a "sit-in" campaign designed to break the color bar in churches, lavatories, post offices, restaurants, and other public facilities. Harry Nkumbula and Kenneth Kaunda, its leading officers, favored the withdrawal of African labor from European-run farms and industrial undertakings. They formed a Youth League and entrusted its oversight to Wilson Chakulya.

During this period, Kaunda attained national prominence for the first time. A man of determined mien, he voiced a new kind of desperate nationalist determination. In a speech at Livingstone, he demanded political equality for Africans, particularly in their own territorial legislature.

These people [Europeans] must be told that we are no longer babies. We do not hate the colour of the man, but his conduct. . . . We want the franchise now. . . . What can we do against people with the mentality of . . . Welensky; they are enemies fighting against us; they must be taught it is our country; we are not afraid of guns or atomic bombs. . . . As long as power remains with the whites it is a police state and no peace can prevail. . . . Unless and until the foreign power is removed, there can be no peace. We want the franchise and we want it now.[12]

But neither the British, the Federal, nor the territorial governments paid serious attention to nationalists. Sir Gilbert Rennie, the governor of Northern Rhodesia, dismissed Kaunda as "an agitator."[13] His government, in concert with Welensky and Huggins on the Federal level, refused to encourage the copper mining companies and the white-run miners' union to advance selected Africans into skilled occupations. It preferred to dismiss the conclusions of a commission, chaired by Andrew Dalgleish, that in 1948 had investigated the advancement of Africans in industry. Dalgleish had then concluded that "Africans could not be held back indefinitely," and that there would soon be trouble on the mines unless

[12] N/0001/2/1: Report of a meeting in Livingstone, 7 October 1953, Lusaka archives.
[13] Ibid., minute of 12 October 1953.

Africans were permitted to advance in status.[14] The British and Northern Rhodesian governments also overrode African opposition and, after prolonged discussion, granted white settlers a further entrenchment of their overweening position in the Protectorate's Legislative Council. For Africans, the word partnership rang hollow.

Both Congresses prepared for an uncompromising attack against the Central African political system in which they found themselves imprisoned. Unfortunately, however, we know little about the manner in which the Congresses organized themselves, and the extent of their following. In Northern Rhodesia, Nkumbula claimed more than one hundred branches; many may have included few paid-up members, others may not have met regularly. Thanks to Kaunda and his successors, the rural Northern Province rivaled Nkumbula's Tonga-Ila area in the strength of its support for the Congress movement. In Lusaka, and on the Copperbelt, its membership was probably even more influential, but the actual number of active Congressmen may still have remained small. In Nyasaland, Blantyre, Limbe, Lilongwe, and Zomba harbored their own militant branches, and the rural Karonga, Mzimba, Nkata Bay, Chiradzulu, and Cholo districts continued to support the Congress movement strongly. Nevertheless, the Nyasaland and the Northern Rhodesian Congresses both remained weak financially and administratively. Nkumbula and Kaunda staffed an office in an African suburb of Lusaka, but organizational skills took time to acquire.

The leaders of both Congresses carried the burden of nationalism almost alone; within the Congresses themselves, they battled the forces of inertia, apathy, and inefficiency—only occasionally gaining major victories. With the help of Wittington K. Sikalumbi and Titus Mukupo, Kaunda began, despite harassment by the police, to distribute a mimeographed monthly, the "Congress News." Meanwhile, the leading nationalists immersed themselves in the lore of political combat. Kaunda carried and studied Gandhian tracts and the political literature of India. Nkumbula and Chinyama corresponded with British socialists and other African nationalists. To further these ties, Nkumbula and Kaunda even convened a regional Pan-African Congress meeting in Lusaka. Eighteen represen-

[14] Sec/Lab/59: Dalgleish to Rennie (1948), Lusaka archives. *Report of the Commission Appointed to Enquire into the Advancement of Africans in Industry* (Lusaka, 1948).

tatives of other African nationalist movements promised to take part, but the Federal government effectively prevented them from entering its domain.

Unable to impress either the British or the two territorial governments with the force of their rhetoric or the sincerity of their opposition, the two Congresses sought by other means to demonstrate the strength of their nationalist case. Earlier, before the Federation began, branches of the Northern Rhodesian Congress in Broken Hill, Kitwe, Ndola, and Lusaka had demonstrated against discrimination. In Broken Hill, many Africans withdrew their custom from a produce store, a bakery, and the main butchery, all of which had customarily refused to serve them in the same way in which they ordinarily served Europeans. In particular, the proprietor of the butchery had for many years aroused resentment. At their monthly meetings, members of the Broken Hill African Urban Advisory Council had regularly denounced the degrading manner in which he treated them. Sikalumbi, who organized the partially successful campaign, later explained that "Africans either had to buy their often highly stinking meat at the back door of the shop or already wrapped in newspaper, which stuck to the meat, from a pigeonhole opposite the European counter." This was the "hatch" system. "No Africans could enter the 'holy place'—the shop where Europeans bought their meat. Buying "pig in a poke," Africans had to buy the rotten and bony meat which was unsuitable even for the dogs of the Europeans. A Farmer would unashamedly claim that he did not want to buy the meat for his dog as it was fit for Kaffirs only."[15]

Both in order to denounce racial discrimination generally and to indicate the strength of their movement, Kaunda and Nkumbula timed the inauguration of a new boycott to coincide with a visit to Lusaka by Lyttleton. Early in 1954, after white proprietors had again refused to serve Africans except through hatches, Congressmen began to picket the butcher shops of Lusaka. Africans respected the picket lines and, despite official interference on the side of the butchers, steadfastly maintained their position until, at the

---

[15] Wittington K. Sikalumbi (ed. Harry W. Langworthy), "The Circumstances which gave rise to the Banning of the Zambia African Congress of Northern Rhodesia" (unpub. typescript, 1959/63), 28. See also 62/1/8: Minutes of the Broken Hill African Urban Advisory Council, 1950–1952, Lusaka archives.

end of seven weeks, butcheries and other shops opened their doors to Africans on a supposedly strictly "first come, first served" basis. The butchers dismantled their partitions and, in almost every case, sealed their hatches.

The boycott had meanwhile spread to Livingstone, Mazabuka, and the Copperbelt towns. In Livingstone and Mazabuka, it met with little success. The police forcibly broke up demonstrations and arrested a number of leading Congressmen. In Ndola, the largest butchery averted a prolonged boycott by promising to meet African objections. Its competitors followed suit. The butchers of Mufulira also avoided a conflict with the Congress. In Luanshya, where the Congress possessed comparatively little identifiable support, the Africans concerned first held two public meetings in order to discuss whether or not they should boycott the local butcheries. To one forceful speaker, the issue appeared clear: whites still refused to consider Africans human. They treated them "like animals," sold them meat weeks after it had been slaughtered, but gladly took their money. He reminded the meeting that Africans had "the same money as Europeans. The money with which we buy meat goes into their banks in the same way as the Europeans' money." There was, he repeated, "no discrimination in Money."[16] He and others favored a boycott, but local Congressmen and the Luanshya Urban Advisory Committee, which had obtained the promise of concessions from the two white butchers concerned, argued against any demonstrations. Finally, despite this apparent confusion of roles, Africans spontaneously withdrew their custom from and picketed the butchers. One firm conceded defeat, the other refused to negotiate and, leaderless, the Africans of Luanshya gradually accepted minor improvements and patronized the butchers. The boycotts, wrote Sikalumbi, "helped to leave on the minds of the people that where a Britisher is concerned . . . this colonized race must fight for every inch of its elementary rights."[17] Of even greater significance, the now militant Congress had, to its own satisfaction, achieved a measure of real success by challenging white rule openly. Although Lyttleton had refused to deal with them, the leaders of the Congress now sought the political kingdom with

[16] Quoted in A. L. Epstein, *Politics in an Urban African Community* (Manchester, 1958), 172.
[17] Sikalumbi, "Banning," 45.

greater determination than ever before. The government, and whites generally, now recognized its importance and Africans in many, but not all, areas welcomed its leadership.

Throughout the next few months, the Northern Rhodesian Congress again urged its followers not to work for European farmers or European-owned construction firms. In Ndola and Lusaka, it opposed the introduction of a new pass system that applied primarily to women. It also attempted to close the municipally run beer hall in Lusaka. But its successes there, and elsewhere, were unimportant. The government arrested leaders who spoke publicly of "non-cooperation" or participated prominently in riotous protests. It carefully watched the activities of Nkumbula and Kaunda and even arrested and deported James Frederick Sangala, then the president of the Nyasaland Congress, when he attempted to visit Lusaka.

The Nyasaland Congress had not yet recovered from the debacle at Cholo. During 1954, it enrolled new members and branches, but otherwise refrained from increasing the effectiveness of its organization. In a number of public statements, the Congress continued to demand self-government. It again condemned the Federation and, on behalf of Nyasas, rejected the notion that Africans should pay a federal income tax until such time as they "shall have attained self-government . . . and when there shall be no discrimination on the basis of colour."[18] Sangala wrote to sympathetic British parliamentarians of the meaninglessness of partnership. He noted the extent to which Europeans had benefited economically by Federal rule. He protested against the denial to Africans of their hitherto unchallenged right to move freely within the three federated territories. Sangala pointed to his own arrest in Northern Rhodesia and to the summary deportation of Nkumbula and Kaunda from Southern Rhodesia.[19] "Federation," he said, "has made African leaders . . . live as if they were in a concentration camp where movements are controlled under the cheap term of prohibited immigrants."[20]

[18] 101020: Resolution of the Nyasaland African Congress, 3 March 1954.

[19] On 24 August 1954, Nkumbula and Kaunda flew to Salisbury purposely in order to test their rights of movement. In Lusaka, they purchased one-way tickets only. See *Central African Post*, 25 August 1954; Kenneth Kaunda, *Zambia Shall Be Free* (New York, 1963), 61.

[20] 101020: James Frederick Sangala to Eirene White, 14 September 1954.

The Nyasaland Congress at this time limited itself to verbal protests. Sangala asked his followers to be patient, and to do nothing
that would provoke the Government to repress their movement.
Congressmen, he wrote to the various branch leaders, were "required to obey all the laws of the government and to refrain from
doing things which will bring the Congress into disrepute or disgrace." He expected them to "fight for the rights of the Africans in
a constitutional manner" and to adopt peaceful methods.[21] Yet, Sangala's organization still remained skeletal. Its central executive exercised little control over the actions of the branches. Neither these
branches, nor the central executive, could raise the funds necessary
to sustain a long campaign for self-rule. The specter of the debt-
collector always hovered nearby. In early 1954, for example, the
Congress owed £146 to various creditors after having expended no
more than £585 during the previous year.

"TOILING AND GOING TO PRISON"

Despite these various handicaps, the Congress vigorously resumed its attack upon settler rule at a time when the Government
of Nyasaland had begun to consider possible alterations in the
composition of the Protectorate's Legislative and Executive Councils. Influenced by younger radicals, the most important of whom
were Henry Masauko Chipembere, a recent graduate of Fort Hare
University College, and Murray William Kanyama Chiume, who
had studied at Makerere College and had taught at a Church Missionary Society high school in Dodoma, Tanganyika, the Congress
in public refused categorically to accept constitutional changes that
fell short of complete self-government and universal suffrage.[22]
In 1955, it adopted *kwaca*, a Cinyanja word connoting "dawn," (i.e.,
"freedom") as its fighting slogan, created and flew on its flagstaff a
new national banner, and mimeographed "Kwaca," a monthly news-
sheet containing strident views and reports of "the struggle" elsewhere. At its annual general meeting in Lilongwe, the Congress
demanded the right to secede immediately from the Federation;
"all our fears," its spokesmen said, had been "well and truly real-

---

[21] *Ibid.*, circular letter of 18 September 1954.

[22] In private, Sangala and a number of the older leaders of the Congress
adopted a more "realistic" approach to the problems of political compromise.
101020: Meeting of 20 February 1955.

ized."[23] It called upon the British government "to make a categorical declaration . . . that Nyasaland [was] an African State" that occupied the same status as Uganda.[24] The followers of Chipembere and Chiume—the "Young Turks"—also urged Wellington Chirwa and Clement Kumbikano, the two Africans who represented Nyasaland in the Federal Assembly, to resign their well-paying positions. By remaining, the Young Turks argued that Chirwa and Kumbikano would unwittingly compromise the movement in favor of secession.

The governments of the protectorates still retained a faith in the federal concept. "Our job and primary object in the next few years," Governor Geoffrey Colby of Nyasaland said, "must be to allay African fears . . . and to convince the African population that Federation is in their best interests and indeed is in the interest of all communities in this territory."[25] To this end, his government amended the 1907 Order-in-Council so as to give Africans a greater representation in the Legislative Council of the Protectorate. Hitherto, ten white officials and ten unofficials—three Africans nominated by the Protectorate Council, one Asian delegate of the Asian Association, five whites nominated by the various white associations, and one white nominee of the governor—had joined the Governor in Council. In 1955, the Government of Nyasaland decided that twenty-two members, including eleven officials, should henceforth sit with the governor. Of the other eleven, whites (voters then numbered 1866) should elect six directly, and the three provincial councils should together select five Africans. Two white unofficials, as heretofore, but no Africans, would sit on the Executive Council. When the government announced these revisions, and called for an election in 1956, both whites and Africans, each aggrieved, complained that the new constitution favored the other race. Nonetheless, both groups took part, and the Young Turks, in particular, saw in the 1956 election an attempt to advance the cause of nationalism constitutionally. Chipembere, Chiume, and others sponsored by the Congress stood as candidates and campaigned

[23] *Ibid.*, minutes of the meetings of 8–11 April 1955.

[24] *Ibid.*, telegram from the Congress to the Secretary of State for the Colonies, 11 April 1955. By this time the British government had conceded many demands made by supporters of the exiled Kabaka of Buganda and had signified its willingness to restore him to his throne.

[25] Nyasaland, *Proceedings*, 11 July 1955.

aggressively throughout the last half of 1955 and the first months of 1956.

The provincial councils voted in their favor. In March 1956, Chiume, Chipembere, Chinyama, and N. D. Kwenje—who staunchly supported the Congress—entered the Legislative Council. Its fifth African member, Dunstan W. Chijozi, also followed the Congress' line. He narrowly defeated D. Richard Katengeza, a fellow Congressman, in the Central Province election.[26] Thereafter these new legislators used every public opportunity to forward the African case. Although such behavior had hitherto seemed unthinkable, Chiume and Chipembere peppered the government benches with leading questions. In his first appearance Chipembere asked if the government would consider appointing a commission to inquire into "wages earned by Africans with a view to having them increased, conditions under which Africans work, [and] the housing of African employees." The Chief Secretary refused to do so "at present." Chipembere also requested an assurance that the government would never alienate African trust land and that it would provide full compulsory education for Africans. He demanded the unification of the civil service and the total abolition of racial discrimination within government employment. Chiume accused the Nyasaland Government of denying to its subjects the freedoms of assembly, speech, and organization. He urged the changing of the old order, and objected strenuously to the continuous use of the word "native" in official or private communications.[27]

The African-elected members continuously ventilated their criticisms of the Federation. In a debate upon its economics, Chipembere looked forward to the time when Africans might derive tangible benefits from Federal expenditures. He contrasted increased taxes and customs duties and the consequently higher costs of goods normally purchased by Africans to the lofty promises made by Federal officials. He warned whites "against the danger of over-emphasising the political arguments and the political considerations when dealing with the question of Nyasaland's membership in the Federation."

[26]See Colin Leys, "An Election in Nyasaland," *Political Studies,* v (1957), 266–268.

[27] Nyasaland Protectorate, *Proceedings of the . . . Legislative Council,* 14 May 1956, 5–7, 10–11, 19, 38.

The idea with the African people . . . is that our people are not so fond
of money as the British people are. We know that materialism is the
curse which Europeans are suffering from. But then we are not patients
suffering from that disease. . . . We believe that the aim of all political
schemes should be to promote the happiness of the people. . . . concerned. . . . Now, is Federation promoting happiness in this country?
It is not.

After a number of interjections, Chipembere contrasted the good
old pre-Federal days with the present.

As a result of Federation there is conflict between the races. . . . Our
. . . membership in the Federation is . . . based [only] on political considerations [and] . . . we shall defend [our political rights] . . . for ever and
ever. I ask the . . . Financial Secretary not to lead us into materialism,
but to deliver us from his own imperialism.

In the same debate, Chiume complained that "whatever the European is earning in [Nyasaland] is earned on the groans and sweat
of the exploited African labourer." Chipembere called Europeans
"bloodsuckers."[28] Together, and with frequent assistance from
Kwenje and Chijozi, they vilified white rule and, until early 1959,
fought a militant parliamentary campaign on behalf of their African
constituents.

Meanwhile, in the Federation generally, and in Northern Rhodesia particularly, the real meaning of "partnership" became more
apparent. When Malcolm Whitfield, the Negro American middle-
distance track champion, toured the Federation, invitations to stay
with selected liberal whites spared him the embarrassment of finding hotels "full." The Municipality of Lusaka tarred a road from the
Government Secretariat to the European hospital, but failed to
make up the next two hundred yards that led to the entrance of
the African hospital. Unlike whites, Africans who received registered parcels could not simply claim them at the post offices in
question. Their employers, if any, first had to stamp the relevant
claim checks. (If they had no employers, elaborate procedures for
furnishing proof of identity were necessary.) The Northern Rhodesian Olympic and Empire Games committee said that the time
"was not yet ripe" for the participation of Africans in white-spon-

[28] Nyasaland Protectorate, *Proceedings*, 17 March 1958, 23–29.

sored sporting events. Instead, the committee hoped that the government would educate Africans in the lore of "true sportsmanship." The Northern Rhodesian Bar Association asked the government not to give Africans bursaries to study law. In June 1955, an Afrikaans-speaking farmer beat and kicked an African employee to death. He received a one-year jail sentence. In August 1955, an African servant assaulted and robbed his white employer. He received a five-year sentence. At about this time, the Lusaka town council and numerous whites indicated their dislike of a proposal to build and sell "middle-class" houses to Africans in an area uncomfortably close to white residences.

Huggins, always capable of speaking to the point, had already clarified any misunderstandings about the meaning of partnership. The white people of the Federation, he explained, had promised to "adopt a liberal policy in respect of the bulk of the people, who happen . . . to be black." "But that does not mean they have got to lose their heads and fondle these people as if they were pets showing off for the benefit of people in the United Kingdom. They are adult . . . very backward, and it is going to take a very long time to improve them. . . . We do not intend . . . to turn them into spoilt children."[29] As Gore-Browne wrote, the African "is learning what utter humbug the Partnership talk all is, and he distrusts us even more than ever. With good reason too."[30]

Early in the same year, Kaunda and Nkumbula spent two months in prison after the Northern Rhodesian police discovered prohibited publications—what the sentencing magistrate called "cheap, disreputable and scandalous literature of a political nature"[31] in the Congress' office. Kaunda had already bundled together for disposal copies of the prohibited *Africa and the Colonial World,* a magazine that Fenner Brockway, a leading British Member of Parliament, had for some time sent to the Congress. The police also discovered sample copies of pamphlets distributed by the British Communist Party, the Berlin Women's International Democratic Federation, and the New York Council of African Affairs.[32] Two days after

[29] *Central African Post,* 9 February 1955.

[30] Gore-Browne Papers: Sir Stewart Gore-Browne to Dame Ethel Locke-King, 26 January 1955.

[31] *Central African Post,* 12 January 1955.

[32] Kaunda, *Zambia,* 64; Philip Mason, *Year of Decision: Rhodesia and Nyasaland in 1960* (London, 1960), 114.

searching the headquarters of the Congress in Lusaka, the police raided its offices in the Eastern Province of Northern Rhodesia. Dominic Mwansa, the provincial president, and Frank Chitambala, a clerk in the office, thereafter received prison sentences for committing the offences similar to those for which Nkumbula and Kaunda had gone to jail.

Later, perhaps by way of retaliation, the Congress determined to defy the authority of the government and the chiefs in the Northern Province of Northern Rhodesia. Kaunda's own Chinsali district had long been a center of disaffection. There, Robert Makasa, the Congress' provincial chairman, Simon Mwansa Kapwepwe, who had recently returned from India, John Sokoni, and other leaders of the local Congress encouraged villagers to take "positive action" against white rule. They disobeyed the orders of chiefs and district commissioners, boycotted the official producers' cooperative organization, and even uprooted a tree that had been planted to celebrate the coronation of Queen Elizabeth II.[33] In this protest campaign, the Congress received support from the Lumpa Church, an African-run separatist sect that had already become the most influential religious movement in the district.[34] But the police mobile unit, or riot squad, managed to pacify the district, the Lumpa Church later had troubles of its own with the administration, and, during 1964, relations between the Church and Kaunda's government grew violent.

On the shores of Lake Tanganyika, the administration decided to deal drastically with those who defied constituted authority. The test came in Chief Tafuna's area. At the behest of the commissioner in charge of the Abercorn district, Tafuna forbade public meetings without his express permission. But Hardings Wind Mzimba, a rather unscrupulous young trader and sometime mission teacher who also served as the organizing secretary of the Congress in the district, addressed gatherings in the Chisanza section of villages near the lake and provoked protests against license fees that Tafuna's Native Authority had imposed upon the ownership of fish nets and the felling of trees—both common pursuits in the area. After all, Wind Mzimba said, "God put fish into the lake and

[33] N/0001/2/15/4: *passim*, Lusaka archives.
[34] See Robert I. Rotberg, "The Lenshina Movement of Northern Rhodesia," *The Rhodes-Livingstone Journal*, xxix (1961), 63–78.

planted the trees around it."[35] He also accused Tafuna of "being a servant of the *bwanas*,"—the white administration—and gathered a large group of followers that, on a number of occasions, resisted Tafuna's attempts to arrest them. This group terrorized the lake shore for about two weeks, until the police mobile unit could rush to the rescue of the local officials. Wind Mzimba fled to Tanganyika, but there local Africans refused to befriend him, and the government of Tanganyika, through its district commissioner at Sumbawanga, abruptly returned Wind Mzimba to Northern Rhodesia without a hearing. There he received a two-year sentence for counseling and procuring a riot.

In Kasama, the administrative headquarters of the Northern Province, the Congress had meanwhile organized a boycott of a chain store that discriminated against Africans in an especially obnoxious way. The white manager of the store apparently provided an immediate excuse for the boycott by telling a leading official of the Kasama Congress branch that he and all other Africans were baboons "who had been washed, cleaned, and could [only] wear suits because of the white man's coming to Africa." Whites often expressed these and similar sentiments, but on this occasion, when they objected to his attitude, the manager—whom Gore-Browne called "particularly offensive"—also challenged the Congressmen to do anything about it. "What could munts do?" he sneered.[36] In the event, the Congress successfully persuaded Africans to withhold their custom from his store. But the government effectively ended the boycott by trying and imprisoning Makasa and two of his associates for conspiring to injure the trade of the firm that they had boycotted. Makasa subsequently spent eighteen months in prison.

These actions, and the arrests of other prominent Congressmen, the ever-present atmosphere of discrimination, and the Federal decision to proceed with the Kariba instead of the Kafue hydroelectricity scheme redounded to the benefit of the nationalist movement. In particular, the construction of the Kariba dam presup-

[35] N/0002/15/2: Letter of April 1955.

[36] Sikalumbi, "Banning," 65; N/0002/15/2: Minutes of 29 July 1955; Gore-Browne Papers: Sir Stewart Gore-Browne to Dame Ethel Locke-King, 29 July 1955. Whites called Africans "munts" in the way that white Americans might call Negroes "niggers." The word is a contraction of Muntu, the singular form of Bantu.

posed the movement of about 30,000 Tonga and the flooding of about two-hundred square miles of the Zambezi Valley. This provided an obvious issue, and the Congress then, and regularly thereafter, exploited it whenever possible.[37] Yet, throughout 1955 and 1956, divisions of opinion among the leadership of the Congress vitiated the effectiveness of its appeal. Nkumbula more and more steered a lonely, authoritarian course. A member of the executive committee later wrote: "Under Nkumbula, the executive had no real authority. Nkumbula dictated, was the boss of everything, and dealt with subordinates on an 'I trust you' basis. He knew well how to play at politics: a curious and intricate web of intrigue, deception and bluff, all in secret and behind the veil."[38] He spent funds belonging to the Congress recklessly and, from this time, quarreled continuously with his various treasurers and accountants. He and Kaunda continued to cooperate, but they more and more demonstrated different political styles. Kaunda, who forswore meat and spirits, and wore a toga in the Ghanaian manner, tended to tour the provinces and to pay attention to problems of organization more than Nkumbula, who had meanwhile gained a reputation for excessive living. But the former avoided the limelight, and Nkumbula remained the dominant public figure of the Northern Rhodesian nationalist movement. Even so, when he traveled to London in the latter part of 1955, the Secretary of State for the Colonies, by now Alan Lennox-Boyd (later Lord Boyd), refused to grant him an interview; he eventually returned home aggrieved and chagrined.

Nkumbula and Kaunda grew farther apart politically during 1956, a year that, more than any other, marked the end of an era during which the Congress still hoped to persuade whites to change their prejudiced ways and the white-run governments of Central Africa to share real power with Africans. In January, Kaunda warned the government that it could not hope to keep the black masses in their "right place" indefinitely. Later he countered the charge that the Congress movement followed a Communist line. Its nationalism, he said, rested upon the premise that Africans, like whites, wanted

[37] For a discussion of the problems relating to the removal of Africans from the Zambezi Valley, see *Report of the Commission Appointed to Inquire into the Circumstances Leading up to and Surrounding the Recent Deaths and Injuries caused by the Use of Firearms in the Gwembe District and Matters Relating Thereto* (Lusaka, 1958).

[38] Sikalumbi, "Banning," 95–96.

security for themselves and their children. "If to ask for bread and butter and . . . better conditions for our people is communism," he wrote, "then we are 100% so."[39] He and Nkumbula urged whites to meet African aspirations half way. Instead, Governor Sir Arthur Benson, who had earlier served successively as a Northern Rhodesian district commissioner, the secretary of the Central African Council, and the Chief Secretary in Nigeria, announced that both he and the Colonial Secretary looked forward keenly to the day when they could transfer their responsibilities to a locally elected, presumably settler, government.[40] This speech electrified African opinion. The events of the months prior to the formation of the Federation had scarred their memories; anxious in the extreme, the Congress tried once again to make economic weapons serve the ends of protest.

Two weeks after the speech by the governor, Kaunda called upon Africans to unite in order to form a force that no military power could break. He feared that the Colonial Office would soon leave Africans helpless in the hands of the settlers. Pressed to enunicate a policy, he proclaimed a campaign against the color bar that, initially, took the form of a non-violent boycott of all European- and Asian-owned shops.[41] Kaunda hoped that the campaign would rally the supporters of the Congress and test their strength. He also wanted to teach Africans thrift in order to prepare them for "the uphill struggle ahead." Economic grievances provided additional excuses for the boycott. Prices seemed high. Most proprietors (except for the butchers) still served Africans through hatches, and took advantage generally of their naïveté. Moreover, Asian traders —in the eyes of some Africans, unfairly—undercut their African competitors in the "locations" that surrounded the towns of Northern Rhodesia. In Lusaka, where it began early in April, the boycott virtually paralyzed the so-called second-class trading area. No

---

[39] *Central African Post*, 20 January, 15 February 1956.

[40] *Ibid.*, 5 March 1956.

[41] *Ibid.*, 19, 21 March 1956; Sikalumbi, "Banning," 78. See also *Report of the Committee appointed to Investigate the Extent to which Racial Discrimination is Practised in Shops and in Other Business Premises* (Lusaka, 1956). Simultaneously, and apparently only because the Lusaka municipality proposed to charge them 50 percent more in stall fees than before, vendors boycotted the Lusaka African market. See Ackson A. Nyirenda, "African Market Vendors in Lusaka with a note on the recent boycott," *The Rhodes-Livingstone Journal*, xxii (1957), 57–59.

pickets paraded. Instead, women known as "watchdogs" for three weeks effectively dissuaded Africans from buying from non-Africans.

The boycott served its economic purposes impressively; hatches disappeared permanently, and the local bus company began to provide service to the main locations. But, before the campaign could accomplish all of the goals that Kaunda had enumerated, Nkumbula compromised its effectiveness by patronizing a European-owned delicatessen and then allowed Harry Franklin, a white member of the Northern Rhodesian Executive Council, to persuade him to call off the boycott. Franklin apparently argued that the Congress movement could best achieve its desired political ends by gradual, respectable means. He may also have suggested that the Government of Northern Rhodesia would help the Congress only if it adopted "responsible" tactics.[42] For the next few months, Nkumbula accepted the logic of Franklin's suggestion and urged his followers to moderate their attacks against existing injustices.

Meanwhile, the campaign against the color bar had spread to other towns along the line-of-rail. In Broken Hill, Alex Masala and Dixon Konkola organized a brief, almost totally effective boycott of European and Asian-owned grocery stores, the butchery against which Africans had demonstrated in 1953, and a cinema. The butcher improved his services, and the manager of the largest white-owned store promised in future to be more courteous to Africans. The district commissioner in charge of the town later admitted that he had underestimated the power of the Congress in Broken Hill and had, naïvely, attempted and failed to crush the boycott simply by sending police into the main areas affected.[43] In Monze, Mazabuka, and Livingstone, the Congress similarly managed to make its presence felt. Reuben Kamanga, then the chairman of the Congress' Eastern Province branch, organized a boycott in Fort Jameson. In Ndola, the Congress branch informed the local European and Asian chambers of commerce that Africans would shun their places of business if a number of enumerated grievances remained uncorrected. When the Copperfields Cold Storage Com-

---

[42] Sikalumbi, "Banning," 80; Franklin, Wedlock, fails to mention his part in the boycott.

[43] MN/2154/2: L. E. Bradbury to F. M. Thomas, 28 May 1956, Lusaka archives.

pany refused to cease wrapping meat sold to Africans with news-print, a boycott followed. A week later, the Congress branch in Mufulira offered to discuss a list of African complaints with local European shopkeepers. The Congress accused the proprietors of overcharging or giving short weight to African buyers of maize meal, of refusing to permit Africans to examine the contents of pre-wrapped parcels, of delivering only to whites, and of continuing to to sell to Africans through hatches.[44] The Mufulira Chamber of Commerce refused to meet with or to recognize the Congress. Africans therefore withdrew their custom, and presented the shop-keepers with an almost solid phalanx of opposition. As a result, the government tried Edward Mungoni Liso, then the president of the Congress in the Western Province, Andrew Mutemba, his deputy, Amonson Mugala, the Mufulira chairman, and Emmanuel Chala-besa, the Mufulira secretary, for conspiring to injure the traders of Mufulira. But, to the surprise of many, the trial in the Mufulira magistrate's court resulted in the acquittal of the four Congressmen. The magistrate believed that the cause of the boycotters possessed sufficient justification.[45]

The campaign had successfully accomplished its main aims. Yet, at Franklin's suggestion, Nkumbula ordered the branches of the Congress to conclude their local boycotts by the end of June 1956. Despite strong opposition from Kaunda, Chimba, and other mem-bers of his executive committee, Nkumbula inaugurated a policy of moderation—what he and others termed the "New Look." Accord-ing to one member of the Congress executive, Nkumbula turned against boycotts because he feared that they might lead to out-breaks of violence that "might put him in prison."[46] Some weeks

[44] Sikalumbi, "Banning," 84. Three European tradesmen were later con-victed of giving short weight.

[45] Kaunda, *Zambia*, 77; Edward Clegg, *Race and Politics: Partnership in the Federation of Rhodesia and Nyasaland* (London, 1960), 191. In another case, the Northern Rhodesian High Court upheld an appeal by Kapwepwe, then acting president of the Congress in the Northern Province, and James Sinyangwe, the secretary of its Abercorn branch, against convictions in the Lungu Appeal and the Kasama magistrate's courts. The three Congressmen had originally incurred arrest for holding a meeting in Abercorn township against the expressed wishes of Chief Tafuna. N/0002/15/2: Telegram from Kaunda to T. S. L. Fox-Pitt, 25 July 1956.

[46] Sikalumbi, "Banning," 81. Job Mayanda, treasurer-general of the Con-gress, and Titus Mukupo, its chief clerk, resigned in opposition to the "New Look." Mukupo later rejoined the Congress.

later Nkumbula, Kaunda, Chimba, and Sikalumbi met the leaders of the white elected members of the Legislative Council to discuss the "New Look." At this time, Nkumbula committed the Congress only to gradual reform. He promised to control his own followers and to join the settlers and the government of Northern Rhodesia in their attempts to better race relations. "We will do our best to work for the development of Northern Rhodesia and all its people," he said, "but for this we need the help and sympathy of all liberal-minded Europeans."[47] Rodney Malcolmson, the deputy-leader of the elected members, then asked Nkumbula what the Congress really hoped to achieve. Supposedly, Nkumbula indicated that the Congress wanted "respect" from Europeans.

This reply suggested the extent to which Nkumbula had compromised his earlier militancy. His policies profoundly dissatisfied Kaunda, Chimba, Sikalumbi, and other radicals. "Is it true," Chimba evidently asked Sikalumbi, "that we have been toiling and going to imperialist prisons because we want respect from the white nincompoops?"[48] Dismayed, Kaunda and his cohorts argued vainly against the "New Look" and, for the most part, refused to believe that it could accomplish any of the major objectives for which they had long fought. They suspected that Nkumbula had been "bought." But Nkumbula controlled the purse strings of the Congress and, at the time, commanded the support of the African masses. The more militant leaders of the Congress consequently avoided an open break with their leader, and dissension in public. Nevertheless, Nkumbula's decision to blunt the edge of the successful boycott weapon, and his subsequent dismissal of those Congressmen who refused to moderate their political approach and pronouncements, foreshadowed some of the many issues that later resulted in the creation of the Zambia African National Congress.

While the Congress contemplated its "New Look," African miners had begun to take matters into their own hands. The African Mineworker's Union, which had been formed in 1949, was then engaged in a bitter struggle for survival against the Mines African Staff Association, a union of foremen and clerical workers that the various copper companies had created in 1953. In order to strengthen its own relationship *vis-à-vis* the Union, the companies had assigned

[47] *Central African Post,* 3 August 1956.
[48] Quoted in Sikalumbi, "Banning," 82a.

to the Staff Association rather than to the Union the right to represent those important Africans whom they had recently advanced to surface and underground jobs previously held by whites. Between April and September 1956, the antagonism between these rival bodies, the color bar in general, and the close ties between the younger leadership of the Union and the militant members of the executive council of the Congress, found expression in a series of eighteen brief, so-called "rolling" strikes that disrupted the even production of copper and lead during a period of peak demand.

Lawrence Katilungu, the president of the Union, had welcomed Nkumbula's "New Look," but Matthew Deluxe Nkoloma, its strong-willed secretary, favored policies of the kind that Kaunda, Mungoni Liso, and others had enunciated for the Congress. In a very real sense, therefore, the strikes and the boycotts of 1956 both brought into focus the same kinds of discontent and hostility. The miners wanted higher wages, better housing, and all of the benefits that whites customarily received. As strikes *qua* strikes, however, they involved superficially token, to Europeans seemingly trivial issues —whether African underground workers only should wear protective leggings, for example—that failed to advance the Union cause very far. But the strikes nevertheless annoyed the companies, and the atmosphere of African agitation frightened whites and created a "general feeling of panic."[49] In September, after the African miners had refused to work overtime on Sundays and a number had gone on strike, the government declared a state of emergency on the Copperbelt. The police detained forty-five leaders of the union, including Nkoloma and Mungoni Liso. Nkoloma spent the next three years in restriction, despite a favorable decision by the Chief Justice of Northern Rhodesia in a case brought against the government.[50]

[49] *Central African Post,* 17, 20 August 1956.

[50] ZP/25: Material and memoranda collected for the Commission of Inquiry into Industrial Unrest. Memorandum by E. W. Dunlop, Assistant Labour Commissioner, 11 October 1956; African National Congress memorandum, 29 October 1956, Lusaka archives. The verbatim evidence heard by the Commission occupies fourteen loose volumes. For unsympathetic views of the Union's case, see Mason, *Decision,* 116–117; William Rendall, 18 July 1956, in Northern Rhodesia, *Debates,* 88 (1956), cc. 511–512.

The action of the government ended Nkumbula's first attempt to introduce the nationalist "New Look." "I've extended the hand of friendship to the government," he told a meeting of Congressmen, "but nothing happened."

The white people cannot keep hanging on to their privileged positions in society without hurting themselves. By this I mean the whites must accept the Africans as their fellow human beings and allow them to advance by removing the present artificial barriers. In so doing the whites of Central Africa have everything to gain. The Blacks will certainly take the Whites into their confidence if a genuine approach to the problems which confront them all is made.[51]

Kaunda later reminded the same gathering of delegates that "partnership" was a farce—that it was the "partnership of the slave and the free." The delegates demonstrated their sympathy with the policy of non-violent cooperation that had been advocated by Kaunda, eschewed cooperation with whites, demanded equality of political opportunity in their own country, and asked the British government to permit Northern Rhodesia to secede from the Federation. Immediately thereafter, the Northern Rhodesian Government refused to permit Kaunda to attend a conference of socialists in Rangoon (the Nyasaland Government similarly withheld a passport from T. D. T. Banda), and Welensky, upon succeeding Huggins (now Lord Malvern) as Prime Minister of the Federation, comforted white opinion by denouncing African aspirations. In these circumstances, Kaunda realistically advised settlers to build schools and hospitals, to advance Africans economically, and to dispel the heartfelt African sense of frustration instead of arming themselves in order to crush an "imaginary army" of rebels. He warned the Colonial Office that its failure to accede to the requests made by the Congress might result in a wave of popular unrest. "As everyone knows," he concluded an article in the *Congress Newsletter*, "the next five years are going to be epochal politically. It is a period in which it will be decided whether the races which inhabit Central Africa are indeed going to live together in peace and harmony or otherwise."[52]

[51] "President's speech at the Seventh Annual Conference" (mimeographed), 8 October 1956. Misquoted in *Central African Post*, 8 October 1956.
[52] Quoted in *ibid.*, 19 November 1956.

For Africans, the five "epochal" years began inauspiciously. Lennox-Boyd, who visited Central Africa early in 1957, announced that the Federation had come to stay. "It is good for you," he told Africans, "and you must accept it."[53] He rejected constitutional proposals submitted by the Congress that would have given Africans representational parity with whites in the Legislative Council. "Taking into consideration the relative populations of the two races," Nkumbula said, "what could be more moderate and civilized?"[54] But, neither the Secretary of State for the Colonies, his governors, nor the settler politicians of the Rhodesias and Nyasaland saw any need to satisfy African aspirations. "Let us make it quite clear," Welensky said, "we will never tolerate the creation of a second class State with second class principles for the purpose of political expediency." He went on to tell a Southern Rhodesian white audience that he was "convinced that to hand over the backward mass of African people to the tender mercies of some of their demagogic leaders is little less than a betrayal and I shall not be a party to it."[55] The Federal government supported the British government strongly over Suez and, in turn, the British government permitted the Federal government to alter its constitution in ways that discriminated against Africans.

Although none could admit it officially, partnership was dead. Even the more moderate Africans recognized its demise; Congressmen could no longer even hope that white-run governments might begin to act according to the liberal precepts that had been enshrined in the preamble to the Federal constitution. Gore-Browne, who understood the nature of African discontent, had already publicly decried "this partnership fraud." "Those of us . . . who live in Central Africa," he wrote to the *Manchester Guardian*, "know very well that partnership between white and black at the present time anyhow is at best a pious hope, at worst a disingenuous myth propagated for political purposes."

[53] N/0049/19/2: Lennox-Boyd, address to a meeting of the Western Provincial Council, 4 January 1957.
[54] Quoted in Sikalumbi, "Banning," 107.
[55] *The Times* (London), 16 November 1957.

We are always being told one of the most urgent needs of the day for Europeans in Africa is to retain, or rather regain, the confidence of Africans, and the sooner the partnership myth is dropped the better. It will be time enough to revive it when something has been done about the colour-bar. . . . Partnership between races is a fine ideal, fraternity is perhaps a finer one, but nothing is gained and much is lost by pretending that either the one or the other is being attempted when actually nothing of the sort is happening.[56]

To Lennox-Boyd, Gore-Browne gently said that "the long and short of the trouble is that the African has lost confidence in the European, and no amount of talking will alter this, though not many Europeans seem to realise this."[57]

Settler politicians, and the British government, naturally hoped that Rhodesians could somehow make the Federal experiment work even if the much abused concept of partnership meant, in practice, nothing. But affairs elsewhere in Africa affected Rhodesia and Nyasaland. The wind of political change had begun to blow briskly throughout Africa. Ghana's independence also heartened many. A few months before, Chipembere, Chiume, and Dunduzu Chisiza— a northern Nyasa who, before being deported home in late 1956, had been active in nationalist politics in Southern Rhodesia—and other Young Turks had managed in January 1957 to persuade Sangala to resign his position as president of the Congress. In his stead, they installed Thamar Dillon Thomas Banda, a younger man and a Tonga who had been the secretary-general of the Congress throughout most of 1956.

With Nkumbula, T. D. T. Banda attended the celebrations in Ghana in 1957. There he met Dr. Banda, his namesake, but no relation and, on behalf of the Congress, evidently begged him to return home to lead the nationalist movement. Chipembere had already corresponded with Dr. Banda along similar lines; "human nature is such," Chipembere had written, "that it needs a kind of hero to be hero-worshipped if a political struggle is to succeed."

---

[56] Gore-Browne Papers: Sir Stewart Gore-Browne to the editor of the *Manchester Guardian,* 6 February 1956; Gore-Browne to Patrick Monkhouse, 6 February 1956.

[57] Gore-Browne Papers: Gore-Browne to Alan Lennox-Boyd, 15 February 1957.

He suggested that Dr. Banda should return home "to fill the vacuum" that neither himself, Chiume, Chisiza, or T. D. T. Banda —all of whom Chipembere considered too young and too immature —could adequately fill. He proposed to inflate Dr. Banda's reputation so that Nyasas would eventually welcome him as a political messiah.[58]

"I have inspiring news," T. D. T. Banda announced upon his arrival from Ghana. To the applause of a crowd that welcomed him at the Chileka airport, he reported that Dr. Banda had agreed to return to Nyasaland "within a few years to come."[59] Thereafter, Chiume and others extolled Dr. Banda's virtues throughout Nyasaland and carefully prepared their followers for the day when he might return home. At the same time, the Young Turks obtained Dr. Banda's support for their campaign against the continued presence of Kumbikano and Wellington Chirwa in the Federal Assembly. In July 1957, after both Kumbikano and Chirwa had again refused to resign, Chipembere, Chiume, and Chisiza procured their dismissal from the Congress.[60] A delegation from the Congress also visited Governor Sir Robert Armitage, but he refused to discuss the possibility that Nyasaland might some day secede from the Federation. He thought that their proposals for the reform of the Nyasaland constitution—T. D. T. Banda and Chisiza wanted the Legislative Council to contain a majority of African members by 1960—were hopelessly impractical.

In Northern Rhodesia, the Congress had meanwhile launched yet another campaign to dramatize the color bar in Lusaka. Their followers tried to obtain service in selected restaurants and cafes. Proprietors ignored their presence or threw them out, but there were few important incidents. Later, at Kaunda's urging, the Con-

---

[58] Quoted in *Report of the Nyasaland Commission of Inquiry*, Cmnd. 814 (1959), 12–13. Clyde Sanger, *Central African Emergency* (London, 1960), 198–199, says, but does not explain why the Rev. Mr. Andrew Doig and Major Peter Moxon, who farmed in Nyasaland and had married an African, exerted a greater influence upon Dr. Banda's decision to return home than Chipembere. Major Moxon (interview with the author, 7 July 1964) evidently visited Dr. Banda in Kumasi, Ghana, in early 1958 and, in general terms, discussed the political prospects for Nyasaland. Major Moxon felt that Dr. Banda wanted to make sure that it was the right time for him to return home.

[59] 101020: Report of a meeting of 19 March 1957.

[60] *Ibid.*, C. B. B. Kanchunjulu (Secretary-General of the Congress) to Clement Kumbikano and Wellington Chirwa, 9 July 1957.

gress again sponsored a beer-hall boycott on the line-of-rail. It achieved a reasonable degree of success, but before it could provide publicity for the Congress or results beneficial to Africans, both Nkumbula and Kaunda flew off to London to put a new demand for a "one man, one vote" constitution to Lennox-Boyd. Unfortunately, Nkumbula's penchant for the "good life" obstructed the performance of his political mandate. He avoided meeting the Colonial Secretary, and then flew home, leaving Kaunda to discuss the Congress' position with lesser officials at the Colonial Office.

Kaunda remained in Britain for six months as a guest of the Labour party; he studied its organization, investigated political procedures, and toured Britain. Meanwhile, in Northern Rhodesia, Nkumbula had attempted unsuccessfully to end the beer-hall boycotts; lesser leaders defied him, and Africans generally continued to follow their lead. In the Abercorn district, Wind Mzimba renewed his controversy with Chief Tafuna; he held meetings without permission, insulted the chief, encouraged Africans not to pay their taxes, and received a sentence of fourteen months in jail. In the Luwingu district, Festus Mukuka Nkoloso, a sometime Roman Catholic seminarian, used similar tactics in an area ruled by Chief Shimumbi. He urged his Congress followers to withhold any form of cooperation from the government and to break Native Authority rules. He resisted arrest, and it was only after the outbreak of hostilities that a police unit finally captured Nkoloso and purged the district of its more influential Congressmen.[61]

Nyasas had also chosen to follow an insurgent line. Since Governor Armitage's implicit rejection of their constitutional proposals, Chisiza, Chipembere, and Chiume had redoubled their efforts to transform the financially and administratively weak Congress into an organization capable of making an impression upon local and British opinion. (In April 1957, it claimed about 60,000 members. A few months before, however, its registered branches totaled only eighteen, of which six had been established by Nyasas living outside of Nyasaland.) They repeatedly urged Dr. Banda to agree to command their movement; he offered them tactical advice but, until early 1958, continued to question whether or not he could really give them the kind of leadership that they needed and wanted. The

[61] N/0001/2/15/3: *passim.*

British government's willingness to back Welensky, and the implication that it would help him to create an independent Central African dominion in 1960—with all that such a course of action meant for African rights—ultimately influenced his receptiveness to the entreaties from Nyasaland. The ease with which Nkrumah and the several Nigerian leaders had persuaded Britain to devolve authority to Africans may also have encouraged Dr. Banda to think that he could do for Nyasas what other British colonial subjects had done for their own peoples. For whatever combination of reasons, early in 1958 Dr. Banda let it be known that he would probably be willing to come home sometime within the next six months. The Young Turks widely advertised his qualities as a messiah. In March, after T. D. T. Banda had been accused of misappropriating Congress funds, they engineered his suspension from office. B. W. Matthews Phiri became the acting president-general of the Congress until Dr. Banda could return.

First Dr. Banda, Chipembere, and Chisiza attempted to understand the views of the British government. In June 1958, with Chief Kuntaja, they interviewed the Colonial Secretary in London. To him they offered the constitutional changes that Governor Armitage had refused to consider seriously. They communicated their dislike of the Federation and their hope that the territorial legislature, if not the Federal Assembly, could fully represent African opinion before 1960. But while Lennox-Boyd "took note" of their views, he preferred to believe that they spoke only for the Congress, not for the African people of Nyasaland. In short, he gave Dr. Banda and the others little comfort. Nevertheless, a few weeks later Chipembere told his fellow legislators that, although they knew that British imperialism only understood "the language of extreme confidence," Africans still hoped to achieve their objectives by following proper constitutional channels. "That is not to say that we are being weak," he repeated. "We too, for the sake of this country, will be quite prepared to lay down our lives, but we believe that there is still a chance to win what we want by constitutional means." He realized that the African cause might be harmed if they indulged in "disloyal methods of winning our independence." Right-wing Southern Rhodesians were then threatening to organize a "Boston Tea Party" and to declare their own independence unilaterally. "We leave it,"

Chipembere concluded, "to the Southern Rhodesian ambassadors of the Angel Lucifer to indulge in such devilish practices."[62]

Two afternoons later, after a false report and his failure to arrive in June had precipitated a riot at the Chileka aerodrome, Dr. Banda returned home triumphantly after an absence of about forty-two years. Attired in a neat suit covered with the skin of a civet cat (it gave him the symbolic attributes of a traditional chief) and festooned with party-crackers, he cheerfully proclaimed the coming of the new dawn. At a press conference later that day, he pointed to his black medical bag. "Everyone expects that I have come with self-government in my hand-bag, but we will have to struggle for it. I do not hate the white man—how could I? I have lived most of my life in their countries, and individually they are very nice—but I hate Federation."[63] In a public rally at Soche, he emphasized that negotiation, and not the spear, would serve as the weapon of freedom. During the first days after his arrival, Dr. Banda spoke thus to members of the administration. The governor apparently welcomed his return, and hoped that he would somehow be able to control the Congress' more unruly elements. Evidently, also, Dr. Banda remained unsure of his own role in Nyasaland's nationalist future; for a few weeks, at least, he continued to have reservations about his own effectiveness in the local situation. He refused, figuratively speaking, to unpack his bags immediately.

From the beginning of August 1958, Dr. Banda personally began to shape the destiny of Nyasaland. At Nkata Bay, he became the undisputed leader of the Congress. There delegates to the annual general meeting of the Congress enthusiastically elected him president-general on his own terms. He obtained, and ever since has retained, the power singly to appoint all of the other officers and the members of the executive committee of the Congress. He selected Chipembere to be its new treasurer-general and summoned Chisiza —then studying economics at Fircroft College in Birmingham, England—to be its secretary-general. Chiume became publicity secretary; Mrs. Rose Chibambo, the sister-in-law of Qabaniso Chibambo,

---

[62] Nyasaland Protectorate, *Proceedings . . . of the Legislative Council,* 4 July 1958, 160–161, 182. Cf. Cmnd. 814 (1959), 23. See also the *Manchester Guardian,* 19 July 1958.

[63] Quoted in Sanger, *Emergency,* 8.

became the leader of the women's branch of the Congress; and two elderly businessmen, Lawrence Makata and Lali Lubani (a Muslim), joined the others on the executive committee. Thereafter, Dr. Banda, who developed great demagogic talents, toured the Protectorate, everywhere emotionally denouncing the Federation and exhorting Africans to swell the membership rolls of the Congress. "He conceived his task as being that of organising the people of Nyasaland behind him to bring about the degree of pressure required to right the basic wrong regarding political rights."[64] Crowds greeted him enthusiastically. To them, he was a charismatic messiah. Meanwhile Chisiza and his brother Yatuta, a former policeman in Tanganyika, undertook to transform the Congress into an efficient instrument of change. They opened a number of new branches and instilled in their subordinates a remarkable respect for discipline.

Africans began to assert themselves in ways that alarmed whites. They showed less than the traditional respect for Europeans. In white eyes, they became "cheeky," and therefore frightening. Their enthusiasm for "freedom" and the end of the "stupid so-called Federation"—to use Dr. Banda's description—translated itself into belligerence. The white-owned press magnified the importance of scattered incidents. Nonetheless, on several occasions the African mood did turn ugly. During late September, Africans in the Fort Johnston district intensified their opposition to the enforcement of a range of agricultural rules after Dr. Banda had noted their complaints in a speech. The government accused Congressmen of intimidating others to violate the rules in question and, in October, the police attempted to arrest a supposed intimidator. Their action provoked a riot at Mputa, near Fort Johnston, during which a platoon of the police mobile force saw action. Later in the month, after Dr. Banda had addressed a large gathering in the market square of Blantyre, Africans waiting near the Clock Tower for transportation home stoned automobiles driven by Europeans and Asians. It was after these incidents that Dr. Banda wrote that things "are hot." "I have the whole of Blantyre and Zomba on fire," he said. "Very soon, I hope to have the whole of Nyasaland on fire."[65] The *Nyasaland Times* treated what was, nevertheless, no more than a

[64] Cmnd. 814 (1959), 28.
[65] *Ibid.*, 35.

show of hooliganism as a major instance of mob rule. The paper excited its white readers and, unfortunately for the future peace of the Protectorate, they may have encouraged the police subsequently to treat all gatherings of Africans as inherently dangerous. Several times thereafter, the police prevented even small groups of peaceful Africans from seeing Dr. Banda informally. They made a fetish of keeping Africans away from the main road junctions whenever he made his way to or from Zomba.

During the last months of 1958, Dr. Banda frequently conferred and attempted to negotiate with the governor and his subordinates. He continuously put forward the constitutional changes offered to Armitage and to Lennox-Boyd months before. He apparently showed a willingness to compromise on details if the British government would grant him principles. Instead, Governor Armitage continued to postpone such decisions. The Government of Nyasaland was cordial to Dr. Banda; but it and the British government still believed in the fixed nature of the Federation. The forces of Nyasan nationalism, more mature than ever before, had at last collided head on with the inflexible, unimaginative wall of official reaction. The impasse sought its own solution.

In Northern Rhodesia, a number of younger nationalists had meanwhile challenged Nkumbula's leadership of the Congress movement. Throughout 1957, his subordinates grew increasingly restless. They deplored his personal habits and disagreed with his political tactics. His lapses in London disturbed them. His opponents charged Nkumbula with "keeping Congress at a snail's pace."[66] In Kaunda's absence, he dillied and dallied and fraternized with whites whose motives seemed suspect. Now and then, Nkumbula tried to revive the "New Look." By the end of 1957, the undercurrent of distrust had become a ground swell of disillusion. But Kaunda, upon his return home from Britain, refused to attack his erstwhile mentor. At that time, Kaunda believed that the Congress movement must, at all costs, be held together.

During the early months of 1958, Kaunda worked loyally with Nkumbula. Together they opposed changes that the Government of Northern Rhodesia proposed to introduce a year hence in the com-

[66] Sikalumbi, "Banning," 109.

position of its Legislative Council. Governor Benson suggested that whites and Africans should vote separately, and under a series of complicated arrangements, for their representatives. Although the Africans had of late consistently demanded "one man, one vote," the governor had instead given them only a minority of the available seats. He refused to accept the Congress' counterproposals lest white settlers should "paralyse" the government. "Are you implying," Kaunda asked, "that for our demands to be met we have got to be in a position to paralyse Government?" "My question," Kaunda later wrote, "was never answered."[67] Nkumbula burned the White Paper that embodied Benson's proposed constitution, and Kaunda, Kapwepwe, Kamanga, Mukupo, Chimba, and Solomon Kalulu refuted the constitutional proposals in a Congress "Black Paper."[68] But, when Nkumbula later went to London to protest personally to the Colonial Secretary, he again managed to avoid his official engagements; instead, he posted a memorandum to the Colonial office and slept through an appointment with Lennox-Boyd. During a period when Kaunda visited India, Nkumbula attempted to purge the Congress of those provincial and branch leaders whose loyalty to himself seemed suspect. He demanded authoritarian powers within the party of a kind similar to those obtained by Dr. Banda in Nyasaland. He quarreled regularly with Kapwepwe, the treasurer of the Congress, over finances. Kapwepwe apparently demanded a stricter accounting of party funds than the president-general could abide. Finally, despite his public opposition to the constitutional proposals, Nkumbula suggested that the Congress should run its own candidates— of whom he would be one—either alone or in consort with the Constitution Party that had recently been formed by a number of white liberals. He flirted politically with whites, and, in the eyes of the more militant members of his executive committee, rapidly lost his claims upon their loyalty and respect.

In October 1958, Nkumbula sought to persuade delegates attending a hastily called "emergency conference" of the Congress to accept the proposed changes to the constitution of the Protectorate

[67] Kaunda, *Zambia*, 87.

[68] *Proposals for Constitutional Change in Northern Rhodesia* (Lusaka, 28 March 1958); *Proposals for Constitutional Change*, Cmd. 530 (1958); Kaunda, *Zambia*, 176–186, contains the text of the "Black Paper."

and to give him greater personal powers within the Congress. His opponents criticized Nkumbula's heavy-handed methods of rule, and his "hedonistic love of bright lights and fast living." A majority of the delegates, many of whom Nkumbula had hand-picked, gave him a rousing vote of confidence without endorsing his specific political demands. But, even before the ballots had been counted, several of the more influential militant Congressmen, led by Kapwepwe and Chimba, had walked out of the conference. Kaunda and Kamanga followed, and on 24 October, after Kapwepwe had refused to stand in the way of his close colleague, the breakaway group elected Kaunda the first president of the new Zambia African National Congress. At Kapwepwe's suggestion, they took Zambia, after which they later named their republic, from a contraction of Zambezia, the earlier term for the general area of Northern Rhodesia.[69]

In November, the Zambia Congress held its inaugural meeting in Broken Hill. There, in addition to Kaunda, Munukayumbwa Sipalo, a fiery Lozi who had studied in India and whom Nkumbula had earlier expelled from the Congress, Sikalumbi, Paul Kalichini, Kamanga, and Kapwepwe all became its officers. Sikota Wina, a Lozi journalist, and Grey Zulu and Lewis Changufu, two Bemba businessmen, filled the remaining places on the executive committee. Thereafter, the leaders of the Zambia Congress campaigned vigorously throughout the urban and rural areas of the Protectorate. They gained an immediate following in the Northern and Luapula provinces and in a number of the Copperbelt towns, but Nkumbula maintained his strength for a few months in Lusaka and the Southern, Eastern, and Northwestern provinces of Northern Rhodesia. He and a number of his followers agreed to stand for election in 1959; Kaunda and the Zambia supporters urged Africans to boycott the balloting.

[69] Simon M. Kapwepwe, interview with the author, 16 November 1962; Kenneth D. Kaunda, interviews with the author, 15 August 1961, 4 November 1962, 22 November 1962; Kaunda, *Zambia,* 98. Arthur Wina, later Zambia's first Minister of Finance, apparently used the word Zambia to connote Northern Rhodesia in a poem that he wrote while a student at Makerere College. The poem appeared in a student magazine in 1953. Arthur and Sikota Wina and Wesley Nyirenda, later the Speaker of Zambia's first Parliament, in 1958 had—prior to the Kaunda-Kapwepwe split with Nkumbula—formed their own anti-Nkumbula political discussion group in Ndola.

THE STRUGGLE FOR POWER

By the end of 1958, an atmosphere of tension pervaded Central Africa. In the eyes of their leaders, the Nyasaland African Congress and the Zambia African National Congress had exhausted the available channels of constitutional protest. The Nyasaland and Northern Rhodesian governments had ignored African protests and petitions, and the Secretary of State for the Colonies had refused to give nationalist delegations any cause to rejoice. Instead, each of the Protectorates had offered to change the composition of their respective Legislative Councils in ways that seemed to entrench the overweening position of the white settlers. Welensky's threat to demand dominion status for the Federation added to nationalist fears. They envisaged that another cynical round of British-sponsored conferences, and the subsequent approval of their conclusions by settler-controlled legislatures would, in the absence of action by Africans, doom the indigenous inhabitants forever to a second-class status within their own countries. Moreover, as the settlers ceaselessly imprecated the nationalists, and demanded repression of their governments (Welensky flew Federal troops into Nyasaland "on maneuvers"), so the nationalists of Nyasaland and Northern Rhodesia grew increasingly restless.

Banda and Kaunda returned in early 1959 from the sessions of the Accra All-African People's Conference more determined than before to carry the battle against white rule forward to its ultimate conclusion—whatever that might be. Both received ample moral support from other African nationalists at the conference; Prime Minister Nkrumah, President Gamal Abdul Nasser, and others may have promised to supply some of the funds necessary before the Nyasas and Rhodesians could organize themselves for victory. With regard to Northern Rhodesia alone, the delegates in Accra favored Kaunda's brand of leadership over that of Nkumbula, who also attended the conference. In any event, the meetings in Accra gave Banda, who participated little in the actual deliberations, and Kaunda an added mandate to challenge the whole elaboration of settler power with vigor.

From this time, Banda and Kaunda launched an aggressive verbal attack upon the various forces responsible for "betraying and oppressing Africans." Banda foresaw, and welcomed, the possibility that he might be imprisoned on behalf of the nationalist cause. In Salisbury, on his way back to Nyasaland from Ghana, the Southern Rhodesian government treated him as though he were a suspected criminal; its police frisked him for weapons and questioned him at length. Later that day, in an African suburb of the Federal capital, Banda ascended the heights of oratory. "To Hell with Federation," he repeated. He attacked whites and African "stooges"—"for tea and whisky in white men's houses they have betrayed their country"— and promised to die for the nationalist cause. "If I die," he said, "my ghost will fight from the grave . . . let us fill their prisons with our thousands, singing Hallelujah."[70] A few days later, in Nyasaland (where the police had refused to permit Africans to greet his arrival at the airport), Banda said that he meant to fight the Federation with violence only if all other avenues to freedom appeared to be blocked. He invited arrest, and thereafter repeatedly reiterated his willingness to die, to go to prison, to endure exile in the Seychelles or St. Helena "or anywhere" if it would further the African opposition to white rule.[71] Meanwhile, Dunduzu Chisiza and Chipembere carefully constructed an organization more powerful than any previously known to Central Africans.

Kaunda refused to rest until he had removed the Union Jack from Northern Rhodesia. "Whatever the consequences," he told his followers in Lusaka, "we are prepared to pay the price of freedom in this country." If the government banned the Zambia Congress, "as I hear they intend doing," he promised that Africans would continue the struggle. "Zambia may be banned, public meetings may be banned, but the spirit of Zambia will march on until independence is obtained."[72] His followers, like those of Dr. Banda, took up similar themes. They exhorted Africans to "begin to hate everything white which had two legs" and, in familiar terms, vilified settler domination. In Chingola, Sipalo repeated the reasons for African anxiety: "We must have self-government and a democratic Constitution now in Northern Rhodesia. We must get it before 1960 or face the prospect of Dominion status, and that means perpetual subjugation to the British." If the struggle meant "creating nonsense then we

[70] Quoted in *Central African Examiner*, 3 January 1959. See also Enoch Dumbutshena, letter in *ibid.*, 17 January 1959.
[71] Cmnd. 814 (1959), 42.
[72] *Northern News*, 16 February 1959.

must create a nonsense."[73] In general, the Zambia Congress stepped up its attack upon the proposed constitution and warned Africans not to vote in the March elections.

Dr. Banda held another round of abortive discussions with senior officials and settlers in Zomba and Blantyre. After one of these meetings, Africans threw stones at a few passing motorists. Two days later, the police arrested thirty-six women who had insisted upon viewing Dr. Banda's arrival at Government House in Zomba. After his talks with Governor Armitage and Alan Dixon, the settler leader, Banda addressed a public meeting of African congressmen. He urged them to be very patient. But he condemned laws like those that brought about the arrest of women who had only wanted to wave to him in the street. "No one," the Commission of Inquiry paraphrased his talk, "arrested women in the streets of London for waving to the Royal Family or to Churchill." Chipembere, who followed Banda onto the platform, urged his audience forcibly to effect the release of the women at once. "We were hot," he wrote to Chiume, "red hot." A crowd of about five hundred Africans thereafter surrounded the Zomba police station; a district commissioner read the riot act, and the police mobile force finally dispersed the menacing crowd with tear gas and a baton charge.[74]

Within another two days, Dunduzu Chisiza convened a private meeting of the executive committee of the Congress to decide upon the future course of its campaign for self-government. With or without Dr. Banda's approval and/or knowledge, Chisiza, the theoretician, and Chipembere may have urged their colleagues to drop the non-violent approach to political change. That policy had brought little amelioration in the conditions of African life. It promised nothing for the future, and Chisiza presumably understood that the threat of force had already accelerated the pace of constitutional devolution in various parts of the old British Empire. In the event, after its own sessions the executive committee hastily summoned more than two hundred delegates from the branches of the Congress to an "emergency" general conference in Limbe. In a series of secret meetings, one of which for sheer need of space took place in

[73] *Ibid.*, 17 February 1959. Many statements were made without Kaunda's approval.

[74] Cmnd. 814 (1959), 44; Chipembere to Chiume, 2 February 1959, in *ibid.*, 145.

the bush a few miles from the heart of Limbe, they apparently, possibly unanimously, sanctioned "action"—"and 'action' in the real sense of action"—as official policy.[75] It is not clear whether or not Banda and Chisiza either contemplated or planned a program of violence. At the same time, there seems little doubt that the conferees agreed deliberately to defy the authorities. If such defiance provoked the Government to retaliate, then, they realized, Africans might well resist violently. At the emergency conclave, Chisiza may also have assigned definite roles in the campaign of defiance to branches represented by the delegates. Thereafter, the deliberate disobedience of instructions issued by the police and/or district commissioners appeared to form a part of a carefully coordinated plan.

During the next two weeks, Banda's own speeches seemed no more inflammatory than before. At Dedza, he urged a crowd to behave "like ladies and gentlemen so that the police will know that we are a disciplined organisation."[76] But, in various parts of the protectorate, branches of the Congress began to hold public meetings either without official permission or in the face of an explicit denial of such permission. Early in February, in Chisiza's own area, the Karonga district, the Congress held a conspicuous illegal assembly. The police arrested the ringleaders. A few days later, Akogo Kanyanya, a branch leader, addressed about three hundred Africans in the Karonga market. He told the district commissioner that he did not really see why he should need a white man's permission to speak to fellow Africans in his own country. Nonetheless, he and three other leaders let themselves be arrested. A crowd surrounded the police station, however, and the district commissioner thought that it might be prudent to release the accused. On a succeeding day, the Congress again convened an unauthorized meeting in the market place and, although the district commissioner read the riot act and the police threw tear-gas grenades, the crowd successfully defied the government and, in the disturbances that followed, it injured Africans sympathetic to the government and did considerable damage to property. The next day, Congressmen attempted to hinder the landing of police reinforcements at the Fort Hill airport, sixty

[75] Chipembere to Chiume, 2 February 1959, in *ibid.*, 144. See also D. K. Chisiza, "Four Answers from Dr. Banda," *Central African Examiner*, 31 January 1959. But see Welensky, *4000 Days*, 118.

[76] Quoted in Cmnd. 814, 53.

miles northwest of Karonga. In a pitched battle with the police mobile force, stones thrown by supporters of the Congress injured several Europeans, and four of their number suffered wounds when the police opened fire. On the same day, Africans stoned missionaries and a white-owned store at Livingstonia.

Africans had taken matters into their own hands in the Central and Southern provinces. During the second week in February, in the Dowa district, Congressmen assaulted an African veterinary assistant, a sub-chief, and the members of the latter's staff who had attempted to enforce certain veterinary regulations. In the Kota Kota district, Congressmen who had consciously cultivated land in breach of agricultural regulations beat an African soil ranger. The police later moved into this area in force, and after the parties involved had exchanged stones and tear gas, forty-five persons were placed under arrest. Road blocks subsequently appeared in this district, and Africans continued to defy the law by cultivating riverine lands. In the Ncheu district, Congressmen held several illegal meetings, one of which the police mobile force broke up with a baton charge and tear gas. About twenty-three persons incurred arrest.

After 20 February 1959, the disturbances took a more serious turn. On the next day, to Banda's acute dismay, the Federal government decided to fly white Rhodesian troops into Nyasaland. Chipembere made a number of provocative statements that might well have encouraged his fellow Congressmen to continue their harassment of authority. After one of his speeches at Ndirande, Africans stoned motorists and the police used tear gas and batons to clear the nearby road. Yatuta Chisiza, as always, refused to equivocate: "We mean to embarrass the local government, Nyasaland Government and the British Government about our demands. This is the only way. Negotiations won't do. But we mean to create disturbances from Port Herald to Karonga even if it means every person in the country dies."[77] With his brother, he toured a part of the Southern and Central provinces of the Protectorate; invariably, whether or not by chance, disturbances occurred subsequently in the places in which they had tarried.

---

[77] Quoted in *ibid.*, 71. Newspaper accounts of the period discussed above appear to be nearly always unreliable.

In Lilongwe, the action of a white bank employee who had become a special constable may equally have provoked Africans. With insufficient reason, he fatally wounded an African cyclist who, at night while under the influence of alcohol, had erratically pedaled his unlighted machine down one of the town's main thoroughfares. On the next day, when the Congressmen who had been arrested in Kota Kota arrived, a large crowd of Africans surrounded the local prison. They stoned the police and refused to disperse after a district commissioner precipitately read the riot act to them. As police squads were unavailable, he summoned a platoon of the King's African Rifles. Its commander gave the order to shoot and, in separate affrays shortly before dusk, two Africans lost their lives. A few days later, the police dispersed a small crowd of Congress sympathizers in Fort Manning. In the South, troops opened fire, killing one African among a crowd that had menaced the court of Chief Chigaru, who was then trying offenders against agricultural rules. Meanwhile, in the north, Africans burned buildings at the Loudon mission, stoned the police at Mzimba, destroyed property and threatened African employees of the government in Rumpi, attacked the police and cut the water mains in Mzuzu, and temporarily assumed control at the Ekwendeni mission.

By the beginning of March, Africans had demonstrated their ability to tie up the security resources of the Government of Nyasaland. They had also committed Southern Rhodesian troops, and on 26 February, the prime minister of that colony had therefore declared an emergency, banned the territorial African National Congress, and arrested about five hundred of its members.[78] In Northern Rhodesia, the leaders of the Zambia Congress had continued to urge Africans to boycott the "unjust" elections of 20 March. A few of its branch chairmen had also convened public meetings without holding the necessary permits. At their meetings, they spoke of the dire consequences that might befall Africans who voted. There were a few cases of arson for which members of the Zambia Congress might or might not have been responsible. In February, Sipalo and one or two others apparently met secretly with the Chisiza brothers and, conceivably, with George Nyandoro of the Southern

[78] *Rhodesia Herald*, 27 March 1959.

Rhodesian Congress. Together they may have discussed a joint campaign upon the citadels of white power. But, few important incidents had, up to the first days of March, punctuated the comparative quiet of Northern Rhodesia.[79] Kaunda and most of his followers remained true to the official policy of non-violence.

The Government of Nyasaland, with Federal encouragement, banned its Congress movement and, in the early hours of 3 March 1959, arrested Dr. Banda and more than two hundred of his alleged co-conspirators (more than 1300 suspects eventually were imprisoned). At the time, Governor Armitage said that he had taken such steps because "day by day [it had] become increasingly apparent that [the Congress were] bent on pursuing a course of violence, intimidation and disregard of lawful authority. . . ."[80] Later, perhaps as an added embellishment, his Government accused the Congress of having plotted the murder of all of the whites then resident in Nyasaland.[81] Many Europeans honestly believed that Dr. Harry Bwanausi and Dr. Banda had intended, as part of a sub-plot, to poison leading whites with arsenic; according to the local white rumor mongers, a lorry had delivered forty tons of arsenic to Dr. Banda's surgery late on one January evening. In any event, the Government possessed abundant reason to declare an emergency and to arrest the leading African "agitators." The Congress had paralyzed at least the outlying arms of the central administration. Its activities constituted a threat to law and order whether or not any coordinated program of violence had actually been implemented. Moreover, in the last analysis the Government of Nyasaland, whether it acted autonomously or not, had little choice. If it did not attempt to crush dissidence, it could only compromise and seek to come to terms with Dr. Banda. And, for this later course of action, the day

[79] But see N. C. A. Ridley, *Report of an Inquiry into all the Circumstances which Gave Rise to the Making of the Safeguard of Elections and Public Safety Regulations, 1959* (Lusaka, 1959), 16–25, 29, 31–32; Government Notice No. 81 of 1959, in *ibid.*, 37–38.

[80] Quoted in Cmnd. 814 (1959), 87; *Northern News,* 24 March 1959.

[81] *The Times* (London), 24 March 1959; Nyasaland, *State of Emergency,* Cmnd. 707 (1959). The Commission of Inquiry found absolutely no firm evidence to substantiate the allegations of a "murder plot." Much of the Government's information about the plans of the Congress came from a few not necessarily reliable police informers. Cmnd. 814, 86–88. See also *The Observer,* 8 March 1959.

had not yet come. Neither the British nor the Nyasaland governments then appreciated the extent to which the existence of the Federation mortgaged their continued connection with the peoples of the Protectorate.

The actual "Operation Sunrise," as the round-up of Congressmen was called, proceeded smoothly. Most of the important leaders of the Congress offered no resistance. Indeed, Congressmen generally cooperated willingly at the time, but in a number of instances, the police forces abused their authority and apparently attacked, injured, and otherwise mistreated those on the "wanted" list.[82] Later in the day, throughout the Protectorate, Africans retaliated. They blocked roads, threatened individual whites, attacked the police, and attempted to effect the release of detainees. On several occasions, particularly at Nkata Bay, the policemen and soldiers of the King's African Rifles and the Royal Rhodesian Regiment felt that they had to shoot. As a result, more than fifty African civilians lost their lives. Only one African policeman and one European sustained serious injuries. For the next few weeks, Africans continued to block roads, burn huts, and destroy property, especially in the Northern Province. But, by the beginning of April, the "most dangerous" Congressmen occupied prison cells in Southern Rhodesia, and others who posed less of a threat to peace and order occupied, without benefit of trial, a hastily constructed detention camp at Kanjedza, near Blantyre.[83] Ostensibly, the Government of Nyasaland had stilled the voice of the Congress.

In Northern Rhodesia, the speeches and actions of the Zambia Congress had continued as before. Nkumbula, however, and several of his colleagues were standing for election. During early March, members of the Zambia Congress held unauthorized meetings and, particularly after the arrest of nationalists in Nyasaland, Kaunda and many of the branch chairmen may conceivably have courted arrest.[84] But, if a concerted plan existed, few knew of it or acted in accord with its dictates. Nevertheless, press accounts of the public

---

[82] Cmnd. 814, 93–99. See also Griff Jones, *Britain and Nyasaland* (London, 1964), 240–241. "Sunrise" was a play upon *kwacha*.

[83] For their conditions, see *Dissent*, v (4 June 1959), 6–10; xii (22 October 1959), 1–7.

[84] See *Northern News*, 10 March 1959.

utterances of Sipalo and Kaunda had aroused white fears. White politicians begged Governor Benson to do something. John Roberts, the leader of the local settlers, called upon the governor to dispel any "illusion of black self-government." "The forebearance of, patience and good humour of Europeans and reliable Africans," he warned, "are fast running out."[85] Yet Kaunda had never advocated violence; privately he shrank from its use, while remaining aware that he could not always control those of his restless followers who might, under provocation, take matters into their own hands. Two weeks before election day, he told his supporters that they should boycott the election without being violent. In his eyes the election appeared a "hollow mockery," but he asked them to give no excuse "for the use of armed force upon innocent victims."[86] Nevertheless, Governor Benson, who apparently derived his information from police informers, assumed that the Zambia Congress would disrupt the election and that serious violence would erupt on polling day. Before dawn on 12 March, his government arrested and exiled to remote rural *bomas* the leading officers and forty-five of the most dangerous followers of the Zambia movement.

In a private letter, Kaunda described the exercise at length:

I was arrested at 1 a.m. on the 12th. My hut [in Chilenje] was swept clean of my books, papers and diaries. They handcuffed my right hand to that of a white officer and my left to that of an African officer. We drove off to the Woodlands [Lusaka] Police Post where they took my thumb print. From there [we went] to a . . . point on the Lusaka–Broken Hill Road. . . . Then I . . . joined Kapwepwe in a big van . . . together with . . . [others]. We waited for some more but apparently the chaps had decided not to accept these free lifts from the cops that hot and wet morning. So we were off . . . towards Broken Hill . . . [then back] to Lusaka. . . . At the roundabout we went round and round and then made for the airport where we found an aeroplane already spitting fire . . . we were off into the unknown. We landed—it was Ndola. One of us . . . left . . . but this place was more than filled. Here some senior Western Province Zambia officials joined us . . . with . . . shouts of that terrifying [Congress cheer] ZAA! ZAA! ZAA! Small wonder Colonial Governor Benson found it a bit nauseating.[87]

[85] *Northern News*, 19 February 1959.

[86] *Ibid.*, 7 March 1959.

[87] Kenneth Kaunda to Simon Katilungu, 15 March 1959, privately held. See also Kaunda, *Zambia*, 105–108.

Eventually Kaunda landed in Kabompo, but he later received a nine-month sentence for "conspiring to effect an unlawful purpose" and for holding an unauthorized meeting, and he spent the rest of the year in the Salisbury and Lusaka prisons.[88] Sipalo was jailed for sedition. Kapwepwe resided in Mongu, Wina's home district, and Wina lived near the Luwingu boma in the Northern Province. Others similarly spent their days far from their real homes in what the government called "rustication."

Governor Benson justified the banning of Zambia by analogy. To him, Kaunda's organization and its plans smacked of the American "Murder Inc." Zambia seemed "on all-fours with what happened to millions of law-abiding Americans when the comparatively few Chicago racketeers established their protection rackets, corrupted the local governments, ruled by the gun, the sap, the knuckle-duster, the bicycle chain, and went on to establish the organisation of killers which was known as Murder Incorporated."[89] But neither the governor, nor the subsequent, rather disappointing, inquiry could produce any real evidence to support either the governor's words or his actions. The banning of the Zambia Congress assisted Nkumbula and several moderate Africans in their attempts to win legislative seats on 20 March, when the peoples of the Protectorate went to the polls peacefully. It also provoked sporadic outbreaks of violence in Lusaka, on Chilubi Island in Lake Bangweulu, and throughout the Northern and Luapula provinces. The police later arrested more than one hundred Zambians for their parts in the post-ban disturbances.

Whites hoped that life could continue as before. They saw in the actions of the three Central African governments what they had long hoped to see—the death of nationalism and the vindication of the decisions that had resulted in the formation of the Federation. On the contrary, unbeknown to them, the violence and retaliation of 1959 marked the beginning rather than the end of the last phase of the nationalist struggle. The British cabinet thereafter realized that it could only hope to govern the two protectorates with the consent of the governed. It at last understood the depth of African

[88] The magistrate sentencing Kaunda also took "into the account the arrogant and impudent way" in which he defied the law. "No government that expects to survive can tolerate this." *Northern News,* 22 June 1959.
[89] Quoted in Sanger, *Emergency,* 290; *Central African Post,* 13 March 1959.

resistance to the Federation and to settler rule in general. As Banda and Kaunda knew, British governments traditionally only respected those of their subjects who had actually shown the stuff of contention and the potential of leadership. Banda and Kaunda confidently expected that months spent in prisons would qualify them —like many others—to accede, in decent time, to prime ministerships.

Chapter XI

THE TRIUMPH OF NATIONALISM

They have banned the great name of Zambia but the greater
name of *freedom now* is spiritual. It is beyond their reach
and so they cannot ban it. We shall organize our people when
we get out of [detention] in the name of *freedom now*. Africa,
our mother Africa must be free and it has fallen to our lot to
free this part. Be of good cheer, we are just beginning.

—Kenneth Kaunda in a letter to his
"Dear Comrades," 28 April 1959

Thus wrote the leader of the banned Zambia African National Congress from his place of detention near the Kabompo *boma* in northwestern Rhodesia. For him and his followers and for Dr. Banda and the Nyasa Congressmen, imprisonment and obloquy proved the penultimate stage on the road to independence. The fervor with which Africans in both protectorates had declared and continued to demonstrate their opposition to the Federation and to alien rule impressed the British government. Many of its leaders realized that states of emergency, detention, rustication, and all the other techniques of colonial control could be temporary expedients only. By the simple act of banning the two Congress movements, the governments of Northern Rhodesia and Nyasaland had given to them and their leaders an added dimension of importance.

From remote Kabompo, Kaunda wrote letters of encouragement to his fellow detainees in their scattered places of exile. He tried to bolster their spirits. He urged them to meditate, to make new converts to the cause of nationalism, and to plan for the time when they might continue their struggle against Federal and colonial rule. He saw the months of detention ahead in historical perspective. To him they represented no more than an interlude after which the pot of nationalism would come to a boil even more rapidly than before. "Comrades," he wrote, "victory is certain and grand if we all do our very best."

Victory is for the men of vision, courage and determination—I know you are equipped. . . . You know comrades that the British will always pat stooges at their backs, but at the bottom of their hearts it is the rough guys they have both respect and consideration for. They will put them in jail, they will rusticate them but all these are tests to see if they are ready to rule because to govern is no small job and needs to be handed over to people who can stand the ups and downs of life. British colonists do not send fools to political prisons—only those they want to try for the job of governing others do they send to . . . prisons. So you are being tested, comrades. I have no doubt you will pass.[1]

During their days in detention, Zambians learned whom they could and could not trust. As members of a prestigious national movement, they also gained the sense of mutual solidarity that later stood them in such good stead. Surreptitiously, but nonetheless successfully, they spread the nationalist gospel in areas—like Kabompo and Senanga—where such proselytizers had previously been rare. The more numerous Nyasas likewise made much of their period of detention. To the subsequent benefit of nationalism in Nyasaland, they profited from a new sense of confraternal well-being. And, in different ways, they prepared themselves intellectually for a continuation of the struggle. At Khami prison in Bulawayo, Southern Rhodesia, a number of the supposedly more dangerous "threats to peace and good order"—many of whom had previously been unacquainted both with each other and with Dr. Banda—organized a school for their less well-educated fellow detainees. David Rubadiri, an honors graduate of Makerere College (he took another degree at the University of Cambridge) who later became ambassador to the United States, taught English. Augustine Bwanausi, John Msonthi, Willie Chokani, and Orton Ching'oli Chirwa, all of whom possessed university degrees, and all of whom subsequently became members of Dr. Banda's first cabinet, comprised the nucleus of the staff.[2] Sometimes their lessons included hidden messages of nationalist indoctrination. Chirwa, at least, used lessons in Latin as a cover for political conversations with several of the younger Nyasas. By this means he became acquainted with Aleke Banda, a fellow Tonga who had been born in Northern Rhodesia of Nyasa parents and brought up in Southern Rhodesia. Although he was then only

[1] Kenneth Kaunda to his "comrades," 28 April 1959, privately held.
[2] See also *Tsopano*, 12 (November 1960), 7.

nineteen and a student in a mission school, the Southern Rhodesian authorities had imprisoned this Banda—who was unrelated either to Dr. Banda or, directly, to T. D. T. Banda—for his activities on behalf of the nationalist movement of the colony. He subsequently occupied a number of important positions in Dr. Banda's government.

THE NEW PARTIES

Although few—least of all the Africans themselves—appreciated the extent of their victory during the months immediately after the 1959 disturbances, the nationalist movements of Nyasaland and Northern Rhodesia had already compromised the colonial position there beyond repair. The banning of the Zambia and Nyasaland Congresses had arrested nationalist agitation only temporarily. Within two months of the rustication of Kaunda and his followers, Nkumbula, who, in the interim, had posed for milk-drinking advertisements, reassumed a publicly militant posture and a number of other Northern Rhodesians, most of whom professed sympathy with the cause espoused by Kaunda, began to form new political movements similar in outlook to the Zambia Congress. Early in May, Barry Banda, a young clerk and no relation to the other previously mentioned Bandas, resigned from Nkumbula's Congress and, with Dauti Yamba and Paskale Sokota, founded the African National Freedom Movement. At about the same time, Dixon Konkola, the president of the Rhodesian African Railway Workers' Union, established the United African Congress. Konkola, a maverick who frequently expressed eccentric views, had very briefly held the office of vice-president in the Zambia Congress. In June, these two organizations, neither of which possessed many followers, amalgamated to form the United National Freedom Party. Solomon Kalulu, who became its vice-president-general (Konkola became the president-general and Barry Banda its secretary-general), reminded the delegates to the inaugural meeting of the Freedom Party that Kaunda remained their leader. He and many of his colleagues simply hoped to keep alive the ideals and goals enunciated by Kaunda, Kapwepwe, and Sipalo.

The leaders of the new party were united in their opposition both to Nkumbula's "dictatorship," and to the existence of the Federal government. In the usual fashion, they demanded "immediate self-government." According to Barry Banda, they wanted "democracy of the majority." "We would wait for ten years for self-government," he said, "if there was no Federation. But with Federation we want it now." The delegates to the inaugural meeting of the party agreed that they would work assiduously "towards a take over of the government one day, and perhaps in a nearer future." They eschewed the use of "any form of violence whatever," hoping to deal only through the "proper constitutional channels."[3]

The United National Freedom Party exerted little immediate influence upon the political history of Northern Rhodesia. Its leaders failed to elicit the support of the African masses during a time of difficult relations between nationalist politicians and the police. Meanwhile, however, Nkumbula and some of the remaining younger leaders of the Northern Rhodesian African National Congress designed yet another campaign against the color bar. With intermittent support from Nkumbula, Titus Mukupo, the secretary-general of the Congress, and Dominic Mwansa, the Congress president for the Central Province (which included Lusaka) intensified their efforts to compel white-owned hotels, restaurants, cafes, cinemas, and other publicly used facilities to "put partnership into practice."[4] Throughout the African winter months of 1959, whites turned Congressmen away from swimming pools, churches, and schools "for European children." In Kitwe, the proprietor of a fish-and-chip shop told Mukupo and an African businessman that he would only serve them "outside." In Ndola and Mufulira, Congressmen tried to "sit-in" cafes without success. Only one restaurant served them tea, but they were forced to pay £5 for the privilege. At a Ndola tea-garden, a European set three bulldogs upon Finas N. Bulawayo, then the propaganda secretary of the Congress on the Copperbelt, when he requested service. In Lusaka, a white man knocked an African off a bar stool for ordering a beer in an important hotel. When another white man offered his own glass to an African who had been denied service in a milk bar, a waitress slapped it to the floor. Even Sir Francis Ibiam, a prominent lay Anglican churchman and physician

[3] Private Report of the Inaugural meeting of the United National Freedom Party, 20 June 1959, lent to the author by Patrick Mumba. See also the *Central African Mail* (17 July 1964), 5.

[4] *Northern News*, 8 May 1959.

who subsequently became the governor of the Eastern Region of Nigeria, was denied tea in Chingola because of his color. He was then traveling from Lagos via Elisabethville to chair a meeting of the provisional council of the All-Africa Churches Conference in Salisbury. In Lusaka, when a group of Congressmen tried to obtain seats in his movie theater, the proprietor told them that there were "no black films for Africans." He said that Africans were "useful in kitchens but not in cinemas."[5]

The Congress succeeded in embarrassing the Government of Northern Rhodesia. Even Sir Roy Welensky began to promise that the Federal government would seek to make partnership real. At the same time, he told whites that he would resist any attempts "to debase our standards, just as I would resist any tendency to resort to what have been called measures of panic partnership in the face of pressure being put upon us." Later he expressed his confidence that the British government would, in 1960, grant the Federation its independence and "full nationhood."[6] He also threatened to dismantle the African Affairs Board. In fact, while the Congress' campaign against the color bar helped in minor ways to encourage racial integration, it brought Africans no closer to the gates of the political kingdom. Welensky and the settler oligarchy continued to bar the way.

Nkumbula had long ceased to provide what other politically minded Africans considered effective leadership. For a combination of many of the same reasons that had earlier driven Kaunda, Kapwepwe, Kamanga, and Chimba to break with Nkumbula, Mukupo attempted unsuccessfully to purge the Congress of Nkumbula. Instead of leading a schism, his own supporters "removed" Nkumbula from the presidency. But Nkumbula naturally refused to recognize or to countenance Mukupo's tactics. On several occasions, he "suspended" Mukupo and lesser officials. The internecine battle raged inconclusively from June to September, 1959. Mukupo's Congress could claim the support of the more militant members of the old Congress, including Mwansa, Bulawayo, and Mainza Chona, a barrister who returned during the year from London. Meanwhile,

[5] Quoted in the *New York Times*, 24 May 1959. See also *Northern News*, 29 April, 15 May, 21 May, 31 August 1959.
[6] *Northern News*, 18 September 1959.

in September, the small African National Independence Party, which Paul Kalichini had started in July, merged with the United National Freedom Party. Finally, in October, Mukupo, Chona, and the other Congressmen who had been unable to obtain a clear victory within Nkumbula's Congress, joined the United National Independence Party that had emerged from the amalgamation meetings in September. Its leaders consciously played a caretaker's role; they wanted to keep the embers of nationalism warm until the time when Kaunda could walk from prison into the presidency of their party.

Nationalist activity resumed in Nyasaland during July 1959, after the Government of Southern Rhodesia had, because of his youth, released Aleke Banda from prison and deported him home to the land of his parents—which he himself had never seen. With the help of Andrew Doig of the Church of Scotland and George Loft, then the representative in Central Africa of the American Friends' Service Committee, young Banda found a good position with a firm managed by Philip Howard, a European who was sympathetic to African political activity. Banda introduced himself into the ranks of the local Trades' Union Congress. Soon, despite the existence of the emergency regulations of the Government of Nyasaland, he founded and began to edit "Ntendere pa Nchito," an outspoken mimeographed broadsheet of the labor movement. It criticized the government and, on a number of occasions, the administration threatened to suppress it. Undeterred, young Banda quickened his largely covert efforts to keep alive the nationalist fervor for which the Nyasaland Congress had been banned. Together with Orton Chirwa, whom the Government of Nyasaland released from prison in August, Banda sought more positive ways in which to further the movement toward indigenous self-government. Somehow they communicated with and consulted Dr. Banda and other Congressmen still in detention. Throughout September, Dr. Banda remained privy to their discussions with members of the elite in Blantyre-Limbe, Zomba, Lilongwe, and other centers of African opinion. At the end of that month, Chirwa, Aleke Banda, Sydney Somanje, Chechiwa Bwanausi (later Mrs. Shadrach Khonje), Augustine Mtambara, and several other prominent African professional and business people formed the Malawi Congress Party as a replacement for the banned Nyasaland African Congress. Chirwa became its president-general and Banda its secretary-general.

In prison, Dr. Banda had chosen significantly to give the new party the name that he hoped later to use for an independent Nyasaland. Historically, the tribes inhabiting much of modern Nyasaland had all been aMalawi, the component peoples of the Malawi nation.[7] Like Nkrumah, Dr. Banda wanted to erase colonial misnomers. To him, the name "Nyasaland" appeared as inappropriate as the "Gold Coast" had seemed to Nkrumah and Joseph Danquah.

The Malawi Congress Party made no pretense of being anything other than the old Congress with a new, more modern title. Indeed, the stated aims and objects of the new party appeared to be identical to those elaborated by the old Congress in innumerable printed statements. The Malawi Congress promised "to work relentlessly to achieve self-government and ultimate independence for the people of Nyasaland" and "to serve as the vigorous conscious political vanguard for removing all forms of oppression, racial, economic, social and otherwise, and for the establishment of a democratic national government in Nyasaland." Orton Chirwa, whom *The Central African Examiner* labeled "The Reluctant Locum," made it abundantly clear that he had no desire to rival Dr. Banda's national leadership.[8] His was a caretaker leadership, and both Chirwa and Aleke Banda promised to resign their positions whenever other detainees might be returned home.

The Malawi Congress achieved prominence almost overnight. Within two days of its formation, more than one thousand Africans had joined its ranks. By the end of November, the new Congress claimed about fifteen thousand paid-up members. Chirwa meanwhile devoted his efforts to seeking the release from prison of his colleagues. In November, he pleaded their case unsuccessfully in London. At home, Aleke Banda replaced "Ntendere pa Nchito" with *The Malawi News,* an at first duplicated, and later printed, weekly organ of the party. With a strident, aggressive tone, it soon achieved

[7] The use of the name Malawi in that sense is foreshadowed in T. Cullen Young and H. Kamuzu Banda (trans. and eds.) *Our African Way of Life* (London, 1946), 10.

[8] *Central African Examiner,* iii (24 October 1959), 12–13; *Dissent,* 12 (22 October 1959); text in Lucy Mair, *The Nyasaland Elections of 1961* (London, 1962), 83–86.

a circulation larger than any other Nyasaland newspaper.[9] Together young Banda and Chirwa carefully laid an administrative groundwork in preparation for the arrival of Dr. Banda. When he eventually returned, he found a well-organized political machine that, like the United National Independence Party in Northern Rhodesia, subsequently provided the ruling class of an independent African government.

THE STAGES OF VICTORY

Both Dr. Banda and Kaunda emerged from their stretches of enforced confinement stronger politically than before. In Kaunda's case, the decision of the government of Northern Rhodesia to attack Zambia and to incarcerate him made of a sectional leader a national hero. As a result, Kaunda's star eclipsed Nkumbula's in the eyes of his potential supporters. While Nkumbula remained an elected legislator, Kaunda retained an aura of nationalist legitimacy. Africans knew of his imprisonment and, simultaneously, learned that Nkumbula more and more chose to fraternize with whites and to be a part of the structure of officialdom.

In most areas of Northern Rhodesia, the United National Independence Party, of which Kaunda became president, could count upon the support of African masses. It also commanded the allegiance of the politically minded intelligentsia, and Kaunda gathered a cadre of devoted prison and university graduates into the "cabinet" of his party. From early 1960, he began to agitate afresh for African self-government and a universal franchise. He and his colleagues denounced the Federation and repeatedly, in meetings throughout the country, they thundered the nationalist slogan—"one man, one vote." Tirelessly, they attempted to build up the party and to persuade the British government to give Africans the political rights to which successive nationalist spokesmen had long aspired. They feared that any delay would mean a further increase in white political power and, with it, the possibility that Welensky, if they relaxed even for a moment, might find a way forever to keep them from obtaining their freedom. Then, for a combination of the old, stereotyped reasons, Africans in Northern Rhodesia vented their frustrations upon schools and other public property. During the months of

[9] See Robert I. Rotberg, "The Malawi News," *Africa Report* (December 1963), 24–26.

July, August, and September 1960, they set fire to schools and hospitals and skirmished with units of the police.

In Northern Rhodesia, the struggle between black and white remained essentially unresolved and unhopeful. But in Nyasaland, Africans had, in all but name, already won their freedom. By July 1960, Orton Chirwa and Aleke Banda had regrouped the peoples of Nyasaland solidly behind the Malawi Congress Party. They had demonstrated overwhelming support for Dr. Banda and his proposals for rapid emancipation. Iain Macleod, who had become the British Secretary of the State for the Colonies, furthermore realized that Dr. Banda's leadership would prove essential during any period of colonial devolution of power. Accordingly, he released Dr. Banda from prison in April 1960, and almost immediately invited him to confer in London. There Dr. Banda refused to compromise on essentials. At a time when the independence of the Congo had begun to exert an influence upon the affairs of emergent Africa, Macleod and the British government willingly cooperated, and the resultant constitution provided for an election after which Dr. Banda, if his party won, might reasonably expect to form a government composed of fellow nationalists. For the time being, however, it would remain ultimately responsible to the governor of the Protectorate.[10] To everyone concerned, this period of so-called "responsible government" represented a first stage on the road to African independence.

Thereafter, political change in the protectorates required only time and further, often over-elaborate constitutional discussion. Africans had, in fact, won the game. (Even the Monckton Commission tended to agree.[11]) But they still had to play by antiquated rules that called for patience, a certain amount of intrigue, and sharp verbal combat. The white settlers refused to give in easily. Throughout the first half of 1961, while Dr. Banda, Dunduzu Chisiza, Aleke Banda and numerous others instilled a remarkable, elsewhere unequaled, drive, discipline, and organization into their campaign for electoral victory, Kaunda and his followers tried to persuade Macleod to grant to them a constitution as forward-looking as that

[10] Report of the Nyasaland Constitutional Conference held in July and August, 1960, Cmd. 1132 (1960); Mair, Elections, 10–21.

[11] See Report of the Advisory Commission on the Review of the Constitution of Rhodesia and Nyasaland, Cmnd. 1148 (1960), 22, 29, 33, 113, 115, 119–120.

obtained by Dr. Banda. At one point Macleod did just that. But, Welensky, and Julian Greenfield, his Federal Minister of Law, threatened and blustered and, perhaps largely because other members of the British Cabinet wanted Welensky's party to obtain a favorable result in a Southern Rhodesian constitutional referendum that had been scheduled for July 1961, Macleod later amended the previously published Northern Rhodesian constitution to meet settler objections. He altered the crucial provisions that had been expected to provide Kaunda's party with a number of important "multiracial" seats in the new Legislative Council. Instead, Macleod devised an exceedingly complicated formula which devaluated African votes for these seats and, in the event, permitted white electors to exercise a virtual veto over prospective African candidates. As a result, Africans on the Copperbelt and in the Northern and Luapula provinces again demonstrated their frustration. They blocked roads and, for a number of months, protested violently, but without the loss of white life. Kaunda believed that he had been double-crossed by the British government and, during much of the remainder of the year, he made several futile trips to London, Accra, and Dar es Salaam in order to discuss his problems with political leaders. Finally, early in 1962, Reginald Maudling, the new Colonial Secretary, persuaded the British government to reverse itself slightly, the last draft of the constitution that had been discussed interminably for more than a year proving a compromise between the two earlier ones.[12]

Already, the Malawi Congress Party had won an overwhelming victory in the August 1961 elections. Dr. Banda had personally canvassed the country, everywhere condemning the "stupid so-called Federation," leading song-fests, and calling upon Africans to vote *en bloc* for the Malawi Party candidates. The Chisiza brothers had meanwhile raised the required campaign funds by regular subscriptions (the Party claimed more than a million members in early 1961), *ad hoc* levies, and the sale of badges bearing the beaming face of Dr. Banda. When the time came, more than 98 percent of those eligible voted in the country's first direct election. The Malawi Congress Party won all twenty of the lower roll (African) seats and

[12] *Northern Rhodesia, Proposals for Constitutional Change,* Cmd. 1295 (1961); *Statement by the Secretary of State for the Colonies on Proposals for Constitutional Change,* Cmd. 1301 (1961).

two of the eight upper roll seats in the Legislative Council.[13] Soon the governor granted five, and later seven of the ten available places on the Protectorate's Executive Council to Dr. Banda's party. And, by the beginning of 1962, Dr. Banda, nominally only the Minister of Land, Natural Resources, and Local Government, had emerged as Nyasaland's *de facto* prime minister. Sir Glyn Jones, the governor, permitted Dr. Banda to initiate and to execute reasonable policies. Decisions of national importance, officially within the governor's prerogative, were made by Dr. Banda; his fellow African ministers and parliamentary secretaries conferred with him daily and ran their departments to his satisfaction.

White colonials expected that the new Malawi ministers would sit back and enjoy the spoils of office—a large house on the side of Zomba mountain, a shining black limousine, and an annual salary of about £3000—and would gladly permit the white permanent secretaries to run the various ministries in the traditional bureaucratic manner. But Dr. Banda and his colleagues immediately made known their will to govern. Within months of taking office, they proceeded to reform the existing administrative machinery and to plan seriously, and on many fronts, for the future. Their industry and ability to learn became legendary. In many positive ways, they sought to demonstrate to skeptics that home rule would confer abundant benefits upon the African population. They expanded the long-neglected system of secondary education, revamped the Native Courts, ended the *tangata* abuses traditionally suffered by agricultural laborers, reformed the existing produce-marketing arrangements, introduced popularly elected district councils in place of chiefs, and began to seek new ways in which to inject the fluid of development into the sluggish body of the Protectorate's economy. Before his untimely death, Dunduzu Chisiza prepared an ambitious five-year plan and organized a successful economic symposium at which experts from throughout the world read papers and discussed the critical needs of underdeveloped countries.

Within a year of its triumphant electoral success, the Malawi Congress Partly ruled Nyasaland in all but name. Dr. Banda became the Chief Minister, and he and his associates prepared to shed the formal coat of "responsible government" for that of "self-government," the

[13] For a detailed, if occasionally questionable, discussion of the campaign, see Mair, *Elections*, 66–79.

last stage before independence. With ritual precision, the British government agreed, at a conference in London during November 1962, that Nyasaland should become self-governing early in the new year. A month later, R. A. Butler, then the Secretary of State for Central African Affairs, promised in principle to permit Nyasaland to secede from the Federation. He confirmed what many had long realized: that the Federation was dead.

In Northern Rhodesia, Kaunda and his followers had meanwhile campaigned vigorously—but with fewer financial, organizational, and emotional resources—against the remnants of Nkumbula's Congress and the white-led United Federal Party. For this election the British and Northern Rhodesian governments had ingeniously constructed perhaps the most complicated regulations ever used anywhere. Whites, Asians, and some Africans—depending upon their literacy and income qualifications—voted for fifteen upper-roll representatives in single-member constituencies. The others, if they earned at least £120 a year and could complete the registration application unaided, chose fifteen lower-roll members, again in single-member constituencies. More than 34,000 persons registered on the upper and 92,000 on the lower roll. Both groups next voted together on the "national" roll, selecting fourteen more representatives in seven double-member constituencies. In four of these constituencies, voters had to cast ballots for one African and one European. Successful candidates could be elected only if they managed to obtain at least 10 percent of the votes cast by members of each race and at least 20 percent of all those cast by one race. Asians separately chose the forty-fifth member of the Legislative Council.

Before the election, Kaunda, ever optimistic, persuaded himself that whites would be sufficiently realistic to vote in reasonable numbers for members of his own party. In the weeks before the polls opened in late October, he therefore attempted to bring white and black together in order to make a difficult constitution work. In speeches to white and mixed audiences, he tried patiently to eliminate the fears of Europeans that African self-government would mean "another Congo" in Rhodesia. He explained candidly that he could only promise whites a secure future if his party received white electoral support. Everywhere he wooed whites assiduously. His carefully chosen or supported white candidates included Sir Stewart

Gore-Browne, two Methodist ministers, a lawyer, and a surgeon. But, in the end, the whites, both civil servants and farmers alike, voted solidly for the United Federal Party.

Almost 90 percent of the electorate cast ballots. More than 60,000 persons voted for the United National Independence Party, 17,000 for the African National Congress, 21,000 for the United Federal Party, and 1,500 for the small Liberal Party.[14] These figures gave the United National Independence Party twelve lower-roll seats (the African National Congress won three in Nkumbula's home area), the special Asian seat, and one on the upper roll. The Federal Party won the thirteen urban upper-roll places and, with the help of the Congress, two more "national seats" in areas in which its Congress allies also won places. In those two areas, the Congress proved able to deliver at least 10 percent of the African vote to the Federal Party. In other areas, Kaunda's candidates received impressive African majorities but proved unable to obtain more than 4 or 5 percent of the total white vote. Even Gore-Browne failed to win. After two subsequent "run-off" elections for the unfilled "national" seats had been held, the final composition of the parties in the Legislative Council was: National Party, fourteen; Federal Party, sixteen; Congress, seven. The electors had managed to fill only thirty-seven of the forty-five places.

Kaunda eventually persuaded Nkumbula, despite the antagonism between their parties, to form a coalition of convenience. Otherwise, Nkumbula might have agreed to establish a government with the Federal Party. Nkumbula and two of his supporters received choice positions on the Executive Council, and Kaunda tried hard to make the best of an awkward arrangement. It held together until a further constitution, and the elections of early 1964, gave the National Party fifty-five of sixty-five African seats in a seventy-five-man Legislative Assembly. Ten whites occupied reserved seats and, this time at least, universal suffrage and simple single-member constituency arrangements contributed to the overwhelming nature of the National Party's victory.

Like Dr. Banda, Kaunda became the prime minister of a self-governing country. On the last day of 1963, the British government

[14] For detailed figures, see Robert I. Rotberg, "Inconclusive Election in Northern Rhodesia," *Africa Report* (December 1963), 4–5; David C. Mulford, *The Northern Rhodesia General Election, 1962* (Nairobi, 1964), 145–155.

had dissolved the Federation that it had begun ten years before. On that occasion, Lord Malvern told newsmen that he would have his "usual whiskey with dinner. Then I shall go to bed and allow the Federation to pass away quietly in my sleep."[15] At the same time, Dr. Banda symbolically buried a Federal coffin, and hurried to prepare his country for the trials of its forthcoming independence. On 6 July 1964—six years to the day after he had returned from the proverbial wilderness of the United States, Great Britain, and Ghana —Nyasaland became the Commonwealth of Malawi. On 24 October 1964—six years to the day after Kaunda had founded the Zambia African National Congress—Northern Rhodesia became the new Republic of Zambia.

[15] Quoted in *The Times* (London), 1 January 1964.

POSTSCRIPT

In the months that have elapsed since this book was sent to the printer, although Zambia—where observers anticipate the imminent announcement of a one-party state—remains seemingly politically serene, the rush of events has dramatically changed the political complexion of Malawi. Within its borders, the sounds of rebellion disturb the anticipated peace and quiet of the post-independence period. Without, exiled former cabinet ministers and friendly white pro-nationalists nurse their grievances and political wounds; some-time colleagues have become bitter enemies. Prime Minister Dr. H. Kamuzu Banda denounces them as he once denounced the Welen-skyites.

The cleavage in the Malawi leadership became apparent at the time of independence. (A fuller analysis must await a subsequent occasion.) For long, the members of the Malawi cabinet had resented being treated by Dr. Banda as if they were schoolchildren (he often referred to them publicly as "my boys"); they wanted the attributes of responsibility and power that befitted their positions of prominence. Dr. Banda made virtually all of the decisions affecting state and party; they wanted to influence the decision-making process more directly. Ideological differences existed: Despite the objections of his younger colleagues, Dr. Banda, a realist, exchanged diplomats with Portuguese-controlled Moçambique and strengthened the mutual economic links that had long ago been forged by his colonial predecessors. (There were unconfirmed rumors that Dr. Banda had been prepared to swap the southernmost tip of Malawi for a slice of Moçambique along the Rovuma River—thereby giving Malawi an outlet on the Indian Ocean.) He refused to cease trading with South Africa and Rhodesia (formerly Southern Rhodesia). For the moment, he was not prepared to exchange ambassadors with the governments of mainland China or East Germany.

When Dr. Banda flew to London for the conference of Commonwealth Prime Ministers that immediately followed Malawi's independence celebrations, he acknowledged the existence of dissidence
within the upper echelons of the Malawi Congress Party by warning
the mass of his followers to be on the lookout for political saboteurs.
Nothing untoward happened during his absence, but during August
1964, Orton Chirwa, W. Kanyama Chiume, Yatuta Chisiza, Masauko
Chipembere, and other members of the Malawi cabinet became
increasingly disenchanted with Dr. Banda's autocratic grip on the
affairs of the new nation. Chirwa, Chiume, and Chipembere, among
others, may have also disliked the extent to which their own political
power and sources of patronage were being diluted by Dr. Banda's
appointments to statutory boards and by the increasing influence of
Aleke Banda who, in addition to being Dr. Banda's private secretary,
the editor of the *Malawi News,* and the secretary-general of the
party, became the director of the new Malawi Broadcasting Corporation and the National Chairman of the League of Malawi Youth
and Young Pioneers—in time a para-military training scheme for
unemployed adolescents and young adults that was modeled upon
the Ghanaian and Israeli examples. The cabinet ministers also championed the grievances of African civil servants, the group within
Malawi that, compared to its own expectations, had benefited least
by independence. The pace of Africanization (Dr. Banda categorically refused to promote Africans unless they were, by his high
standards, fully qualified and uncorrupt) became an issue together
with Dr. Banda's decisions to refrain from raising salaries significantly and, for the first time, to charge a nominal sum for outpatient
care in Malawi's hospitals. (He also refused to integrate the school
system; this last instance of his reluctance to force the pace of
change did not, however, become an important point of controversy.)

During August, dissidents within the cabinet grew increasingly
restless. They were under some pressure from friends in Tanganyika
and Kenya to urge Dr. Banda to adopt a more militant, non-aligned,
anti-colonial posture than had been apparent. First, however, Colin
Cameron, one of Dr. Banda's staunchest white supporters from the
dark days of 1959, resigned from the cabinet in protest against the
prime minister's determination to sponsor a preventive detention
act. Then, a few weeks later, in late August, the break came: Pre-

cipitated perhaps by their differences on the advisability of accepting a loan from the government of mainland China (Dr. Banda called it a "naked bribe"), Chiume, Chirwa, Augustine Bwanausi, Willie Chokani, and Chisiza (Chipembere was on a visit to Canada) forced a confrontation with Dr. Banda. They presented a list of grievances that included the items listed above and pleaded with him to reform. They particularly wanted him to accelerate the pace of Africanization within the civil service and to accord them greater personal respect.

At first Dr. Banda agreed to consider their requests. But then, perhaps influenced by his supporters, including many long-time party stalwarts who for many years had resented the paramount influence of the "intellectuals" and who saw opportunities for themselves in the aftermath of any split, Dr. Banda changed his mind, disregarded the efforts of mediators, and dismissed Chiume, Chirwa, and Bwanausi from the cabinet. He also dismissed Mrs. Rose Chibambo, a parliamentary secretary. As a gesture of solidarity, Chokani and Chisiza resigned. When Chipembere returned from Canada, he too dramatically resigned.

Dr. Banda asked the Malawi Parliament for a vote of confidence. In the ensuing debate, he explained the reasons for the split within the cabinet, and forswore retributions. "What are the four cornerstones on which our Party, our Government, our State, was built?," Dr. Banda asked Parliament. "Here they are. Unity, loyalty, discipline and obedience. . . . Once these four cornerstones are broken away . . . there is no . . . Malawi Government in this country, and there is no State. . . . What do we get? Another Congo? Is that what anyone in this country wants?"[1]

The former ministers, whose places in the Cabinet were soon taken by party stalwarts,[2] joined in assuring Dr. Banda of their loyalty. More in sorrow than in accusation, they also told Parliament why they had challenged Dr. Banda's hitherto unquestioned authority. Chisiza said that he refused to be a sychophant and only tell the prime minister what he wanted to hear. "We are building a

[1] Parliament of Malawi, *Official Report of the Proceedings* (8 September 1964), 10.

[2] John Msonthi had already returned to the cabinet after having been dismissed at the time of independence. John Tembo, the minister of finance, retained his position.

nation and if we really mean what we say, let us build it with honesty and sincerity and dedication," he declared.[3] Chipembere recognized the tragedy and the irony: "It gives me a really heavy heart that Malawi, which people were regarding as a paragon of political organization and discipline and understanding, has now broken down. Broken down to the extent of members of the one . . . mighty Malawi Congress Party, attacking one another in public here in the presence of *atsamunda*, or our former enemies, calling one another traitors. Wherever Welensky is today, he must be rejoicing. He must be celebrating. There must be a cocktail party somewhere in Salisbury as a result of what is taking place here. We are in utter disgrace."[4]

Parliament gave Dr. Banda an overwhelming vote of confidence. Impartial observers assumed that the rift would somehow soon be healed. Few could envisage Chipembere—who had once commanded widespread popular support—quietly accepting his place as a back-bench member of Parliament. Observers also imagined that Dr. Banda would be unable to find ministerial replacements sufficiently capable to help him govern the country.

But the breach widened. The new ministers and parliamentary secretaries were determined to maintain their positions of influence. Dr. Banda suspected that his former colleagues were plotting the violent overthrow of the government. Civil servants remained dissatisfied. There were clashes in Zomba between supporters of the ousted ministers and those still loyal to Dr. Banda. The party became irreparably rent as the atmosphere of enmity everywhere became more ominous. In October, Chokani, Bwanausi, and their families and relatives (including Dr. Harry Bwanausi) fled to Zambia, where Chokani and Dr. Bwanausi obtained employment. Chisiza and Chiume went to Dar es Salaam. (Cameron and Major Peter Moxon were also advised to leave.)

Chipembere went home to the Fort Johnston district. There he gained control of the eastern section of the district. His followers harassed the government; in February—possibly as the spearhead of a revolution that failed—two hundred of them attacked the *boma* at Fort Johnston and sent a raiding party as far as the Liwonde ferry, where white-officered troops loyal to Dr. Banda forced them

[3] *Proceedings* (8 September 1964), 40.
[4] *Ibid.* (9 September 1964), 89.

to retreat. More recently, Chipembere's supporters have continued to clash with the government. Dr. Banda meanwhile has armed the Young Pioneers, deposed disloyal chiefs, and detained several hundred civil servants and other supposed supporters of Chipembere. As this is written (8 May 1965), although Dr. Banda has materially strengthened his grip upon the loyalties of the citizens of Malawi and Chipembere has left Fort Johnston for the United States, ripples of dissent continue to disturb the surface calm of a nation uneasy.

A Note on the Sources

Select Bibliography

Index

A NOTE ON THE SOURCES

The records of the various departments of the governments of Northern Rhodesia and Nyasaland provided the main sources for the present study and, wherever appropriate, the footnotes cite the most important individual files by number. The archives in Zomba contained important material on the Rising of 1915, on the early administration of the Protectorate, and on the growth of African and European religious and political organizations. Although a fire swept the Zomba Secretariat in 1919, it apparently failed to consume as much important material as the standard guide to the archival resources of Central Africa, and a number of writers, have reported. Moreover, after the fire, successive administrators brought duplicate files and other materials from the outlying *bomas* into Zomba. Unlike Lusaka, in Zomba the archives held the back files of all of the provincial and district headquarters. In Northern Rhodesia, however, many of the rural administrative centers possessed their own small caches of historically valuable records; by now termites have probably devoured their contents.

For the period between the two World Wars, both the Zomba and Lusaka archives contained a wealth of documentation on the political, social, and economic history of the two protectorates. Copies of the correspondence and memoranda of the East African Governors' Conference and full reports on the closer association movements also found their way into the two archives. A further group of records never entered the archives, however, and for administrative and security reasons, remained within the respective secretariats. Moreover, during the post-World War II era, administrators often refused to deposit "sensitive" files in the archives. Many of these documents are now lost. Unfortunately, too, a large proportion of the more important secret and confidential files (some of which must remain unacknowledged), and a number of the unclassified files used herein have since been destroyed and/or removed from their repositories in Lusaka and Zomba by the retreating colonial authorities. (Elsewhere, when the British withdrew from their African colonies they characteristically destroyed a vast array of historically valuable material. In Kenya, sources on the emergency, and on recent history in general, fueled bonfires; in Uganda, an entire room of secret and confidential files vanished on the eve of independence.) In the period before the emergence of Northern Rhodesia and Nyasaland as Zambia and Malawi, British officials apparently denied to posterity the records of the 1959 emergency and, in large measure, the secret and confidential accounts that depicted the early growth of the modern nationalist movements in both countries. Police Special Branch reports have, for the most part, also disappeared.

In addition to the records in Lusaka and Zomba, the files of several of the offices of the British South Africa Company, the Administrator of Southern Rhodesia, the High Commissioner for South Africa and his Resident Commissioner in Salisbury, and police reports on religious and political movements—all of which may be found in the Salisbury archives —contribute significantly to an understanding of the early colonial history of Northern Rhodesia and Nyasaland. The British Public Record Office holds the important Foreign and Colonial Office files that pertain to this period.

Of the private papers and unpublished documents consulted, those of Lt. Col. Sir Stewart Gore-Browne were of the greatest importance and bulk. They covered the years from 1920 to 1956, and illuminated many of the darker corners of the recent history of Central Africa. The papers of Haya Peters shed a certain amount of light on the mood of John Chilembwe, with whom Peters corresponded in the years before the Rising of 1915. The late George Simeon Mwase wrote an important unpublished book about John Chilembwe—"A Dialogue of Nyasaland, Record of Past Events, Environments, and the Present Outlook within the Protectorate"—that contains an apparently eyewitness account (or a collage of eyewitness accounts) of the events that preceded and caused the rising. Mwase wrote in about 1932, however, and may have supplemented his report from documents conceivably then available to clerks in either the Secretariat or one or more of the provincial bomas. The Mombera Association notebook contains a detailed record of the activities and deliberations of that politically important organization from 1920 to 1936. The papers of Mr. Archibald H. Elwell relate to the period immediately before the formation of the Northern Rhodesian Federation of African Welfare Societies in 1946. For the modern period, the papers of G. G. S. J. Hadlow—who was active in settler politics after World War II—include several important unpublished memoranda. Wittington K. Sikalumbi's unpublished "The Circumstances which gave rise to the Banning of the Zambia African Congress of Northern Rhodesia" (1959–63), deals with the period from 1953 to 1959. The papers of Patrick Mumba contained material on the origin of the Zambia Congress and the formation of several successor parties. Having been raided on a number of occasions by the Northern Rhodesian Police, the files of the African National Congress lacked the depth and the interest that was no doubt found in the records seized by the Police Special Branch from the leaders of the Zambia and Nyasaland African Congresses at the time of the 1959 arrests.

Interviews with a number of persons who helped to shape the recent history of Malawi and Zambia corrected or amplified the written evidence. On numerous occasions between 1959 and 1963, and in a variety of settings, I discussed the rise of nationalism with Mr. (now President) Kenneth D. Kaunda, Dr. (now Prime Minister) H. Kamuzu Banda, Sir Stewart Gore-Browne, and Mr. Sikota Wina, now a member of the cabinet of Zambia. With Augustine Bwanausi, McKinley Qabaniso Chibambo, W. Kanyama Chiume, Willie Chokani, Mainza Chona, Reuben Kamanga, Simon M. Kapwepwe, John Msonthi, and Arthur Wina, all present or recent members of the Malawi and Zambia cabinets. I had further discussions either in Africa or the United States during 1962/63. The late Mr. Dunduzu Kaluli Chisiza; Aleke Banda, who succeeded Mr. Chisiza as the secretary-general of the Malawi Congress Party, and Mr. J. David Rubadiri, the Malawi Ambassador to the United States, shared their own experiences and views. Mr. James Sangala, the founder of the Nyasaland African Congress; the Rev. Mr. Charles C. Chinula, one of the earliest Nyasa association leaders; Mr. Donald Siwale, who played a similar role in Northern Rhodesia; and Chief Mwase Kasungu all spoke of the many events with which they were familiar. I also obtained the personal views of Messrs. Mtalika Banda, sometime secretary of the Nyasaland African Congress; Sir Kenneth Bradley, a sometime Rhodesian administrative officer; Ronald Bush, sometime Secretary for Native Affairs of Northern Rhodesia; Ralph N. Chinyama, sometime president of the Nyasaland African Congress; T. S. L. Fox-Pitt, sometime provincial commissioner, Northern Rhodesia; G. G. S. J. Hadlow; Rowland S. Hudson, sometime Secretary for Native Affairs of Northern Rhodesia; Mrs. Chechiwa Khonje, of the Malawi Congress Party; Iain Macleod, M. P., sometime Secretary of State for the Colonies; Major Peter Moxon; Harry Nkumbula, president of the Northern Rhodesian African National Congress; the Rev. Mr. Hanock Msokera Phiri; Sydney Somanje, of the Nyasaland African Congress and the Malawi Congress Party; Simon ber Zukas, of the Ndola Anti-Federation Action Committee, and others who wish to remain nameless.

SELECT BIBLIOGRAPHY
OF PRINTED MATERIALS

For additional books and periodicals relevant to the political, social, and economic history of Malawi and Zambia, see J. Gus Liebenow and Robert I. Rotberg, "Federalism in Rhodesia and Nyasaland," in William S. Livingston (ed.), *Federalism in the Commonwealth: A Bibliographical Commentary* (London, 1963), 193–222. Private papers are cited only in the footnotes to the text.

Allighan, Garry, *The Welensky Story* (Cape Town, 1962).

Arnot, Frederick Stanley, *Garenganze; or, Seven Years Pioneer Mission Work in Central Africa* (London, 1889).

Baldwin, Robert E., "Wage Policy in a Dual Economy—The Case of Northern Rhodesia," *Race*, iv (1962), 73–87.

Banda, H. Kamuzu, and Harry Nkumbula, *Federation in Central Africa* (London, 1951).

Banton, Michael, "African Prophets," *Race*, v (1963), 42–55.

Baragwanath, Orlando, "The First Copper Mines in Northern Rhodesia," *The Northern Rhodesia Journal*, v (1964), 209–222, 380–388.

Barber, William J., *The Economy of British Central Africa: A Case Study of Economic Development in a Dualistic Society* (Stanford, 1961).

———— "Economic Rationality and Behavior Patterns in an Underdeveloped Area: A Case Study of African Economic Behavior in the Rhodesias," *Economic Development and Cultural Change*, viii (1960), 237–251.

Barnes, Bertram H., *Johnson of Nyasaland* (London, 1933).

Barnes, John A., *Politics in a Changing Society: A Political History of the Fort Jameson Ngoni* (Cape Town, 1954).

Baxter, T. William, "The Angoni Rebellion and Mpeseni," *The Northern Rhodesia Journal*, ii (1950), 14–24.

———— "The Concessions of Northern Rhodesia," *Occasional Papers of the National Archives of Rhodesia and Nyasaland*, i (1963), 3–41.

———— "More about Mpeseni," *The Northern Rhodesia Journal*, vi (1955), 46–52.

Bettison, David G., *Cash, Wage and Occupational Structure in Blantyre-Limbe, Nyasaland* (Lusaka, 1958).

Booth, Joseph, *Africa for the African* (Baltimore, 1897).

Bradley, Kenneth, *Copper Venture: The Discovery and Development of Roan Antelope and Mufulira* (London, 1952).

Brown, Godfrey N., "British Educational Policy in West and Central Africa," *The Journal of Modern African Studies,* ii (1964), 365–377.

Bruce, A. Livingstone, *The Cape-to-Cairo: or Britain's Sphere of Influence* (Edinburgh, 1892).

Buchanan, John, *The Shire Highlands as Colony and Mission* (London, 1885).

—— "The Industrial Development of Nyasaland," *Royal Geographical Journal,* i (1893), 245–252.

Burles, R. S., "The Katengo Council Elections," *The Journal of African Administration,* iv (1952), 14–17.

Burnett, Hugh (ed.), *Face to Face* (London, 1964).

Cardew, Claude Algernon, "Nyasaland in the Nineties," *The Nyasaland Journal,* viii (1955), 57–63.

Chadwick, Owen, *Mackenzie's Grave* (London, 1959).

Chandos, Oliver Lyttleton Viscount, *The Memoirs of . . .* (London, 1962).

Chibambo, Yesaya Mlonyeni (trans. Charles Stuart), *My Ngoni of Nyasaland* (London, 1942).

Chingota, Jailos, "An Autobiography," *The Nyasaland Journal,* xiv (1961), 13–26.

Chisiza, Dunduzu K., *Africa: What Lies Ahead?* (New York, 1962).

—— "The Outlook for Contemporary Africa," *The Journal of Modern African Studies,* i (1963), 25–38.

Chiume, M. W. Kanyama, "The Nyasaland Crisis," *Africa South,* iii (July-September 1959), 45–51.

—— *Nyasaland Demands Secession and Independence* (London, 1959).

—— *Nyasaland Speaks* (London, 1959).

Chona, Mainza, "Northern Rhodesia's Time for Change," *Africa South in Exile,* v (January-March 1961), 72–76.

Clay, Gervas, "African Urban Advisory Councils in the Northern Rhodesia Copperbelt," *The Journal of African Administration,* i (1949), 33–38.

Clegg, Edward M., *Race and Politics: Partnership in the Federation of Rhodesia and Nyasaland* (London, 1960).

Clutton-Brock, Guy, *Dawn in Nyasaland* (London, 1959).

Coillard, François (trans. and ed. Catherine Winkworth Mackintosh), *On the Threshold of Central Africa* (London, 1897).

Conyngham, L. D., "African Towns in Northern Rhodesia," *The Journal of African Administration,* iii (1951), 113–117.

Coupland, Reginald, *Kirk on the Zambesi: A Chapter of African History* (Oxford, 1928).

Crawford, Daniel, *Thinking Black: Twenty-two Years without a Break in the Long Grass of Central Africa* (London, 1913).

Creighton, Thomas R. M., *The Anatomy of Partnership: Southern Rhodesia and the Central African Federation* (London, 1960).

Davidson, J. W., *The Northern Rhodesian Legislative Council* (London, 1948).

Davis, J. Merle (ed.), *Modern Industry and the African* (London, 1933).

Denny, S. R., "Leopold Moore versus the Chartered Company," *The Northern Rhodesia Journal*, iv (1960), 219–230, 335–346.

——— "Val Gielgud and the Slave Traders," *The Northern Rhodesia Journal*, iii (1957), 331–338.

Duff, Hector, *African Small Chop* (London, 1932).

——— *Nyasaland under the Foreign Office* (London, 1906).

Elmslie, W. A., *Among the Wild Ngoni* (Edinburgh, 1899).

Epstein, A. L., *Politics in an Urban African Community* (Manchester, 1958).

——— *The Administration of Justice and the Urban African* (London, 1953),

——— "Urban Native Courts on the Northern Rhodesian Copperbelt," *The Journal of African Administration*, iii (1951), 117–124.

Faber, Michael, "Southern Rhodesia Alone? A Look at the Economic Consequences," *The South African Journal of Economics*, xxviii (1960), 283–303.

Fotheringham, L. Monteith, *Adventures in Nyassaland: A Two Years' Struggle with the Arab Slave Dealers in Central Africa* (London, 1891).

Fraenkel, Peter, *Wayaleshi* (London, 1959).

Franck, Thomas M., *Race and Nationalism: The Struggle for Power in Rhodesia-Nyasaland* (New York, 1960).

Franklin, Harry, *Unholy Wedlock: The Failure of the Central African Federation* (London, 1963).

Fraser, Donald, *African Idylls: Portraits and Impressions of Life on a Central African Mission Station* (London, 1923).

——— *The Autobiography of an African: Retold in Biographical Form and in the Wild African Setting of the Life of Daniel Mtusu* (London, 1925).

——— *Winning a Primitive People: Sixteen Years Work among the War-like Tribe of the Ngoni and the Senga and Tumbuka Peoples of Central Africa* (London, 1914).

Fraser, R. H., "Land Settlement in the Eastern Province of Northern Rhodesia," *The Rhodes-Livingstone Journal*, iii (1945), 45–50.

Frost, David, "The Economic Outlook for Nyasaland," *Race*, iv (1963), 59–72.

Gadd, K. G., "The Lusitu Tragedy," *Central African Journal of Medicine*, viii (1962), 491–508.

Gann, Lewis H., *The Birth of a Plural Society* (Manchester, 1958).

——— *A History of Northern Rhodesia: Early Days to 1953* (London, 1964).

——— "The Northern Rhodesian Copper Industry and the World of Copper: 1923–1952," *The Rhodes-Livingstone Journal*, xviii (1955), 1–18.

——— and Michael Gelfand, *Huggins of Rhodesia: The Man and His Country* (London, 1964).

Gelfand, Michael, *Lakeside Pioneers: Socio-Medical Study of Nyasaland* (*1875–1920*) (Oxford, 1964).

────── "Migration of African Labourers in Rhodesia and Nyasaland," *The Journal of Local Administration Overseas*, ii (1963), 149–153.

────── *Northern Rhodesia in the Days of the Charter: A Medical and Social Study, 1878–1924* (Oxford, 1961).

────── (ed.), *Doctor on Lake Nyasa, Being the Journal and Letters of Dr. Wordsworth Poole* (*1895–1897*) (Salisbury, 1961).

Glennie, A. F. B., "The Barotse System of Government," *The Journal of African Administration*, iv (1952), 9–13.

Gore-Browne, Stewart, "The Anglo-Belgian Boundary Commission, 1911–1914," *The Northern Rhodesia Journal*, v (1964), 315–329.

────── "Legislative Council in Northern Rhodesia Twenty Years Ago," *The Northern Rhodesia Journal*, iv, 2 (1954), 39–45.

────── "The Relations of Black and White in Tropical Africa," *Journal of the Royal African Society*, xxxv (1935), 378–386.

Graham-Jolly, H. G., "The Progress of Local Government in Nyasaland," *The Journal of African Administration*, vii (1955), 188–192.

Gray, J. A., "A Country in Search of a Name," *The Northern Rhodesia Journal*, iii (1956), 75–78.

Gray, Richard, *The Two Nations: Aspects of the Development of Race Relations in the Rhodesias and Nyasaland* (London, 1960).

Hailey, William Malcolm Baron, *Native Administration in the British African Territories. Part II. Central Africa* (London, 1950).

Hall, Richard, *Kaunda: Founder of Zambia* (Lusaka, 1964).

Hancock, W. Keith, *Survey of British Commonwealth Affairs, II: Problems of Economic Policy, 1918–1939* (London, 1942), ii.

Hanna, Alexander John, *The Beginnings of Nyasaland and North-Eastern Rhodesia, 1859–1895* (Oxford, 1956).

────── *The Story of the Rhodesias and Nyasaland* (London, 1960).

Harding, Colin, *Far Bugles* (London, 1933).

────── *In Remotest Barotseland* (London, 1905).

Hazlewood, Arthur, and P. Arthur Henderson, *Nyasaland: The Economics of Federation* (Oxford, 1960).

Heath, F. M. N., "The Growth of African Councils on the Copperbelt of Northern Rhodesia," *The Journal of African Administration*, v (1953), 123–132.

Heaton Nicholls, George, *South Africa in My Time* (London, 1961).

Hetherwick, Alexander, *The Gospel and the African* (Edinburgh, 1932).

────── "Nyasaland Today and Tomorrow," *Journal of the African Society*, xvii (1917), 11–19.

Hine, John Edward, *Days Gone By: Being Some Account of Past Years Chiefly in Central Africa* (London, 1924).

Hoffman, Carl von (ed. Eugene Löhrke), *Jungle Gods* (London, 1929).

Jack, James W., *Daybreak in Livingstonia: The Story of the Livingstonia Mission, British Central Africa* (Edinburgh, 1901).

Johnson, William Percival, *My African Reminiscences, 1875–1896* (London, 1924).

—— *Nyasa: The Great Water* (London, 1922).

Johnston, Harry H., *British Central Africa* (New York, 1897).

—— *The Story of My Life* (Indianapolis, 1923).

Johnston, James, *Reality versus Romance in South Central Africa* (London, 1893).

Jones, Griff, *Britain and Nyasaland* (London, 1964).

Jordan, E. Knowles, "Namwala in 1906," *The Northern Rhodesia Journal,* ii (1953), 24–37.

Kaunda, Kenneth, "Rider and Horse in Northern Rhodesia," *Africa South,* iii (July-September 1959), 52–56.

—— "Some Personal Reflections," *Africa's Freedom* (London, 1964), 24–37.

—— *Zambia Shall Be Free* (New York, 1963).

—— and Colin Morris, *Black Government?* (Lusaka, 1960).

Keatley, Patrick, *The Politics of Partnership: The Federation of Rhodesia and Nyasaland* (Harmondsworth, 1963).

Kidney, E., "Native Sons of Nyasaland," *Journal of the African Society,* xx (1921), 116–126.

Lane-Poole, F. H., "Mpeseni and the Exploration Companies, 1885–1898," *The Northern Rhodesia Journal,* v (1963), 221–232.

Langworthy, Emily Booth, *This Africa Was Mine* (Stirling, 1952).

Laws, Robert, "Native Education in Nyasaland," *Journal of the African Society,* xxvii (1929), 347–368.

—— *Reminiscences of Livingstonia* (Edinburgh, 1934).

Lessing, Doris, *Going Home* (London, 1957).

Leys, Colin, "An Election in Nyasaland," *Political Studies,* v (1957), 258–280.

—— and R. Cranford Pratt (eds.), *A New Deal in Central Africa* (London, 1960).

Livingstone, David, *Missionary Travels and Researches in South Africa* (London, 1857).

—— and Charles, *Narrative of an Expedition to the Zambesi and Its Tributaries, and of the Discovery of the Lakes Shirwa and Nyasa, 1858–1864* (London, 1865).

—— (ed. Horace Waller), *The Last Journals of David Livingstone in Central Africa* (London, 1874).

Livingstone, William P., *Laws of Livingstonia* (London, 1923).

—— *A Prince of Missionaries: Alexander Hetherwick* (London, 1931).

Lugard, Frederick D., *The Rise of Our East African Empire: Early Efforts in Nyasaland and Uganda* (London, 1893), 2 vols.

McCracken, K. J., "Livingstonia as an Industrial Mission, 1875–1900: A Study in Commerce and Christianity in Nyasaland," *Religion in Africa* (Edinburgh, 1964), 75–96, mimeo.

MacDonald, Duff, *Africana: Or the Heart of Heathen Africa* (London, 1882), 2 vols.

Mackay, Peter, *A Portrait of Malawi* (Zomba, 1964).

Mackintosh, Catherine Winkworth, *Coillard of the Zambesi* (London, 1907).

Macrae, F. G., "Some Footnotes to the History of Mporokoso District," *The Northern Rhodesia Journal*, iii (1956), 26–33.

Mair, Lucy P., *Native Administration in Central Nyasaland* (London, 1952).

—————— *The Nyasaland Elections of 1961* (London, 1962).

Marwick, M. G., "Another Modern Anti-Witchcraft Movement in East Central Africa," *Africa*, xx (1950), 100–112.

Mason, Philip, *Year of Decision: Rhodesia and Nyasaland in 1960* (London, 1960).

Masters, Henry and Walter, *In Wild Rhodesia* (London, 1920).

Maugham, R. C. F., *Africa as I Have Known It* (London, 1929).

—————— *Nyasaland in the Nineties* (London, 1935).

Melland, Frederick A. (using the pseudonym "Africanus"), "A Central African Confederation," *Journal of the African Society*, xvii (1918), 276–306.

Mitchell, J. Clyde, "The Political Organization of the Yao of Southern Nyasaland," *African Studies*, viii (1949), 141–160.

—————— and A. L. Epstein, "Occupational Prestige and Social Status Among Urban Africans in Northern Rhodesia," *Africa*, xxix (1959), 22–40.

Moir, Frederick L. M., *After Livingstone: An African Trade Romance* (London, 1924).

Mortimer, M. C., "History of the Barotse National School—1907 to 1957," *The Northern Rhodesia Journal*, iii (1957), 303–310.

Mulford, David C., *The Northern Rhodesia General Election, 1962* (Nairobi, 1964).

Mumba, Levi, "The Religion of My Father," *The International Review of Missions*, xix (1930), 362–376.

Murray, S. S. (ed.), *A Handbook of Nyasaland* (London, 1932).

Norman, L. S., *Nyasaland Without Prejudice* (London, 1934).

—————— "Rebellion," *Blackwood's Magazine*, ccxxx (1931), 862–873.

North, A. C., "Rural Local Government Training in Northern Rhodesia: an account of the work of the Native Authority Development Centre, Chalimbana," *The Journal of African Administration*, xiii (1961), 67–77.

Ntara, Samuel Yosia, *Headman's Enterprise: An Unexpected Page in Central African History* (London, 1949).

—————— (trans. and ed. T. Cullen Young), *Man of Africa* (London, 1934).

Nyirenda, Ackson A., "African Market Vendors in Lusaka with a note on the recent boycott," *The Rhodes-Livingstone Journal*, xxii (1957), 31–63.

Oliver, Roland, *Sir Harry Johnston and the Scramble for Africa* (London, 1957).

Oliver, Roland, " 'Too Cheaty, Too Thefty . . .'—The Seeds of National-ism in Nyasaland," *The Twentieth Century*, clxv (1959), 365–368.
Padmore, George (ed.), *History of the Pan-African Congress* (London, 1963).
Page, Thomas, "Early Days in Fort Jameson," *The Northern Rhodesia Journal*, iii (1956), 1–7.
Perham, Margery, *Lugard: The Years of Adventure, 1858–1898* (London, 1956).
Powdermaker, Hortense, *Coppertown: Changing Africa—The Human Situation on the Rhodesian Copperbelt* (New York, 1962).
Prain, Ronald L., "The Copperbelt of Northern Rhodesia," *The Journal of the Royal Society of Arts*, ciii (1955), 196–216.
Quick, Griffith, "Some Aspects of the African Watch Tower Movement in Northern Rhodesia," *The International Review of Missions*, xxix (1930), 216–226.
Rangeley, W. H. J., "Early Blantyre," *The Nyasaland Journal*, vii, 1 (1954), 37–42.
Rankin, Daniel, *Zambesi Basin and Nyasaland* (Edinburgh, 1893).
Read, Margaret, *The Ngoni of Nyasaland* (London, 1956).
Rennie, Gilbert, "Kafue or Kariba: The Facts Recalled," *East Africa and Rhodesia* (22 October 1964), 188–187.
Richards, Audrey I., "A Modern Movement of Witch-Finders," *Africa*, viii (1935), 448–460.
Robertson, Wilfrid, *Mandala Trail: A Tale of Early Days in Nyasaland* (London, 1956).
Robins, J. W., "Development of Rural Local Government for Nyasaland," *The Journal of African Administration*, xiii (1961), 148–158.
Ross, Andrew C., "The Foundations of the Blantyre Mission, Nyasaland," *Religion in Africa* (Edinburgh, 1964), 97–113, mimeo.
——— "The African—A Child or a Man," *Conference of the History of the Central African Peoples* (Lusaka, 1963), no pp., mimeo.
Rotberg, Robert I., *Christian Missionaries and the Creation of Northern Rhodesia, 1880–1924* (Princeton, 1965).
——— "The Federation Movement in British East and Central Africa, 1889–1953," *Journal of Commonwealth Political Studies*, ii (1964), 141–160.
——— "Inconclusive Election in Northern Rhodesia," *Africa Report* (December 1962), 3–6.
——— "The Lenshina Movement of Northern Rhodesia," *The Rhodes-Livingstone Journal*, xxix (1961), 63–78.
——— "Malawi—1963," *Africa Report* (January 1963), 7–9.
——— "The Malawi News," *Africa Report* (December 1963), 24–26.
——— "Missionaries as Chiefs and Entrepreneurs: Northern Rhodesia, 1882–1924," *Boston University Papers in African History* (Boston, 1964), i, 197–215.
——— "The Rise of African Nationalism: The Case of East and Central Africa," *World Politics*, xv (1962), 75–90.

Rowland, H. R., "Nyasaland General Elections, 1964," *The Journal of Local Administration Overseas*, iii (1964), 226–240.

Rukavina, Kathaleen Stevens, *Jungle Pathfinder* (London, 1951).

Saffery, A. L., *A Report on some Aspects of African Living Conditions on the Copperbelt of Northern Rhodesia* (Lusaka, 1943).

Samkange, Stanlake, "How to be a Partner," *The Twentieth Century*, clxv (1959), 365–368.

Sampson, Richard, *So This Was Lusaakas* (Lusaka, 1959).

Sanderson, F. E., "The Development of Labour Migration from Nyasaland, 1891–1914," *The Journal of African History*, ii (1961), 259–271.

Sanger, Clyde, *Central African Emergency* (London, 1960).

Scott, G. Michael, *A Time to Speak* (London, 1958).

Sharpe, Alfred, "Travels in the Northern Province and Katanga," *The Northern Rhodesia Journal*, iii (1957), 210–219.

Shepperson, George, "Abolitionism and African Political Thought," *Transition*, iii (1964), 22–26.

———— "Church and Sect in Central Africa," *The Rhodes-Livingstone Journal*, xxxiii (1963), 82–94.

———— "David Livingstone the Scot," *The Scottish Historical Review*, xxxix (1960), 113–121.

———— (ed.), *David Livingstone and the Rovuma* (Edinburgh, 1964).

———— "Ethiopianism and African Nationalism," *Phylon*, xiv (1953), 9–18.

———— "External factors in the development of African nationalism, with particular reference to British Central Africa," *Historians in Tropical Africa* (Salisbury, 1962), 317–332, mimeo.

———— "The Literature of British Central Africa," *The Rhodes-Livingstone Journal*, xxiii (1958), 12–46.

———— "The Military History of British Central Africa," *The Rhodes-Livingstone Journal*, xxvi (1959), 23–33.

———— "Negro American Influences on the Emergence of African Nationalism," *The Journal of African History*, i (1960), 299–312.

———— "Nyasaland and the Millennium," in Sylvia L. Thrupp (ed.), *Millennial Dreams in Action* (The Hague, 1962), 144–159.

———— "Pan-Africanism and 'Pan-Africanism': some historical notes," *Phylon*, xxiii (1962), 346–358.

———— "The Politics of African Church Separatist Movements in British Central Africa, 1892–1916," *Africa*, xxiv (1954), 233–246.

———— and Thomas Price, *Independent African. John Chilembwe and the Origins, Setting and Significance of the Nyasaland Native Rising of 1915* (Edinburgh, 1958).

Stokes, Eric T., "Barotseland: The Survival of an African State, 1890–1911," and "Early European Administration and African Political Systems in Nyasaland, 1891–1897," *Conference of the History of the Central African Peoples* (Lusaka, 1953), no pp., mimeo.

Stonehouse, John, *Prohibited Immigrant* (London, 1960).

Summers, Roger, and L. H. Gann, "Robert Edward Codrington, 1869–1908," *The Northern Rhodesia Journal*, iii (1956), 44–50.

Swann, Alfred J., *Fighting the Slave Hunters in Central Africa* (London, 1910).

Tabler, Edward C. (ed.), *Trade and Travel in Early Barotseland* (London, 1963).

Taylor, Don, *The Rhodesian: The Life of Sir Roy Welensky* (London, 1955).

Taylor, John V., and Dorothea Lehmann, *Christians of the Copperbelt: The Growth of the Church in Northern Rhodesia* (London, 1961).

Temple, Merfyn, and John Sokoni, *Kaunda of Zambia* (Lusaka, 1964).

Terry, P. T., "African Agriculture in Nyasaland, 1858–1894," *The Nyasaland Journal*, xiv (1961), 27–35.

Tew, Mary, *Peoples of the Lake Nyasa Region* (London, 1950).

Tilsley, G. E., *Dan Crawford: Missionary and Pioneer in Central Africa* (London, 1929).

Varian, H. F., *Some African Milestones* (Wheatley, England, 1953).

Van Velsen, Jaap, "Labour Migration as a Positive Factor in the Continuity of Tonga Tribal Society," *Economic Development and Cultural Change*, viii (1960), 265–278.

—— "The Establishment of the Administration in Tongaland," *Historians in Tropical Africa* (Salisbury, 1962), 177–196, mimeo.

—— "The Missionary Factor among the Lakeside Tonga of Nyasaland," *The Rhodes-Livingstone Journal*, xxvi (1959), 1–22.

—— *The Politics of Kinship: A Study of Social Manipulation among the Lakeside Tonga of Nyasaland* (Manchester, 1964).

Wallace, Lawrence Aubrey, "The Beginnings of Native Administration in Northern Rhodesia," *Journal of the African Society*, xxi (1922), 165–176.

Welensky, Roy, "Toward Federation in Central Africa," *Foreign Affairs*, xxxi (1952), 142–149.

—— *Welensky's 4000 Days: The Life and Death of the Federation of Rhodesia and Nyasaland* (London, 1964).

Wells, James, *Stewart of Lovedale: The Life of James Stewart* (London, 1908).

White, C. M. N., "The Place of Training in the Development of African Local Government in Northern Rhodesia," *The Journal of African Administration*, ii (1950), 29–31.

Williams, Shirley, *Central Africa: The Economics of Inequality* (London, 1960).

Wills, A. J., *An Introduction to the History of Central Africa* (London, 1964).

Wilson, Godfrey, *An Essay on the Economics of Detribalization in Northern Rhodesia* (Livingstone, 1941/42), 2 vols.

Wood, Anthony St. John, *Northern Rhodesia: The Human Background* (London, 1961).

Young, Edward D. (ed. Horace Waller), *Nyassa: A Journal of Adventures* (London, 1877).
Young, T. Cullen, *African Ways and Wisdom: A Contribution Toward Understanding* (London, 1937).
—— "The Battle of Karonga," *The Nyasaland Journal*, viii (1955), 27–30.
—— *Notes on the Speech of the Tumbuka-Kamanga Peoples in the Northern Province of Nyasaland* (London, 1932).
—— and Frank Melland, *African Dilemma* (London, 1937).
—— and H. Kamuzu Banda (trans. and eds.), *Our African Way of Life* (London, 1946).

NEWSPAPERS AND PERIODICALS

In addition to the articles cited individually in the Select Bibliography of Printed Materials or in the notes to the text, the major newspaper and periodical sources for any study of the colonial period in Nyasaland and Northern Rhodesia and Nyasaland include:

The Rhodesia Herald (Salisbury), 1892–
The Bulawayo Chronicle, 1894–
The British Central Africa Gazette (Zomba), 1894–1899
The Central African Times (Blantyre), 1895–1908
The Livingstone Mail, 1906–
The Nyasaland Times (Blantyre), 1908–
The Copperbelt Times (Chingola), 1932–1943
The Northern Rhodesia Advertiser (Ndola), 1935–1955
Mutende (Lusaka), 1936–1952
The Northern News (Ndola), 1943–
The Central African Post (Lusaka), 1948–1962
The Malawi News (Limbe), 1959–
The African Mail (Lusaka), 1960–1962
The Central African Mail (Lusaka), 1962–

Of the locally published periodicals, the most relevant for the recent period include:

The Central African Examiner (Salisbury), 1957–
Dissent (Salisbury, mimeographed), 1959–1961
Tsopano (Salisbury), 1959–1961

SELECT LIST OF PUBLISHED OFFICIAL REPORTS, ARRANGED CHRONOLOGICALLY

Report of the Commission . . . to Inquire into . . . the Native Rising Within the Nyasaland Protectorate, 6819 (Zomba, 1916).
Second Report of the Committee Appointed . . . to Consider Certain Questions Relating to Rhodesia, Cmd. 1417 (1921).
Agreement . . . for the Settlement of Outstanding Questions Relating to Southern and Northern Rhodesia, Cmd. 1984 (1923).
Report of the East Africa Commission, Cmd. 2387 (1925).

Future Policy with Regard to Eastern Africa, Cmd. 2904 (1927).

Report of the Commission on Closer Union, Cmd. 3234 (1929).

Memorandum on Native Policy in East Africa, Cmd. 3573 (1930).

Statement of the Conclusions of His Majesty's Government in the United Kingdom as Regards Closer Union in East Africa, Cmd. 3574 (1930).

Correspondence with Regard to Native Policy in Northern Rhodesia, Cmd. 3731 (1930).

Report of the Commission Appointed to Enquire into the Financial and Economic Position of Northern Rhodesia, col. no. 145 (1938).

Rhodesia–Nyasaland Royal Commission Report, Cmd. 5949 (1939).

Reports of the [two] Commissions Appointed to Enquire into the Disturbances in the Copperbelt, Northern Rhodesia (Lusaka, 1935 and 1940).

Confidential Reports . . . Concerning the Copperbelt Disturbances of March–April 1940 (Lusaka, 1940).

Statement by the Government of Northern Rhodesia on the Recommendations of the Report of the Copperbelt Commission, 1940 (Lusaka, 1941).

Report of the Commission Appointed to Enquire into the Advancement of Africans in Industry (Lusaka, 1948).

Central African Territories: Report of the Conference on Closer Association, Cmd. 8233 (1951).

Central African Territories: Comparative Survey of Native Policy, Cmd. 8235 (1951).

Closer Association in Central Africa: Statement by His Majesty's Government in the United Kingdom, Cmd. 8411 (1951).

Southern Rhodesia, Northern Rhodesia, and Nyasaland: *Draft Federal Scheme,* Cmd. 8573; *Report of the Judicial Commission,* Cmd. 8671; *Report of the Fiscal Commission,* Cmd. 8672; *Report of the Civil Service Preparatory Commission,* Cmd. 8673 (1952).

Southern Rhodesia, Northern Rhodesia, and Nyasaland: *Report by the Conference on Federation Held in London in January, 1953,* Cmd. 8753 (1953).

The Federal Scheme for Southern Rhodesia, Northern Rhodesia and Nyasaland Prepared by a Conference Held in London, January 1953, Cmd. 8754 (1953).

Report of the Committee Appointed to Investigate the Extent to which Racial Discrimination is Practised in Shops and in Other Business Premises (Lusaka, 1956).

Report of the Commission Appointed to Inquire into the Circumstances Leading up to and Surrounding the Recent Deaths and Injuries Caused by the Use of Firearms in the Gwembe District and Matters Relating Thereto (Lusaka, 1958).

Proposals for Constitutional Change [Northern Rhodesia], Cmd. 530 (1958).

Report of the Nyasaland Commission of Inquiry, Cmnd. 814 (1959).

Report of an Inquiry into all the Circumstances which Gave Rise to the Making of the Safeguard of Elections and Public Safety Regulations, 1959 (Lusaka, 1959).

Nyasaland: State of Emergency, Cmnd. 707 (1959).

Report of the Nyasaland Constitutional Conference held in July and August, 1960, Cmd. 1132 (1960).

Report of the Advisory Commission on the Review of the Constitution of Rhodesia and Nyasaland, Cmnd. 1148 (1960).

Northern Rhodesia: Proposals for Constitutional Change, Cmd. 1295 (1961).

Statement by the Secretary of State for the Colonies on Proposals for Constitutional Change, Cmd. 1301 (1961).

Northern Rhodesia: Proposals for Constitutional Change, Cmnd. 1423 (1961).

Report of the Constitutional Working Party (Zomba, 1961).

Report of the Delimitation Commission (Lusaka, 1962).

Report of the Central Africa Conference Held at Victoria Falls (Lusaka, 1963).

Report of the Northern Rhodesia Independence Conference Held in London in May, 1964 (Lusaka, 1964).

INDEX

This index does not include reference matter from the footnotes, entries in the bibliography, or names cited only in the preface. The colonies of Nyasaland and Northwestern, Northeastern, and Northern Rhodesia, each of which is mentioned on almost every page of the text, are accordingly not indexed separately.

Draper, Charles Richard Eardley, administrator, 137–138
Duff, Hector Livingston, administrator, 16, 40–41, 43–44, 45
Dundas, (Sir) Charles, Chief Secretary of Northern Rhodesia (later governor of Uganda), 46
Durban, South Africa, 66, 68
Dutch Reformed Church Mission, 8, 147

East Africa, union with, 97–100. See also relevant individual countries
Eastern Province of Northern Rhodesia, 262, 273, 277, 291. See also Fort Jameson; Petauke
Economic development: of Northern Rhodesia, 9, 38, 44, 99; of Nyasaland, 24, 44, 62, 118, 313; and Federationist arguments, 105–107, 114, 217, 227, 233, 236–237, 241, 245; and copper, 157–158, 168; during Federation, 256–258
Edinburgh Royal College Medical School, 188
Education, 45, 123; missionaries, 7–8, 9–10, 65; village, 10; secondary, 10, 52–53, 65, 313, 318; and separatists, 58, 62, 63, 71, 77, 150; for Europeans, 105, 216–217, 257; African agitation for, 118–119, 126, 128, 190, 196, 198, 202, 208, 212–213, 222, 270, 281; on the Copperbelt, 159; of politicians, 181, 183, 304
Eklesia Lananga, 150
Ekwendeni mission, 40, 297
Elections: 1956, 269–270; 1959, 290, 294, 297, 300, 301, 311–315
Elisabethville, Katanga, 158
Elites, African, 115–116, 121–122, 123, 192–196, 304, 308
Elizabeth II, Queen of England, 248n, 249, 251–252, 273
Elwell, Archibald H., social welfare officer, x, 204–206, 326
Emergency, states of: 1956, 80; 1959, 297–300, 303, 326
Equality of races, 59, 61, 72, 80, 82, 100–101, 103–104, 129, 134, 196, 208, 228, 234, 254, 262, 281
Ethiopian Church of Barotseland, 56, 58–60

Ethiopian Church of South Africa, 58
European Protection League, 113
Executive Council: of Northern Rhodesia, 110–111, 127, 277, 315; of Nyasaland, 262, 268–269, 313
Exploration of Central Africa, 2–6. See also Livingstone, David

Fabian Colonial Bureau, 197, 198, 235, 246n
Federation, campaign for: of East and Central Africa, 97–98, 99–100, 102–104; of Central Africa, 99–100, 104–106, 110–111, 114, 214–223, 227–233, 235–252; African opposition to, 111–114, 123, 190, 197, 211, 213, 214–226, 228–252; propaganda war, 243–245
Federation of African Societies of Northern Rhodesia, 206–207, 209, 211–212, 230
Federation of African Welfare Societies of Southern Rhodesia, 206
Federation of Rhodesia and Nyasaland, 253–302; constitution of, 247–248; and partnership, 253–256, 264, 267, 271–272, 282–283, 307; opposition to, 253, 258–314; the Federal assembly, 254–256, 269, 284, 286; economics of, 256–258, 263–264, 270; Kariba dam and resettlement scheme, 274–275; demise, 314, 315–316
Ferguson, Robert, 88
Fernandes, António, Portuguese degredado, 2
Fife, boma and district, 20, 25, 136–138, 141
Fircroft College, 287
Foot, Captain C. E., consul, 11–12
Florence Bay (now Chitimba), village, 149
Fort Hare Native (later University) College, 198n, 268
Fort Hill (now Chitipa), settlement, 295–296
Fort Jameson, boma and district, 25, 38, 141, 166, 206, 277
Fort Johnston, boma and district, 17, 18, 19, 194n, 288, 320
Fort Manning (now Mchinji), boma, 297

Publications Written under the Auspices of the
Center for International Affairs
Harvard University

Created in 1958, the Center for International Affairs fosters advanced study of basic world problems by scholars from various disciplines and senior officials from many countries. The research at the Center focuses on economic and social development, the management of force in the modern world, and the evolving roles of Western Europe and the Communist bloc. The published results appear here in the order in which they have been issued. The research programs are supervised by Professors Robert R. Bowie (Director of the Center), Hollis B. Chenery, Samuel P. Huntington, Alex Inkeles, Henry A. Kissinger, Edward S. Mason, Thomas C. Schelling, and Raymond Vernon.

BOOKS

The Soviet Bloc, by Zbigniew K. Brzezinski (jointly with the Russian Research Center), 1960. Harvard University Press.

The Necessity for Choice, by Henry A. Kissinger, 1961. Harper & Bros.

Strategy and Arms Control, by Thomas C. Schelling and Morton H. Halperin, 1961. Twentieth Century Fund.

Rift and Revolt in Hungary, by Ferenc A. Váli, 1961. Harvard University Press.

United States Manufacturing Investment in Brazil, by Lincoln Gordon and Engelbert L. Grommers, 1962. Harvard Business School.

The Economy of Cyprus, by A. J. Meyer, with Simos Vassiliou (jointly with the Center for Middle Eastern Studies), 1962. Harvard University Press.

Entrepreneurs of Lebanon, by Yusif A. Sayigh (jointly with the Center for Middle Eastern Studies), 1962. Harvard University Press.

Communist China 1955–1959: Policy Documents with Analysis, with a Foreword by Robert R. Bowie and John K. Fairbank (jointly with the East Asian Research Center), 1962. Harvard University Press.

In Search of France, by Stanley Hoffmann, Charles P. Kindleberger, Laurence Wylie, Jesse R. Pitts, Jean-Baptiste Duroselle, and François Goguel, 1963. Harvard University Press.

Somali Nationalism, by Saadia Touval, 1963. Harvard University Press.

The Dilemma of Mexico's Development, by Raymond Vernon, 1963. Harvard University Press.

Limited War in the Nuclear Age, by Morton H. Halperin, 1963. John Wiley & Sons.

The Arms Debate, by Robert A. Levine, 1963. Harvard University Press.

Africans on the Land, by Montague Yudelman, 1964. Harvard University Press.

Counterinsurgency Warfare, by David Galula, 1964. Frederick A. Praeger, Inc.

People and Policy in the Middle East, by Max Weston Thornburg, 1964. W. W. Norton & Co.

Shaping the Future, by Robert R. Bowie, 1964. Columbia University Press.

Foreign Aid and Foreign Policy, by Edward S. Mason (jointly with the Council on Foreign Relations), 1964. Harper & Row.

Public Policy and Private Enterprise in Mexico, by M. S. Wionczek, D. H. Shelton, C. P. Blair, and R. Izquierdo, ed. Raymond Vernon, 1964. Harvard University Press.

How Nations Negotiate, by Fred Charles Iklé, 1964. Harper & Row.

China and the Bomb, by Morton H. Halperin (jointly with the East Asian Research Center), 1965. Frederick A. Praeger, Inc.

Democracy in Germany, by Fritz Erler (Jodidi Lectures), 1965. Harvard University Press.

The Troubled Partnership, by Henry A. Kissinger (jointly with the Council on Foreign Relations), 1965. McGraw-Hill Book Co.

The Rise of Nationalism in Central Africa, by Robert I. Rotberg, 1965. Harvard University Press.

OCCASIONAL PAPERS (Published by the Center for International Affairs)

1. *A Plan for Planning: The Need for a Better Method of Assisting Underdeveloped Countries on Their Economic Policies,* by Gustav F. Papanek, 1961.

2. *The Flow of Resources from Rich to Poor,* by Alan D. Neale, 1961.

3. *Limited War: An Essay on the Development of the Theory and an Annotated Bibliography,* by Morton H. Halperin, 1962.

4. *Reflections on the Failure of the First West Indian Federation,* by Hugh W. Springer, 1962.

5. *On the Interaction of Opposing Forces under Possible Arms Agreements,* by Glenn A. Kent, 1963.

6. *Europe's Northern Cap and the Soviet Union,* by Nils Örvik, 1963.

7. *Civil Administration in the Punjab: An Analysis of a State Government in India,* by E. N. Mangat Rai, 1963.

8. *On the Appropriate Size of a Development Program,* by Edward S. Mason, 1964.

9. *Self-Determination Revisited in the Era of Decolonization,* by Rupert Emerson, 1964.

10. *The Planning and Execution of Economic Development in Southeast Asia,* by Clair Wilcox, 1965.